THE ROUTLEDGE INTERNATIONAL HANDBOOK OF THE PSYCHOLOGY OF MORALITY

This cutting-edge handbook examines moral psychology and behavior, uncovering layers of human morality through a comprehensive overview of topics and approaches.

Featuring an array of expert international contributors, the book addresses five key themes: moral reasoning, moral judgments, moral emotions, moral behavior and moral self-views. Each section includes empirical chapters that address these themes at the intrapersonal, interpersonal, intragroup or intergroup level. Each section starts with a reflective chapter from a leading scholar in this field of study who shares their personal vision on key issues and future developments. Drawing on emerging research and featuring real-world examples, the book offers a deeper understanding of the social psychological factors that shape our moral behavior and how this plays out in our daily lives.

The Routledge International Handbook of the Psychology of Morality will be essential reading for academics and students in social psychology, the psychology of morality, business ethics and related areas. It will also be a compelling resource for legal and HR professionals, policy makers and anyone interested in understanding the complex and multi-faceted nature of human morality.

Naomi Ellemers is Distinguished University Professor at Utrecht University, Netherlands, elected member of the Netherlands Royal Academy of Arts and Sciences, the American Academy of Arts and Sciences, and corresponding Fellow of the British Academy. Her research focuses on the way people live together in groups and work together in organizations. She examines how individual behaviors and moral choices are influenced by social concerns and group norms.

Stefano Pagliaro is Associate Professor of Social Psychology at the University of Chieti-Pescara, Italy, where he is Head of the GPM-Lab (Group Processes and Morality Lab). His main research interests relate to social perception and group dynamics. In particular, he is interested in understanding the way in which moral concerns regulate interpersonal, intragroup and intergroup dynamics.

Félice van Nunspeet is Assistant Professor at Utrecht University, Netherlands. She is research leader of the program on Integrity & Ethics in the Organizational Behaviour Research Group, at the department of Psychology. Her research is focused on how social contexts affect people's moral perceptions and motivations. She takes a psychophysiological and neuroscientific research approach to examine people's implicit behavior and the underlying cognitive and affective processes.

THE ROUTLEDGE INTERNATIONAL HANDBOOK OF THE PSYCHOLOGY OF MORALITY

Edited by Naomi Ellemers, Stefano Pagliaro and Félice van Nunspeet

LONDON AND NEW YORK

Designed cover image: © Getty Images

First published 2024
by Routledge
4 Park Square, Milton Park, Abingdon, Oxon OX14 4RN

and by Routledge
605 Third Avenue, New York, NY 10158

Routledge is an imprint of the Taylor & Francis Group, an informa business

© 2024 selection and editorial matter, Naomi Ellemers, Stefano Pagliaro and Félice van Nunspeet; individual chapters, the contributors

The right of Naomi Ellemers, Stefano Pagliaro and Félice van Nunspeet to be identified as the authors of the editorial material, and of the contributors for their individual chapters, has been asserted in accordance with sections 77 and 78 of the Copyright, Designs and Patents Act 1988.

All rights reserved. No part of this book may be reprinted or reproduced or utilized in any form or by any electronic, mechanical, or other means, now known or hereafter invented, including photocopying and recording, or in any information storage or retrieval system, without permission in writing from the publishers.

Trademark notice: Product or corporate names may be trademarks or registered trademarks, and are used only for identification and explanation without intent to infringe.

British Library Cataloguing-in-Publication Data
A catalogue record for this book is available from the British Library

ISBN: 9780367647209 (hbk)
ISBN: 9780367647308 (pbk)
ISBN: 9781003125969 (ebk)

DOI: 10.4324/9781003125969

Typeset in Times New Roman
by Newgen Publishing UK

CONTENTS

List of figures   x
List of contributors   xi

1 Introduction: what is right and what is wrong relates to who you are and where you belong—unpacking the psychology of morality   1
Naomi Ellemers, Stefano Pagliaro, and Félice van Nunspeet

PART I
A vision on morality   7

2 Forward: the century of moral psychology   9
Jonathan Haidt

PART II
Moral reasoning   17

PART IIA
A vision on moral reasoning   19

3 Moral reasoning: my personal journey   21
Linda Klebe Treviño

PART IIB
Empirical review chapters on moral reasoning   27

4   The intrapersonal level: intrapersonal moral reasoning   29
    Paul Conway

5   The interpersonal level: impartial beneficence—the forgotten core of
    utilitarian psychology   40
    Jim Everett

6   The intragroup level: how social identity tunes moral cognition   51
    *Jay J. Van Bavel, Dominic J. Packer, Jennifer L. Ray, Claire Robertson
    and Nick Ungson*

7   The intergroup level: human = moral—the boundary conditions for
    moral reasoning engagement in intergroup contexts   63
    Lasana T. Harris and Ramandeep Mungur

PART III
Moral judgments   73

PART IIIA
A vision on moral judgments   75

8   Moral judgment: what makes it unique?   77
    Andrea E. Abele

PART IIIB
Empirical review chapters on moral judgments   85

9   The intrapersonal level: how power shapes the judgment of others'
    moral character—a social context perspective   87
    Marlon Mooijman

10   The interpersonal level: interpersonal consequences of moral judgments
     about others   97
     Christopher W. Bauman and Erik G. Helzer

11   The intragroup level: moral character in group perception   109
     Marco Brambilla and Simona Sacchi

12 The intergroup level: social neuroscience of intergroup decision-making *Jennifer Kubota, Richa Gautam, and Jasmin Cloutier*	118

PART IV
Moral emotions — **135**

PART IVA
A vision on moral emotions — **137**

13 A vision (and definition) of moral emotions *Roger Giner-Sorolla*	139

PART IVB
Empirical review chapters on moral emotions — **145**

14 The intrapersonal level: beyond contamination and disgust—the role of moral emotion in threat monitoring and moral judgment *Simone Schnall and Robert K. Henderson*	147
15 The interpersonal level: what is shame? Shame as a relational network of emotion-experience *Nicolay Gausel*	157
16 The intragroup level: moral emotions, empathy, and acceptance of others as ingroup members—a social neuroscience perspective *Eric J. Vanman*	168
17 The intergroup level: moral emotions in intergroup relations—the motivations and consequences of advantaged group members' aims to challenge the intergroup inequality *Bertjan Doosje, Hanna Szekeres, Enzo Cáceres Quezada, Michael Boiger and Judit Kende*	179

PART V
Moral behaviour   **191**

PART VA
A vision on moral behaviour   **193**

18 Behavioural ethics: a retrospective reflection and prospective prescription   195
Ann E. Tenbrunsel

PART VB
Empirical review chapters on moral behavior   **201**

19 The intrapersonal level: from feelings to moral actions—a working memory model of emotional influences on people's own moral behaviours   203
Lotte F. van Dillen

20 The interpersonal level: affirming transgressors' morality as a strategy to promote apologies and interpersonal reconciliation—the promise and potential pitfalls   212
Nurit Shnabel

21 The intragroup level: when and why reputational concerns influence immoral behaviour   223
Bianca Beersma, Annika S. Nieper, Maria T. M. Dijkstra, and Gerben A. van Kleef

22 The intergroup level: the strategic use of morality in intergroup relations   234
Susanne Täuber

PART VI
Moral self-views   **245**

PART VIA
A vision on moral self-views   **247**

23 On the vertical: how the moral self pursues its highest good   249
Karl Aquino

PART VIB
Empirical review chapters on moral self-views — **255**

24 The intrapersonal level: the moral self — 257
Jennifer Jordan, Elizabeth Mullen and Marijke C. Leliveld

25 The interpersonal level: moral self-views, at the interpersonal level of analysis — 267
Maryam Kouchaki and Rajen Anderson

26 The intragroup level: morally motivated intragroup deviance and dissent — 280
Jolanda Jetten and Charlie R. Crimston

27 The intergroup level: moral self-views — 291
Matthew J. Hornsey

PART VII
A concluding vision — **301**

28 How morality shapes research: a conversation with the editors — 303
Susan T. Fiske

Index — *309*

FIGURES

4.1	The difference between traditional versus modelling approaches and the hard versus soft dual process models	32
5.1	Utilitarianism	44
6.1	Moral tuning	52
7.1	Distal, mixed, and proximal model of the self	64
9.1	Perceived cooperative and perceived competitive norms	93
10.1	A conceptual model of why morality influences interpersonal interactions	99
11.1	The primacy of morality in group perception	115
12.1	Standard computational model vs intergroup value computational model	128
12.2	Salience network and social cognition network	129
14.1	Experience of threat	153
15.1	Event, the self, criticisms and motivations	159
16.1	Moral group responses	169
17.1	Orientations, emotions, attitudes and behavior	181
17.2	Appraisal, emotions, behavior	184
19.1	Working memory as a central hub for affective processing and for the regulation of affective influences on people's moral choices and actions	204
20.1	Main findings of mediation analysis	217
21.1	Interventions targeting reputational concerns can have positive, negative or no effect on (im)moral behaviour	229
22.1	Different actors (A) involved in maintaining and reproducing existing power differentials through different forms of power exertion (Panel B). Responses to power exertion by the powerless group (Panel C) make these processes dynamic and interactive	237
24.1	Moral self image	260
25.1	Moral behavior, moral self, and immoral behavior	273
26.1	Questions to consider that might help to determine the drivers of why someone becomes a moral rebel	285
27.1	An attributional gatekeeper model of delivering moral feedback to groups	294

CONTRIBUTORS

Andrea E. Abele is a senior professor in social psychology at Erlangen university and vice-president of the Bavarian Academy of Science. Her research interests are focused on both issues of occupational psychology and especially on social cognition and social evaluation. She is perhaps best known for her work on the fundamental dimensions of social judgment (together with Bogdan Wojciszke).

Rajen Anderson is currently a postdoctoral fellow at the Kellogg School of Management at Northwestern University. His research interests include moral psychology, political attitudes, and general problems of judgment and social cognition. In the spring of 2023 he joined the University of Leeds as a Lecturer (Assistant Professor).

Karl Aquino is the Richard Poon Professor of Organizations and Society at the Sauder School of Business at the University of British Columbia. His conducts research on moral psychology, revenge and forgiveness, victimization, person perception and motivated reasoning. He received his Ph.D. in Organizational Behavior at Northwestern University.

Jay J. Van Bavel is Professor of Psychology and Neural Science at New York University. He studies how collective concerns shape the mind, brain and behavior. He is co-author of *The Power of Us: Harnessing Our Shared Identities to Improve Performance, Increase Cooperation, and Promote Social Harmony*.

Christopher W. Bauman is Associate Professor of Organizations and Management at the Paul Merage School of Business at the University of California, Irvine. Much of his research examines how people perceive and respond to social rules, including morality, justice and norms.

Bianca Beersma is a professor of Organizational Behaviour at the Department of Organization Sciences at Vrije Universiteit Amsterdam. Her research focuses on the dilemmas of cooperation and competition in organizations. Specific research topics she studies are gossip, negotiation, team work and conflict management.

Michael Boiger is Assistant Professor at the University of Amsterdam (The Netherlands) and an emotion-focused and systemic therapist in private practice. In his research, he studies the cultural dynamics of emotion in close relationships. In particular, he is interested in how intercultural couples navigate potential cultural differences in emotion.

Marco Brambilla is Full Professor of Social Psychology at the University of Milano-Bicocca. He studies social cognition, specifically how we think about other people and groups. Most of his work examines the role of morality in the impression-formation process and in shaping person perception, stereotypes, prejudice and emotions.

Paul Conway is Associate Professor at the University of Southampton Centre for Research on Self and Identity. His work focuses on sacrificial moral dilemmas, examining the processes giving rise to such judgments, the interpersonal consequences deriving from them, and the connection between morality and the self-concept.

Jasmin Cloutier is Associate Professor at the University of Delaware in the Department of Psychological and Brain Sciences. He is broadly interested in social cognition and social neuroscience with an emphasis on research questions related to person perception, person evaluation and impression formation.

Charlie R. Crimston is Research Fellow in moral psychology at the University of Queensland. Her research explores the nature of our moral boundaries, group polarization and identity change. Dr Crimston is best known for her work on the psychology of moral expansiveness.

Maria T.M. Dijkstra is an assistant professor at the Department of Organization Sciences at Vrije Universiteit Amsterdam. Her research focuses on conflict and gossip in organizations at the individual and small-group level.

Bertjan Doosje is Social Psychologist at the University of Amsterdam in the Netherlands. His teaching and research interest includes intergroup processes such as radicalization and terrorism, misrecognition of minorities, acculturation of ethnic minorities and perceived discrimination by members of minority groups.

Naomi Ellemers is Distinguished University Professor at Utrecht University, the Netherlands, elected member of the Netherlands Royal Academy of Arts and Sciences, the American Academy of Arts and Sciences, and corresponding Fellow of the British Academy. Her research focuses on the way people live together in groups and work together in organizations. She examines how individual behaviors and moral choices are influenced by social concerns and group norms.

Jim Everett is Reader (Associate Professor) at the University of Kent, specializing in moral judgment, perceptions of moral character and the moral psychology of trust in artificial intelligence. Jim's work takes a highly interdisciplinary approach, combining social psychological approaches with insights from philosophy, evolutionary theory and behavioral economics.

Nicolay Gausel is Full Professor of Social and Emotion Psychology at the University of Stavanger. He studies morality and emotions, specifically how moral failures are appraised, felt and coped with on intrapersonal, interpersonal and intergroup level. Most of his work examines the role of shame and rejection after moral failures.

Richa Gautam is a graduate student at the University of Delaware interested in discriminatory behavior and its antecedents. She employs behavioral, computational and neuroscientific methods. Prior to graduate school, she engaged in social and physiological research at Vassar College, clinical research at Weill Cornell Medicine and market research at YouGov.

Roger Giner-Sorolla is Professor of Social Psychology at the University of Kent. His main research interests are in anger, disgust, guilt and shame, in addition to dehumanization and apology as they relate to emotions. He addresses these issues in his 2013 monograph, *Judging Passions: Moral Emotions in Persons and Groups*.

Susan T. Fiske is Eugene Higgins Professor, Psychology and Public Affairs, Princeton University. Her research addresses how stereotyping, prejudice and discrimination are encouraged or discouraged by social relationships, such as cooperation, competition and power.

Jonathan Haidt is a social psychologist at New York University's Stern School of Business. He studies the intuitive foundations of morality, and how morality varies across cultural and political divisions. He is the author of *The Righteous Mind* and the co-author of *The Coddling of the American Mind*.

Lasana T. Harris is a social neuroscientist who takes an interdisciplinary approach to understand human behavior. He explores the brain and physiological correlates of social cognition, including person perception, social learning, emotions, dehumanization, anthropomorphism, punishment and decision-making. His research addresses perceptions of humans and non-humans, and social, legal, ethical and economic decision-making.

Erik G. Helzer is Associate Professor of Management and Organizations at the Naval Postgraduate School in Monterey, CA. Dr. Helzer develops and applies psychological, organizational and behavioral science insights to understand three facets of practical wisdom for leading: ethical behavior and moral judgment, self-knowledge, and personal agency and adjustment.

Robert K. Henderson is a recent graduate of the University of Cambridge. His research interests are focused on how physical and social threats fortify moral judgments.

Matthew J. Hornsey is Professor of Social Psychology at the University of Queensland. He researches in the areas of group processes and intergroup relations, with particular interests in how people respond to criticisms and recommendations for change. He is perhaps best known for his work on climate change communication.

Jolanda Jetten is Professor of Social Psychology and Australian Research Council Laureate Fellow at The University of Queensland. Her research focuses on social identity and intergroup relations. She is best known for her work on how group processes impact a range of outcomes including deviance, dissent and conformity.

Contributors

Jennifer Jordan is Professor of Leadership and Organizational Behavior at IMD. She researches the topics of power, morality and the intersection of both. Her most notable work is on moral compensation and power instability. She is interested in how these topics are affecting and affected by the modern world.

Judit Kende is Social Psychologist at the Université libre de Bruxelles, Belgium. Her research focuses on intergroup relations and equality. She is interested in how inequality influences how people from different social groups relate to each other and how people from different social groups can challenge inequalities together.

Maryam Kouchaki is Professor of Management and Organizations at Kellogg School of Management, Northwestern University. Her research interests are focused on understanding the dynamic nature of moral decision-making, charitable giving and receiving, and the complexity and challenges of managing ethnic and gender diversity for organizations.

Jennifer Kubota is Associate Professor and Senior Ford Fellow in the Departments of Psychological and Brain Sciences and Political Science and International Relations at the University of Delaware. Dr. Kubota's research crosses disciplinary boundaries, bridging psychology, political science, neuroscience and decision-making.

Marijke C. Leliveld is Associate Professor in marketing at the University of Groningen. Her research interest is focused on the role of morality in consumer decision-making. Her work addresses topics like charitable donations, cause-related marketing and sustainable consumption.

Marlon Mooijman is Assistant Professor at the Jones Graduate school of Business at Rice University in Houston, Texas (USA). He studies power dynamics, trust and distrust development, and the consequences of moral beliefs.

Elizabeth Mullen is Associate Professor of Management at San José State University. She conducts research about justice and morality. She investigates how people's emotions and moral convictions influence their fairness perceptions and reactions to transgressions. She also investigates how individuals regulate and evaluate their own and others' moral behavior.

Ramandeep Mungur is a Ph.D. student at University College London. He is interested in the role of disgust in social behavior, particularly in the spheres of intergroup interactions, humor and morality.

Annika S. Nieper is a Ph.D. candidate at the Department of Organization Sciences at Vrije Universiteit Amsterdam. Her research focuses on unethical behaviour and corruption, and the role of gossip and reputation therein.

Félice van Nunspeet is Assistant Professor at Utrecht University, the Netherlands. She is research leader of the program on Integrity & Ethics in the Organizational Behaviour Research Group, at the department of Psychology. Her research is focused on how social contexts affect people's moral perceptions and motivations. She takes a psychophysiological and neuroscientific research approach to examine people's implicit behavior and the underlying cognitive and affective processes.

Dominic J. Packer is Professor of Psychology and the Associate Vice Provost for Research at Lehigh University. He studies how people's social identities influence their thoughts, feelings and decisions. He is co-author of *The Power of Us: Harnessing Our Shared Identities to Improve Performance, Increase Cooperation, and Promote Social Harmony*.

Stefano Pagliaro is Associate Professor of Social Psychology at the University of Chieti-Pescara, Italy, where he is Head of the GPM-Lab (Group Processes and Morality Lab). His main research interests relate to social perception and group dynamics. In particular, he is interested in understanding the way in which moral concerns regulate interpersonal, intragroup and intergroup dynamics.

Enzo Cáceres Quezada is a Ph.D. candidate at the University of Amsterdam. He studies profiles of dominant and marginalized identities management strategies across ethnicity, sexual orientation and gender identity lines, how they relate to appraisals of inequality and appreciation of intergroup differences, and their consequences for the status quo.

Jennifer L. Ray is the Employee Surveys and Cultural Measurement Lead at Takeda Pharmaceuticals. She develops and implements Takeda's enterprise-wide employee listening strategy and delivers valuable business via surveys and other research methodologies. Her work innovates ways to measure Takeda's employee experience and culture through technology and analytics.

Claire Robertson is a Ph.D. student at NYU. Her research interests focus on the ways that social processes change in online contexts. She is best known for her work on negativity bias in news consumption.

Simona Sacchi is Full Professor of Social Psychology at the University of Milano-Bicocca. Her research interests primarily focus on social cognition and, specifically, on information search process and social-hypothesis testing, both in moral and non-moral domains. She studies how people form and update impressions of individuals and groups.

Simone Schnall is Professor of Experimental Social Psychology at the University of Cambridge, and Director of the Cambridge Body, Mind and Behaviour Laboratory. She investigates how bodily states, including emotions, influence various judgments and behaviors. Topics have included morality, risky decision-making and perception of physical space.

Nurit Shnabel is Full Professor at Tel Aviv University. She is best known for her work on the needs-based model, a theoretical framework that identifies the social psychological processes that facilitate or hinder reconciliation between individuals and groups. Her other work examines subtle processes that hinder gender equality.

Contributors

Hanna Szekeres is Assistant Professor of Social Psychology at Eotvos Lorand University in Budapest, Hungary. She studies intergroup relations, specifically prejudice towards minorities in society, women and the LGBTQ+ community, prejudice reduction interventions, and collective action.

Susanne Täuber is Associate Professor at the University of Groningen. Her research focuses on factors that obstruct the translation of policy into actual organizational and societal change, for instance in the context of gender quotas. As an expert in moral motivation, Täuber combines empirical research with conceptual and theoretical contributions.

Ann E. Tenbrunsel is the David E. Gallo Professor of Business Ethics at the University of Notre Dame. Her research focuses on the psychology of ethical decision-making, examining why people behave unethically, despite their best intentions to behave to the contrary. Ann is the author, co-author and co-editor of numerous articles and books on this topic.

Linda Klebe Treviño is Distinguished Professor of Organizational Behavior and Ethics at the Pennsylvania State University. Her research has focused on understanding ethical and unethical conduct in organizational context including work on ethical decision-making, ethical climate and culture, ethical and unethical leadership, and ethical voice.

Nick Ungson is Assistant Professor of Psychology at Susquehanna University. His research interests are on interaction between identity, behavior and decision-making. For example, how does identity affect decisions to engage in non-normative behavior, react to deviance and dissent, and shape our perceptions of right and wrong?

Eric J. Vanman is Associate Professor in the School of Psychology at the University of Queensland, Australia. His research interests include the social neuroscience of emotion and intergroup prejudice, human-robotic interaction and negative behaviors involved in social media usage. His studies have incorporated several kinds of psychophysiological and neuroimaging methods.

Lotte F. van Dillen works as Associate Professor at the Social, Economic, and Organizational Psychology Unit of Leiden University. A central theme in her research concerns the influence of people's limited mental capacity on their feelings, judgments and decisions, and how they can make the best use of this capacity.

Gerben A. van Kleef is Professor of Social Psychology at the University of Amsterdam. His research seeks to illuminate how people relate to each other in a deeply social world. His main research programs revolve around emotion, power, social norms, conflict and cooperation.

1
INTRODUCTION

What is right and what is wrong relates to who you are and where you belong—unpacking the psychology of morality

Naomi Ellemers, Stefano Pagliaro, and Félice van Nunspeet

The topic of morality – generally referring to the distinction between "right" versus "wrong" ways to behave (Haidt & Kesebir, 2010) – is undoubtedly one of the hottest and most investigated in contemporary social psychology. A recent review highlights the exponential increase in the interest of researchers in the psychology of morality since 2005, the rate of which is disproportionately larger than the overall increase in publications in social psychology (Ellemers, Van der Toorn, Paunov, & Van Leeuwen, 2019). This handbook aims to capture and give credit to the considerable advances that have been made in current insights on the topic of morality in social psychology. We organize this body of knowledge through an interpretative key that distinguishes between relevant sub-themes in this area of inquiry and systematically compares insights targeting intrapersonal, interpersonal, intragroup, and intergroup levels of analysis.

Before elaborating on these aspects, as editors of this handbook we will share how we approached the theme of morality in our own research, how our personal stories led us on this path, and why we are passionate to pursue moral questions through our scientific work.

Naomi Ellemers: My ambition has always been to understand why individuals are treated differently because of their group memberships, and why inequalities between social groups persist. This led me on the path of examining group processes and intergroup relations, which I began to study from a Social Identity perspective. I have been using this framework from my PhD project onwards, to advance basic insights in the psychology of the group self as a way to benefit the analysis of real-life problems. Initially, my attention was focused on structural determinants (e.g., permeability of group boundaries, legitimacy, and stability of the social structure) that define status relations between groups in society, and guide the thoughts and behaviors of individuals (Ellemers, 1993). For many years I worked with the assumption that individuals and groups could derive social status from any characteristic that would allow them to distinguish themselves from others in that situation. A collaborative project with Colin W. Leach and Manuela Barreto systematically assessing and comparing different sources of group pride and identification opened my eyes to the fact that morality was not just another indicator of social standing, nor should it be seen as a 'second rate' source of group value. Our joint publication (Leach et al., 2007) opened up a whole new perspective on issues I had been examining for many years, revealing the power and pervasiveness of moral concerns and moral motives in group processes and intergroup relations. This view on the social meaning and group-level implications of moral reasoning and moral decisions was widely acknowledged in existing theories on morality. However, when I delved into the empirical literature I discovered the interests of researchers were very skewed favoring the intrapersonal level of analysis, mainly charting people's ideas about right vs wrong with hypothetical dilemmas in the moral reasoning (Ellemers et al., 2019). This reinforced my motivation to further examine the role of morality as a fundamental concern that serves different regulatory functions in group life, in organizations, and in intergroup relations in society (Ellemers, 2017; Ellemers & De Gilder, 2022; Ellemers & Van den Bos, 2012).

Around the time that I was starting to see the importance of morality for the collective self, Stefano Pagliaro visited the University of Leiden, NL, to work with me as a PhD student.

Stefano Pagliaro: I have always been passionate about studying low-status groups, in particular understanding the motivations that pushed the members of these groups to mobilize to improve the situation of their group as a whole (i.e., collective change), rather than their own situation (i.e., individual mobility). In Leiden, during a meeting with Naomi and Manuela Barreto, the idea was born to consider the evaluative dimension (in this case, morality vs. competence) among the factors that could influence the effect of group norms on the behavior of its members. This gave a strong impetus to my doctoral project and other projects in the following years. With different colleagues, I examined the differential effect of considerations related to morality or competence investigated in relation to intra-group and inter-group dynamics (Ellemers, Pagliaro, & Barreto, 2013; Ellemers, Pagliaro, Barreto, & Leach, 2008; Pagliaro, Ellemers, & Barreto, 2011), in the evaluation of victims of gender-based violence (for a review, Pagliaro et al., 2020) and, more recently, in organizational contexts (Giannella, Pagliaro, & Barreto, 2022; Pagliaro et al., 2018; Teresi et al., 2019). In many of these projects, the scientific partnership started in Leiden has represented and still represents a point of common reflection and collaboration, as in the case of the present handbook. I realized through ongoing cooperations with different groups of colleagues and students who are not (yet) aware of this literature that the field could benefit from an overview of relevant strands of research, perspectives, and relevant scholars in this area. Indeed, I thought that although there is a large literature on many of the topics covered in this volume, it is not easy to find this type of overview, especially highlighting the relevance for the group, organizational and social problems I have been working on – that is, intragroup and intergroup processes, organizational climate, virtuous leadership. This is why I joined Naomi and Félice in this endeavor to put together such an overview that systematically addresses a broad catalogue of topics, approaches and authors.

After Naomi and Stefano had started their collaboration, Félice van Nunspeet became a research assistant at the Social and Organizational Psychology Unit at Leiden University.

Félice van Nunspeet: My interest in morality arose when thinking about a research question for a Master's course in Developmental Cognitive Neuroscience: I was intrigued by what happens in peoples' brains when (or hence why) they do bad things. Bad things in a legal sense that was, a perspective sparked by the occupations some of my family members held within the police department – among which my parents. Relatedly, as a thesis student, I proposed to examine the neural underpinnings of moral reasoning in juvenile delinquents. This led me to work with my supervisors Eveline Crone and Wouter van den Bos on a study of the neural correlates of social decision-making in severely antisocial adolescents (Van den Bos et al., 2014). After graduating, my work as as a research assistant with Naomi Ellemers gave me the opportunity to continue to use social neuroscience – to explore people's moral motivations beyond their self-reported intentions and perceptions. This work soon turned into my PhD, which was focused on people's (implicit and explicit) motivation to act in line with their own, as well as their group members', moral values (Van Nunspeet, 2014). The triangulation of combining neuroscientific methods with self-report and behavioral measures yielded both insightful as well as complex findings, which I continued to pursue and unravel in the years thereafter. The scientific partnership with Naomi is still active at Utrecht University, where we investigate the psychological processes associated with integrity (e.g., how people respond to and process moral criticism; Rösler, Van Nunspeet, & Ellemers, 2023), responsibility, and (im)moral behavior (see also Ellemers & van Nunspeet, 2020). My current research not only addresses these basic mechanisms but also examines how these reveal and explain the behavioral responses in applied settings. I have done this, for instance, with regard to organizational rule and norm compliance, and the implementation of public policies on social responsibility (van Nunspeet & Ellemers, 2021). Translating our psychophysiological and neuroscientific lab experiments into field studies is one of the exciting challenges I happily wrap my head around. Going beyond what people say and do when it comes to their moral attitudes and actions fascinates me, and I'm very pleased the neuroscientific perspective is covered in some of the chapters in this handbook.

Our personal stories summarized above bear witness to the common interest of the editors of this handbook in the theme of morality but also highlight the range of themes and methodological approaches to the study of this topic. This also reflects current research on morality, with different scholars and research groups addressing different facets of morality and its pervasive effects on reasoning, social judgment, emotions, and behavior, analyzing these issues from different perspectives and at different levels. The aim of this handbook therefore is to give shape and structure to this vast body of research.

One giant umbrella: different topics, different levels

The present handbook is structured around five main themes, each of which addresses four level of analysis. This mirrors the organization used to structure a comprehensive literature review using expert content analysis to classify empirical publications into five different themes: Moral Reasoning, Moral Judgment, Moral Emotions, Moral Behavior, and Moral Self-Views (Ellemers et al., 2019). We will now explain how we define and consider these topics that shape the five sections of this book.

Moral reasoning relates to the application of abstract moral principles as well as specific life experiences or religious and political identities, that people use to locate themselves in the world. Moral reasoning research addresses moral standards people can adhere to, for instance, in the decision guidelines they adopt or in the way they respond to moral dilemmas or evaluate specific behavioral choices. *Moral judgments* refer to the perceived dispositions and behaviours of other individuals, groups, or companies in terms of their morality. Research on moral judgements considers the characteristics and actions of other individuals and groups. People can use these as examples of behaviour to follow or avoid, or as a source of information to extract social norms and guidelines for their own behaviour. *Moral emotions* concern the emotional responses that are seen to characterize moral situations. They are commonly used to diagnose the moral implications in terms of emotional rewards and punishments of different events. Moral emotions research typically addresses feelings of guilt and shame (vs. pride) that people experience about their own behaviour, or outrage and disgust (vs. admiration) in response to the moral transgressions of others. *Moral behaviour* includes the behavioural displays that convey the moral tendencies of individuals or groups. These include implicit indicators of moral preferences, such as efforts to achieve more fairness or willingness to make cooperative choices, as well as more deliberate displays of helping, cheating, or standing up for one's principles. *Moral self-views* concern the self-reflective aspirational and self-justifying tendencies associated with moral choices and moral lapses. Moral self-views research addresses the mechanisms people use to maintain self-consistency and think of themselves as moral persons, even when they realize that their behaviour is not in line with their moral principles.

Within each of these five thematic sections, the book structure further defines four levels of analysis. Different chapters highlight studies that examine intrapersonal, interpersonal, intragroup, or intergroup mechanisms. Research on *intrapersonal* mechanisms addresses how a single individual considers, evaluates, or makes decisions about rules, objects, situations, and courses of action. Research on *interpersonal* mechanisms examines how individuals perceive, evaluate, and interact with other individuals. Research on *intragroup* mechanisms investigates how people perceive, evaluate, and respond to norms or behaviours displayed by other members of the same group, work or sports team, religious community, or organization. Research on *intergroup* mechanisms focuses on how people perceive, evaluate, and interact with members of different cultural, ethnic, or national groups.

To complete the structure of the book, each section opens with a vision chapter. written by scholars whose pathbreaking work has come to define and guide later work on one of the five themes we identified. In these vision chapters they share their personal intellectual journey and perspective on current and future developments on the theme they have been working on for much of their careers. We are privileged to be able to include two exceptional chapters as 'bookends.' In his opening chapter Jonathan Haidt reflects upon his perspective on the field of morality and how this developed in social psychology. He highlights the timeliness and relevance of the breadth of topics and perspectives covered in this handbook, proposing that the 21st century deserves to become *the century of moral psychology*. In closing, we include an interview with Susan Fiske in which she reflects on how her own thinking about the issues presented in the book developed over time. In this final chapter, Fiske shares her own intellectual journey and how it resulted in her current perspective on the topics described in the previous chapters.

With this structure and composition this handbook aims to provide a comprehensive overview of the variety of topics and issues represented in psychological research on morality, highlighting different levels of analysis, offering a broad variety of methodologies, and sharing how personal experiences and real life problem have inspired research questions and scholarly insights. In this way we hope to offer a collection of chapters that not only provides a review of the relevant literature but also to encourage people to be inspired by their personal stories to do science.

There are many people we wish to thank at the conclusion of this journey. First of all, *all the colleagues* who generously contributed to the writing of the various chapters, especially in a period characterized by the Corona pandemic in which taking on new commitments was certainly not easy. Nonetheless, all of them showed enthusiasm for the project from the very beginning, and did their utmost to bring it to fruition. Eleanor Taylor at Routledge encouraged us to believe this enterprise was possible from the start and assisted us in every possible way. Karin Dirks-Hansen helped us keep track of all the different authors, manuscripts, and materials that had to be put together. We thank Douwe Hoendervanger for harmonizing the designs of all the visuals in this volume.

A final consideration concerns the editorial process that led to the creation of this handbook. The three editors of this text have shared every aspect of this process, from the generation of the initial idea to the structure of the book, from the choice of contributors to the editorial work on the chapters. This was a highly fruitful cooperation, which allowed them to constructively manage the critical issues that emerged. For this reason, the editors wish to declare that they share the first authorship for all aspects concerning the publication of this introductory text as well as the volume as a whole: their names are therefore presented in alphabetical order.

References

Ellemers, N. (1993). The influence of socio-structural variables on identity enhancement strategies. *European Review of Social Psychology, 4*, 27–57. https://doi.org/10.1080/14792779343000013

Ellemers, N. (2017). *Morality and the regulation of social behavior: Groups as moral anchors*. Milton Park, UK: Routledge/Taylor & Francis.

Ellemers, N., & De Gilder, D. (2022). *The moral organization: Key issues, analyses and solutions*. Cham: Springer publishers.

Ellemers, N., Pagliaro, S., & Barreto, M. (2013). Morality and behavioural regulation in groups: A social identity approach. *European Review of Social Psychology, 24*(1), 160–193. https://doi.org/10.1080/10463283.2013.841490

Ellemers, N., Pagliaro, S., Barreto, M., & Leach, C. W. (2008). Is it better to be moral than smart? The effects of morality and competence norms on the decision to work at group status improvement. *Journal of Personality and Social Psychology, 95*, 1397–1410. https://doi.org/10.1037/a0012628

Ellemers, N., & Van den Bos, K. (2012). Morality in groups: On the social-regulatory functions of right and wrong. *Social and Personality Psychology Compass, 6*, 878–889. https://doi.org/10.1111/spc3.12001

Ellemers, N., & van Nunspeet, F. (2020). Neuroscience and the social origins of moral behavior: How neural underpinnings of social categorization and conformity affect everyday moral and immoral behavior. *Current Directions in Psychological Science, 29*(5), 513–520. https://doi.org/10.1177/0963721420951584

Ellemers, N., van der Toorn, J., Paunov, Y., & van Leeuwen, T. (2019). The psychology of morality: A review and analysis of empirical studies published from 1940 through 2017. *Personality and Social Psychology Review, 23*(4), 332–366. https://doi.org/10.1177/1088868318811759

Giannella, V.A., Pagliaro, S., & Barreto, M. (2022). Leader's morality, prototypicality, and followers' reactions. *The Leadership Quarterly, 33*(4), 101596. https://doi.org/10.1016/j.leaqua.2021.101596

Haidt, J., & Kesebir, S. (2010). Morality. In S. Fiske, D. Gilbert, & G. Lindzey (Eds.), *Handbook of social psychology*, 5th Edition (pp. 797–832). Hoboken, NJ: Wiley.

Leach, C. W., Ellemers, N., & Barreto, M., (2007). Group virtue: The importance of morality (vs. competence and sociability) in the positive evaluation of in-group. *Journal of Personality and Social Psychology, 93*, 234–249. https://doi.org/10.1037/0022-3514.93.2.234

Pagliaro, S., Ellemers, N., & Barreto, M. (2011). Sharing moral values: Anticipated ingroup respect as a determinant of adherence to morality-based (but not competence based) group norms. *Personality and Social Psychology Bulletin, 37*, 1117–1129. https://doi.org/10.1177/0146167211406906

Pagliaro, S., Lo Presti, A., Barattucci, M., Giannella, V.A., & Barreto, M. (2018). On the effects of ethical climate(s) on employees' behavior: A social identity approach. *Frontiers in Psychology, 9*, 960. https://doi.org/10.3389/fpsyg.2018.00960

Pagliaro, S., Pacilli., M.G., & Baldry, A. C. (2020). Bystanders' reactions to intimate partner violence: An experimental approach. *European Review of Social Psychology, 31* (1), 149–182. https://doi.org/10.1080/10463283.2020.1776031

Rösler, I. K., van Nunspeet, F., & Ellemers, N. (2023). Falling on deaf ears: The effects of sender identity and feedback dimension on how people process and respond to negative feedback – an ERP study. *Journal of Experimental Social Psychology, 104*, 104419. https://doi.org/10.1016/j.jesp.2022.104419

Teresi, M., Pietroni, D. D., Barattucci, M., Giannella, V.A., & Pagliaro, S. (2019). Ethical climate(s), organization identification, and employees' behaviour. *Frontiers in Psychology, 10*, 1356. https://doi.org/10.3389/fpsyg.2019.01356

van den Bos, W., Vahl, P., Güroğlu, B., van Nunspeet, F., Colins, O., Markus, M., Rombouts, S. A. R. B., van der Wee, N., Vermeiren, R., & Crone, E. A. (2014). Neural correlates of social decision-making in severely antisocial adolescents. *Social Cognitive and Affective Neuroscience, 9*(12), 2059–2066. https://doi.org/10.1093/scan/nsu003

Van Nunspeet, F. (2014). *Neural correlates of the motivation to be moral* (Doctoral dissertation, Leiden University).

van Nunspeet, F., & Ellemers, N. (2021). Alarmbellen in het brein: De invloed van sociale normen op het belang van regelnaleving en op de cognitieve processen onderliggend aan regelnalevend en-overtredend gedrag. *[Red flags in the brain: The influence of social norms on the importance of rule compliance and the cognitive processes underlying rule-compliant and rule-violating behavior]*. Boom criminologie.

PART I

A vision on morality

2
FORWARD

The century of moral psychology

Jonathan Haidt

Introduction

In 2004, two of the geneticists who first decoded the human genome declared that the 21st century would be the "century of biology" (Venter & Cohen, 2004). Since then, various scientists and professional groups have vied for funding and attention by declaring that the next decade or century will be all about robots, artificial intelligence, blockchain, the metaverse, or some other technology.

I have a better idea. Let's look at the next decade and the 21st century as a whole from the demand side—what do we *need*—rather than the supply side—what is technology *offering us?* I suggest that the area where humanity most desperately needs scientific progress is moral psychology, for two reasons.

First, in the 21st century, humanity's greatest problems are no longer purely technical challenges, such as curing cholera or increasing agricultural productivity. They are largely social and moral problems—even if they seem to be technical or scientific challenges—and it is in these areas where we are making little progress (See Rittel & Webber's [1973] analysis of "wicked problems" for an earlier statement of this idea). Take the COVID pandemic. Producing vaccines turned out to be much easier and faster than first predicted. Getting people to take it in numbers high enough to achieve herd immunity turned out, in some countries, to be much harder. And throughout the pandemic, battles emerged in many countries between COVID maximalists (generally on the left) who favored lockdowns, school closures, and strict masking policies that far exceeded any supporting evidence, versus covid minimalists (generally on the right) who opposed almost any restrictions or vaccination mandates, even when those were supported by evidence. Why does this polarization happen? How can leaders and public health authorities do better in the next pandemic? Moral psychology offers answers.

The second reason why progress in moral psychology is desperately needed is that the technologies that are candidates for dominating the 21st century are generally being developed by people who have very little understanding of human nature. Some of them even have little concern for the social and moral consequences of what they are doing. We saw this most clearly in the design of Web 2.0 and the major social media platforms, which were built within a Silicon Valley ecosystem that generally embraced libertarian politics (with its aversion to regulation) and an explicit ethos, stated by Facebook founder Mark Zuckerberg, of "move fast and break things." Well, they broke things. There was little concern for privacy or security, leading to open architectures that supported an ever-expanding ring of exploitation and crime, from sex trafficking and child pornography through drug and weapons bazaars to electoral manipulation and the networking of terrorists who live-stream their atrocities.

But what if the internet had been designed with humans—in all their variety, vulnerability, and tribalism—in mind?

What moral psychology was

I entered the field of moral psychology in 1987 when I enrolled in the psychology PhD program at the University of Pennsylvania. I arrived as a young and hopeful cognitive psychologist—or, at least, I was a 23-year-old philosophy major who had worked as a computer programmer and harbored naïve dreams of combining those skills to study artificial intelligence from the psychology side, rather than the computer science side. But I didn't really know what I was doing, and I changed my focus after a great conversation with the cognitive psychologist Jonathan Baron, who studies thinking and decision-making, and who had a side interest in moral thinking. At Penn, every student had to design, conduct, and write up an empirical study within eight months of arriving, so I conducted my first psychology experiment on the question of when and why people judge harm caused by *omission* (doing nothing) to be as bad as harm caused by *commission* (doing something). My report (eventually published as Haidt & Baron, 1996) was somewhat dry and dull, which was typical of moral psychology at that time.

But as I began to read widely, I discovered that morality had once been a major crossroads and battleground of psychology, one that every major school had tried to conquer. So many of the 20th century's greatest figures had issued pronouncements about where morality came from. The one thing that nearly all agreed upon was that the child's mind was effectively a blank slate, and so the challenge was to explain how morality got "in." In one of the earliest social psychology textbooks, William McDougall wrote that "The fundamental problem of social psychology is the moralization of the individual by the society into which he is born as a creature in which the non-moral and purely egoistic tendencies are so much stronger than any altruistic tendencies" (McDougall, 1998/1908, p. 18).

A few years earlier, Sigmund Freud (1976/1900) had offered his own account of how morality got "in" with his complicated story of psycho-sexual development: the young boy's "Oedipal conflict"—rivalry with his father over the affections of the mother—resolves itself when the boy "internalizes" the father's moral beliefs, giving birth to the boy's new superego. (Don't even ask about how it was supposed to work for girls).

The behaviorists were bitter rivals of the Freudians, and they offered a radically different account. Forget all that sexual stuff, they said, and all those unmeasurable internal constructs like the superego. Morality is whatever behaviors society reinforces, said B. F. Skinner (1971), who had shown how easy it is to teach pigeons to play ping pong, if you can just reinforce them fast enough for each specific behavior.

Nonsense, said the insurgents of the cognitive revolution, which began in the 1950s with Noam Chomsky's (1959) devastating critique of Skinner's behaviorist theory of language learning. An important second line of attack was Lawrence Kohlberg's (1969) research on moral development. Building on the earlier work of Jean Piaget (1932), he argued that you can't explain moral development without focusing on the cognitive structures that children construct as they interact with others and gradually create—for themselves—more adequate understandings of their social worlds.

By 1987, the Freudians and behaviorists had faded into history, and the cognitive developmentalists had won the day. Moral psychology had become a subfield of developmental psychology, focused on cognitive development: how do children develop ever more adequate understandings of justice? Tragically, Kohlberg died by suicide in January of that year, and so when I arrived at Penn in September, it felt like the last of the giants had left the arena, and the heroic age had ended.

The new synthesis in moral psychology

But as I continued to learn and read widely, I discovered other giants in neighboring fields whose work on morality generally pointed to emotions and intuitions, thereby calling out for integration with psychology. One of these was the evolutionary biologist Edward O. Wilson, who built on Darwin's keen interest in the origin of morality in emotions such as anger, shame, sympathy, and disgust. Wilson had predicted, in 1975, that ethics would soon become part of the "new synthesis" of sociobiology, in which distal mechanisms (such as evolution), proximal mechanisms (such as neural processes), and the socially constructed web of meanings and institutions (as studied by the humanities and social sciences) would all be integrated into a full explanation of human morality. But Wilson's book and term "sociobiology" ran afoul of the progressive politics of the academy in the 1970s. By 1987, it was somewhat taboo to suggest that evolution had shaped human nature because such a claim could be used to justify existing power structures (see discussion in Pinker, 2002).

In primatology, however, there was no such taboo on evolutionary thinking. Frans de Waal's highly readable books, such as *Good Natured* (de Waal, 1996) presented evidence that many of the "building blocks" of human morality are already visible in the societies of chimpanzee and bonobos. Many of these building blocks were (as Darwin had said) emotional responses such as feelings of sympathy, fear, anger, and affection.

In 1992, a group of evolutionists and psychologists challenged the taboo with a bold edited volume titled *The Adapted Mind: Evolutionary Psychology and the Generation of Culture* (Barkow, Cosmides, & Tooby, 1992). The book contained essays on the origins of cooperation, sharing, nurturance, gossip, and other elements of morality. More importantly, it launched the modern field of evolutionary psychology, which has been an essential part of the new synthesis. It is now common for moral psychologists to refer to evolution, adaptation, and "human nature" in a way that was not common before the 1990s.

The 1990s was truly "the decade of the brain," in that functional MRI became far more widely used, and it was immediately applied to the study of morality, most notably by Antonio Damasio (1994) in his landmark book *Descartes's Error*. Everyone studying morality suddenly had to become familiar with the difference between the lateral prefrontal cortex (where cool and "rational" deliberation takes place) and the ventromedial prefrontal cortex (which integrates emotional responses into thinking and decision-making).

But what made the 1990s truly a "new synthesis" of the sort Wilson had hoped for was that the new interest in morality wasn't just coming from the natural-science side of the academy (neuroscience, evolution, primatology). Morality and the role of the emotions was also becoming a central topic in the social sciences and several humanities departments. For example, cultural differences in morality was a major focus of the emerging field of cultural psychology (Markus & Kitayama, 1991; Shweder, 1990). The role of moral emotions in moral judgments was a growth field in moral philosophy (Flanagan, 1996; Gibbard, 1990), and there was even a new movement called Experimental Philosophy (or "X-Phi"), in which philosophers conducted psychological experiments, often on moral intuitions (e.g,. Petrinovich and O'Neill 1996; and later Greene et al. 2001).

My own work in moral psychology grew out of all of these intersecting and sometimes conflicting streams of research and scholarship. My dissertation (Haidt, Koller, & Dias, 1993) was a test of a debate between the anthropologist Richard Shweder and the developmental psychologist Elliot Turiel over their competing claims about whether the moral domain is (descriptively) circumscribed by the concepts of harm, rights, and justice (as Turiel, 1983, had proposed) or whether it was broader, in many societies, including an "ethic of community" and an "ethic of divinity" (as Shweder, Mahapatra, & Miller, 1987, had proposed). My cross-cultural study of "harmless taboo violations" (such as a family that eats its already-dead pet dog) across cultures and social classes strongly supported Shweder's claims—it was only the highly educated groups that limited the moral domain to harm, rights, and justice.

The rest of my career has been an effort to study the expanded and culturally variable moral domain that Shweder had helped me to see, to ground its origins in evolution, to explain its operation and its quirks using neuroscience and cognitive psychology, and then to (carefully, gingerly) explore the normative ramifications of an expanded and culturally variable moral domain, especially as these variations help to explain the "culture war" currently rocking the USA and many Western democracies.

I wrote up my vision of what a cross-disciplinary moral psychology would look like in a 2001 essay in *Psychological Review* titled "The Emotional Dog and its Rational Tail: A Social Intuitionist Theory of Morality." I then teamed up with Craig Joseph (a former Shweder student) and Jesse Graham (now at the University of Utah) to expand the Social Intuitionist Model by specifying what, exactly, the intuitions were (Haidt & Graham, 2009; Haidt & Joseph, 2007). We proposed that there were at least five innate "foundations" upon which all societies build their variable moralities: care/harm, fairness/cheating, loyalty/betrayal, authority/subversion, and purity/degradation. Graham and I then began a collaboration to test and improve this new "Moral Foundations Theory" with Ravi Iyer, Sena Koleva, Pete Ditto, and Sean Wojcik. We created an online site where anyone with access to the internet could take the Moral Foundations Questionnaire and many other morality surveys. The site is at YourMorals.org, which is now run by Morteza Dehghani at the University of Southern California (for a review of our findings, and of MFT, please see Graham et al. 2013).

My essay on the social intuitionist model was published in September, 2001—the same month that Joshua Greene published his landmark fMRI study showing that when people choose the "deontological" choice in trolley dilemmas (to respect the autonomy of the potential victim rather than sacrificing them for the greater utilitarian good), their decisions depend on the emotional integration centers that Damasio had pointed to, not on the areas involved in cool rational deliberation. These two articles, published at the same time, are sometimes pointed to as a turning point in the trajectory of moral psychology. Unfortunately, that same month saw hijackers crash airliners into the World Trade Center and the Pentagon, which, by a tragic chain of events, became the launching point for three very long wars: in Afghanistan, in Iraq, and against "terror." That attack and those wars mark a turning point in many Western nations from the exuberant and hopeful post-Cold War 1990s to the darker, more conflict-ridden 21st century. Now, in the early 2020s, with so much political turbulence, great power politics, and a loss of confidence in liberal democracy among younger generations, many are asking: what went wrong, and what do we do now? Moral psychology can help us understand why it is so hard for people to live together, find truth together, and build widely trusted institutions together.

The next decade (or century) of moral psychology

What will the future bring? As Phil Tetlock's work on prediction shows, experts armed with detailed information can't usually predict the future much better than a coinflip or a monkey throwing darts (Tetlock & Gardner, 2015), so I'll stick close to the present and just talk about two trends that may matter for the community of researchers in moral psychology.

1) Social Media and Epistemic Chaos

In the science fiction novel Neuromancer, the matrix is defined as "a consensual hallucination" (Gibson, 1982). That's a good description of social reality too. But when social media platforms such as Facebook and Twitter blossomed, and became far more viral in the early 2010s, it greatly sped up the process of social construction and made widely shared and stable social understandings nearly impossible to maintain. I have argued that social media knocked over the (metaphorical) Tower of Babel (Haidt, 2022) around 2014, condemning humanity for the foreseeable future to an inability to understand one other. I think that the most urgent task for social scientists in the next decade is to study the phase change or social rewiring that happened in the 2010s, plunging us into an era of epistemic chaos in which everyone is drowning under a waterfall of "content" that confirms their pre-existing beliefs and prejudices. With so much confirmation that the other side is truly evil, I believe that moral conflict and culture wars will get ever more intense. As AI begins to create far more of this "content," things will get much worse. I believe that the study and mitigation of social media's effects on human relationships and democratic functioning should be among the top research priorities of democratic nations and science funding organizations.

2) Political Polarization and Distrust of Social Science

In 2011, I became concerned that there was essentially no political diversity in my field, social psychology. After a long search, I was able to find just one politically conservative professor. I and five colleagues then wrote an article explaining why the absence of political diversity damaged the quality of research in social psychology (Crawford et al., 2015). In 2015 I grew far more alarmed as the United States and other English-speaking countries experienced a wave of activism and moralism on college campuses in which students, professors, and visiting speakers who merely *questioned* the beliefs and policies most cherished on the left were actively persecuted, shamed, silenced, and in a few cases physically attacked (Lukianoff & Haidt, 2018). This rapid conversion (sometimes called "the great awokening"; Yglesias, 2018) is disastrous for universities, because they must have public trust both for the credibility of academic research and for their financial survival as recipients of taxpayer support. Yet as professors, universities, and professional organizations in the English-speaking countries have become more explicit in their support for left-wing values, parties, and candidates, they are, predictably, earning the distrust and enmity of citizens, organizations, and legislators on the right. If I am correct that the Western world is heading in to a period of much greater epistemological and political chaos, then it is urgent that universities and researchers reverse their politicization, focus on their truth-seeking missions, do their jobs well, and regain public trust (Haidt, 2022).

In conclusion: I believe that the 21st century will turn out to be the century of moral psychology.
There will be extraordinary material progress coming out of the natural sciences and engineering, but it may all be for naught if we cannot understand the forces of moralism, judgmentalism,

hatred, and division that are part of human nature, that are weakening democracies, and that might even be warping the social sciences.

Will we rise to the challenge? This volume offers a comprehensive look at the current state of the field, and points ahead to the work we must do.

References

Barkow, J. H., Cosmides, L., & Tooby, J. (Eds.). (1992). *The adapted mind: Evolutionary psychology and the generation of culture*. New York: Oxford.

Chomsky, N. (1959). Review of Skinner's "Verbal Behavior." *Language, 35*, 26–58.

Crawford, J. T., Duarte, J. L., Haidt, J., Jussim, L., Stern, C., & Tetlock, P. E. (2015). It may be harder than we thought, but political diversity will (still) improve social psychological science. *Behavioral and Brain Sciences, 38*, e164.

Damasio, A. (1994). *Descartes' error: Emotion, reason, and the human brain*. New York: Putnam.

de Waal, F. B. M. (1996). *Good natured: The origins of right and wrong in humans and other animals*. Cambridge, MA: Harvard University Press.

Flanagan, O. (1996). Ethics naturalized: Ethics as human ecology. In L. May, M. Friedman & A. Clark (Eds.), *Mind and Morals: Essays on ethics and cognitive science* (pp. 19–43). Cambridge, MA, MIT Press:.

Freud, S. (1976/1900). *The interpretation of dreams* (J. Strachey, Trans.). New York: Norton.

Gibbard, A. (1990). *Wise choices, apt feelings*. Cambridge, MA: Harvard University Press.

Gibson, W. (1993) *Neuromancer*. London: Harper.

Graham, J., Haidt, J., Koleva, S., Motyl, M., Iyer, R., Wojcik, S., & Ditto, P. H. (2013). Moral foundations theory: The pragmatic validity of moral pluralism. *Advances in Experimental Social Psychology, 47*, 55–130.

Greene, J. D., Sommerville, R. B., Nystrom, L. E., Darley, J. M., & Cohen, J. D. (2001). An fMRI investigation of emotional engagement in moral judgment. *Science, 293*, 2105–2108.

Haidt, J. (2001). The emotional dog and its rational tail: A social intuitionist approach to moral judgment. *Psychological Review, 108*, 814–834.

Haidt, J. (2022). When truth and social justice collide, choose truth. *Chronicle of Higher Education*, Sept. 23, 2022.

Haidt, J., & Baron, J. (1996). Social roles and the moral judgment of acts and omissions. *European Journal of Social Psychology, 26*, 201–218.

Haidt, J., & Graham, J. (2009). Planet of the Durkheimians, where community, authority, and sacredness are foundations of morality. In J. Jost, A. C. Kay, & H. Thorisdottir (Eds.), *Social and psychological bases of ideology and system justification* (pp. 371–401). New York: Oxford.

Haidt, J. & C. Joseph (2007). The moral mind: How 5 sets of innate intuitions guide the development of many culture-specific virtues, and perhaps even modules. In P. Carruthers, S. Laurence & S. Stich (Eds.)*The innate mind, Vol. 3.* (pp. 367–391). New York, Oxford.

Haidt, J., Koller, S., & Dias, M. (1993). Affect, culture, and morality, or is it wrong to eat your dog? *Journal of Personality and Social Psychology, 65*, 613–628.

Kohlberg, L. (1969). Stage and sequence: The cognitive-developmental approach to socialization. In D. A. Goslin (Ed.), *Handbook of socialization theory and research* (pp. 347–480). Chicago: Rand McNally.

Lukianoff, G. & Haidt, J. (2018). *The coddling of the American mind: How good intentions and bad ideas are setting up a generation for failure*. London: Penguin.

Markus, H. R., & Kitayama, S. (1991). Culture and the self: Implications for cognition, emotion, and motivation. *Psychological Review, 98*, 224–253.

McDougall, W. (1998/1908). *An introduction to social psychology*. Boston: John W. Luce.

Petrinovich, L., & O'Neill, P. (1996). Influence of wording and framing effects on moral intuitions. *Ethology and Sociobiology, 17*, 145–171.

Piaget, J. (1965/1932). *The moral judgement of the child* (M. Gabain, Trans.). New York: Free Press.

Pinker, S. (2002). *The blank slate: The modern denial of human nature*. New York: Viking.

Rittel, H. W. J., & Webber, M. (1973). Dilemmas in a general theory of planning. *Policy Sciences, 4*, 155–169.

Shweder, R. A. (1990). Cultural psychology: What is it? In J. W. Stigler, R. A. Shweder, & G. Herdt (Eds.), *Cultural psychology: Essays on comparative human development* (pp. 1–43). New York: Cambridge University Press.

Shweder, R. A., Mahapatra, M., & Miller, J. (1987). Culture and moral development. In J. Kagan & S. Lamb (Eds.), *The emergence of morality in young children* (pp. 1–83). Chicago: University of Chicago Press.
Skinner, B. F. (1971). *Beyond freedom and dignity*. New York: Alfred A. Knopf.
Tetlock, P. E., & Gardner, D. (2015). *Superforcasting: The art and science of prediction*. New York: Crown.
Turiel, E. (1983). *The development of social knowledge: Morality and convention*. Cambridge, England: Cambridge University Press.
Venter, C., & Cohen, D. (2004). The century of biology. *New Perspectives Quarterly, 21*, 73–77.
Wilson, E. O. (1975). *Sociobiology*. Cambridge, MA: Harvard University Press.

PART II

Moral reasoning

PART IIA

A vision on moral reasoning

3
MORAL REASONING
My personal journey

Linda Klebe Treviño

Introduction

To think about what sparked my interest and work related to moral reasoning, I delved back decades to my doctoral program in management at Texas A&M University. True confessions – starting out, I wasn't interested in moral reasoning at all. But I was intrigued (for some reason I didn't yet understand) by the many business ethics scandals in the early to mid-1980s (scandals that were thought to be a "fad," by the way). I wondered what we knew about the thinking and behaviour of those involved. Over time, I became even more interested in understanding ethical and unethical behaviour in an organizational (work) context. I discovered after an extensive search that the management literature had little to offer from a behavioural perspective. There had been normative pieces written by philosophers about what businesspeople "should" and "should not" do and a few survey studies that asked managers about their experiences, but there was little theoretical or empirical work on the question of what employees think and do and why they behave as they do. That presented an opportunity for a curious doctoral student looking for a way to contribute.

While searching related literatures to see what I could learn, I discovered cognitive moral development theory (CMD) (Kohlberg, 1969) developed by Lawrence Kohlberg, a Harvard cognitive psychologist who interviewed a set of young boys over a number of years as they developed in their thinking about hypothetical moral issues. I was intrigued by what the theory told me, especially when I learned that some of Kohlberg's students, Rest among others, had extended the work to adults (e.g., Rest, 1986). Critical to me was learning that, according to Kohlberg's theory, most adults were at the conventional level of CMD and were looking outside themselves for guidance in ethical dilemma situations. That helped to explain why most adults at work were so open to external influence from peers, authority figures, and organizational cultures including incentive systems. I was also interested to learn that some people were more advanced and autonomous in their thinking and action, making justice and rights-based decisions. That helped me to explain the action of people such as those who reported misconduct, often at great risk to themselves. And I learned that some adults were "stuck" in pre-conventional thinking where only rewards and punishments (or tit for tat thinking) matter. But most important was the notion that this theory explained why factors external to the individual were SO crucial to understanding employee ethical thinking and action. With CMD in hand, I was inspired to write a paper that became my first major publication, a conceptual paper published in the *Academy of Management Review* entitled "Ethical Decision Making in Organizations: A Person-Situation Interactionist Perspective (Treviño, 1986). Cognitive moral development was prominent in the model but I used it to explain that most employees would be quite open to those external influences noted above. That paper went on to inspire my doctoral dissertation, and I was able to test and support part of the proposed model (Treviño & Youngblood, 1990). The remainder of this chapter will highlight other aspects of my research stream related to ethical decision making, from cognitive processes to affective processes.

Cognitive processes: ethical awareness

When I arrived at Penn State in 1987 (for my first and sole academic position), I had become familiar with the work of Kohlberg's student, James Rest and his four-stage model that extended beyond moral judgment to acknowledge the importance of ethical recognition as a first step. But that first step had received little research attention and I hadn't given it much thought. My dissertation had begun with the assumption that people knew that they were facing an ethical dilemma, as Kohlberg had done. A hallway encounter set me straight. My colleague Denny Gioia thought I was missing something important. He relayed that, prior to his academic career, he had been the recall coordinator at Ford Motor Company when Ford was producing Pintos and considering whether to recall a car that exploded in slow rear-end collisions. Although they considered recalling Pintos twice while Denny was there, they didn't recall until years later, well after Denny had left and after the case hit the press (and the courts). Denny said something revelational – that, while at Ford, he had never thought about the decision to recall or not as an "ethical" decision. According to him (now a social cognition expert) it was a decision driven by the dominant cognitive scripts that he followed to do his very difficult, information intensive job. For example, in order to initiate a safety recall, he needed a number of cases (he had very few), and traceable cause to a problem that could and should be fixed by the company. And for a long time, Ford didn't know why the cars exploded at low impact other than that they were little cars being hit in the rear by big ones. At that point, a light bulb went on in my head and I realized that more attention needed to be paid to researching the notion of what we termed ethical awareness. It seemed obvious that "moral reasoning" or judgment couldn't happen unless the person was consciously aware that the situation involved ethical concerns of harm/care, fairness, etc. This seemed particularly important in business settings where one could easily, intentionally or not, fail to "see" the ethical concerns. Decisions could be seen as "business" decisions (as in the Challenger disaster) (Vaughan, 1996). During the decision about whether to launch the Challenger space shuttle in cold weather in 1986, engineers were told to put on their manager hats, which arguably moved them away from prioritizing safety (ethical) concerns as engineers are taught to do. The Challenger blew up seconds after launch with multiple astronauts inside including the first "teacher in space." In follow-up research on ethical awareness, my colleagues and I found that three factors influenced ethical awareness among competitive intelligence professionals: the amount of harm they thought was involved, whether social consensus existed that the behaviour under consideration was ethically problematic, and whether ethical language (instead of business language) was used (Butterfield, Treviño, & Weaver, 2000).

Some in behavioral ethics in organizations have studied a related concept they refer to as bounded ethicality, "ethical blind spots" and "ethical fading" (Bazerman & Tenbrunsel, 2011). The authors argue that, in work organizations, many simply are blind to the ethical implications of their decisions and their "want selves" win over their "should selves" at decision time as the ethical import remains out of view in favor of the business implications of a decision. That is somewhat consistent with the research described above that found the importance of using ethical language to increase ethical awareness and Diane Vaughn's finding that when managers were exhorted to make a "management" decision, the decision criteria to launch the Challenger changed. But, ethnographic research I conducted with colleagues (den Nieuwenboer, de Cunha & Treviño, 2017) also showed that, often, employees who are pressured by managers to engage in unethical actions, are absolutely aware that what they're doing is wrong and they are willing to say so. The ethical implications do not fade but are rather overwhelmed by situational factors. If the employees need the job and can't get a comparable one, most will comply with the request to behave unethically despite expressed (and continued) discomfort.

Cognitive processes: moral disengagement at work

I became interested in another relevant moral cognition process termed moral disengagement, theorized by Bandura (2016). Moral disengagement is based upon the notion that human behaviour is directed by internalized moral standards that generally keep our behavior in line with those standards because we anticipate that we would experience guilt or sanction if we engaged in the contemplated unethical action. But importantly, those internalized moral standards can be cognitively disengaged to allow individuals to behave unethically without guilt. Bandura theorized moral disengagement as an individual difference – some individuals are more inclined toward moral disengagement than others and he developed a measure of it. The moral disengagement process seemed relevant to my work because several of the eight theorized moral disengagement mechanisms are highly related to the rationalizations we see organizational members use to justify unethical behavior. For example, organizations are authority structures and *displacement of responsibility* to an authority figure is a common rationalization used to justify unethical action – "my boss made me do it." *Diffusion of responsibility* to a group is also relevant as when an employee might say, "this was a group decision. I didn't have much say." Organizational actors are also known to blame the victim (e.g., *attribution of blame* – "it's their own fault for not checking the fine print"). Other moral disengagement mechanisms include moral justification, euphemistic labeling, advantageous comparison, distortion of consequences and dehumanization. My colleagues and I studied moral disengagement in adults in work contexts and related it to a variety of types of unethical conduct including fraud. We also developed a highly reliable measure that was designed for adults in work settings and can be used to predict who will be more likely to engage in it (Moore, Detert, Treviño, Baker, & Mayer, 2012). We treated moral disengagement as an individual difference in this research (as Bandura did). However, in other research, we also found that it could be triggered by different types of work situations (Kish-Gephart, Detert, Treviño, Baker, & Martin, 2014).

Affective processes: moral outrage

Finally, tracking work in moral psychology, my work moved in the direction of considering the importance of affect (rather than just cognition). So, my interest in moral reasoning moved to focus on moral thinking *and* feeling. Multiple projects focused on moral outrage (a combination of anger and disgust) and its powerful effects on behaviour. For example, my colleagues and I applied qualitative methods to study the media's treatment of Joe Paterno, long-time head (American) football coach at Penn State University who was known for decades for his integrity and for being a moral beacon in a sea of misconduct in college football. A scandal surfaced in 2001 when a state grand jury indicted former defensive football coach Jerry Sandusky for molesting young boys who were associated with the charity he had started. At least one event occurred on Penn State's campus in the football facility shower. That event had been reported to Paterno, which he then reported up the chain as was required. Yet, despite much ambiguity about his role, many in the press and the public held Joe Paterno responsible for not doing more, and his moral beacon image was besmirched in less than a week and never recovered (Bishop, Treviño, Gioia & Kreiner, 2021).

Affective processes: fear, elevation and voice

I have long been interested in speaking up in organizations and I co-authored a paper on how the emotion, fear, stops people from speaking up (Kish-Gephart, Detert, Treviño & Edmondson, 2009). My co-authors and I viewed silence as the default because of the paralysis that accompanies the widely reported fear of retaliation. More recently, my work has focused on what we are terming ethical voice (speaking up about ethical issues within groups and work units). In some of that work, we became interested in understanding the consequences for the voicer who does choose to speak up. There, we hypothesized and found that those who voice ethical issues within work groups and units can get support from co-workers because the ethical voice leads to moral elevation in observers, a positive emotional response that makes co-workers regard the voicer highly and wish to emulate him or her. In that research, we used survey, experimental, and qualitative methods (Chen & Treviño, 2022). More and more, I believe, as I think most would agree, that cognition and emotion go hand in hand and need to be understood together as we attempt to move knowledge forward about moral reasoning.

Conclusion

A concluding note about methodology. Much moral psychology and behavioral ethics research published in the top journals is experimental and conducted in the behavioural lab. We have certainly learned a great deal from that work. But I see experiments as somewhat limited for my own work because, generally, they have limited ability to capture the organizational context that I continue to believe is so important. So, multiple research methods have guided my work, including qualitative methods which I am using increasingly. In reflecting, I find it fascinating that the work of Kohlberg that initially inspired me was qualitative. But most of the subsequent work on moral reasoning has not been. I encourage others to explore this avenue going forward, although I offer fair warning to get training on how to do qualitative research right.

One more note – While writing the preface to my textbook, I had a revelation about why I have been driven for almost 40 years to understand why people do good and bad things. My parents were Holocaust survivors, German Jews who fortunately found their way to the US in the late 1930s. They didn't dwell on the past. They were too focused on hard work and the good fortune that allowed them to survive and to make a good life for themselves and their children in the US. But questions about those who harmed and those who helped always lurked in the background for me and I came to realize that my family's powerful narrative helps to explain my decades-long motivation.

References

Bandura, A. 2016. *How do people harm and live with themselves*. New York: Worth Publishing.
Bazerman, M. H. & Tenbrunsel, A. E. 2011. *Blind spots: Why we fail to do what's right and what to do about it*. Princeton, NJ: University Press.

Bishop, D.G., Treviño, L.K., Gioia, D.A., & Kreiner, G.E. 2021. Leveraging a recessive narrative to transform Joe Paterno's image: Media sensebreaking, sensemaking, and sensegiving during scandal. *Academy of Management Discoveries*, *6*(4): 572–608.

Butterfield, K., Treviño, L. K., & Weaver, G. R. 2000. Moral awareness in business organizations: Influences of issue-related and social context factors. *Human Relations*, *53*(7): 981–1018.

Chen, A. & Treviño, L. K. 2022. Promotive and prohibitive ethical voice: Coworker emotions and support for the voice. *Journal of Applied Psychology*, *107*(11), 1973–1994.

Den Nieuwenboer, N., Vieira da Cunha, J., & Treviño, L. K. 2017. Middle managers and corruptive routine translation: The social production of deceptive performance. *Organization Science*, *28*(5): 781–803.

Kish-Gephart, J., Detert, J. R., Treviño, L. K., & Edmondson, A. C. 2009. Silenced by fear: The nature, sources, and consequences of fear at work. *Research in Organizational Behavior*, *29*: 163–193.

Kish-Gephart, J., Detert, J., Treviño, Baker, V., & Martin, S. L. K. 2014. Situational moral disengagement: Can the effects of self-interest be mitigated? *Journal of Business Ethics, 125*: 267–285.

Kohlberg L. (1969). Stage and sequence: The cognitive-developmental approach to socialization. In Mischel T. (Ed.), *Cognitive development and epistemolog*, pp. 151–235. New York, NY: Academic Press.

Moore, C., Detert, J. R., Treviño, L. K., Baker, V. L., Mayer, D. V. 2012. Why employees do bad things: Moral disengagement and unethical organizational behavior. *Personnel Psychology*, *65*(1): 1–48.

Rest, J. 1986. *Moral development: Advances in research and theory*. NY: Praeger.

Treviño, L. K. 1986. Ethical decision making in organizations: A person-situation interactionist Model. *Academy of Management Review*, *11*(3): 601–617.

Treviño, L. K. & Youngblood, S. A. 1990. Bad apples in bad barrels: A causal analysis of ethical decision-making behavior. *Journal of Applied Psychology, 75*: 378–385.

Vaughan, D. 1996. *The Challenger launch decision: Risky technology, culture, and deviance at NASA*. Chicago: University of Chicago Press.

PART IIB

Empirical review chapters on moral reasoning

4
THE INTRAPERSONAL LEVEL
Intrapersonal moral reasoning

Paul Conway

Abstract

Sacrificial moral dilemmas comprise cases where people decide to cause some harm to prevent greater harm. Hence, they entail a trade-off between moral concerns about avoiding harming others and concerns about maximizing overall wellbeing. Though these dilemmas originated in philosophy, decades of research suggests that dilemma decisions arise from various psychological mechanisms. Here, I review the development of models of intrapersonal moral reasoning and decision-making, examining both traditional analytic approaches—measuring relative preferences for rejecting harm versus maximizing outcomes—and modelling approaches—which disentangle multiple response tendencies underlying relative decisions. Regarding theory, I raise doubts about the classic "hard" dual process model that contrasts rapid affective processing with slower deliberative processing. Instead, I suggest findings are best explained by a "soft" reinterpretation of the dual process model, where multiple processes contribute to each decision, but responses nonetheless reflect a different preponderance of affective and cognitive processing.

- Research on moral reasoning examines how people prioritize clashing moral concerns in dilemmas where maximizing overall outcomes (upholding utilitarian perspectives) requires causing sacrificial harm (violating deontological perspectives).
- Traditional approaches examine only *relative preferences* for rejecting harm versus maximizes outcomes.
- Alternatively, modelling approaches independently estimate harm rejection and outcome maximization tendencies, allowing for more nuanced insight into empirical relationships.
- Data raise doubts about the original "hard" dual process model contrasting rapid affective reactions to harm with slower deliberative evaluations of outcomes
- Instead, data remain consistent with a "soft" dual process model, where multiple processes contribute to each judgment, with a different relative preponderance of affective and deliberative processing

Introduction

Should you sacrifice a baby to save a village? Should you deploy troops to defend your people? Should you limit freedoms to contain a deadly disease? Such cases exemplify *sacrificial dilemmas*, cases where harmful outcomes can only be prevented by actions causing lesser harm—a sacrifice for the greater good. In sacrificial dilemmas, the same action produces both objectionable and laudable outcomes. Hence, unlike research on prosocial or antisocial behavior which contrasts moral concern with self-interest, sacrificial dilemma research examines how people prioritize clashing moral concerns—when people feel sacrifice is worthwhile to secure overall wellbeing.

Although sometimes derided as fanciful *trolleyology*—after the famous case where a trolley will kill five people unless redirected to kill one—sacrificial dilemmas unfortunately describe many real-world problems involving questions of whose rights may be trampled to protect others' rights or when suffering can be morally justified (e.g., Truog et al., 2003). Hence, clarifying the psychology involved in such dilemmas is of paramount societal importance.

The intrapersonal psychological mechanisms leading to sacrificial decisions may be described as *moral reasoning*.[1] In the current work, I first describe sacrificial dilemmas, considering their origins and connection to philosophy. Next, I compare traditional approaches examining dilemma judgments directly with modelling approaches that estimate the independent contributions of response tendencies underlying judgments. Then I raise questions about the original "hard" dual process model, suggesting instead that evidence instead remains consistent with a "soft" reinterpretation of the dual process model. Finally, I consider important future directions for the field. For interpersonal elements of moral reasoning and decisions made in sacrificial dilemmas see Everett (this volume).

Sacrificial dilemmas

Moral psychology is a vast and multifaceted area of inquiry, including thoughts and feelings about abstract moral principles, rights and duties, the social anchoring of right and wrong, the moral character of oneself and others, and moral decisions of specific acts and behaviors (Krebs, 2008; Ellemers et al., 2019). Here I focus on intrapersonal reasoning about whether actions are right or wrong—specifically addressing sacrificial actions where causing harm maximizes overall outcomes.

Sacrificial dilemmas originated in philosophy (Foot, 1967). The classic *trolley dilemma* involves potentially redirecting a runaway train: "A runaway trolley is headed for five people who will be killed if it proceeds on its present course. The only way to save them is to hit a switch that will turn the trolley onto an alternate set of tracks where it will kill one person instead of five. Ought you to turn the trolley in order to save five people at the expense of one?" (Greene et al., 2001, p. 2105).

Dilemmas originated as rhetorical arguments to illustrate the *doctrine of double effect*, the acceptability of harm as a focal goal versus byproduct of action (Foot, 1967). Yet, subsequent theorists began describing decisions in terms of mainstream philosophical positions. Specifically, sacrificial actions cause harm, and therefore violate the principle of *deontology*, which judges the morality of actions by their intrinsic nature: doing harm itself is wrong and immoral, regardless of outcomes (e.g., Kant, 1785). Yet, sacrificial actions also prevent suffering or death of many more people, leading to a net gain in total wellbeing. Hence, they uphold *consequentialist* or *utilitarian* ethics that prioritize the consequences or utility of actions: actions that produce the greatest benefits for the most people are judged most moral from this perspective (Mill, 1861/1998).

Accordingly, theorists often characterize sacrificial dilemmas as a conflict between deontological and utilitarian ethics. This conceptualization sometimes leads theorists to assume that people who arrive at a decision adhere to the philosophical principle that would explain that decision. From a psychological point of view, decisions are better described as *aligning with* but not *caused by* philosophical theory. Indeed, a multitude of psychological processes may lead people to arrive at a given decision, few of which reflect philosophical concerns. Originally, researchers conceptualized two such processes—affective reactions to harm and cognitive evaluations of outcomes—pitted against one another in the "hard" dual process model. Research now identifies many such processes, that loosely align in a revised "soft" dual process model we will consider below.

Analytic approaches

Traditional approach: relative preference for harm rejection versus outcome-maximization

Traditionally, researchers have examined moral reasoning in sacrificial dilemmas by presenting participants with dilemmas where causing harm maximizes outcomes and assessing their responses. Researchers might offer participants a single dilemma and code whether they indicate that sacrificial harm is *appropriate* or *not appropriate*. Researchers may also sum responses across a battery of dilemmas or assess relative degrees of accepting sacrificial harm on seven-point scales. Sometimes they examine other wording, like "would you" sacrifice?

Much work using the traditional approach manipulates dilemma elements to test how responses shift. For example, researchers compare responses to *impersonal* dilemmas, where harm is mechanically mediated—as in hitting a switch in the trolley dilemma—with *personal* dilemmas where harm is "up close and personal," such as pushing a heavy person off a footbridge to stop a runaway trolley. People are more averse to using their physical muscles than mechanical force for sacrifices (e.g., Greene et al., 2009). People are also more averse to harming ingroup members and members of disadvantaged groups than outgroup or advantaged members (Uhlmann et al., 2009). In addition, much work examines how response patterns correlate with individual difference variables—for example, people high in empathic concern tend to reject sacrificial harm (Gleichgerrcht & Young, 2013). Other work tracks how different groups of people respond—for example, people in Asia and South America tend to reject harm more often than those in North America and Europe, perhaps due to tighter social norms against harm (e.g., Awad et al., 2020).

Although the traditional approach is useful for assessing responses to dilemmas, it suffers from a key problem: people only face decisions pitting sacrificial harm against maximizing outcomes. Responses are treated as direct opposites: accepting sacrificial harm requires not rejecting sacrificial harm, and vice versa. This means the traditional approach cannot assess how much people want to reject harm independently of how much they want to maximize outcomes—responses reflect a *relative preference* for each response. Hence, it is unclear whether a given response (say, reject sacrificial harm) reflects a strong unilateral preference for rejecting harm, a weak preference for rejecting harm, or an internal debate between rejecting harm and maximizing outcomes. These cases have radically different implications for the underlying mechanisms, yet traditional analyses treat them as equivalent. Moreover, any measure related to both response tendencies will not show up because these competing effects will cancel one another out, which is called *suppression*. Therefore, researchers developed modelling approaches which increase sensitivity by independently estimating the strength of harm-rejection and outcome-maximization response tendencies.

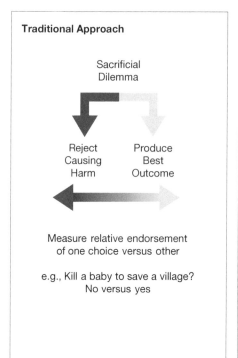
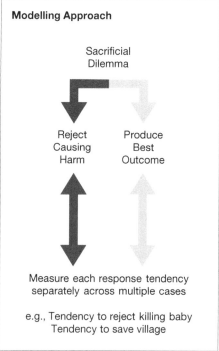
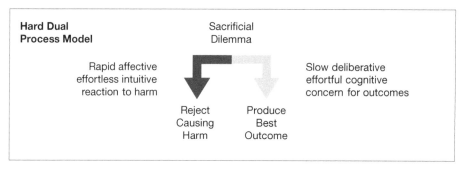
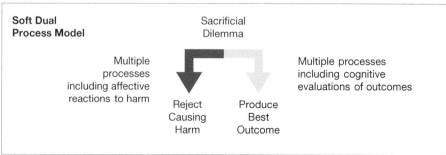

Figure 4.1 The difference between traditional versus modelling approaches and the hard versus soft dual process models.

This approach clarifies whether someone has a strong or weak preference for rejecting harm and can detect cases of suppression.

Modelling approaches: independently assessing harm rejection and outcome-maximization

Whereas traditional models assess people's judgments on dilemmas where causing harm maximizes outcomes, modelling approaches aim to estimate the unique tendency to reject harm and maximize outcomes underlying responses. They achieve this by examining not only cases where harm maximizes outcomes—such as killing a baby to save a village from death—but also parallel cases where harm (arguably) does not maximize overall outcomes—such as killing a baby to save a village from labor. They then use linear algebra or multinomial modelling to estimate patterns of responding across cases: the degree to which people *maximize outcomes*, regardless of harm, and *reject sacrificial harm*, regardless of outcomes (and sometimes other patterns). See Figure 4.1 for an illustration of the difference between traditional and modelling approaches.

Conway and Gawronski (2013) developed the first modelling approach by adapting a technique from the memory literature called process dissociation. This technique examines responses to dilemmas where causing harm does and does not (arguably) maximize outcomes, creating one estimate of harm rejection (called the *deontology parameter*) and one of outcome maximization (called the *utilitarian parameter*).[2] Although process dissociation proved useful (see below), critics noted that someone could reject harm either because they care about the focal target or because they simply wish to avoid getting involved whatsoever. Hence, Gawronski et al. (2017) later expanded to the *consequences norms inaction (CNI) model*, which estimates sensitivity to consequences (*consequences parameter*), concern for moral norms (*norms parameter*), and general inaction tendencies (*inaction parameter*). Like process dissociation, the CNI model assesses responses across cases where harmful action does and does not maximize overall outcomes, but it adds cases where inaction likewise does and does not maximize overall outcomes (for a debate over the meaning of these parameters see Baron & Goodwin, 2020 and Gawronski et al., 2020).

Rather than treating responses as relative preferences for harm rejection and outcome maximization responses, modelling approaches separately estimate how much people show each response pattern. The advantage of this approach is twofold. First, this allows modelling approaches to clarify where findings detected via traditional methods impact one response pattern versus the other. Second, this allows greater sensitivity in cases of suppression, where something simultaneously impacts both response tendencies. Let us consider some examples.

The clearest case involves antisocial personality traits like psychopathy, egoism, and acceptance of ethics violations. Numerous studies using the traditional approach have demonstrated that such antisocial traits predict increased willingness to sacrifice people to achieve overall outcomes (e.g., Bartels & Pizarro, 2011). Typically, this finding is reported as "people high in psychopathy are more utilitarian" and has led some researchers to suggest that dilemma research fails to assess genuine concern for utilitarian outcomes (e.g., Kahane et al., 2018). However, as traditional approaches measure only relative preferences, this finding could also be reported as "people high in psychopathy are less deontological," i.e., especially willing to accept sacrificial harm. Modelling approaches can clarify which description is more accurate.

Indeed, modelling studies find no evidence for the claim that "people high in psychopathy are more utilitarian"—instead, this pattern in relative judgments reflects reduced concerns about causing harm (e.g., Conway et al., 2018; Luke & Gawronski, 2021). That is, people high in antisocial traits accept harm *both* when doing so harm maximizes outcomes and when it does not. Moreover, modelling approaches reveal suppression: they show that people high in antisocial personality traits also often score low in concern for outcomes—though this effect size is somewhat smaller than rejecting harm (they also score low in inaction, i.e., high impulsivity). Therefore, people high in antisocial traits only appear to prefer utilitarian judgments in traditional measures—they actually care little about maximizing outcomes *and even less* about rejecting harm. "Relatively more utilitarian" traditional scores here reflect low absolute utilitarian concerns coupled with even lower absolute deontological concerns. This suggests that the problem of utilitarian judgments among antisocial people is not with dilemmas as a paradigm but rather with interpreting traditional relative measures. For more information on antisociality and sacrificial decisions, see Everett (this volume).

In another important case of suppression, measures of moral concern such as moral identity and moral conviction about harm show the opposite pattern: they predict both increased harm rejection and increased outcome maximization (Conway et al., 2018; Körner et al., 2020). These effect sizes are typically similar, so these effects completely cancel one another out in traditional analyses. In other words, people high in moral concern do not show a relative preference for rejecting harm versus maximizing outcomes *because they are equally concerned with both*—a pattern only visible using modelling. Similar cases of suppression can occur for emotional concern for victims (Reynolds & Conway, 2018), logical reasoning (Byrd & Conway, 2019), and stable childhood environments that promote ethical concern (Maranges, et al., 2021). Therefore, modelling approaches buy increased precision and sensitivity over traditional approaches and suggest dilemma studies are more useful than some critics claim.

That said, some theorists have challenged modelling approaches on conceptual grounds (e.g., Baron & Goodwin, 2020). Modeling approaches must specify using theory which actions are conceptualized as maximizing outcomes; there may be cases where researchers and participants disagree. Modelling parameters reflect patterns of judgment and should not be taken as direct measures of philosophical thinking or psychological processes (Gawronski et al., 2020).

Theoretical models of moral reasoning

Two decades of research has produced a vast body of evidence from both traditional and modelling methods. Despite initial support, evidence casts doubt on the original "hard" dual process model. Instead, evidence remains consistent with a "softer" reinterpretation.

Original "Hard" dual process model

Greene (e.g., 2007) originally described the dual process model in terms of rapid, automatic processing motivating harm rejection versus slower, controlled processing motivating outcome-maximization—i.e., a battle of moral intuition versus reasoning (see Haidt, 2001). Greene drew on classic social cognitive models of dual process systems, where harmful actions presumably evoke efficient, unconscious, unintentional, and uncontrollable aversion (Bargh, 1994). Given sufficient time and motivation to deliberate, people may subsequently engage in expensive, conscious, intentional, and controllable reasoning regarding outcomes, which favors sacrifice for the greater good. The hard version of the dual process model is sometimes described as the *default-interventionist* model (Evans & Stanovich, 2013), insofar as automatic processes are assumed to drive moral responses by default unless there is sufficient time and motivation to engage in deliberation. The model is "hard" in the sense that it posits two and only two processes, and specifies the exact way they interact—rapid, automatic, and affective versus slower, controlled, and cognitive (see Cushman, 2013 for a reinterpretation using computational algorithms).

Support for the hard dual process model stems from (a) manipulations like the personal-impersonal distinction that theoretically manipulate affective or cognitive processing, (b) individual differences in affective or cognitive measures related to affect and cognition like empathic concern and need for cognition, (c) differences in reaction times for different responses, and (d) fMRI data suggesting different brain regions involved in each decision (e.g., Conway & Gawronski, 2013; Gleichgerrcht & Young, 2013; Greene et al., 2001; Greene et al., 2009).

However, critics have noted confounding factors in manipulations like the personal-impersonal distinction (e.g., Körner et al., 2019), demonstrated more complexity than previously appreciated in individual differences (e.g., Reynolds & Conway, 2018; Byrd & Conway, 2019), cast doubt on time differences between accepting versus rejecting sacrificial harm (e.g., Baron & Gürçay, 2017), and criticized the clarify of the fMRI findings (e.g., Klein, 2011). Moreover, modern social cognitive research casts doubt on the simplistic claims of earlier dual process theories (Corneille & Hütter, 2020). Hence, there remains little support for the simplistic, hard, default-interventionist dual process model describing rapid automatic intuition versus slower deliberative reasoning.

Revised "Soft" dual process model

Nonetheless, it would be an error to throw the proverbial baby out with the bathwater—despite many criticisms, considerable evidence remains broadly (though not perfectly) consistent with dual process claims (see below). I suggest evidence may be better conceptualized as supporting a revised "soft" dual process model. This version is "soft" because it posits a variety of processes drive dilemma judgments rather than just two and does not specify a rigid way that processes theoretically interact. Yet, it retains the insight that a relative preponderance of affect-laden processes may promote harm-rejection, a relative preponderance of cognitive-laden processes may promote outcome-maximization.

The soft dual process model abandons claims of "automatic" or "implicit" processing or a temporal order in favor of more general claims about relatively affective versus cognitive processing. It conceptualizes affective reactions to harm and cognitive evaluations of outcomes as just two of many processes that contribute to decisions. Hence, rejecting sacrificial harm may often result from a confluence of relatively affective or emotional considerations, whereas accepting sacrificial harm (to maximize outcomes) may often result from a confluence of relatively cognitive or deliberative processes. Yet, the distinction is relative, not absolute—some affective processes contribute to concern for outcomes and some deliberative processes to harm rejection. Moreover, other processes may play a role, such as heuristic rule following, general inaction, and self-presentation. From this perspective, the hard dual process model is not so much *incorrect* as *incomplete*.

Plenty of evidence corroborates the soft dual process model claim of relative preponderance of affective and cognitive processing. Manipulations that increase emotional aversion to harm, such as making harm vivid, close, and personal (Bartels, 2008; Greene et al., 2009) increase harm rejection decisions, whereas reducing sensitivity to harm through emotional reappraisal reduces harm rejection (Lee & Gino, 2015). Moreover, people who tend to experience stronger emotional processing tend to reject sacrificial harm, such as those high in empathic concern (Gleichgerrcht & Young, 2013) and people who struggle to regulate emotions (Szekely & Miu, 2015). Conversely, people who struggle to understand or experience emotions tend to accept sacrificial harm, such as people high in alexithymia (Patil & Silani, 2014). Incidentally, modelling approaches have isolated such effects to differences in harm-rejection rather than outcome-maximization responding (Conway

& Gawronski, 2013; Christov-Moore et al., 2017; Zhang et al., 2017, 2020). Further consistent with the soft dual process model, measures of deliberative processing typically predict acceptance of sacrificial harm (e.g., Bartels, 2008), as do manipulations such as increasing the ratio of lives gained by sacrifice (Trémolière & Bonnefon, 2014). People who demonstrate stronger mathematical reasoning skills (e.g., performance on the cognitive reflection task) also tend to accept sacrificial harm more—findings that modelling approaches show are unique to outcome-maximization responding (Patil et al., 2021). Hence, on average, affective processing seems to promote harm rejection and cognitive processing outcome maximization.

However, unlike the classic hard dual process model, the soft model recognizes more complexity: some affective processes promote both harm rejection and outcome-maximization, as do some cognitive processes. For example, Reynolds and Conway (2018) found that aversion to *performing* harmful actions uniquely predicted harm rejection in sacrificial dilemmas—but aversion to *witnessing* others suffer simultaneously predicted both harm rejection and outcome maximization responses. Likewise, Byrd and Conway (2019) found that cognitive reflection performance and other measures of *mathematical reasoning* uniquely predicted outcome maximization, whereas performance on *general logical reasoning* tasks predicted both harm rejection and outcome maximization. Hence, affective processing may favor harm rejection overall and cognitive processing may favor outcome maximization overall, but these relations are not exclusive (see also Białek & De Neys, 2017). Moreover, a variety of other processes can influence dilemma responding, including general inaction (Gawronski, et al., 2017), prevention mindsets (Gamez-Djokic & Molden, 2016), and self-presentation (Rom & Conway, 2018). The soft dual process model recognizes this complex array of processes and situates affective reactions to harm and cognitive evaluations of outcomes as just two of many processes. No account of sacrificial decision-making will be complete without addressing the full spectrum of relevant work.

Future directions

By now it should be clear that research on sacrificial dilemmas is fascinating and complex. Research has only scratched the surface of the full range of considerations influencing such decisions. Amid so much focus on basic affective and cognitive processes, only recently have researchers acknowledged social considerations, such as self-presentation and how people view themselves. Recent work shows people accurately infer how their dilemma decisions make them appear to others and strategically adjust choices to present themselves favorably (Rom & Conway, 2018). Yet, only a few inferences and social contexts have been explored thus far.

Another promising direction is to increase the external validity of dilemma research. The structure of sacrificial dilemmas characterizes many real-world conflicts, including military operations and pandemic medical decision-making (Truog et al., 2020). Such real-world decisions can have massive ramifications: for example, Truman's decision to drop nuclear weapons to hasten the end of the Second World War arguably saved many lives—yet it remains a reviled moment in human history and likely cost him reelection (Burnes, 2003). Dilemmas have been frequently criticized for implausible assumptions that undermine validity (Körner et al., 2019), but recent work has provided dilemmas drawn from real-world events (Körner & Deutsch, 2022). Yet, work needs to be done to clarify how well psychological mechanisms from classic dilemmas map onto realistic dilemmas.

Finally, researchers should clarify the exact role of cognitive processing in dilemma judgments. Whereas individual difference findings replicate robustly, manipulations of cognitive processing during tasks (e.g., cognitive load) appear far less reliable. Despite work originally suggesting load reduces concern for outcomes (e.g., Conway & Gawronski, 2013), recent studies suggest that load may instead increase general hesitation to act (Gawronski et al., 2017). Yet, the impact of load may depend on other factors such as abstraction (e.g., Körner & Volk, 2014) or religious beliefs (McPhetres et al., 2018; see also Van Dillen, this volume, about the effects of cognitive load on moral behavior). Hence, much work remains to be done to clarify how cognitive processing during decision-making tasks affects sacrificial decision-making.

Conclusion

Over the past two decades, moral dilemma research has exploded, leading to a plethora of methods, models, approaches, and assumptions that often contradict one another. A number of early "hard" model assumptions have been overturned, yet there remains evidence for a "softer" model that makes more flexible assumptions largely consistent with the evidentiary record. Dilemmas should not be taken as barometers of broad philosophical principles, but they remain interesting and important to study in their own right—after all, doctors, military officers, and others frequently face them. Despite much progress over the past two decades, much remains to be done in this evolving area of work.

Notes

1 *Moral reasoning* here is used broadly, and potentially includes affective, intuitive, and automatic processes.
2 Note the terms *deontology* and *utilitarian parameters* do not imply that psychological mechanisms match philosophical assumptions—i.e., selecting utilitarian choices does not mean one 'is' a utilitarian person, simply that response patterns are *consistent with* relevant philosophies.

References

Awad, E., Dsouza, S., Shariff, A., Rahwan, I., & Bonnefon, J. F. (2020). Universals and variations in moral decisions made in 42 countries by 70,000 participants. *Proceedings of the National Academy of Sciences, 117*(5), 2332–2337.
Bargh, J. A. (1994). The four horsemen of automaticity: Intention, awareness, efficiency, and control as separate issues. In R. Wyer & T. Srull (eds.), *Handbook of social cognition*. Hillsdale, NJ: Lawrence Erlbaum.
Baron, J., & Goodwin, G. P. (2020). Consequences, norms, and inaction: A critical analysis. *Decision and Decision Making, 15*, 421–442.
Baron, J., & Gürçay, B. (2017). A meta-analysis of response-time tests of the sequential two-systems model of moral decision. *Memory & Cognition, 45*, 566–575.
Bartels, D. M. (2008). Principled moral sentiment and the flexibility of moral decision and decision-making. *Cognition, 108,* 381–417. doi:10.1016/j.cognition.2008.03.001
Bartels, D. M., & Pizarro, D. A. (2011). The mismeasure of morals: Antisocial personality traits predict utilitarian responses to moral dilemmas. *Cognition, 121*(1), 154–161.
Białek, M., & De Neys, W. (2017). Dual processes and moral conflict: Evidence for deontological reasoners' intuitive utilitarian sensitivity. *Decision and Decision Making, 12*, 148–167.
Burnes, B. (2003). *Harry S. Truman: His life and times.* Kansas City, MO: Kansas City Star Books.
Byrd, N., & Conway, P. (2019). Not all who ponder count costs: Arithmetic reflection predicts utilitarian tendencies, but logical reflection predicts both deontological and utilitarian tendencies. *Cognition, 192*, 103995.
Christov-Moore, L., Conway, P., & Iacoboni, M. (2018). Deontological dilemma response tendencies and sensorimotor representations of harm to others. Front. *Integr. Neurosci., 11*, 34. doi:10.3389/fnint.2017.00034
Conway, P., & Gawronski, B. (2013). Deontological and utilitarian inclinations in moral decision-making: a process dissociation approach. *Journal of Personality and Social Psychology, 104*, 216–235.

Conway, P., Goldstein-Greenwood, J., Polacek, D., and Greene, J. D. (2018). Sacrificial utilitarian decisions do reflect concern for the greater good: Clarification via process dissociation and the decisions of philosophers. *Cognition, 179*, 241–265. doi:10.1016/j.cognition.2018.04.018

Conway, P., Weiss, A., Burgmer, P., & Mussweiler, T. (2018). Distrusting your moral compass: The impact of distrust mindsets on moral dilemma processing and decisions. *Social Cognition. 36*, 345–380. doi:10.1521/soco.2018.36.3.345

Corneille, O., & Hütter, M. (2020). Implicit? What do you mean? A comprehensive review of the delusive implicitness construct in attitude research. *Personality and Social Psychology Review, 24*(3), 212–232.

Cushman, F. (2013). Action, outcome, and value: A dual-system framework for morality. *Personality and Social Psychology Review, 17*(3), 273–292.

Ellemers, N., Van Der Toorn, J., Paunov, Y., & Van Leeuwen, T. (2019). The psychology of morality: A review and analysis of empirical studies published from 1940 through 2017. *Personality and Social Psychology Review, 23*, 332–366.

Evans, J. St. B. T., & Stanovich, K. E. (2013). Dual-process theories of higher cognition: Advancing the debate. *Perspectives on Psychological Science, 8*, 223–241, 263–271.

Foot, P. (1967). The problem of abortion and the doctrine of double effect. *Oxford Review, 5*, 1–7.

Gamez-Djokic, M., & Molden, D. (2016). Beyond affective influences on deontological moral decision: The role of motivations for prevention in the moral condemnation of harm. *Personality and Social Psychology Bulletin, 42*, 1522–1537.

Gawronski, B., Armstrong, J., Conway, P., Friesdorf, R., & Hütter, M. (2017). Consequences, norms, and generalized inaction in moral dilemmas: The CNI model of moral decision-making. *Journal of Personality and Social Psychology, 113*(3), 343–376. https://doi.org/10.1037/pspa0000086

Gawronski, B., Conway, P., Hütter, M., Luke, D., Armstrong, J., & Friesdorf, R. (2020). On the validity of the CNI model of moral decision-making: Reply to Baron and Goodwin (2020). *Decision and Decision Making, 15*, 1054–1072.

Gleichgerrcht, E., & Young, L. (2013). Low levels of empathic concern predict utilitarian moral decision. *PLOS ONE, 8*, 1–9. doi:10.1371/journal.pone.0060418

Greene, J. D. (2007). Why are VMPFC patients more utilitarian? A dual-process theory of moral decision explains. *Trends in Cognitive Sciences, 11*, 322–323.

Greene, J. D., Cushman, F. A., Stewart, L. E., Lowenberg, K., Nystrom, L. E., & Cohen, J. D. (2009). Pushing moral buttons: The interaction between personal force and intention in moral decision. *Cognition, 111*, 364–371. doi:10.1016/j.cognition.2009.02.001

Greene, J. D., Sommerville, R. B., Nystrom, L. E., Darley, J. M., & Cohen, J. D. (2001). An fMRI investigation of emotional engagement in moral decision. *Science, 293*, 2105–2108. doi:10.1126/science.1062872

Haidt, J. (2001). The emotional dog and its rational tail: a social intuitionist approach to moral decision. *Psychological Review, 108*, 814.

Kahane, G., Everett, J. A., Earp, B. D., Caviola, L., Faber, N. S., Crockett, M. J., & Savulescu, J. (2018). Beyond sacrificial harm: A two-dimensional model of utilitarian psychology. *Psychological Review, 125*, 131–164.

Kant, I. (1959). *Foundation of the metaphysics of morals* (L. W. Beck, Trans.). Indianapolis, IN: Bobbs-Merrill. (Original work published 1785)

Klein, C. (2011). The dual track theory of moral decision-making: A critique of the neuroimaging evidence. *Neuroethics, 4*(2), 143–162.

Körner, A., & Deutsch, R. (2022). Deontology and utilitarianism in real life: A set of moral dilemmas based on historic events. *Personality and Social Psychology Bulletin*, 01461672221103058.

Körner, A., Deutsch, R., & Gawronski, B. (2020). Using the CNI model to investigate individual differences in moral dilemma decisions. *Personality and Social Psychology Bulletin*, 0146167220907203.

Körner, A., Joffe, S., & Deutsch, R. (2019). When skeptical, stick with the norm: Low dilemma plausibility increases deontological moral decisions. *Journal of Experimental Social Psychology, 84*, 103834.

Körner, A., & Volk, S. (2014). Concrete and abstract ways to deontology: Cognitive capacity moderates construal level effects on moral decisions. *Journal of Experimental Social Psychology, 55*, 139–145.

Krebs, D. L. (2008). Morality: An evolutionary account. *Perspectives on Psychological Science, 3*, 149–172.

Lee, J. J., & Gino, F. (2015). Poker-faced morality: Concealing emotions leads to utilitarian decision making. *Organizational Behavior and Human Decision Processes, 126*, 49–64.

Luke, D. M., & Gawronski, B. (2021). Psychopathy and moral dilemma decisions: A CNI model analysis of personal and perceived societal standards. *Social Cognition, 39*, 41–58.

Maranges, H. M., Hasty, C. R., Maner, J. K., & Conway, P. (2021). The behavioral ecology of moral dilemmas: Childhood unpredictability, but not harshness, predicts less deontological and utilitarian responding. *Journal of Personality and Social Psychology, 120*(6), 1696.

McPhetres, J., Conway, P., Hughes, J. S., & Zuckerman, M. (2018). Reflecting on God's will: Reflective processing contributes to religious peoples' deontological dilemma responses. *Journal of Experimental Social Psychology, 79*, 301–314

Mill, J. S. (1998). *Utilitarianism* (R. Crisp, ed.). New York, NY: Oxford University Press. (Original work published 1861)

Patil, I. & Silani, G. (2014). Reduced empathic concern leads to utilitarian moral decisions in trait alexithymia. *Frontiers in Psychology, 5*, 2014, 501.

Patil, I., Zucchelli, M. M., Kool, W., Campbell, S., Fornasier, F., Calò, M., ... & Cushman, F. (2021). Reasoning supports utilitarian resolutions to moral dilemmas across diverse measures. *Journal of Personality and Social Psychology, 120*(2), 443.

Reynolds, C. J., & Conway, P. (2018). Not just bad actions: Affective concern for bad outcomes contributes to moral condemnation of harm in moral dilemmas. *Emotion*. doi:10.1037/emo0000413

Rom, S. C., & Conway, P. (2018). The strategic moral self: Self-presentation shapes moral dilemma decisions. *Journal of Experimental Social Psychology, 74*, 24–37.

Szekely, R. D., & Miu, A. C. (2015). Incidental emotions in moral dilemmas: The influence of emotion regulation. *Cognition and Emotion, 29*, 64–75.

Trémolière, B., & Bonnefon, J.-F. (2014). Efficient kill–save ratios ease up the cognitive demands on counterintuitive moral utilitarianism. *Personality and Social Psychology Bulletin, 40*, 923–930.

Truog, D.R., Mitchell, R.N., & Daley, G.Q. (2020). The toughest triage—allocating ventilators in a pandemic. *The New England Journal of Medicine, 382*(21), 1973–1975.

Truog, R. D., & Robinson, W. M. (2003). Role of brain death and the dead-donor rule in the ethics of organ transplantation. *Critical Care Medicine, 31*(9), 2391–2396.

Uhlmann, E. L., Pizarro, D. A., Tannenbaum, D., & Ditto, P. H. (2009). The motivated use of moral principles. *Decision and Decision making, 4*, 479–491.

Zhang, L., Li, Z., Wu, X., & Zhang Z. (2017). Why people with more emotion regulation difficulties made a more deontological decision: The role of deontological inclinations. *Frontiers in Psychology, 8*, 2095. doi:10.3389/fpsyg.2017.02095

Zhang, X., Wu, Z., Li, S., Lai, J., Han, M., Chen, X., ... & Ding, D. (2020). Why people with high alexithymia make more utilitarian decisions. *Experimental Psychology, 67*(1), 23.

5
THE INTERPERSONAL LEVEL

Impartial beneficence—the forgotten core of utilitarian psychology

Jim Everett

Abstract

Prior work on moral reasoning has relied on sacrificial moral dilemmas to study utilitarian versus non-utilitarian decision-making. This research has generated important insights into people's attitudes toward instrumental harm—the sacrifice of an individual to save a greater number. But this approach has serious limitations. Most notably, it ignores impartial beneficence—the positive, altruistic core of utilitarianism, characterized by a radically impartial concern for the well-being of others. Here, I describe the two-dimensional model of utilitarianism, showing that instrumental harm and impartial beneficence are both conceptually and psychologically distinct. I review evidence showing they have different patterns of individual differences, associated underlying processes, and consequences for how moral decision-makers are perceived. Acknowledging the dissociation between instrumental harm and impartial beneficence in the thinking of ordinary people has helped clarify existing debates about the nature of moral psychology, its relation to moral philosophy, and helps generate fruitful avenues for further research.

- In utilitarian decision-making, both instrumental harm and impartial beneficence need to be considered.
- Whereas instrumental harm characterizes the sacrifice of an individual to save a greater number, impartial beneficence characterizes the radically impartial concern for the wellbeing of others.
- Both the instrumental harm and impartial beneficence components of reasoning are conceptually and psychologically distinct.
- They have different patterns of individual differences, associated underlying processes, and consequences for how moral decision-makers are perceived by others.

Introduction

Utilitarianism in its purest form is a radically simple moral philosophy: it holds that the whole of morality can be deduced from the single general principle that we should always act in the way that would impartially maximize aggregate well-being. It is at first glance a highly attractive philosophy, intuitively appealing from the start—who *wouldn't* want to maximize the "greatest good for the greatest number"? Utilitarianism has attracted its devotees, people inspired by the theory's deceptively simple basis and its role in progressive calls to do *more* good for *more* people—for example by calling for wealthy Westerners to donate more of their income to those in the developing world or advocating for animals to be included within our typical moral circle and therefore refrain from eating meat (e.g. Singer, 2015). But utilitarianism has also been resoundingly criticized for the way it can seemingly be used to justify terrible decisions that harm others—torture, murder, even infanticide. Utilitarianism remains deeply controversial: beloved and detested in equal measure.

Utilitarianism is a philosophical theory, primarily discussed by ethicists debating the nature of right and wrong. But it has also been highly influential in moral psychology, with psychologists often describing ordinary people as engaging in *utilitarian reasoning* or making *utilitarian decisions*. When it comes to traditional moral psychological work on utilitarianism, however, one will read little about charity, animal rights, or self-sacrifice. Instead, one will read about runaway trolleys, torturing terrorists, and strange medical experiments. This research has generated important insights into people's attitudes toward instrumental harm—harm to some to help a greater number. However, this approach also has serious limitations. Most notably, it ignores impartial beneficence—the positive, altruistic core of utilitarianism, characterized by the impartial and equal concern for the well-being of others. In this chapter I will attempt to plug that gap, highlighting the importance of taking a multidimensional approach to understanding utilitarian psychology. I will show that these two dimensions, of instrumental harm and impartial beneficence, are conceptually and psychologically distinct; that they exhibit different patterns of individual differences; that they seem to rely on different underling psychological processes; and that they have distinct social consequences. I will show that by moving beyond sacrificial dilemmas to this positive, forgotten core of utilitarian psychology, we can shed new light on old questions, and see glimpses of new questions to be asked.

Trolleyology

Sacrificial moral dilemmas are a staple of literature, theatre, films, and—in the last two decades—moral psychology. Whether it is runaway trolleys, burning buildings, or highly dubious medical procedures, philosophy undergraduates have long been forced to grapple with a central question in ethics: When, if ever, is it acceptable to cause harm to some for the benefit of a greater number? Philosophers have long engaged in vigorous debates how we *should* respond to such questions, contemplating when and why it is acceptable to endorse instrumental harm. But in the last 20 years, psychologists have jumped in too.

To try and understand how, when, and why people engage in (non)utilitarian reasoning,[1] moral psychologists have used sacrificial dilemmas like the "trolley problem". Inspired by—and originally directly using—the trolley dilemmas from philosophy (Foot, 1967), in the sacrificial dilemma paradigm participants are typically asked whether it is morally right to sacrifice one person to save the lives of five people. The classic finding is that when the sacrifice is achieved by "impersonal" means (e.g. switching a runaway trolley to a different track), most people endorse it, though when it is requires "personal" means (e.g. pushing someone off a footbridge), a large majority rejects it as immoral (e.g. Greene et al., 2001). While classic utilitarianism says we should always sacrifice one to save the greater number, then, troublesome humans do not agree—at least in more direct, personal, physically confronting cases. This, in psychological terms, can be described as the "trolley problem": why it is that we endorse instrumental harm in sacrificial dilemmas in some cases, but not others?

The classic and highly influential answer comes from the dual process model of morality (DPM, e.g. Conway et al. 2018; Greene, 2008, 2014; Greene et al. 2001, 2004; see also Conway, this volume). Dual process models in psychology describe cognition as resulting from the competition between quick, intuitive, and automatic processes, and slow, deliberative, and controlled processes (e.g. Chaiken & Trope, 1999). In the classic trolley problem, Greene et al. (2001) have argued that in impersonal dilemmas the utilitarian-consistent decision to sacrifice is driven by controlled, cognitive processes, while automatic, intuitive processes are activated exclusively in personal dilemmas because of the emotional aversion to harm that such dilemmas involve. When individuals make the pro-sacrificial decision—often called *utilitarian decisions*—it is thought that they employ deliberative processing to repress their initial intuition and solve the dilemma using utilitarian cost-benefit analysis. Building on this, the DPM suggests non-utilitarian (often referred to as *deontological*) aspects of our moral decision-making are based in intuitive gut-reactions, while utilitarian decisions (e.g. sacrificing one to save a greater number) are uniquely attributable to effortful moral reasoning (see also Conway, this volume, for differences between hard vs. soft dual process models).

As can be seen in Conway's chapter in this same volume, moral psychology has adopted the sacrificial dilemma paradigm with vigor in the 20 years since Greene et al. published their seminal *Science* paper. Research shows, for example, that participants typically take longer to make pro-sacrificial decisions—suggesting these decisions are dependent on more controlled, deliberative processes—and pro-sacrificial decisions are associated with stronger activation in brain regions that support controlled, deliberative processes, such as the dlPFC. Most recently (and impressively), recent work by Patil et al. (2021) shows across eight studies using a variety of self-report, behavioral performance, and neuroanatomical measures, that individual differences in reasoning ability and cognitive style of thinking are associated with increased pro-sacrificial decisions. Part of the reason that the sacrificial dilemma paradigm and DPM has been so influential is that it aims to shed light not just on how people respond to artificial trolley dilemmas, but how, when, and why people do—or do not—engage in utilitarian reasoning more generally. Sacrificial dilemmas are typically taken as being the central source of conflict of utilitarian and non-utilitarian ethical approaches, with the idea that through studying sacrificial decisions we can understand why people engage in utilitarian reasoning in general (see Kahane & Everett 2022 for extended discussion on the role of the sacrificial dilemma paradigm in psychology). But there is a piece of the puzzle missing, the central, positive core of utilitarianism: impartial beneficence.

A missing piece: impartial beneficence

From its conception, utilitarianism has been a radically demanding and progressive ethical view. Philosophically, classical utilitarianism is neither solely about sacrificial harm or the rather mundane view that we should think about whether actions have positive consequences for well-being. Utilitarianism makes the much more radical claim that we must impartially maximize the well-being of all persons, rather than the rights of any specific individual, regardless of our personal, emotional, spatial, or temporal distance from the people involved (the *positive dimension,* or what we call *"impartial beneficence"*); and that this aim is not constrained by any other moral rule, including those forbidding us from intentionally harming innocent others (the *negative dimension,* or what we call *"instrumental harm"*). This, in a simplified form, is utilitarianism philosophically. The two dimensions are connected, but dissociable. They are connected because instrumental harm can be seen as consequence of impartial beneficence in utilitarianism: if all that matter is impartially maximising overall, aggregate welfare (impartial beneficence), then sometimes that might mean we have to harm some people in order to bring about a better state of affairs for a greater number of people (instrumental harm). But they are also dissociable: Kantian ethics might, for example, endorse some aspects of impartial beneficence by saying that we must give equal respect to all rational beings (see Mihailov, 2022) but reject instrumental harm by saying it is not acceptable to use one person as a means to an end, as in the classic footbridge dilemma.

Much work on utilitarianism over the last two decades has focused on decisions in the negative dimension of instrumental harm, measured in sacrificial dilemmas. But this is far from the central motivating claim of utilitarianism, nor is it even the only interesting claim. Utilitarianism tells us to not only maximize our own well-being, or those close to us, but rather to maximize the well-being of all other sentient beings on the planet (Bentham, 1789). It is for this reason that utilitarians have historically been leading figures in efforts against sexism, racism, and "speciesism"; key advocates of political and sexual liberty; and key actors in attempts to eradicate poverty in developing countries. Take the leading utilitarian philosopher Peter Singer, who argued extensively for the more "positive" aspects of utilitarianism theory through advocating for animals to be included within our moral circle (Singer, 1975) and highlighting the demands of relatively affluent Westerners to do much more good to help those in other countries, even at significant personal cost (Singer, 2015). As I will show in the remainder of this chapter, understanding this positive core dimension of impartial beneficence is central to understanding utilitarian psychology more generally.

The two-dimensional model of utilitarian psychology

The *two-dimensional (2D) model of utilitarian psychology* (Everett & Kahane 2020; Kahane et al. 2018, Kahane & Everett, 2022) brings together this missing piece in the psychology study of utilitarianism. The model is based on the recognition that there are at least two primary ways in which utilitarianism, as a philosophical theory, departs from our common-sense moral intuitions: first, it permits harming innocent individuals when this maximises aggregate utility (*instrumental harm*); and second, it tells us to treat interests of other individuals as equally morally important, without giving priority to oneself or those to whom one is especially close (*impartial beneficence*).

There is a growing amount of evidence that as well as being conceptually distinct, these two dimensions of utilitarianism are psychologically distinct too. For example, if utilitarianism is a single, unitary psychological construct (which is necessary for us to make conclusions about utilitarianism in general on the basis of questions about sacrificial dilemmas specifically), then we should see similarities in how people respond to different kinds of questions reflecting paradigmatic utilitarian judgments. Unfortunately, the existing evidence suggests that we do not (Kahane & Everett et al. 2015; 2018; see also Conway et al. 2018). For example, people who endorse "utilitarian" sacrifice of one person to save five in trolley-style dilemmas are *not* more likely to also endorse "utilitarian" maximization of welfare in questions about helping people in far off countries, reducing suffering of animals, or making sacrifices now for future generations. In fact, sometimes people who make the first kind of "utilitarian" judgments are *less* likely to make the second kind of "utilitarian" judgment.

If the psychology of instrumental harm is meaningfully different from the psychology of impartial beneficence, it means that much of our previous work on "utilitarian psychology" has only told half the story at best. By focusing on the sacrificial dilemma paradigm, we have gained important insights into when, why, and how people endorse the instrumental harm of some in pursuit of the greater good. But we cannot assume that these findings about the psychology of instrumental harm generalize to the psychology of impartial beneficence (the "generalizability question": Everett & Kahane, 2020). In fact, as I will show in the remainder of this chapter, there is significant emerging

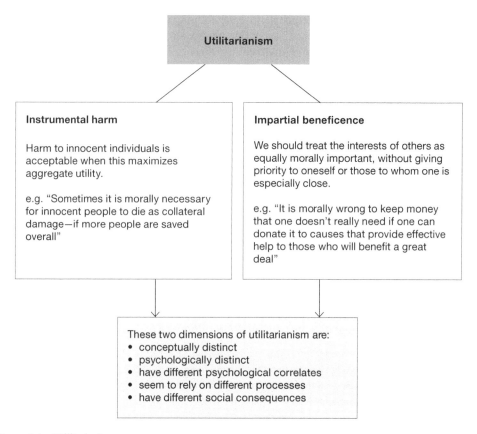

Figure 5.1 Utilitarianism.

evidence that the findings cannot generalize: that just as someone who endorses instrumental harm is not necessarily more likely to endorse impartial beneficence, the two dimensions are associated with contrasting patterns of individual differences; seemingly dependent on different psychological processes; and result in distinct social perceptions of others.

This insight, that instrumental harm and impartial beneficence are not only conceptually but also psychologically distinct, therefore sets up both a challenge and an opportunity for moral psychology. The disunity of "utilitarian psychology" results in a challenge because it means we need to revisit our conclusions about utilitarian psychology, where findings must be more appropriately reinterpreted as elucidating the psychology of instrumental harm specifically. But it also offers an opportunity: an opportunity to reconsider established findings, shed new light on seemingly settled questions in moral psychology, and an opportunity to come to a more complete understanding of how people come to endorse different aspects of utilitarianism.

Individual differences

Distinguishing between instrumental harm and impartial beneficence encourages us to reconsider what individual differences have been associated with "utilitarian psychology." Much work, for example, has discussed the association between both clinical and subclinical psychopathy and pro-sacrificial instrumental harm decisions (Bartels & Pizarro, 2011; Kahane et al., 2015; Koenigs et al., 2012; Wiech et al., 2013—but see Conway et al. 2018 for a contrasting view, as well as Conway, this volume). This has led to a rather unflattering picture in the moral psychology of utilitarians as cold, unfeeling, even anti-social. But when we look at the endorsement of utilitarian impartial beneficence, we see a very different pattern. Indeed, participants' scores on the instrumental harm sub-scale of the Oxford Utilitarianism Scale (OUS) are positively associated with subclinical psychopathy and negatively associated with empathic concern (Kahane & Everett et al. 2018). But we find the opposite pattern is for impartial beneficence: people who endorse the utilitarian impartial maximization of welfare (e.g. "It is morally wrong to keep money that one doesn't really need if one can donate it to causes that provide effective help to those who will benefit a great deal") are actually *less* likely to agree with statements tapping subclinical psychopathy (e.g. "For me, what's right is whatever I can get away with": Levenson et al. 1995) and *more* likely to agree with statements tapping empathic concern (e.g. "I often have tender, concerned feelings for people less fortunate than me": Davis, 1980). That is, people who feel greater empathy and concern for others can indeed be more likely to endorse utilitarian principles—just in the domain of impartial beneficence, not instrumental harm.

What about socio-ideological attitudes, such as religiosity or political ideology? Religious systems have often focused on the importance of rule-based moral decision making, and utilitarianism has historically conflicted with religious views (Mill, 1863). In line with this, research using sacrificial dilemmas has reported that religiosity is associated with reduced utilitarian endorsement of instrumental harm (e.g. Piazza, 2012; Piazza & Sousa, 2014; Szekely, Opre, & Miu, 2015). When using our OUS measure of impartial beneficence, however, we have shown that religiosity is associated with increased utilitarian endorsement of impartial beneficence (Kahane & Everett et al., 2018). This makes sense when one thinks about the impartial, welfare maximizing nature of some religious injunctions, and particularly standard accounts of Christian ethics, which generally involve quite radical demands for self-sacrifice and impartiality. Indeed, upon his appointment, Pope Francis said that "It hurts me when I see a priest or a nun with the latest model car; you can't do this ... please, choose a more humble one. If you like the fancy one, just think about how many children are dying of hunger in the world" (Francis, 2013). As we have noted before, Peter Singer has said almost identical things.

When it comes to political ideology, we again see the dissociation between instrumental harm and impartial beneficence. While political liberals are less likely to endorse utilitarian instrumental harm (e.g. thinking it is sometimes morally necessary for innocent people to die as collateral damage if more people are saved overall), they are actually more likely than their conservative counterparts to endorse utilitarian impartial beneficence (e.g. thinking that from a moral perspective, people should care about the well-being of all human beings on the planet equally, Kahane & Everett et al., 2018).

Underlying processes

Just as treating utilitarianism as a non-unitary psychology construct sheds greater light on how different kinds of utilitarianism-consistent moral decisions are associated with different individual differences, there is also some evidence that the same is true for considering psychological processes underlying these decisions. According to the influential dual process model of utilitarian decision-making, deliberation favors "utilitarian" reasoning whereas intuition favors "deontological" decisions (e.g. Greene et al., 2001; Conway et al., 2018; Patil et al., 2021). As with much of the work, however, this has been conducted almost exclusively in the context of attitudes about instrumental harm, measured in sacrificial dilemmas. Would the same pattern emerge for impartial beneficence?

We have tested this in previous work, looking at how using classic manipulations of cognitive process might shift participants' endorsement of both impartial beneficence and instrumental harm (Capraro, Everett, & Earp, 2020). We conducted three studies in which we manipulated participants' cognitive process by priming intuition or deliberation (Levine et al., 2018), telling participants to answer based "on your first, emotional response and your 'gut-feeling' … just focus on what your intuition tells you" or "on reason, rather than intuition. Focus on thinking and reasoning about the question … think carefully about each question." We then had participants complete both the instrumental harm and impartial beneficence items from the OUS. Across three studies and in line with past research, we found that those participants in the intuition-primed conditions endorsed utilitarian statements about instrumental harm significantly less than those who were encouraged to make their decisions through careful deliberation. Importantly, however, this was not the case for impartial beneficence. That is, priming intuition (vs. deliberation) reduced utilitarian decisions about instrumental harm, but had no effect on impartial beneficence. Again, studying only sacrificial dilemmas but generalizing to utilitarian psychology at large can give a misleading picture.

Social perceptions

Finally, just as utilitarian reasoning about instrumental harm and impartial beneficence exhibit different psychological profiles with individual differences and potentially rely on different processes, there is also increasing evidence that they have different social consequences for how someone is perceived, and how trustworthy they are seen to be by others.

There is a large body of evidence now showing that people who endorse utilitarian instrumental harm in sacrificial dilemmas (e.g. endorsing sacrificing one person to save five) are seen as less moral and trustworthy, chosen less frequently as social partners, and trusted less in economic exchanges than those who reject it (Bostyn & Roets, 2017; Everett et al., 2016, 2018; Rom et al., 2017; Sacco et al., 2017; Uhlmann et al., 2013: see Crockett et al. 2021 for a review). We have explained this through reference to partner choice models (Everett et al. 2016; 2018), noting that the demands that utilitarianism makes in instrumental harm—the demand to break moral norms and even cause harm when it maximizes the greater good—are seemingly incompatible with what we look for in social partners. When looking for friends or thinking about our family, we want to be able to trust that they will support us and do us no harm—even when hurting us would bring about the greater good.

But what about impartial beneficence dilemmas? Should, for example, someone spend their weekend cheering up their lonely mother or instead help re-build houses for families who have lost their homes in a flood? Or should someone give money to help a family member or donate it to charity to provide life-saving help to many more individuals in a far-off country? Such dilemmas also seem to raise conflicts with what we seek in social partners. The impartial utilitarian standpoint seems to depart from what we want from friends and families because it denies the existence of "special obligations" to those with whom we have a close relationship. Saving my own child over two stranger's children may not maximize the good, but many deontological ethical approaches suggest that it is morally permissible (even required), because I have *special* obligations to my child, ones that I do not have towards a stranger's children (see Jeske, 2014).

There is evidence that those who help a stranger instead of family members are judged as less morally good and trustworthy than those who did the opposite (McManus et al., 2020), and that this pattern of results is seen even when it is clear that helping strangers would maximize the greater good. For example, Hughes (2017) presented participants with a description of someone facing a dilemma between spending the weekend comforting their lonely mother or instead using the time to help rebuild homes for poor families through Habitat for Humanity. They found that participants who made the impartially beneficent welfare-maximizing decision to volunteer instead of see their mother were seen as having a worse moral character. Similarly, Law et al. (2022) show that socially distant altruists (e.g. endorsing donating money to save the life of a distant stranger in another country) tend to be seen as having a worse moral character than those who are socially close altruists (e.g. endorsing spending their money on a dream vacation for their terminally ill child). Interestingly, however, it appears that this potential negativity towards those who endorse impartial beneficence may be at least somewhat dependent on the type of social role these people have, with people who endorsed impartial beneficence being seen as a worse friend but a *better* political leader (Everett et al., 2018).

We have recently explored the way that endorsing instrumental harm and impartial beneficence might have distinct consequences in trust in political leaders specifically (Everett et al., 2021). We conducted a Registered Report experiment, recruiting 23,000 participants in 22 countries over six continents. Participants completed both self-reported and behavioral measures of trust in leaders who endorsed utilitarian or non-utilitarian principles about instrumental harm or impartial beneficence in a series of real-world inspired dilemmas concerning the COVID-19 pandemic. For example, one instrumental harm dilemma concerned the permissibility of mandatory privacy-invading tracing devices to reduce the spread of the virus, and one impartial beneficence dilemma concerned whether resources such as medicine should be sent wherever in the world they should do the most good or reserved first for a country's own citizens. Our results showed that across both the self-reported and behavioral measures, endorsement of instrumental harm decreased trust, while endorsement of impartial beneficence increased trust. Just as impartial beneficence and instrumental harm are associated with different individual differences and seem to rely on different psychological processes, so too do they seem to have distinct social consequences for how people are perceived—all of which would be obscured if we treated utilitarianism as a unitary phenomenon, studying only sacrificial dilemmas.

Future directions

The study of impartial beneficence, this forgotten but central core of utilitarian psychology, is woefully neglected when compared to the astonishing amount of research studying instrumental harm and sacrificial dilemmas. Luckily for the ambitious new researcher, this means that the fruit is ripe for picking. In this final section, I will briefly review just some of many future directions that could be especially exciting.

One particularly important new direction that is already happening is looking at how the endorsement of utilitarian impartial beneficence relates to real-world examples of impartial welfare maximization. For example, we know that greater concern for animal suffering is positively correlated with impartial beneficence, but not instrumental harm (Caviola et al., 2021), and it will be interested to explore how real-world animal suffering activists think about these utilitarian principles. Similarly, there are strong links between the Effective Altruism movement (MacAskill, 2015) and the utilitarian principle of impartial beneficence, though it remains to be seen how those who fully embrace these principles (e.g. by pledging certain amounts of their income to effective charities in the developing world) come to hold their impartially beneficent views. In this vein, exciting recent work has looked at how real-world extraordinary altruists—those who donated a kidney to a stranger—scored higher on utilitarian impartial beneficence, but not instrumental harm (Amormino et al., 2022). It will be fruitful for future work to consider in more detail the psychology of impartial beneficence in such real-world contexts.

Another open area for future research is to understand the developmental trajectory of the (lack of) endorsement of impartial beneficence, and how early environments might influence adult moral judgments about the impartial maximization of welfare. While some work has been done looking the development of sacrificial judgments (Caravita et al., 2017; Pellizzoni et al., 2010) or how unpredictable child environments shape adult judgments about instrumental harm (Maranges et al., 2021), we know little about impartial beneficence. How do children start thinking about (im)partiality in moral judgments when this conflicts with motivations to help more people? How and when might children develop ideas about the importance of undergoing small sacrifices for themselves to benefit strangers? It will be interesting for future research to consider such questions.

Finally, it will be interesting to understand "interventions" that promote impartial beneficence and encourage real-world behavior that impartially maximizes overall welfare. By building on our existing knowledge about the psychological barriers to effective altruism (e.g. see Berman et al., 2018; Caviola et al., 2021) we can start to consider interventions that can promote the endorsement of impartial beneficence in other behavioral contexts beyond charitable donations.

Conclusion

In this chapter I hope to have convinced you of the conceptual importance and psychological informativeness of treating utilitarianism not as a unitary construct in which we can base conclusions solely on the sacrificial dilemma paradigm. Instead, I hope to have shown the way that treating utilitarianism as a multidimensional construct, consisting of at least two main dimensions of both instrumental harm and impartial beneficence, can shed light on established topics in moral psychology and generate new directions in the field. Compared to instrumental harm, the endorsement of impartial beneficence is correlated with different patterns of individual differences, seems to rely on different underlying processes, and has different consequences for how moral decision-makers are perceived. We have spent two decades studying utilitarianism through focusing on sacrificial dilemmas and this work has generated many important insights. But I believe that this is only part of the story. There is another part of the study which is woefully underwritten—the story of the psychology of impartial beneficence.

Note

1 For consistency with other chapters in this volume I use the terms moral reasoning and moral decisions or moral decision-making, instead of the more commonly used "moral judgments"—which is used in this handbook to indicate how people evaluate others and others' moral choices. This should not be taken as indicating that when people are responding in sacrificial dilemmas they are (always) engaging in any deliberative reasoning process.

References

Amormino, P., Ploe, M., & Marsh, A. (2022). Moral foundations, values, and reasoning in extraordinary altruists. *Pre-print.* 10.21203/rs.3.rs-1762722/v1
Bartels, D. M., & Pizarro, D. A. (2011). The mismeasure of morals: Antisocial personality traits predict utilitarian responses to moral dilemmas. *Cognition, 121*(1), 154–161.
Bentham, J. (1789). *An introduction to the principles of morals.* London: Athlone.

Berman, J. Z., Barasch, A., Levine, E. E., & Small, D. A. (2018). Impediments to effective altruism: The role of subjective preferences in charitable giving. *Psychological Science, 29*(5), 834–844.

Bostyn, D. H., & Roets, A. (2017). Trust, trolleys and social dilemmas: A replication study. *Journal of Experimental Psychology. General*. https://doi.org/10.1037/xge0000295

Caviola, L., Schubert, S., & Greene, J. D. (2021). The psychology of (in) effective altruism. *Trends in Cognitive Sciences, 25*(7), 596–607.

Caravita, S. C., De Silva, L. N., Pagani, V., Colombo, B., & Antonietti, A. (2017). Age-related differences in contribution of rule-based thinking toward moral evaluations. *Frontiers in Psychology, 8*, 597.

Chaiken, S., & Trope, Y. (Eds.). (1999). *Dual-process theories in social psychology* (Vol. xiii). New York: Guilford Press.

Capraro, V., Everett, J. A. C., & Earp, B. D. (2020). Priming intuition decreases instrumental harm but not impartial beneficence. *Journal of Experimental Social Psychology, 83*, 142–149.

Conway, P., & Gawronski, B. (2013). Deontological and utilitarian inclinations in moral decision making: A process dissociation approach. *Journal of Personality and Social Psychology, 104*(2), 216.

Conway, P., Goldstein-Greenwood, J., Polacek, D., & Greene, J. D. (2018). Sacrificial utilitarian judgments do reflect concern for the greater good: Clarification via process dissociation and the 4 of philosophers. *Cognition, 179*, 241–265. https://doi.org/10.1016/j.cognition.2018.04.018

Crockett, M. J., Everett, J. A., Gill, M., & Siegel, J. Z. (2021). The relational logic of moral inference. In *Advances in experimental social psychology* (Vol. 64, pp. 1–64). New York: Academic Press.

Davis, M. H. (1980). A multidimensional approach to individual differences in empathy. *JSAS Catalog of Selected Documents in Psychology, 10*, 85.

Everett, J. A. C., Colombatto, C., Awad, E., Boggio, P., Bos, B., Brady, W. J., Chawla, M., Chituc, V., Chung, D., Drupp, M., Goel, S., Grosskopf, B., Hjorth, F., Ji, A., Lin, Y., Ma, Y., Maréchal, M., Mancinelli, F., Mathys, C., … Crockett, M. J. (2021). Moral dilemmas and trust in leaders during a global health crisis. *Nature Human Behaviour, 5*(8), 1074–1088.

Everett, J. A. C., Faber, N. S., Savulescu, J., & Crockett, M. J. (2018). The costs of being consequentialist: Social inference from instrumental harm and impartial beneficence. *Journal of Experimental Social Psychology, 79*, 200–216. https://doi.org/10.1016/j.jesp.2018.07.004

Everett, J. A. C., & Kahane, G. (2020). Switching tracks? Towards a multidimensional model of utilitarian psychology. *Trends in Cognitive Sciences*. https://doi.org/10.1016/j.tics.2019.11.012

Everett, J. A. C., Pizarro, D. A., & Crockett, M. J. (2016). Inference of trustworthiness from intuitive moral judgments. *Journal of Experimental Psychology. General, 145*(6), 772–787. https://doi.org/10.1037/xge0000165

Foot, P. (1967). The problem of abortion and the doctrine of double effect. *Oxford Review, 5*, 5–15.

Francis, Pope (2013, July 6). What would Jesus drive? Pope tells priests to buy "humble" cars. *Reuters*. Retrieved from www.reuters.com/article/pope-cars-idUSL5N0FC0IR20130706

Greene, J. D. (2008). The secret joke of Kant's soul. In *Moral psychology, Vol 3: The neuroscience of morality: Emotion, brain disorders, and development* (pp. 35–80). Cambridge: MIT Press.

Greene, J. D. (2014). *Moral tribes: Emotion, reason and the gap between us and them*. London: Atlantic Books Ltd.

Greene, J. D., Nystrom, L. E., Engell, A. D., Darley, J. M., & Cohen, J. D. (2004). The neural bases of cognitive conflict and control in moral judgment. *Neuron, 44*(2), 389–400. https://doi.org/10.1016/j.neuron.2004.09.027

Greene, J. D., Sommerville, R. B., Nystrom, L. E., Darley, J. M., & Cohen, J. D. (2001). An fMRI investigation of emotional engagement in moral judgment. *Science, 293*(5537), 2105–2108.

Hughes, J. S. (2017). In a moral dilemma, choose the one you love: Impartial actors are seen as less moral than partial ones. *British Journal of Social Psychology, 56*(3), 561–577.

Jeske, D. (2014). Special obligations. In E. N. Zalta (Ed.). *The Stanford encyclopedia of philosophy* (Spring 2014) Metaphysics Research Lab, Stanford University. Retrieved from https://plato.stanford.edu/archives/spr2014/entries/special-obligations/.

Kahane, G & Everett, J.A.C (2022). Trolley dilemmas: From moral philosophy to cognitive science and back again. In Lillehammer, H. (Ed.) *The trolley problem: Classic philosophical arguments series*. Cambridge, UK: Cambridge University Press.

Kahane, G., Everett, J. A. C., Earp, B. D., Caviola, L., Faber, N. S., Crockett, M. J., & Savulescu, J. (2018). Beyond sacrificial harm: A two-dimensional model of utilitarian psychology. *Psychological Review, 125*(2), 131–164. https://doi.org/10.1037/rev0000093

Kahane, G., Everett, J. A. C., Earp, B. D., Farias, M., & Savulescu, J. (2015). 'Utilitarian' judgments in sacrificial moral dilemmas do not reflect impartial concern for the greater good. *Cognition, 134*, 193–209. https://doi.org/10.1016/j.cognition.2014.10.005

Koenigs, M., Kruepke, M., Zeier, J., & Newman, J. P. (2012). Utilitarian moral judgment in psychopathy. *Social Cognitive and Affective Neuroscience, 7*(6), 708–714.

Law, K. F., Campbell, D., & Gaesser, B. (2022). Biased benevolence: The perceived morality of effective altruism across social distance. *Personality and Social Psychology Bulletin, 48*(3), 426–444.

Levine, E. E., Barasch, A., Rand, D., Berman, J. Z., & Small, D. A. (2018). Signaling emotion and reason in cooperation. *Journal of Experimental Psychology: General, 147*(5), 702–719. https://doi.org/10.1037/xge0000399

Levenson, M. R., Kiehl, K. A., & Fitzpatrick, C. M. (1995). Assessing psychopathic attributes in a noninstitutionalized population. *Journal of Personality and Social Psychology, 68*(1), 151.

MacAskill, W. (2015). *Doing good better: Effective altruism and a radical new way to make a difference*. London: Guardian Faber Publishing.

McManus, R. M., Kleiman-Weiner, M., & Young, L. (2020). What we owe to family: The impact of special obligations on moral judgment. *Psychological Science, 31*(3), 227–242.

Maranges, H. M., Hasty, C. R., Maner, J. K., & Conway, P. (2021). The behavioral ecology of moral dilemmas: Childhood unpredictability, but not harshness, predicts less deontological and utilitarian responding. *Journal of Personality and Social Psychology, 120*, 1696–1719.

Mihailov, E. (2022). Measuring impartial beneficence: A Kantian perspective on the Oxford Utilitarianism Scale. *Review of Philosophy and Psychology*, 1–16.

Mill, J. (1863). Of the ultimate sanction of the principle of utility. *Utilitarianism*, Web.

Patil, I., Zucchelli, M. M., Kool, W., Campbell, S., Fornasier, F., Calò, M., Silani, G., Cikara, M., & Cushman, F. (2021). Reasoning supports utilitarian resolutions to moral dilemmas across diverse measures. *Journal of Personality and Social Psychology, 120*(2), 443–460. https://doi.org/10.1037/pspp0000281

Piazza, J. (2012). "If you love me keep my commandments": Religiosity increases preference for rule-based moral arguments. *International Journal for the Psychology of Religion, 22*(4), 285–302.

Piazza, J., & Sousa, P. (2014). Religiosity, political orientation, and consequentialist moral thinking. *Social Psychological and Personality Science, 5*(3), 334–342.

Pellizzoni, S., Siegal, M., & Surian, L. (2010). The contact principle and utilitarian moral judgments in young children. *Developmental Science, 13*(2), 265–270.

Rom, S. C., Weiss, A., & Conway, P. (2017). Judging those who judge: Perceivers infer the roles of affect and cognition underpinning others' moral dilemma responses. *Journal of Experimental Social Psychology, 69*, 44–58.

Sacco, D. F., Brown, M., Lustgraaf, C. J. N., & Hugenberg, K. (2017). The adaptive utility of deontology: Deontological moral decision-making fosters perceptions of trust and likeability. *Evolutionary Psychological Science, 3*(2), 125–132. https://doi.org/10.1007/s40806-016-0080-6

Singer, P. (1975) *Animal liberation: A new ethics for our treatment of animals*. New York: The New York Review.

Singer, P. (2015). *The most good you can do: How effective altruism is changing ideas about living ethically*. New Haven, CT: Yale University Press.

Szekely, R. D., Opre, A., & Miu, A. C. (2015). Religiosity enhances emotion and deontological choice in moral dilemmas. *Personality and Individual Differences, 79*, 104–109.

Uhlmann, E. L., Zhu, L. L., & Tannenbaum, D. (2013). When it takes a bad person to do the right thing. *Cognition, 126*(2), 326–334.

Wiech, K., Kahane, G., Shackel, N., Farias, M., Savulescu, J., & Tracey, I. (2013). Cold or calculating? Reduced activity in the subgenual cingulate cortex reflects decreased emotional aversion to harming in counterintuitive utilitarian judgment. *Cognition, 126*(3), 364–372.

6
THE INTRAGROUP LEVEL
How social identity tunes moral cognition

*Jay J. Van Bavel, Dominic J. Packer, Jennifer L. Ray,
Claire Robertson and Nick Ungson*

Abstract

In this chapter, we move beyond the treatment of intuition and reason as competing systems and outline how social contexts, and especially social identities, allow people to flexibly "tune" their cognitive reactions to moral contexts—a process we refer to as "*moral tuning*." Collective identities—identities based on shared group memberships—significantly influence *judgments and decisions* of many kinds, including in the moral domain. We explain why social identities influence all aspects of moral cognition, including processes traditionally classified as intuition and reasoning. We then explain how social identities tune preferences and goals, expectations, and what outcomes care about. Finally, we propose directions for future research in moral psychology.

- Social identities allow people to flexibly tune their cognitive reactions within moral contexts.
- The social environment shapes moral intuitions, tuning decisions to reflect the moral norms of the group or community to which people belong.
- Our model assumes that people's moral decisions are based on weighing the probability of certain outcomes as well as people's preferences, goals, and expectations—and that these considerations are shaped by social identities and group norms.
- Moral group norms are dynamic and may change over time.
- Future research is needed to investigate more precisely how shifting norms influence moral decisions through social preferences, expectations and/or salient outcomes.

Introduction

For centuries, philosophers and scientists have argued whether emotional intuition or deliberative reasoning is the dominant—or appropriate—force in determining whether things are morally right or wrong. Kant (1785/1993) saw reason as the primary imperative in moral judgment, whereas Hume (1751/1983) argued that reason is, and ought to be, ruled by the passions. Classic psychological accounts of morality emphasized the role of *reasoning* in moral judgment (Kohlberg, 1969; Piaget, 1932/1965; Turiel, 1983), whereas more recent approaches emphasize the role of emotional *intuitions* and relegate reason to the role of *post hoc* justification (Haidt, 2001) or corrective control

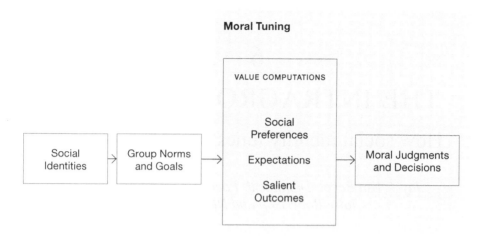

Figure 6.1 Moral tuning.

(Feinberg et al., 2012; Greene et al., 2001). However, much less has been said about the intragroup and intergroup dynamics that shape these processes (see Ellemers, Van Der Toorn, Paunov, & Van Leeuwen, 2019)—creating a "moral psychology of raceless, genderless strangers" (Hester & Gray 2020, p. 216). Here, we explore the role the role of social identity in moral cognition.

In this chapter, we outline how social contexts, and especially social identities, allow people to flexibly "tune" their cognitive reactions to moral contexts—a process we refer to as "moral tuning" (Bocian et al., 2021; Ellemers & van den Bos, 2012; Ellemers et al., 2019; Cohen, 2015; Graham et al., 2009; Koleva et al., 2012; Xiao et al., 2016). Our approach is based on extensive evidence that collective identities—identities based on shared group memberships—significantly influence *judgments and decisions*[1] of many kinds (Ellemers et al., 2019; Ellemers et al., 2013; Hester & Gray, 2020; Oakes et al., 1994; Turner et al., 1994). We argue that this framework is critical to understand moral judgment and decision making.

Moral tuning by social identities is an intragroup phenomenon in the sense that identified group members are motivated to conform to and enforce group norms, as well as pursue group interests and goals (Terry & Hogg, 1996; Van Bavel & Packer, 2021). However, these processes often have intergroup implications because group norms frequently prescribe how ingroup *and* outgroup members should be viewed or treated (e.g., Crandall et al., 2002; Murrar et al., 2020). Further, group norms and goals can themselves be shaped by the intergroup context, emphasizing distinctiveness from outgroups (e.g., Berger & Heath, 2008; Turner et al., 1994). As such, moral psychology requires a richer understanding of both the *intragroup* and *intergroup* context.

In this chapter, we explain why we argue that social identities influence all aspects of moral cognition, including processes traditionally classified as both intuition and reasoning. We then describe how social identities tune preferences and goals, expectations, and the outcomes people care about (see also Figure 6.1). We end the chapter with directions for future research.

Moving Beyond Intuition versus Reason

Rationalist approaches, long dominant in moral psychology, stress that moral judgments and decisions are made through a process of reasoning and reflection (Kohlberg, 1984; Piaget, 1932/

1965; Turiel, 1983). According to these models, moral action is—and should be—driven by reason (Kohlberg, 1975). In the past few decades, intuitionist models have challenged the view that moral reasoning is the sole or even primary mover in moral cognition. The Social Intuitionist Model, for example, argues that certain situations automatically elicit moral intuitions, which in turn guide moral judgments and decisions (Haidt, 2001; Haidt, 2012). This approach assumes that intuitions about moralized issues are based on a combination of evolutionary, cultural, and developmental influences that accumulate over long periods of time and are often difficult to change through reasoning. An overlooked feature of the social intuitionist model is that moral intuitions are shaped by the *social* environment–tuning judgments and decisions to reflect the moral norms of the community in which humans are embedded. Our chapter explains how the social environment shapes moral cognition through the lens of social identities and group norms.

Inspired by dual process theories of human cognition (Chaiken & Trope, 1999; Kahneman, 2003), other models of morality have bridged these two perspectives (see also Conway, this volume). Dual process models acknowledge the importance of emotional intuitions, while arguing that corrective controlled processes can override these automatic responses (Feinberg et al., 2012; Greene et al., 2001). According to these models, people with the requisite motivation and opportunity can regulate and replace their emotional intuitions. However, dual process theorists acknowledge that moral psychology, and real-world conflict, is often derived from differences in social identity (Greene, 2013). Thus, both perspectives acknowledge the power of group dynamics to shape moral cognition.

Social intuitionist and dual process models of morality both assume that moral intuitions arise from automatic evaluation of an eliciting situation. Although automatic evaluations (e.g., attitudes) were originally charactered as relatively static or fixed—activated almost inevitably in response to relevant stimuli—there is considerable research demonstrating that they exhibit rapid tuning as a function of goal states and contextual factors (see Blair, 2002). Researchers are continuing to uncover the malleability of automatic evaluations, and their susceptibility to influence from various top-down processes and contextual factors (Cesario & Jonas, 2014; Ferguson & Wojnowicz, 2011; Lin & Packer, 2017). For instance, automatic evaluations of group members reflect the currently relevant social identities (Van Bavel & Cunningham, 2009) and social norms (Sinclair, Lowery, Hardin, & Colangelo, 2005) of the immediate social context. These studies, as well as accumulating knowledge about brain function, support a more dynamic approach to automatic evaluation (Cunningham & Zelazo, 2007; Cunningham et al., 2007; Van Bavel, Xiao, et al., 2012; Van Bavel, Packer, et al., 2012). As such, we propose an alternative approach to moral cognition that combines these more recent dynamic understandings of evaluation with research on social identity and self-categorization (Turner et al., 1994).

We argue that collective identity processes tune moral cognition, which can occur automatically as different self-categorizations become salient. Group norms and goals—consensual understandings of how we should behave and what we are trying to achieve—alter moral cognition by influencing a person's preferences, their expectations for others' behavior (which matter in many morally relevant situations), and the outcomes they care about. The same person can perceive themselves in terms of multiple identities (e.g., their race, gender, citizenship, occupation, religion, political affiliation, favorite sports team, etc.) and when an identity is salient, the norms and goals associated with that identity can influence what they want, what they expect, and what elements of possible behavioral choices capture their attention (Van Bavel & Packer, 2021). This, in turn, influences their own decisions, as well as how they judge the actions of others. Each of these elements can be understood as parameters in a value-computation framework—representing the process of moral tuning (see Van Bavel, Pärnamets, Reinero, & Packer, 2022; for a visualization see Figure 6.1).

Our approach to moral cognition is informed by value-based models of decision making from the neuroeconomics and cognitive neuroscience (Pärnamets, Shuster, Reinero, & Van Bavel, 2020; Van Bavel, et al., 2022). These models argue that multiple mental processes supported by multiple brain systems give rise to moral judgments and decisions. Our model assumes that *potential outcomes* associated with different choices are weighted by *estimates of their probability* and the *preferences and goals* of the decision-maker (Van Bavel et al., 2022) and that these computations are shaped by social identities (see Van Bavel & Pereira, 2018). The overall computations of the value of choices and actions is thus sensitive to information that feeds into computations of these three parameters. Of course, many factors, like social network structure and social institutions, can shape these parameters, and, ultimately, moral decision-making (Van Bavel et al., 2022). However, here, we focus on how social identities can influence moral judgments and decisions by affecting the following three parameters: preferences/goals, expectations, and what sorts of outcomes are taken into consideration.

Social Identities Tune Preferences and Goals

Morally relevant situations often involve conflicts between choices about which the interests of different parties are in tension. Moral transgressions typically involve an agent putting their own desires ahead of the interests, needs, or rights of others, thus causing them harm (e.g., Gray et al., 2012), whereas acts worthy of moral praise usually involve an agent sacrificing self-interest for the sake of someone else's or the greater good. Value-computation frameworks of cooperation model how much people weigh the interests of different parties (e.g., their own versus others') in terms of social preferences (see Van Bavel et al., 2022). Social preference parameters can, for example, capture individual differences in how much people prioritize their own outcomes over others' (e.g., pro-selfs versus pro-socials as indexed by social value orientation; Balliet et al., 2009). These preferences, along with social norms, inform the computations that underlie decisions to engage in selfish or pro-social behavior (Hackel, Wills, & Van Bavel, 2020).

We argue that social identity also influences social preferences, such that people tend to care more about outcomes incurred by in-group than out-group members (Tajfel & Turner, 1979; Van Bavel & Packer, 2021). For instance, highly identified group members appear to experience vicarious reward when they observe in-group (but not out-group) members experiencing positive outcomes, as indexed by activity in ventral striatum, a brain region implicated in hedonic reward (Hackel et al., 2017). Intergroup competition may exacerbate differences in concern for in-group versus out-group targets, causing people to feel empathy when in-group targets experience negative outcomes but schadenfreude (pleasure in others' pain) when out-group members experience these same events (Cikara et al., 2014). Shared social identities can also lead people to put collective interests ahead of their own individual interests in social dilemmas. For instance, making collective identities salient causes selfish individuals to contribute more to their group than when these same people were reminded of their individual self (De Cremer & Van Vugt, 1999). This shift in behavior was not necessarily because they were less selfish, but rather because their sense of self had shifted from the *individual* to the *collective* level.

In a paper on the relationship between social identity and moral judgment, students from Dartmouth and Princeton watch video of a college football game between their two schools (Hastorf & Cantril, 1954). They asked students to report the number and severity of rule infractions committed by players on each team. Students from each school differed in their reported perceptions: Princeton students recalled that the Dartmouth team made more than double the number of infractions than Princeton, whereas Dartmouth students recalled that both teams made about the same number of infractions. This suggests that collective identities can tune moral judgments—even altering their attention and memory for events (see Xiao, Coppin, & Van Bavel, 2016).

Researchers have found that people more readily excuse moral transgressions committed by in-group members compared to out-group members (Uhlmann et al., 2009; Valdesolo & DeSteno, 2007, see Jetten & Crimston, this volume). Indeed, the influence of groups on moral cognition may extend to children as young as three years old, leading kids to perceive within-group (but not between-group) harm as an intrinsic moral transgression (Rhodes & Chalik, 2013). People are more willing to punish out-group than in-group norm violators when responding reflexively (quickly or under cognitive load), suggesting that group boundaries can shape automatic moral judgments (Yudkin et al., 2016). However, this is not inevitable and people can overcome these biased reactions with deliberation.

An important exception to these findings is the "black sheep effect," in which in-group norm violators are condemned more than out-group violators. This is especially the case when such violations dilute boundaries between groups or threaten the validity of in-group norms (Marques & Paez, 1994). Contrasting with research finding that in-group transgressors are given greater clemency, these findings underscore how collective motivations shape moral evaluation. Goals to preserve positive and distinct social identities may, in different contexts or groups, promote more leniency or harshness depending on relevant collective demands. The punishment of in-group norm violators might be more severe among children of left-wing parents, while the punishment of out-group norm violators might be more severe among children of politically right-wing parents (Leshin et al., 2022). Thus, decisions to engage in in-group favoritism or harsh in-group punishment might be dictated by ideological or partisan influences.

While there is an overall tendency for people to prefer their own groups over others (Tajfel, 1970), the social preferences that people deem appropriate and important to weigh in decision-making are often shaped by social norms. At times and in certain groups, norms may espouse egalitarianism or allyship rather than parochialism, causing people to extend greater concern to out-group interests. Moreover, group norms influence how widely members draw their circles of moral concern, which can include a far larger swathe of humanity than just the in-group (Van Bavel & Packer, 2021). Activating inclusive identities and cultivating these social norms might be key to motivating people to place a greater emphasis on the welfare of a diverse group of strangers. For instance, a study in 67 countries found that people who identified with their nation were more likely to support a variety of costly public health behaviors (e.g., Van Bavel et al., 2022).

Social identities tune expectations

Computations of value are a function of potential outcomes weighted by their likelihood and decision-makers' preferences and goals. The influence of groups on expectations regarding the likelihood of different choices may be most relevant in social dilemma situations, in which outcomes are highly dependent on choices made by others (Van Lange et al., 2015). Shared identities increase cooperative behavior in part through expectations, specifically expectations based on the norm that fellow group members behave in a trustworthy fashion toward one another (Foddy et al., 2009; Platow et al., 2011). One line of research to this effect had people play trust-type games with in-group and out-group members. The players knew the group membership of their partners, but the experimenters varied whether they believed that their partners were aware of the players' social identity. Only when people believed that in-group partners were *aware* of their shared group membership (i.e., that they were in-group members) did they trust them more than an out-group partner (Foddy et al., 2009; Platow et al., 2011).

People are also motivated to conform to moral norms because of how they expect group members to respond if they deviate. Making moral choices that are socially desirable to one's in-group can lead to acceptance and praise, whereas acting in ways deemed immoral often leads to criticism or ostracism (Henrich et al., 2006; DeScioli & Kurzban, 2009; Hui et al., 2020; Fehr & Schurtenberger, 2018; Henrich & Muthukrishna, 2021, see Jetten & Crimston, this volume). Furthermore, concerns about group norms are especially active in moral (vs. non-moral) decisions, where even considering the wrong moral choice may cause a person to be perceived as "tainted" (Tetlock, 2003; Ginges et al., 2007). The expectations of social sanction are powerful motives for group members who care about their inclusion and reputation in a group.

Social identities tune what outcomes matter

People are multifunctional entities who shift between different identities (Turner et al., 1994) and decision-making mindsets (Tetlock, 2002). Thus, the same person may alternate between acting as an "intuitive economist" animated by utilitarian concerns and a "principled theologian" animated by the need to protect sacred values from secular encroachments. When deciding how to spend money we have allocated for travel, for example, we can focus on a variety of desired outcomes. If we are seeking to maximize fun and relaxation, options involving sunshine, beaches, and drinks with umbrellas may seem particularly appealing. If we are thinking about advancing our career goals, options that would allow us to attend a conference are priorities. If we are worried about the environmental future and want to minimize our carbon footprint, we might opt to remain local and enjoy a staycation. As such, these mental frames shape attention and decisions, as well as judgments about other people's choices (Jarudi et al., 2008; Van Bavel, Packer, et al., 2012).

The identities and mindsets we bring to bear have a profound influence on how we make decisions. For instance, asking people to consider the moral (versus pragmatic or hedonic) implications of different actions, led them to make faster, more extreme judgments—and impose their judgments on others (Van Bavel, Packer, et al., 2012). Likewise, assigning people to the perspective of a decision-maker as opposed to a decision-recipient reduced their concern with fair treatment and increased their concern with outcomes (Heuer et al., 2007). The importance and meaning of abstract moral concepts, like procedural justice (Field & House, 1990; Heilman et al., 1984; Houlden et al., 1978; Lissak & Sheppard, 1983) and distributive justice (van Yperen et al., 2005), can be moderated by people's roles and contexts.

Group norms play an important role in shaping which sorts of outcomes people attend to. Norms influence whether a decision or judgment is understood to be one into which moral or ethical values should be incorporated or not. Moberg and Caldwell (2007) described this in terms of "moral imagination" (see also Werhane, 1998).

> Given any decision situation … moral imagination will lead people to identify the ethical implications of that decision more frequently than they would otherwise. In contrast, decision-makers whose moral imagination remains dormant will handle potentially ethical situations without recourse to their personal inventory of ethics-related talents and skills.
>
> (p. 194)

Whether people exhibit moral imagination is shaped by norms regarding appropriate ways of making decisions. For example, in an experiment that manipulated perceptions of organizational culture, they found that people assigned to an organization that ostensibly valued ethical behavior (versus product quality) exhibited greater moral imagination (i.e., greater consideration of ethics in decisions; Moberg & Caldwell, 2007).

Of course, moral sensibilities of groups can change with time. For instance, attitudes towards slavery, smoking, and vegetarianism have all been moralized, changing from activities widely construed as economic or personal decisions to acts rife with moral meaning (Rozin, 1999; Rozin et al., 1997). The process of moralization usually involves a shift in norms about what sorts of outcomes should be attended to, such that choices once evaluated in hedonic or pragmatic terms come to be consistently evaluated in moral terms. These attitudes are known as "moral mandates," because they are rooted in moral convictions and operate differently from other attitudes (Skitka et al., 2005). For example, people's beliefs about the extent to which a specific issue (e.g., abortion) is rooted in morality predict behavior over and above other attitude strength indices (e.g., extremity, accessibility, certainty; see Täuber, this volume). Amoralization, where values become preferences so that people no longer evaluate what was once a moral issue in moral terms (e.g., divorce), can also occur

Directions for future research

Our model of how social identities tune moral cognition raises several prospects for future research. The social identity approach provides a foundation for further studying the role that leaders play in shaping moral cognition, particularly by influencing followers' conceptions of group interests and goals (what we're striving to achieve; Haslam et al., 2020). Identity leadership has clarified why the "guards" in the famous Stanford Prison Experiment engaged in brutality towards the "prisoners" (Haslam, Reicher, & Van Bavel, 2019) and how US President Donald Trump mobilized his supports to engage in a violent insurrection of the Capitol Building (Haslam et al., 2022). More work is needed on the impact of leadership across a much broader array of contexts, and especially on pro-social behavior.

This work should also extend to organizational and institutional contexts where moral imagination has been investigated. Scholars should examine how group identities influence the types of outcomes (e.g., moral, hedonic, economic) actors are attentive to as they render judgments and make decisions. Under what conditions do groups encourage "moral imagination" (Moberg & Caldwell, 2007), focusing members on morally relevant concerns? Shifting attention to moral considerations is an urgent issue in organizations where theft, insider trading, and the mistreatment of others is common. It is also important for organizations that impact society negatively (e.g., producing pollution) and could be motivated to care about human welfare.

Value-based models of decision making are attentive to how multiple mental processes supported by multiple brain systems give rise to judgments and decisions, allowing us to move past heuristic models of human cognition. There is great scope for research on how basic cognitive (e.g., perception, attention), higher order cognitive (e.g., language, memory), and social cognitive (e.g., mind perception) processes shape value computations and thereby influence human morality (Gantman & Van Bavel, 2015; Pärnamets et al., 2015; Van Bavel et al., 2022). However, connecting this work to a unified theoretical model has been missing in the literature. We believe the value-based approach offers one fruitful direction for bridging these levels of analysis. But more empirical work is needed that formally incorporates these elements.

Conclusion

For centuries, philosophers and scientists have debated the role of emotional intuition and reason in moral judgment. Thanks to theoretical and methodological developments over the past few decades, we believe it is time to move beyond these debates. We argue that social identity can tune the intuitions and reasoning processes that underlie moral cognition (Van Bavel et al., 2015). Extensive research has found that social identities have a significant influence on social and moral judgment and decision-making (Oakes et al., 1994; Van Bavel & Packer, 2021). This approach offers an important complement to other theories of moral psychology and suggests a powerful way to shift moral judgments and decisions—by changing identities and norms, rather than hearts and minds.

Acknowledgments

The authors wish to thank Sharareh Noorbaloochi, Lisa Kaggen, and members of the NYU Social Identity and Morality Lab for their comments on this manuscript.

Note

1 Here, we use the term *moral decision* to refer to individuals' own choices and actions and *moral judgment* to refer to their assessments of other people's choices and actions. The terms *moral evaluation* or *moral cognition* are used more generally to describe psychological processes involved in producing decisions or judgments.

References

Balliet, D., Parks, C., & Joireman, J. (2009). Social value orientation and cooperation in social dilemmas: A meta-analysis. *Group Processes & Intergroup Relations, 12*(4), 533–547. https://doi.org/10.1177%2F1368430209105040

Berger, J., & Heath, C. (2008). Who drives divergence? Identity signaling, outgroup dissimilarity, and the abandonment of cultural tastes. *Journal of Personality and Social Psychology, 95*(3), 593–607. https://doi.org/10.1037/0022-3514.95.3.593

Blair, I. V. (2002). The malleability of automatic stereotypes and prejudice. *Personality and Social Psychology Review, 6*(3), 242–261. https://doi.org/10.1207/S15327957PSPR0603_8

Bocian, K., Cichocka, A., & Wojciszke, B. (2021). Moral tribalism: Moral judgments of actions supporting ingroup interests depend on collective narcissism. *Journal of Experimental Social Psychology, 93*, Article 104098. https://doi.org/10.1016/j.jesp.2020.104098 .

Cesario, J., & Jonas, K. J. (2014). Replicability and models of priming: What a resource computation framework can tell us about expectations of replicability. *Social Cognition, 32*, 124–136. https://doi.org/10.1521/soco.2014.32.supp.124

Chaiken, S., & Trope, Y. (1999). *Dual-process theories in social psychology*. New York: Guilford Press.

Cikara, M., Bruneau, E., Van Bavel, J. J., & Saxe, R. (2014). Their pain gives us pleasure: How intergroup dynamics shape empathic failures and counter-empathic responses. *Journal of Experimental Social Psychology, 55*, 110–125. https://doi.org/10.1016/j.jesp.2014.06.007

Cohen, A. B. (2015). Religion's profound influences on psychology: Morality, intergroup relations, self-construal, and enculturation. *Current Directions in Psychological Science, 24*(1), 77–82. https://doi.org/10.1177/0963721414553265

Crandall, C. S., Eshleman, A., & O'Brien, L. (2002). Social norms and the expression and suppression of prejudice: the struggle for internalization. *Journal of Personality and Social Psychology, 82*(3), 359. https://doi.org/10.1037/0022-3514.82.3.359

Cunningham, W. A., & Zelazo, P. D. (2007). Attitudes and evaluations: A social cognitive neuroscience perspective. *Trends in Cognitive Sciences, 11*(3), 97–104. https://doi.org/10.1016/j.tics.2006.12.005

Cunningham, W. A., Zelazo, P. D., Packer, D. J., & Van Bavel, J. J. (2007). The iterative reprocessing model: A multi-level framework for attitudes and evaluation. *Social Cognition, 25*(5), 736–760. https://doi.org/10.1521/soco.2007.25.5.736

De Cremer, D., & Van Vugt, M. (1999). Social identification effects in social dilemmas: A transformation of motives. *European Journal of Social Psychology, 29*(7), 871–893. https://doi.org/10.1002/(SICI)1099-0992(199911)29:7%3C871::AID-EJSP962%3E3.0.CO;2-I

DeScioli, P., & Kurzban, R. (2009). Mysteries of morality. *Cognition, 112*(2), 281–299. https://doi.org/10.1016/j.cognition.2009.05.008

Ellemers, N., & van den Bos, K. (2012). Morality in groups: On the social-regulatory functions of right and wrong. *Social and Personality Psychology Compass, 6*(12), 878–889. https://doi.org/10.1111/spc3.12001

Ellemers, N., Pagliaro, S., & Barreto, M. (2013). Morality and behavioural regulation in groups: A social identity approach. *European Review of Social Psychology, 24*(1), 160–193. https://doi.org/10.1080/10463283.2013.841490

Ellemers, N., Van Der Toorn, J., Paunov, Y., & Van Leeuwen, T. (2019). The psychology of morality: A review and analysis of empirical studies published from 1940 through 2017. *Personality and Social Psychology Review, 23*(4), 332–366. https://doi.org/10.1177%2F1088868318811759

Fehr, E., & Schurtenberger, I. (2018). Normative foundations of human cooperation. *Nature Human Behaviour, 2*(7), 458–468. https://doi.org/10.1038/s41562-018-0385-5

Feinberg, M., Willer, R., Antonenko, O., & John, O. P. (2012). Liberating reason from the passions: Overriding intuitionist moral judgments through emotion reappraisal. *Psychological Science, 23*(7), 788–795. https://doi.org/10.1177/0956797611434747

Ferguson, M. J., & Wojnowicz, M. T. (2011). The when and how of evaluative readiness: A social cognitive neuroscience perspective. *Social and Personality Psychology Compass, 5*(12), 1018–1038. https://doi.org/10.1111/j.1751-9004.2011.00393.x

Field, R. H., & House, R. J. (1990). A test of the Vroom-Yetton model using manager and subordinate reports. *Journal of Applied Psychology, 75*(3), 362–366. https://doi.org/10.1037/0021-9010.75.3.362

Foddy, M., Platow, M. J., & Yamagishi, T. (2009). Group-based trust in strangers: The role of stereotypes and expectations. *Psychological Science, 20*(4), 419–422. https://doi.org/10.1111/j.1467-9280.2009.02312.x

Gantman, A. P., & Van Bavel, J. J. (2015). Moral perception. *Trends in Cognitive Sciences, 19*(11), 631–633. https://doi.org/10.1016/j.tics.2015.08.004

Ginges, J., Atran, S., & Medin, D. (2007). Sacred bounds on rational resolution of violent political conflict. *Proceedings of the National Academy of Sciences, 104*(18), 7357–7360. https://doi.org/10.1073/pnas.0701768104

Graham, J., Haidt, J., & Nosek, B. A. (2009). Liberals and conservatives rely on different sets of moral foundations. *Journal of Personality and Social Psychology, 96*(5), 1029–1046. https://doi.org/10.1037/a0015141

Gray, K., Young, L., & Waytz, A. (2012). Mind perception is the essence of morality. *Psychological Inquiry, 23*(2), 101–124. https://doi.org/10.1080/1047840X.2012.651387

Greene, J. (2013). *Moral tribes: Emotion, reason, and the gap between us and them.* London: Penguin Press.

Greene, J. D., Sommerville, R. B., Nystrom, L. E., Darley, J. M., & Cohen, J. D. (2001). An fMRI investigation of emotional engagement in moral judgment. *Science, 293*(5537), 2105–2108. https://doi.org/10.1126/science.1062872

Hackel, L. M., Wills, J. A., & Van Bavel, J. J. (2020). Shifting prosocial intuitions: Neurocognitive evidence for a value-based account of group-based cooperation. *Social Cognitive and Affective Neuroscience, 15*, 371–381.

Hackel, L. M., Zaki, J., & Van Bavel, J. J. (2017). Social identity shapes social valuation: Evidence from prosocial behavior and vicarious reward. *Social Cognitive and Affective Neuroscience, 12*(8), 1219–1228. https://doi.org/10.1093/scan/nsx045

Haidt, J. (2001). The emotional dog and its rational tail: A social intuitionist approach to moral judgment. *Psychological Review, 108*(4), 814–834. https://doi.org/10.1037/0033-295X.108.4.814

Haidt, J. (2012). *The righteous mind: Why good people are divided by politics and religion.* New York: Pantheon/Random House.

Haslam, S. A., Reicher, S. D., & Platow, M. J. (2020). *The new psychology of leadership: Identity, influence and power*. New York: Routledge. https://doi.org/10.4324/9781351108232

Haslam, S. A., Reicher, S. D., Selvanathan, H.,, P., Gaffney, A. M., Steffens, N. K. Packer, D. J. Van Bavel, J. J., Ntontis, E.,Neville, F., Vestergren, S., Jurstakova, K., & Platow, M. J. (2022). Examining the role of

Donald Trump and his supporters in the 2021 assault on the U.S. Capitol: A dual-agency model of identity leadership and engaged followership. *The Leadership Quarterly*, 101622. https://doi.org/10.1016/j.leaqua.2022.101622

Haslam, S. A., Reicher, S. D., & Van Bavel, J. J. (2019). Rethinking the nature of cruelty: The role of identity leadership in the Stanford Prison Experiment. *American Psychologist, 74*(7), 809–822. https://doi.org/10.1037/amp0000443

Hastorf, A. H., & Cantril, H. (1954). They saw a game: A case study. *Journal of Abnormal and Social Psychology, 49*(1), 129–134. https://doi.org/10.1037/h0057880

Heilman, M. E., Hornstein, H. A., Cage, J. H., & Herschlag, J. K. (1984). Reactions to prescribed leader behavior as a function of role perspective: The case of the Vroom-Yetton model. *Journal of Applied Psychology, 69*(1), 50–60. https://doi.org/10.1037/0021-9010.69.1.50

Henrich, J., & Muthukrishna, M. (2021). The origins and psychology of human cooperation. *Annual Review of Psychology, 72*, 207–240. https://doi.org/10.1146/annurev-psych-081920-042106

Henrich, J., McElreath, R., Barr, A., Ensminger, J., Barrett, C., Bolyanatz, A., Cardenas, J. C., Gurven, M., Gwako, E., Henrich, N., Lesorogol, C., Marlowe, F., Tracer, D., & Ziker, J. (2006). Costly punishment across human societies. *Science, 312*(5781), 1767–1770. https://doi.org/10.1126/science.1127333

Hester, N., & Gray, K. (2020). The moral psychology of raceless, genderless stangers. *Perspectives on Psychological Science, 15*, 216–230.

Heuer, L., Penrod, S., & Kattan, A. (2007). The role of societal benefits and fairness concerns among decision makers and decision recipients. *Law and Human Behavior, 31*(6), 573–610. https://doi.org/10.1007/s10979-006-9084-2

Houlden, P., LaTour, S., Walker, L., & Thibaut, J. (1978). Preference for modes of dispute resolution as a function of process and decision control. *Journal of Experimental Social Psychology, 14*(1), 13–30. https://doi.org/10.1016/0022-1031(78)90057-4

Hui, B. P., Ng, J. C., Berzaghi, E., Cunningham-Amos, L. A., & Kogan, A. (2020). Rewards of kindness? A meta-analysis of the link between prosociality and well-being. *Psychological Bulletin, 146*(12), 1084–1116. https://doi.org/10.1037/bul0000298

Hume, D. (1983). *An enquiry concerning the principles of morals* (J. B. Schneewind, Ed.). Indianapolis: Hackett Publishing Company. (Original work published 1751)

Jarudi, I., Kreps, T. & Bloom, P. (2008). Is a refrigerator good or evil? The moral evaluation of everyday objects. *Social Justice Research, 21*(4), 457–469. https://doi.org/10.1007/s11211-008-0082-z

Kahneman, D. (2003). A perspective on judgment and choice: Mapping bounded rationality. *American Psychologist, 58*(9), 697–720. https://doi.org/10.1037/0003-066X.58.9.697

Kant, I. (1993). *Grounding for the metaphysics of morals* (3rd ed., J. W. Ellington, Trans.). Indianapolis: Hackett Publishing Company. (Original work published in 1785)

Kohlberg, L. (1969). Stage and sequence: The cognitive developmental approach to socialization. In D. A. Goslin (Ed.), *Handbook of socialization theory and research*. Chicago: Rand.

Kohlberg, L. (1975). The cognitive-developmental approach to moral education. *Phi Delta Kappan, 56*(10), 670–677.

Kohlberg, L. (1984). *Essays on moral development: Vol. 2. The psychology of moral development*. New York: Harper & Row.

Koleva, S. P., Graham, J., Iyer, R., Ditto, P. H., & Haidt, J. (2012). Tracing the threads: How five moral concerns (especially Purity) help explain culture war attitudes. *Journal of Research in Personality, 46*(2), 184–194. https://doi.org/10.1016/j.jrp.2012.01.006

Leshin, R., Yudkin, D. A., Van Bavel, J. J., Kunkel, L., & Rhodes, M. (2022). Parents' political ideology predicts how their children punish. *Psychological Science*. https://doi.org/10.31234/osf.io/j8cws

Lin, S-Y, & Packer, D. J., (2017). Dynamic tuning of evaluations: Implicit racial attitudes are sensitive to situationally-variable cooperative affordances. *Social Cognition, 35*(3), 245–272. https://doi.org/10.1521/soco.2017.35.3.245

Lissak, R. I., & Sheppard, B. H. (1983). Beyond fairness: The criterion problem in research on dispute intervention. *Journal of Applied Social Psychology, 13*(1), 45–65. https://doi.org/10.1111/j.1559-1816.1983.tb00886.x

Marques, J. M., & Paez, D. (1994). The 'black sheep effect': Social categorization, rejection of ingroup deviates, and perception of group variability. *European Review of Social Psychology, 5*(1), 37–68. https://doi.org/10.1080/14792779543000011

Moberg, D., & Caldwell, D. F. (2007). An exploratory investigation of the effect of ethical culture in activating moral imagination. *Journal of Business Ethics, 73*(2), 193–204. https://doi.org/10.1007/s10551-006-9190-6

Murrar, S., Campbell, M. R., & Brauer, M. (2020). Exposure to peers' pro-diversity attitudes increases inclusion and reduces the achievement gap. *Nature Human Behaviour, 4*(9), 889–897. https://doi.org/10.1038/s41562-020-0899-5

Oakes, P. J., Haslam, S. A., & Turner, J. C. (1994). *Stereotyping and social reality*. Oxford: Blackwell.

Pärnamets, P., Johansson, P., Hall, L., Balkenius, C., Spivey, M. J., & Richardson, D. C. (2015). Biasing moral decisions by exploiting the dynamics of eye gaze. *Proceedings of the National Academy of Sciences of the United States of America, 112*(13), 4170–4175. https://doi.org/10.1073/pnas.1415250112

Pärnamets, Shuster, Reinero, & Van Bavel, J. J. (2020). A value-based framework for understanding cooperation. *Current Directions in Psychological Science, 29*, 227–234.

Piaget, J. (1965). *The moral judgment of the child*. New York: The Free Press. (Original work published in 1932)

Platow, M. J., Foddy, M., Yamagishi, T., Lim, L. I., & Chow, A. (2011). Two experimental tests of trust in in-group strangers: The moderating role of common knowledge of group membership. *European Journal of Social Psychology, 42*(1), 30–35. https://doi.org/10.1002/ejsp.852

Rhodes, M., & Chalik, L. (2013). Social categories as markers of intrinsic interpersonal obligations. *Psychological Science, 24*(6), 999–1006. https://doi.org/10.1177/0956797612466267

Rozin, P. (1999). The process of moralization. *Psychological Science, 10*(3), 218–221. https://doi.org/10.1111%2F1467-9280.00139

Rozin, P., Markwith, M., & Stoess, C. (1997). Moralization and becoming a vegetarian: The transformation of preferences into values and the recruitment of disgust. *Psychological Science, 8*(2), 67–73. https://doi.org/10.1111/J.1467-9280.1997.TB00685.X

Sinclair, S., Lowery, B. S., Hardin, C., & Colangelo, A. (2005). Social tuning of automatic racial attitudes: The role of affiliative motivation. *Journal of Personality and Social Psychology, 89*, 583–592.

Skitka, L. J., Bauman, C. W., & Sargis, E. G. (2005). Moral conviction: Another contributor to attitude strength or something more? *Journal of Personality and Social Psychology, 88*(6), 895–917. https://doi.org/10.1037/0022-3514.88.6.895

Tajfel, H. (1970). Experiments in intergroup discrimination. *Scientific American, 223*(5), 96–103.

Tajfel, H., & Turner, J. C. (1979). An integrative theory of intergroup conflict. In W. G. Austin & S. Worchel (Eds.), *The social psychology of intergroup relations* (pp. 33–47). Monterey, CA: Brooks/Cole.

Terry, D. J., & Hogg, M. A. (1996). Group norms and the attitude-behavior relationship: A role for group identification. *Personality and Social Psychology Bulletin, 22*(8), 776–793. https://doi.org/10.1177%2F0146167296228002

Tetlock, P. E. (2002). Social-functionalist frameworks for judgment and choice: The intuitive politician, theologian, and prosecutor. *Psychological Review, 109*(3), 451–472. https://doi.org/10.1037/0033-295x.109.3.451

Tetlock, P. E. (2003). Thinking the unthinkable: Sacred values and the taboo tradeoff. *Trends in Cognitive Sciences, 7*(7), 320–324. https://doi.org/10.1016/s1364-6613(03)00135-9

Turiel, E. (1983). *The development of social knowledge: Morality and convention*. Cambridge: Cambridge University Press.

Turner, J. C., Oakes, P. J., Haslam, S. A., & McGarty, C. (1994). Self and collective: Cognition and social context. *Personality and Social Psychology Bulletin, 20*(5), 454–463. https://doi.org/10.1177%2F0146167294205002

Uhlmann, E. L., Pizarro, D. A., Tannenbaum, D., & Ditto, P. H. (2009). The motivated use of moral principles. *Judgment and Decision Making, 4*(6), 476–491. https://doi.org/10.1037/e683162011-049

Valdesolo, P., & DeSteno, D. (2007). Moral hypocrisy: Social groups and the flexibility of virtue. *Psychological Science, 18*(8), 689–690. https://doi.org/10.1111/j.1467-9280.2007.01961.x

Van Bavel, J. J., Cichocka, A., Capraro, V. et al. (2022). National identity predicts public health support during a global pandemic. *Nature Communications, 13*, 517. https://doi.org/10.1038/s41467-021-27668-9

Van Bavel, J. J., & Cunningham, W. A. (2009). Self categorization with a novel mixed-race group moderates social and racial biases. *Personality and Social Psychology Bulletin, 35*, 321–355.

Van Bavel, J.J., FeldmanHall, O., & Mende-Siedlecki, P. (2015). The neuroscience of moral cognition: From dual processes to dynamic systems. *Current Opinion in Psychology, 6*, 167–172. https://doi.org/10.1016/j.copsyc.2015.08.009

Van Bavel, J. J., & Packer, D. J. (2021). *The power of us: Harnessing our shared identities to improve performance, increase cooperation, and promote social harmony.* New York: Little, Brown Spark.

Van Bavel, J. J., Packer, D. J., Haas, I. J., & Cunningham, W. A. (2012). The importance of moral construal: Moral versus non-moral construal elicits faster, more extreme, universal evaluations of the same actions. *PLoS ONE, 7*(11), Article e48693. https://doi.org/10.1371/journal.pone.0048693

Van Bavel, J. J., & Pereira, A. (2018). The partisan brain: An Identity-based Model of Belief. *Trends in Cognitive Sciences, 22*, 213–224.

Van Bavel, J. J., Pärnamets, P., Reinero, D., & Packer, D. J. (2022). How neurons, norms, and institutions shape group cooperation. *Advances in Experimental Social Psychology.* https://doi.org/10.1016/bs.aesp.2022.04.004

Van Bavel, J. J., Xiao, Y. J., & Cunningham, W. A. (2012). Evaluation as a dynamic process: Moving beyond dual system models. *Social and Personality Psychology Compass, 6*(6), 438–454. https://doi.org/10.1111/j.1751-9004.2012.00438.x

Van Lange, P. A. M., Balliet, D., Parks, C. D., & Van Vugt, M. (2015). *Social dilemmas: The psychology of human cooperation.* Oxford: Oxford University Press.

van Yperen, N. W., van den Bos, K., & de Graaff, D. C. (2005). Performance-based pay is fair, particularly when I perform better: Differential fairness perceptions of allocators and recipients. *European Journal of Social Psychology, 35*(6), 741–754. https://doi.org/10.1002/ejsp.273

Werhane, P. H. (1998). Moral imagination and the search for ethical decision-making in management. *Business Ethics Quarterly, 8*(S1), 75–98. https://doi.org/10.1017/S1052150X00400084

Xiao, Y. J., Coppin, G., & Van Bavel, J. J. (2016). Perceiving the world through group-colored glasses: A perceptual model of intergroup relations. *Psychological Inquiry, 27*(4), 255–274. https://doi.org/10.1080/1047840X.2016.1199221

Yudkin, D.A., Rothmund, T., Twardawski, M., Thalla, N., & Van Bavel, J.J. (2016). Reflexive intergroup bias in third party punishment. *Journal of Experimental Psychology: General, 145*(11), 1148–1459. https://doi.org/10.1037/XGE0000190

7
THE INTERGROUP LEVEL

Human = moral—the boundary conditions for moral reasoning engagement in intergroup contexts

Lasana T. Harris and Ramandeep Mungur

Abstract

Humans rely on moral reasoning to determine whether a target belongs to the category human or not. We propose an evolutionary theory of the boundary conditions for moral reasoning engagement, particularly as it relates to ingroups and outgroups. Morality co-opted disgust as an emotional response to protect the ingroup from violation. We argue that moral reasoning—and subsequent attribution of humanity—is gated by the same principle that regulates disgust and more general emotional responding: *contaminant proximity*. Proximity—both physical and psychological—of a violator to a harm determines whether moral reasoning gets engaged or not. This engages *avoidance action-tendencies* that short-circuit moral reasoning, resulting in moral disengagement. Finally, there exist *prepared stimuli* that trigger moral intuition without moral reasoning. We describe gates that determine whether moral reasoning is facilitated or inhibited, explaining moral decisions, and moral behaviour toward ingroups and outgroups driven by whether they are considered fully human.

- Moral reasoning is gated by considered humanity, which in turn affects the perception of outgroups and intergroup relations.
- Moral reasoning occurs more in the context of ingroup than outgroup members because ingroup members may be viewed to be more fully human.
- Whether others are perceived as (fully) human depends on their physical and psychological proximity, moderated by disgust.
- Disengaged moral reasoning towards outgroup members may result in avoidance action tendencies such as dehumanisation and deindividualisation—which may make them the victim of immoral acts.

Introduction

Human beings evolved in small groups. This fundamental truth about human evolution shaped the brains and cognitive processes of modern humans (Dunbar, 1992). In our evolutionary history human beings living in hunter-gatherer societies may have considered 'human' to represent the ingroup since interactions with outgroup members was much rarer than in modern human societies. As such, we argue that morality evolved to safeguard the ingroup, ensuring everyone abided by the social contract or ingroup norms (Harris, 2017). Morality still serves this primary function today.

In this chapter, we will use this evolutionary lens to view moral reasoning in intergroup contexts. We begin by defining moral reasoning and posit that its gating determines who is considered human. We then consider contaminant proximity as an approach to understanding the gating of moral reasoning. Next, we consider how the gating of moral reasoning affect the perception of groups and their behaviour. We then consider avoidance action tendencies—deindividuation and dehumanisation—that facilitate the moral disengagement of outgroups. Finally, we discuss how outgroups might be considered prepared stimuli that elicit moral emotions, before suggesting future directions for research. For a visualisation of the model we propose, see Figure 7.1.

The delineation of 'ingroup' member from not is complex and fluid in human society since people hold multiple identities and belong to many social groups (Linville, 1985). People rely on familiarity and similarity to help determine whether a conspecific is human or not (Harris & Fiske, 2011). Moral protection is reserved for the ingroup, but the delineation of group membership could occur along either of these two dimensions, meaning that morality could be extended beyond the actual members of the ingroup if that group is defined by familiarity. Early human outgroups were unfamiliar, and perhaps dissimilar only in vocal prosody and accent. Therefore, moral protection was reserved just for highly familiar and similar others. This relatively loose delineation of group boundaries allows the perceived in-group and thus moral protection to be extended to previous out-groups, pets, and institutional symbols (Kwan & Fiske, 2008). Further, increased human migration meant some outgroup members were potential future allies, so a strict carving of the world into 'us' and 'them' may not have always been feasible. Here, moral reasoning again played a role in determining who was able to join the ingroup and who was not (Harris, 2017). In short, we argue

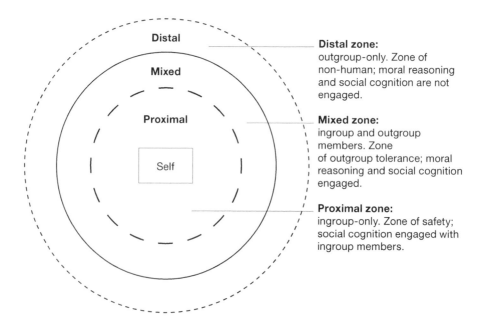

Figure 7.1 Distal, mixed, and proximal model of the self.

that moral reasoning determines whether a conspecific is human or not, and conversely, ingroup members (as full human beings) promote moral reasoning, while outgroup members do not.

Before continuing, we must distinguish concepts commonly conflated in the literature. Here, morality is the set of cognitive and affective tools that result from consideration of potential harm and suffering of others. Moral reasoning is the process of integrating emotional and non-emotional information to make a moral decision. When making such decisions, one must first decide if their toolkit of moral heuristics ought to be used. In contrast, moral judgements require moral reasoning but result in opinions, attitudes, and other forms of self-report instead of behaviour. Given that attitudes and behaviour often differ (LaPiere, 1934), as do hypothetical judgements and consequential decisions (Camerer & Mobbs, 2017; Kang, Rangel, Camus, & Camerer, 2011), moral judgements likely often differ from moral decisions, though not always.

When moral reasoning is engaged, people consider both the suffering that may result from the moral decision (i.e. a utilitarian ethic) and the moral principles that act as axioms of ought behaviour (i.e. a deontological ethic). Moral decisions therefore result from moral reasoning about consequential behaviour, such as donating money to charity or administering electrical shocks as punishment. This involves weighing both the significance of utilitarian and deontological information and using this to resolve any conflict between them.

Moral reasoning relies on mentalising—considering the thoughts and feelings of others—in the context of threat detection and harm avoidance. This makes moral reasoning a form of social cognition. Current theorising suggests social cognition is flexible, that is, people can engage social cognition or not depending on their goals or the social context (Deroy & Harris, under review; Harris, 2017). Therefore, we argue that moral reasoning is also flexibly engaged. Here, we go beyond the traditional approach to moral reasoning and intergroup behaviour that focusses almost exclusively on social exclusion (e.g. Rutland & Killen, 2015) to describe a principle that gates moral reasoning, allowing it to be engaged or not in intergroup contexts.

Moral reasoning is gated by contaminant proximity

Morality evolved to protect social groups from behaviour that causes harm or suffering. As such, it relies on disgust—an emotion evolved to guard against the violation of the 'body envelope'—the parts of the body where chemicals can enter, including the skin, mouth, nose, reproductive and waste organs (Haidt, Rozin, McCauley, & Imada, 1997) and avoid pathogens (Curtis, Aunger & Rabie, 2004; Van Leeuwen et al., 2012). Physiological disgust responses to moral violations overlap with contaminant avoidance (Chapman et al., 2009), suggesting that moral disgust relies on the same mechanisms as physical disgust (see also the section on Moral Emotions, this volume, for more information on disgust). Disgust is a threat detection mechanism or a type of fear (Klucken et al., 2012). As such, it relies on a principle that determines whether a threat is present or not, thus able to contaminate—*contaminant proximity*. Here, we argue that this principle is relevant for moral reasoning as well, influencing whether perceivers engage in moral reasoning, considering a target as human and an ingroup member.

The principle of contaminant proximity states that the closer a person is to a morality-relevant stimulus, the more likely it is that moral reasoning is engaged. If the person is far enough away from a morality-relevant stimulus, moral reasoning is not engaged. Proximity therefore triggers avoidance action-tendencies—cognitive mechanisms that can block moral reasoning engagement. These include cognitive mechanisms that disengage social cognition, a sense of self, and agency, and are captured in theorising regarding dehumanisation and deindividuation—forms of moral disengagement (Bandura, Barbaranelli, Caprara, & Pastorelli, 1996; Harris, 2017; Postmes & Spears,

1998). Such cognitive mechanisms are often triggered by goals or the social context, such as seeing a group of young males approaching you, leading to you crossing the street. Further, certain behaviours will engage a moral intuition independent of moral reasoning, similar to the manner in which prepared stimuli trigger disgust even if people know there is no contaminant threat (e.g. a piece of chocolate shapes like faeces). In an intergroup context, this suggests that people may be less likely to reason about the behaviour of outgroup members than ingroup members because outgroup members are more psychologically and often physically distant.

Proximity plays a central role in construal level theory (CLT). CLT claims that we understand and interact with our environment via construals—cognitive representations ranging from concrete to abstract (Trope & Liberman, 2010). For instance, if we are making our way through a crowd, we may perceive the people who make up the crowd as many individuals, whereas if we were to see a crowd of people from a hill, we may perceive that crowd as a single unit, even though we know that the crowd is made up of many people. These construals can be considered abstract when thinking of the crowd, or concrete when thinking of the individuals. As we zoom in from our vantage point, the crowd becomes individuals. In this sense, the resolution of our perception is inversely proportional to the distance between us and that with which we interact.

Psychological distance measures how far something (a construal) is to the self. It interacts with CLT since as psychological distance increases, the preference for more abstract construals increases (Trope & Liberman, 2010). Lower resolution (more general) rules of the world ought to be more stable with distance, be this distance physical, psychological, or otherwise. Our morals are themselves abstract, hence ought to be more stable with psychological distance; research demonstrates that they are more salient in our reasoning when thinking about the distant future compared to the near future events (Eyal, Liberman, & Trope, 2008; Gong & Medin, 2012; Žeželj & Jokič, 2014). Moreover, abstract construals trigger more stereotyping and group-based biases (McCrea, Wieber, & Myers, 2012), suggesting they play a role in intergroup perception.

How might CLT then influence our judgements with the classic trolley and footbridge problems (e.g. Thomson, 1985)? We would expect that as the scenarios progress from further (distal) to closer (proximal) physical distance, moral emotions and consequently deontological ethics are given a higher weight in the moral reasoning process because of diminishing physical distance between the agent and the patient. Experiments using similar scenarios have found that people find killing one versus five more morally acceptable in the psychologically distal versus proximal condition (Greene et al., 2001; Lanteri et al., 2008). Given that the choice to kill one or five (and by extension save the other(s)), it seems curious that the distal condition elicits the above results.

Through the lens of CLT, one can argue that utilitarian reasoning (e.g. the life of one person is less valuable than the lives of five) becomes most salient in the psychologically distal condition, while the deontological reasoning (e.g. no life should be sacrificed) becomes more likely in the proximal condition. This is akin to Greene et al.'s (2001) personal/impersonal distinction. In deontological judgements, other factors such as the humanness of the patient, social group membership, and indeed the agency of the participant, increase in salience (Cikara, Farnsworth, Harris, & Fiske, 2010), decreasing the palatability of the utilitarian judgement. This suggests that distance moderates the weight ratio of emotional to non-emotional information during moral reasoning, hence moderating the probability that either deontological or utilitarian ethics is used. This is but one example of how CLT can affect moral reasoning extended to social groups.

Moral disgust acts as a moral intuition that inhibits moral reasoning about moral violations that coincide with body envelope violations (Giner-Sorolla & Harris, 2014; Russell & Giner-Sorolla, 2013). Further, in countries with high pathogen densities, disgust sensitivity and the relative weighting of disgust-associated moral foundations are elevated (Van Leeuwen et al., 2012, Graham et al., 2016). Given that, by definition, something that could harbour pathogens is more dangerous as its distance to the self decreases, it follows that moral emotions too will be more readily activated as the psychological distance from a disgusting action decreases (e.g. an agent killing a patient with their bare hands). It may also be the case that the more disgusting one perceives something to be, the more proximal it is perceived to be, demonstrating how our visceral reaction can influence our moral reasoning (and judgements).

Emotional reactivity decreases as psychological distance increases (Van Boven et al., 2010). Therefore, sacrificing a stranger increases the weight of emotional information (deontology) and reduces the weight of non-emotional information (utilitarianism) as psychological distance is reduced because disgust becomes more salient. Indeed, this explains people's reticence to kill a patient to harvest their organs to save five others who need the patient's organs, as in another iteration of the trolley problem (Waldmann & Dieterich, 2007). Here, disgust associated with organ harvesting is salient as one imagines physically cutting out the organs. Nonetheless, disgust itself can slow us down and encourage caution whilst gathering more information to understand whether it is better to approach or avoid a construal. Thus, disgust is an emotion that helps inform the appropriate adaptive psychological distance between us and a construal. This is consistent with outgroups who, by nature of their increased psychologically distance, elicit more disgust responses (Fiske, Cuddy, Glick, & Xu, 2002).

The influence of proximity on moral reasoning for intergroup relations

We now consider the implications of moral reasoning and contaminant proximity for intergroup relations (see also Figure 7.1). Ingroup members—who are psychologically more proximal in part because they are evolutionarily safer to be close to—are morally judged and policed more than out-group members (Meleady, Hodson & Earle, 2021; Wang et al., 2017). It follows that we are more likely to utilise our moral heuristics when reasoning in the context of ingroup members than out-group members, viewing ingroup members to be moral thus fully human. It may also be the case that we are more likely to consider someone to be an ingroup member if we perceive them to be moral.

Consider how proximity predicts moral judgements across three hypothetical moral dilemmas based on the classic trolley problem (Foot, 1967); sacrificing a life to save many lives by: (i) pushing a lever; (ii) pushing a person; and (iii) harvesting organs. In these hypotheticals, proximity is operationalised as both physical and psychological distance, that is, the space between the person engaged in the harmful behaviour (agent) and the victim who incurs suffering or harm (patient). Increased distance results more utilitarian judgements and less moral condemnation of the agent.

While the relationship between moral emotions and proximity is positive for moral judgements and decisions, the relationship may be negative for moral non-emotional information. Consider the case of sentencing blue and white-collar crimes. In these real-world cases, proximity is operationalised in the same manner as hypotheticals, and increased distance also results in less moral condemnation and punishment of the agent. That is, blue-collar crimes (e.g. murder, mugging, etc.) appear more psychologically proximal than white-collar crimes (e.g. money laundering, tax evasion) due to a reduced distance between the agent and patient, and thus emotional information is likely to be given a higher weight. This increases the weight of moral emotions (e.g. disgust, moral outrage) and hence harshness regarding the sentencing decisions for blue-collar crimes (Gottschalk & Rundmo, 2014).

Moreover, those who commit white-collar crimes might be perceived to come from groups perceived as high in competence, eliciting the in-group emotion pride and the ambivalent emotion envy (Fiske et al., 2002). When examining this more closely, one could argue that an ingroup, whilst more likely to be judged via emotional than non-emotional information, may also be forgiven more readily as not all (moral) emotions will be negative. Outgroup criminals on the other hand are more prone to be appraised via emotional responses such as disgust—part of a dehumanised perception—that may play a larger role in judgements about them. This could lead to disproportionate sentences for ingroup versus outgroup criminals.

Additionally, there is more psychological distance between the agent and patient in white-collar crimes; money laundering by a corrupt businessperson (agent) affects the government's tax revenue stream, which affects everyone in the country (patients). This is a very different type of crime from a physical attack at a large public event, where agent and patients are near each other when the harm occurred. This suggests an increased weighting of non-emotional vs emotional information when people decide punishment for white- relative to blue-collar crimes.

Brain imaging and behavioural data illustrate the difference between blue- and white-collar crimes; in one study, participants read vignettes describing blue- and white-collar crimes matched on government sentencing guidelines such that both types of crimes would receive the same sentence in the court of law. Behavioural results reveal that punishment decisions were less severe for white-collar crimes (below the government sentencing guidelines) versus blue-collar crimes (which matched sentencing guidelines). Converging evidence comes from brain activity patterns in regions underlying moral reasoning, showing less engagement by white-collar crimes (Capestany & Harris, 2014). Such evidence is consistent with the contaminant proximity principle, demonstrating that proximity gates moral reasoning.

Another example of non-emotional reasoning following an inverse relationship with contaminant proximity comes from the legal research on dignity takings; these describe instances where government bodies and institutions have enacted legislation that deprives people of their property, schools, hospitals, homes, and even culture (Harris, 2018). Such consequences occur usually to societal outgroups: ethnic minorities, lower class people, or other societal outgroup patients that are often never considered by the governmental agent acting in their professional role. This highlights how psychological distance can affect real-life outcomes for traditionally marginalised societal groups.

Denying outgroup members moral reasoning: avoidance action-tendencies

Flexible social cognition theory states that people's tendency to consider other people's minds is not inevitable in the presence of another (Deroy & Harris, under review; Harris, 2017). Given that an inference of another person's mind allows them to be perceived as fully human, a failure to engage social cognition signifies that the target is not processed as fully human. Such a dehumanised perception excludes the target from the bounds of moral protection, making it easier to justify immoral behaviour towards the target (for review, see Harris & Fiske, 2009). In the context of moral reasoning, flexible social cognition could be viewed as part of the construal construction process. Psychological distance may mediate the extent to which our social cognition is engaged (and thus change the construal of the target), and the process of engaging or disengaging our social cognition may mediate psychological distance consciously, subconsciously, or both.

Dehumanised perception is an avoidance action-tendency—an evolved mechanism for behaviour to distance oneself from, and avoid, others—in the moral domain. Dehumanised perception occurs to people perceived as societal outcasts; people experiencing homelessness and injection drug users (Harris & Fiske, 2006). This highlights how these avoidance action-tendencies affect out-groups, shutting them off from full humanity, and denying them moral reasoning. It also reinforces the idea that people perceived as morally reprehensible are not considered fully human; in legal canon and public discourse, such immoral actors are often referred to as 'monsters' (Nuzzo, 2013; Sharpe, 2007; 2009).

Another avoidance action-tendency is deindividuation. Consider what happens when we perceive groups or when we are physically part of a group. One hypothesis is that we see group members as homogeneous. Such homogeneity may engage deindividuation, seeing oneself or others as solely members of a group (Postmes & Spears, 1998; Reicher, Spears, & Postmes, 1995). To return to the crowd analogy, we do not perceive groups as the individuals of whom they are made up, but as their own entity. Thus, as psychological distance from the individual increases, we may construe them using their group membership rather than their full humanity. For instance, outgroup members' relative distance to the ingroup may increase the likelihood that their construals are deindividuated. This would increase the probability of triggering disgust if the deindividuated individual is close enough in physical distance.

When an outgroup member is perceived to be more distant in the psychological domain, but more proximal in the physical domain, the deindividuated outgroup member may be more likely to be perceived as a threat, hence more likely to trigger a threat response. Here, we would therefore expect emotional reasoning to be more engaged despite the increased psychological distance. This expectation takes the initial CLT model and looks more closely at the concept of psychological distance. Whereas CLT sees all distance as equivalent, here we examine what happens when a construal is more distant in one domain and less distant in another. We argue that with sufficient physical proximity, the emotional reasoning is used (this is in line with CLT) even if the target is psychologically more distant (this contrasts with CLT). Further, in the case we examine, the reasoning engaged is not a simple average of the two distances. The target is more harshly judged precisely because it is a psychologically distant and physically close simultaneously.

Both the avoidance action-tendencies of dehumanisation and deindividuation can lead to moral disengagement, which in this context means the suspension of moral reasoning. Our moral reasoning apparatus thus has a psychological proximity threshold that predicts whether the agent engages passive or active harm to the patient (Cuddy, Fiske, & Glick, 2007). Disgust's role in dehumanisation (Harris & Fiske, 2009) suggests there is a degree of disgust that would motivate the agent to increase psychological distance. The resulting moral disengagement allows the agent to commit otherwise immoral acts to a patient and may be central in outgroup genocide. One of the most infamous cases of this is the Holocaust where one of Hitler's methods of murdering Jewish people was to gas them with the pesticide Zykoln B (Weindling, 1994).

Perceiving outgroups as prepared stimuli

We have covered how psychological distance can impact associated moral emotions, and how these emotions are accessed, as well as moral reasoning and the role of action-tendencies in moral judgements and decisions involving groups. We must now ask if there are certain stimuli that are impermeable to non-emotional moral information, regardless of psychological distance. How might the response to certain prepared stimuli—things in the world that trigger a moral emotion—be resistant to non-emotional moral information? Jonathan Haidt et al. (2000) famously (and in jest) asked people to consider if it was wrong to fornicate with a dead chicken, assuming that the chicken was clean and adequate contraception was used. People's instinctive reactions were to believe it was wrong, but they could not give a reason as to why. This phenomenon is known as moral dumbfounding—a feeling of wrongness that cannot be justified logically —and it seems to have its roots in disgust (Haidt, Bjorklund, & Murphy, 2000). When faced with a scenario where a disgusting action is taking place, it is much harder to override our intuitive emotions in favour of reason (Russell & Giner-Sorrolla, 2013).

Under the appropriate conditions, therefore, it may be argued that certain outgroups act as prepared stimuli. Interaction with members of certain outgroups may trigger a heightened, automatic disgust response that may: (i) lead to the dehumanisation of these members, or; (ii) hijack the construal such that the members are never humanised. This would explain part of the motivations of hate crimes; media portrayal of outgroups may cause people to more easily associate disgust with such groups, a form of cultural learning. This can hack our evolutionarily preserved outgroup threat detection mechanisms, increasing the probability of hate crimes (Müller & Schwarz, 2020), wars, and genocide. It is difficult to propose an effect size for such phenomena because cumulative effects of cultural learning coupled with negative interactions between group members may cause a snowball effect. Positive intergroup interactions and positive media coverage, however, may mitigate such negative impacts (Kubin & von Sikorski, 2021).

Final thoughts and directions for future research

There is certainly conflicting evidence in the literature for our theoretical argument. The contaminant proximity principle seems to contrast with findings of Eyal et al. (2008) who found that psychologically distal moral hypotheticals were judged more harshly than proximal ones. However, Navarette et al. (2012) found that increased emotional arousal was associated with a decrease in utilitarian reasoning (for similar results, see Pan & Slater (2011) and Szekely & Miu, 2015). Further, a recent meta-analysis suggests that the evidence for CLT may not be as strong as previously thought (Maier et al., 2022). Future research is needed to further clarify these concepts.

Future research should also explore our ability to flexibly engage social cognition to manipulate psychological distance (and hence change the ratio of emotional and non-emotional moral information) specifically as it relates to countering injustices arising from outgroup prejudices. A better understanding of this should better inform integration policies regarding immigrants as we would be better able to predict what could cause social harmony and disharmony, especially as this intersects with the legal system.

Flexibly engaging one's social cognition to promote one's professional self and subsequent goals may side-line social biases (Okonofua, Harris, & Walton, 2022), making moral reasoning more appropriately used. For instance, lawmakers may be more objective and more readily engage moral reasoning by focussing on their goal to be impartial, distancing themselves from crimes during deliberation. Professional goals may also affect how legal professionals value lives, facilitating rehabilitation of offenders. Indeed, it could be our environment that dictates our disgust sensitivities and moral foundations that lead to perceptions of justice that are more adaptive to that environment. As our environments change over time therefore, our sense of justice might too. Similarly, social groups also shift over time, suggesting that moral responses to ingroups and outgroups are malleable.

References

Bandura, A., Barbaranelli, C., Caprara, G. V., & Pastorelli, C. (1996). Mechanisms of moral disengagement in the exercise of moral agency. *Journal of Personality and Social Psychology*, 71(2), 364–374. doi/10.1037/0022-3514.71.2.364

Camerer, C., & Mobbs, D. (2017). Differences in behavior and brain activity during hypothetical and real choices. *Trends in Cognitive Sciences, 21*(1), 46–56.

Capestany, B. H., & Harris, L. T. (2014). Disgust and biological descriptions bias logical reasoning during legal decision-making. *Social Neuroscience, 9*(3), 265–277.

Chapman, H. A., Kim, D. A., Susskind, J. M., & Anderson, A. K. (2009). In bad taste: Evidence for the oral origins of moral disgust. *Science, 323*(5918), 1222–1226.

Cikara, M., Farnsworth, R. A., Harris, L. T., & Fiske, S. T. (2010). On the wrong side of the trolley track: Neural correlates of relative social valuation. *Social Cognitive and Affective Neuroscience, 5*(4), 404–413.

Cuddy, A. J., Fiske, S. T., & Glick, P. (2007). The BIAS map: Behaviors from intergroup affect and stereotypes. *Journal of Personality and Social psychology, 92*(4), 631–648.

Curtis, V., Aunger, R., & Rabie, T. (2004). Evidence that disgust evolved to protect from risk of disease. *Proceedings of the Royal Society of London. Series B:Biological Sciences, 271(suppl_4), S131–S133*.

Deroy, O., & Harris, L. T. (Manuscript under review). *Flexible social cognition: A mark of the social in the human brain.*

Dunbar, R. I. (1992). Neocortex size as a constraint on group size in primates. *Journal of Human Evolution, 22*(6), 469–493.

Eyal, T., Liberman, N., & Trope, Y. (2008). Judging near and distant virtue and vice. *Journal of Experimental Social Psychology, 44*(4), 1204–1209.

Fiske, S. T., Cuddy, A. J. C., Glick, P., & Xu, J. (2002). A model of (often mixed) stereotype content: Competence and warmth respectively follow from perceived status and competition. *Journal of Personality and Social Psychology, 82*(6), 878–902.

Foot, P. (1967). The problem of abortion and the doctrine of double effect. *Oxford Review*, 5.

Giner-Sorolla, R., & Harris, L. T. (2014). The negative side of disgust. *The Emotion Researcher*, http://emotionresearcher.com/the-negative-side-of-disgust/

Graham, J., Meindl, P., Beall, E., Johnson, K. M., & Zhang, L. (2016). Cultural differences in moral judgement and behavior, across and within societies. *Current Opinion in Psychology, 8*, 125–130.

Greene, J. D., Sommerville, R. B., Nystrom, L. E., Darley, J. M., & Cohen, J. D. (2001). An fMRI investigation of emotional engagement in moral judgement. *Science, 293*(5537), 2105–2108.

Gong, H., & Medin, D. L. (2012). Construal levels and moral judgement: Some complications. *Judgement & Decision Making, 7*(5), 628–638.

Gottschalk, P., & Rundmo, T. (2014). Crime: The amount and disparity of sentencing—A comparison of corporate and occupational white collar criminals. *International Journal of Law, Crime and Justice, 42*(3), 175–187.

Haidt, J., Bjorklund, F., & Murphy, S. (2000). Moral dumbfounding: When intuition finds no reason. *Unpublished manuscript, University of Virginia, 191–221.*

Haidt, J., Rozin, P., McCauley, C., & Imada, S. (1997). Body, psyche, and culture: The relationship between disgust and morality. *Psychology and Developing Societies, 9*(1), 107–131.

Harris, L. T. (2017). *Invisible mind: Flexible social cognition and dehumanization.* Cambridge: MIT Press.

Harris, L. T. (2018). Dignity takings and dehumanization: A social neuroscience perspective. *Chicago-Kent Law Review, 92*(3), 725–742.

Harris, L. T., & Fiske, S. T. (2006). Dehumanizing the lowest of the low: Neuroimaging responses to extreme out-groups. *Psychological Science, 17*(10), 847–853.

Harris, L. T., & Fiske, S. T. (2009). Social neuroscience evidence for dehumanised perception. *European Review of Social Psychology, 20*(1), 192–231.

Harris, L. T., & Fiske, S. T. (2011). Perceiving humanity or not: A social neuroscience approach to dehumanized perception. *Social Neuroscience: Toward Understanding the Underpinnings of the Social Mind*, 123–134.

Kang, M. J., Rangel, A., Camus, M., & Camerer, C. F. (2011). Hypothetical and real choice differentially activate common valuation areas. *Journal of Neuroscience, 31*(2), 461–468.

Klucken, T., Schweckendiek, J., Koppe, G., Merz, C. J., Kagerer, S., Walter, B., et al. (2012). Neural correlates of disgust-and fear-conditioned responses. *Neuroscience, 201*, 209–218.

Kubin, E., & von Sikorski, C. (2021). The role of (social) media in political polarization: A systematic review. *Annals of the International Communication Association, 45*(3), 188–206.

Kwan, V. S., & Fiske, S. T. (2008). Missing links in social cognition: The continuum from nonhuman agents to dehumanized humans. *Social Cognition, 26*(2), 125–128.

Lanteri, A., Chelini, C., & Rizzello, S. (2008). An experimental investigation of emotions and reasoning in the trolley problem. *Journal of Business Ethics, 83*(4), 789–804.

LaPiere, R. T. (1934). Attitudes vs. actions. *Social Forces, 13*(2), 230–237.

Linville, P. W. (1985). Self-complexity and affective extremity: Don't put all of your eggs in one cognitive basket. *Social Cognition, 3*(1), 94–120.

Maier, M., Bartoš, F., Oh, M., Wagenmakers, E. J., Shanks, D., & Harris, A. (2022). Adjusting for publication bias reveals that evidence for and size of construal level theory effects is substantially overestimated. doi.org/10.31234/osf.io/r8nyu

McCrea, S. M., Wieber, F., & Myers, A. L. (2012). Construal level mind-sets moderate self-and social stereotyping. *Journal of Personality and Social Psychology, 102*(1), 51–68. doi/10.1037/a0026108

Meleady, R., Hodson, G., & Earle, M. (2021). Person and situation effects in predicting outgroup prejudice and avoidance during the COVID-19 pandemic. *Personality and Individual Differences, 172*, 110593.

Müller, K., & Schwarz, C. (2020). From hashtag to hate crime: Twitter and anti-minority sentiment. doi.org/10.2139/ssrn.3149103

Navarrete, C. D., McDonald, M. M., Mott, M. L., & Asher, B. (2012). Virtual morality: Emotion and action in a simulated three-dimensional 'trolley problem'. *Emotion, 12*(2), 364–370.

Nuzzo, L. (2013). Foucault and the enigma of the monster. *International Journal for the Semiotics of Law-Revue internationale de Sémiotique juridique, 26*(1), 55–72.

Okonofua, J. A., Harris, L. T., & Walton, G. M. (2022). Sidelining bias: A situationist approach to reduce the consequences of bias in real-world contexts. *Current Directions in Psychological Science, 31*(5), 395–404. doi.org/10.1177/09637214221102422

Pan, X., & Slater, M. (2011). Confronting a moral dilemma in virtual reality: A pilot study. In *Proceedings of HCI 2011 The 25th BCS Conference on Human Compuer Interaction, 25* (pp. 46–51).

Postmes, T., & Spears, R. (1998). Deindividuation and antinormative behavior: A meta-analysis. *Psychological Bulletin, 123*(3), 238–259.

Reicher, S. D., Spears, R., & Postmes, T. (1995). A social identity model of deindividuation phenomena. *European Review of Social Psychology, 6*(1), 161–198.

Russell, P. S., & Giner-Sorolla, R. (2013). Bodily moral disgust: What it is, how it is different from anger, and why it is an unreasoned emotion. *Psychological Bulletin, 139*(2), 328–351.

Rutland, A., & Killen, M. (2015). A developmental science approach to reducing prejudice and social exclusion: Intergroup processes, social-cognitive development, and moral reasoning: A developmental science approach to reducing prejudice and social exclusion. *Social Issues and Policy Review, 9*(1), 121–154.

Sharpe, A. N. (2007). Structured like a monster: Understanding human difference through a legal category. *Law and Critique, 18*(2), 207–228.

Sharpe, A. (2009). *Foucault's Monsters and the Challenge of Law* (1st ed.). Abingdon and New York: Routledge-Cavendish. doi.org/10.4324/9780203862834

Szekely, R. D., & Miu, A. C. (2015). Incidental emotions in moral dilemmas: The influence of emotion regulation. *Cognition and Emotion, 29*(1), 64–75.

Thomson, J. J. (1985). The trolley problem. *The Yale Law Journal, 94*(6), 1395–1415.

Trope, Y., & Liberman, N. (2010). Construal-level theory of psychological distance. *Psychological Review, 117*(2), 440–463.

Van Boven, L., Kane, J., McGraw, A. P., & Dale, J. (2010). Feeling close: Emotional intensity reduces perceived psychological distance. *Journal of Personality and Social Psychology, 98*(6), 872–885.

Van Leeuwen, F., Park, J. H., Koenig, B. L., & Graham, J. (2012). Regional variation in pathogen prevalence predicts endorsement of group-focused moral concerns. *Evolution and Human Behavior, 33* (5), 429–437.

Waldmann, M. R., & Dieterich, J. H. (2007). Throwing a bomb on a person versus throwing a person on a bomb: Intervention myopia in moral intuitions. *Psychological Science, 18*(3), 247–253.

Wang, Y., Zhang, Z., Bai, L., Lin, C., Osinsky, R., & Hewig, J. (2017). Ingroup/outgroup membership modulates fairness consideration: Neural signatures from ERPs and EEG oscillations. *Scientific Reports, 7*(1), 1–10.

Weindling, P. (1994). The uses and abuses of biological technologies: Zyklon B and gas disinfestation between the first world war and the holocaust. *History and Technology: An International Journal, 11*(2), 291–298.

Žeželj, I. L., & Jokić, B. R. (2014). Replication of experiments evaluating impact of psychological distance on moral judgement. *Social Psychology, 45*(3), 223–231. doi.org/10.1027/1864-9335/a000188.

PART III

Moral judgments

PART IIIA

A vision on moral judgments

8
MORAL JUDGMENT
What makes it unique?

Andrea E. Abele

My interest in moral judgment

Already while studying psychology I was fascinated by research on moral judgments, because I was convinced that a shared understanding of moral values and a shared interpretation of behavior as moral or immoral is essential for harmony and functioning in both interpersonal relations, small groups and larger societies. When studying developmental psychology, I was fascinated by the approaches of Piaget (1932) and Kohlberg (1964), who showed that moral judgment is closely linked to cognitive development and that not every person may reach the "final" level of moral judgment. I was fascinated by Caroll Gilligan's (1982) approach who argued that women and men differ in their moral judgments, because they focus on different aspects of morality, care-based versus justice-based. And I was fascinated by social-psychological approaches because they explicitly or implicitly reveal that moral judgments have a number of unique features that make them different from other forms of social judgment. Keeping my conviction from the beginning of my studies that a shared understanding of moral values and a shared interpretation of behavior as moral or immoral is essential for social life I became increasingly aware of the most complex nature of moral judgments.

According to my view moral judgments are unique with respect to at least five features:

(1) The definition of morality – and of immorality – is far from trivial.
(2) Moral judgments are value-based and values differ between individuals and groups.
(3) The judgmental perspective, being actor or observer of a behavior, is of high importance.
(4) Moral judgments are characterized by a positive–negative asymmetry.
(5) Moral judgments are strongly tied to valence.

In the following, I will first discuss how moral judgments may be integrated into a more general conceptualization of social judgments and social evaluation. Then I will discuss the above mentioned unique features of moral judgments and will deduce some research questions arising from them.

Moral judgments in the context of social judgment and social evaluation

Social judgments and social evaluations are the basis of our understanding and interpretation of the world (Abele, Ellemers, Fiske, Koch & Yzerbyt, 2021). People constantly evaluate themselves, other individuals, their own groups, and other groups in society, and this is functional for guiding behavior. Evaluative dimensions guide the way people organize and feel about social information, for acting on it. Thus, a key question in psychology is which evaluative dimensions may be distinguished. As traced back to ancient philosophical thinking (for an overview, see Markey, 2002), social evaluation is not just one dimensional, good versus bad, but at least two dimensional. Following the classic view, a long tradition distinguishes two basic functions of behavior and consequently its interpretation, namely accomplishing tasks and forming bonds. These issues, forming bonds, also called "getting along" and performing tasks, also called "getting ahead" are the "Big Two" of social evaluation. The "getting ahead" dimension (usually called agency or competence; also "vertical" dimension) can be subdivided into the facets assertiveness- and ability-judgments. This means that with respect to "getting ahead" people want to evaluate if a given behavior is determined (assertiveness) and clever (ability) enough to enhance goal pursuit. The "getting along" dimension (usually called communion or warmth; also "horizontal" dimension) can also be subdivided into two facets, namely friendliness- and morality-judgments. This means that with respect to "getting along" people want to evaluate if a given behavior is warm and empathic (friendliness) and trustworthy and moral (morality). Empirical research has shown that the Big Two dimensions and their facets can be reliably distinguished in different languages and with respect to different targets (Abele et al., 2016).

Moral judgments, hence, are part of the "getting along" dimension and together with friendliness-, ability-, and assertiveness-judgments they form the "Big Two" of social evaluation (other theories, for instance, the Behavior Regulation Model [Ellemers, 2017; Ellemers, Pagliaro, & Barreto, 2013] or the Moral Primacy Model [Brambilla et al., 2021] conceptualize morality as a third dimension complementing the Big Two. I will not discuss the commonalities and differences of both conceptualizations here [see, for instance, Abele et al., 2021; Koch, Yzerbyt, Abele, Ellemers & Fiske, 2021]). There is ample evidence for the particular role moral judgments play in evaluating self, other persons and groups (Abele et al., 2016; Abele & Hauke, 2019; Abele, Cuddy, Judd & Yzerbyt, 2008; Brambilla, Sacchi, Rusconi & Goodwin, 2021; Ellemers, 2017; Ellemers, van der Toorn, Paunov & van Leeuwen, 2019; Leach, Ellemers & Barreto, 2007; Malle, 2021; for a discussion see Abele, et al., 2021).

Moral judgments are unique because the definition of morality is not trivial

The term morality can be used in quite different ways, for instance, in a descriptive versus normative sense. Descriptively, it addresses what a specific society or a specific group (or even a specific individual) sees as moral. Research as well as everyday experience shows that there are quite substantive differences in what specific groups/individuals/societies regard as moral. Take as an example the extreme case of so-called honor-killing, where a person is killed, because they do not comply with some rules of "morality," which are regarded as completely immoral in another culture. Or as a less extreme example, take the case that someone is rated as "trustworthy" (an important item in morality scales), if this person behaves trustworthy to the target, but the target does not care about the other's trustworthiness towards other people or groups. Therefore, any definition of morality in a descriptive sense has to specify the frame of reference.

Normatively, morality refers to behaviors that ought to be performed or ought to be avoided. Again the normative definition is highly dependent on context and frame of reference. It is extremely difficult to establish general normative standards of morality that are shared across cultures, religious groups, or different power and status hierarchies. There are again many examples in history and politics how morality in a normative sense is differently used dependent on, for instance, a powerful person's interests and goals. Moreover, morality in a normative sense has to be distinguished from law and religion. More distinctions are conceivable, for instance, deontological versus utilitarian morality (see also Gilligan, 1982). This distinction is addressed in the section of this handbook on moral reasoning, but will not be discussed here.

Psychological theories focus on how descriptive and prescriptive morality norms shape behavior and social judgments, and they implicitly assume that these processes are independent of the specific norms and ethics in the respective context (see already Piaget, 1932). This assumption has to be further tested, however.

Moral judgments are unique because they are based on values

Moral judgments are based on values. These values may stem from religious conviction and/or from political and cultural beliefs. Depending on specific values different behaviors can be regarded as moral (or not moral). The above example of "honor-killing" shows that behavior is evaluated on the basis of specific cultural values. On a more everyday level, a person might, for instance, value "stimulation" (a value of the Schwartz, 2012, value theory) highly. Then they might evaluate another's risk behavior as more morally adequate than if he/she values "stimulation" lower. Schwartz et al. (2012) showed that endorsement of "basic values" differs both between individuals and between cultures. He structures values into ten broad categories of self-direction, stimulation, self-enhancement, achievement, power, security, conformity, tradition, benevolence, and universalism. Differences between societies can be arranged on three axes of conservatism vs. intellectual and affective autonomy; hierarchy vs. egalitarianism, and mastery vs. harmony. The impact of such different value orientations both between individuals and between cultures on moral judgments should be studied more deeply.

Moral judgments are unique because they depend on perspective

Attribution research has already revealed the high importance of perspective, e.g., if a behavior is evaluated from the perspective of an actor or an observer (Jones & Nisbett, 1971): Actors tend to consider situational circumstances more than observers do. Research into the Big Two has also shown the importance of perspective, as actors regard more the "getting ahead" dimensions, and observers more the "getting along" dimension in forming evaluative judgments of self and others (Abele & Hauke, 2019; Abele & Wojciszke, 2014; Abele, Bruckmüller & Wojciszke, 2014). The same applies to moral judgments: Actors tend to emphasize situational circumstances if they behaved in a morally questionable way (overview see Ellemers et al., 2019). Moreover, people tend to perceive their own morality as generally high and given (Abele & Hauke, 2019). Observers – particularly if they are victims of another's morally questionable behavior – tend to evaluate the other more extremely negative. However, if they gain from others' immorality, then they judge more leniently (Bocian & Wojciszke, 2014). This means that self-judgments of morality and judgments of others' morality are framed differently. Similarly, judgments of one's ingroup's morality vs an outgroup's morality may also be based on different standards due to perspective.

Moral judgments are unique because negative exemplars have a higher weight than positive ones

Research has repeatedly demonstrated that negative stimuli have a higher weight than positive ones and this also applies to moral judgments (Skowronski & Carlston, 1989). First, negative exemplars of moral behavior and morality (you should not steal, you should not harm others, etc.) are easier to define than positive exemplars (be fair, be trustworthy, be honest, etc.). Second, judgments of negative moral deeds are more informative and hence seem more extreme than those of positive ones (Reeder & Brewer, 1979). Guglielmo and Malle (2019), for instance showed that more blame is assigned in case of immorality than praise in case of morality. Moreover, even if the respective research is not conclusive, negative – and particularly negative morality information – is sometimes inferred faster than positive one (Ybarra, Chan & Park, 2001; but see also Abele & Bruckmüller, 2011). Interestingly, actor–observer differences as outlined before are also more pronounced for negative than for positive outcomes (Malle, 2006).

Moral judgments are unique because they are highly related to valence

One final issue here is the association of moral judgments with valence. In his classic study of 555 traits representative of person descriptors in English, Anderson (1968) found that most traits are clearly negative or positive and only few are more or less "neutral". Peabody (1967), moreover, showed that descriptive (Big Two: "getting along" vs "getting ahead") and evaluative meaning (positive/negative) of traits are confounded in natural languages, so it is nearly impossible to describe people without evaluating them. Research in different languages revealed that trait adjectives belonging to the "getting along" dimension (for instance, fair, unfair, warm, cold, reliable, unreliable, etc.) are even more correlated with valence than traits belonging to the "getting ahead" dimension (intelligent, dull, decisive, indecisive, etc.; Abele & Wojciszke, 2007; Suitner & Maass, 2008; Wojciszke, Dowhyluk & Jaworski, 1998). A reanalysis of Abele and Wojciszke (2007) data with respect to the distinction of morality versus friendliness items additionally showed that morality items (particularly negative ones) are more related to valence than friendliness items. Abele (2022) also showed that morality items were rated more positively than friendliness items, and both were rated more positively than items related to ability and assertiveness. Finally, Abele (2022) also analyzed the association of self-ratings on ability/assertiveness/friendliness/morality with socially desirable responding and showed that self-ratings of morality predicted social desirable responding more than the other self-ratings.

Conclusions

What do I conclude from these unique features of moral judgments? I propose that they may be used as an agenda for further research.

The distinction between descriptive and normative judgments of morality could be analyzed. If, for instance, a group is evaluated with respect to morality and it is shown that moral judgments correlate most highly with emotional reactions, are these moral judgments then descriptive ("the group is like that") or normative ("the group follows a normative standard")? Does this distinction make sense psychologically? Are, for instance, emotional reactions stronger in the case of normative than in the case of descriptive moral judgments?

Moreover, if morality judgments are strongly based on values, should research on moral judgments include measures of individuals' or groups' values? Would such an inclusion allow better prediction of approach or avoidance, emotional reactions, praise and blame? Would the inclusion of values allow us to better understand and judge others' moral (immoral) deeds? How is talking about morality possible if the underlying values, norms and rules are not uncovered?

Furthermore, if moral judgments are heavily based on perspective, how can we know that disliking an "unfair" neighbor is based on the same criteria as those applied by the neighbor him-/her-self? It might well be that the neighbor sees their behavior as adequate and that they do not understand why the other describes it as "unfair". So, if we know that people like others, who are fair and reliable, and that people prefer information on others' morality compared to information on their friendliness (see Brambilla et al., 2021), what does that mean with respect to interpersonal behavior? Perspective differences in social evaluation are so common (see above) that it is worth studying them further with respect to moral judgments.

Finally, if the positive – negative asymmetry applies strongly to moral judgments and if additionally moral judgments are specifically loaded with valence (and with social desirability), how would findings change if judgments were made for negative morality items instead of positive ones?

More generally, would there be different findings if moral judgments are not based on adjectives like fair or unreliable, but instead on specific behaviors which are either provided by the researcher or are self-provided by the participants? And: How do conventional moral judgment measures (adjective ratings) predict actual approach vs. avoidance behavior compared to more fine-grained measures like behavioral information combined with information on the participants' values? Does the fuzziness of the morality construct and its lacking sharpness enhance its power in predicting reactions upon moral judgments? It could well be that – similar to values which are also abstract and do not denote specific ways of behaving – due to their abstractness and due to their partly idiosyncratic nature moral judgments are particularly suited to generate a shared – but diffuse – understanding of societal functioning. Should moral judgments be distinguished more with respect to reputational issues versus epistemic issues? These are just a few questions arising from the unique features of moral judgments and more questions could be easily generated.

My motivation to consider these questions continues my early interest in the psychology of morality, but being a social psychologist, it is guided by the above issues. In my point of view moral judgments must be regarded from both an epistemic and a reputational perspective: In the epistemic perspective it is important to have a clear basis for evaluating our social world and for deducing consequences out of these evaluations. In the reputational perspective it is important to present the self or one's ingroup as "moral" since morality is evaluated as highly positive. Reputational issues may be one source for differences in moral judgments between actors (who want to appear moral) and observers (who have an epistemic interest). However, actor/observer differences in moral judgments are based on more than reputational versus epistemic issues. For instance, they may be based on different information with respect to the issue in question or they may be based on different values. I would love to see future research studying the reputation versus epistemic interest issue as well as the actor/observer differences issue in moral judgment.

References

Abele, A. E. (2022). Evaluation of the self on the Big Two and their facets: Exploring the model and its nomological network. *International Review of Social Psychology, 35*(1): *14*, 1–15. DOI: https://doi.org/10.5334/irsp.688.

Abele, A. E. & Bruckmüller, S. (2011). The bigger one of the "Big Two": Preferential processing of communal information. *Journal of Experimental Social Psychology, 47*, 935–948. doi:10.1016/j.jesp.2011.03.028

Abele, A. E. & Hauke, N. (2019). Comparing the facets of the Big Two in global evaluation of self versus other people. *European Journal of Social Psychology, 49,* 969–982. DOI: 10.1002/ejsp.2639

Abele, A. E. & Wojciszke, B. (2007). Agency and communion from the perspective of self versus others. *Journal of Personality and Social Psychology, 93,* 751–763. doi: 10.1037/0022-3514.93.5.751

Abele, A. E. & Wojciszke, B. (2014). Communal and agentic content: A dual perspective model. *Advances in Experimental Social Psychology, 50,* 195–255. doi.org/10.1016/B978-0-12-800284-1.00004-7

Abele, A. E., Bruckmüller, S. & Wojciszke, B. (2014). You are so kind – and I am kind and smart: Actor – Observer Differences in the Interpretation of On-going Behavior. *Polish Psychological Bulletin, 45,* 394–401. doi: 10.2478/ppb-2014-0048

Abele, A. E., Cuddy, A. J., Judd, C. M. & Yzerbyt, V. Y. (2008). Special issue: Fundamental dimensions of social judgment. *European Journal of Social Psychology, 38,* 1063–1224. DOI: 10.1002/ejsp.574

Abele, A. E., Ellemers, N., Fiske, S., Koch, A. & Yzerbyt, V. (2021). Navigating the social world: Shared horizontal and vertical dimensions for evaluating self, individuals, and groups. *Psychological Review, 128,* 290–314. doi: 10.1037

Abele, A. E., Hauke, N., Peters, K., Louvet, E., Szymkow, A. & Duan, Y. (2016). Facets of the fundamental content dimensions: Agency with competence and assertiveness – communion with warmth and morality. *Frontiers in Psychology, 7,* 1810. DOI: 10.3389/fpsyg.2016.01810

Anderson, N. H. (1968). Likableness ratings of 555 personality trait words. *Journal of Personality and Social Psychology, 9,* 272–279. doi: 10.1037/h0025907

Brambilla, M., Sacchi, S., Rusconi, P. & Goodwin, G. (2021). The primacy of morality in impression development: Theory, research, and future directions. *Advances in Experimental Social Psychology, 64.* DOI:10.1016/bs.aesp.2021.03.001

Bocian, K. & Wojciszke, B. (2014). Self-interest bias in moral judgments of others' actions. *Personality and Social Psychology Bulletin, 40,* 898–909. DOI: 10.1177/0146167214529800

Ellemers, N. (2017). *Morality and the regulation of social behavior: Groups as moral anchors.* Milton Park, UK. Routledge.

Ellemers, N., Pagliaro, S. & Barreto, M. (2013). Morality and behavioral regulation in groups: A social identity approach. *European Review of Social Psychology, 24,* 160–193.

Ellemers, N., van der Toorn, J., Paunov, Y. & van Leeuwen, T. (2019). The psychology of morality: A review and analysis of empirical studies published from 1940 through 2017. *Personality and Social Psychology Review, 1–35,* doi: 10.1177/088868318811759

Gilligan, C. (1982). *In a different voice: Psychological theory and women's development.* Cambridge, MA: Harvard University Press.

Guglielmo, S. & Malle, B. (2019). Asymmetric morality: Blame is more differentiated and more extreme than praise. *PLOS, March 12, 2019;* doi: 10.1371

Jones, E. E., & Nisbett, R. E. (1971). *The actor and the observer: Divergent perceptions of the causes of behavior.* Morristown, NJ: General Learning Press.

Koch, A., Yzerbyt, V., Abele, A. E., Ellemers, N. & Fiske, S. (2021). Social evaluation: Comparing models across interpersonal, intragroup, intergroup, several-group, and many-group contexts. *Advances in Experimental Social Psychology, 63,* 1–68.

Kohlberg, L. (1964). Development of moral character and moral ideology. In M. Hoffmann & L. Hoffmann (Eds.), *Review of child development research, 1,* 381–431. New York: Russell Sage.

Leach, C., Ellemers, N. & Barreto, M. (2007). Group virtue: The importance of morality (vs. competence and sociability) in the positive evaluation of ingroups. *Journal of Personality and Social Psychology, 93,* 234–249. Doi: 10.1037/0022-3514.93.2.234

Malle, B. (2021). Moral judgments. *Annual Review of Psychology, 72,* 293–318. DOI: 10.1146/annurev-psych-072220-104358

Malle, B. F. (2006). The actor-observer asymmetry in attribution: A (surprising) meta-analysis. *Psychological Bulletin, 132,* 895–919. doi: 10.1037/0033-2909.132.6.895

Markey, P. M. (2002). The duality of personality: Agency and communion in personality traits, motivation, and behavior. (63), ProQuest Information & Learning, US. EBSCOhost psych database. https://doi.org/10.1006/jrpe.2001.2341

Peabody, D. (1967). Trait inferences: Evaluative and descriptive aspects. *Journal of Personality and Social Psychology Monograph, 7,* No. 4 (Whole No. 644). doi: 10.1037/h0025230

Piaget, J. (1932). *Le jugement moral chez l'enfant.* Paris: Alcan.

Reeder G. D., & Brewer, M. B. (1979). A schematic model of dispositional attribution in interpersonal perception. *Psychological Review, 86*, 61–79.

Schwartz, S. H. (2012). An overview of the Schwartz theory of basic values. *Online readings in Psychology and Culture, 2*(1), 2307–0919.

Schwartz, S. H., Cieciuch, J., Vecchione, M., Davidov, E., Fischer, R., Beierlein, C., Ramos, A., Verkasalo, M., Lönnqvist, J.-E., Demirutku, K., Dirilen-Gumus, O., & Konty, M. (2012). Refining the theory of basic individual values. *Journal of Personality and Social Psychology, 103*(4), 663–688. Doi: 10.1037/a0029393

Skowronski J. J. & Carlston D. E. (1989). Negativity and extremity biases in impression formation: A review of explanations. *Psychological Bulletin, 105*, 131–142.

Suitner, C. & Maass, A. (2008). The role of valence in the perception of agency and communion. *European Journal of Social Psychology, 38*, 1073–1082. doi: 10.1002/ejsp.525

Wojciszke, B., Dowhyluk, M. & Jaworski, M. (1998). Moral- and competence-related traits: how do they differ? *Polish Psychological Bulletin, 29*, 283–294.

Ybarra, O., Chan, E., & Park, D. (2001). Young and old adults' concerns about morality and competence. *Motivation and Emotion, 25*, 85–100.

PART IIIB

Empirical review chapters on moral judgments

9
THE INTRAPERSONAL LEVEL

How power shapes the judgment of others' moral character—a social context perspective

Marlon Mooijman

Abstract

In the current chapter, I discuss how having a position of power changes people—the intrapersonal effects of power—and focus on how power changes individuals' judgments of others' moral character. I suggest that power can have both positive and negative effects on moral judgments of others, depending on whether the social context emphasizes cooperation or competition. I propose that power makes individuals view others' moral character more positively when cooperation is the perceived norm, whereas power makes individuals view others' moral character more negatively when competition is the perceived norm. I discuss the growing body of research that provides evidence for these ideas and lay out a roadmap for future research on the topic.

- Power positions and related concerns influence the way people judge the moral character of others.
- Research suggests that power holders are inclined to suspect subordinates to lie or cheat, causing them to judge others negatively.
- Alternatively, some studies reveal that a position of power can also induce positive judgments of other people's moral character.
- This chapter proposes that competitive contexts are most likely to induce power holders to judge other people's moral character negatively, while cooperative contexts will more often induce positive moral judgments.

Introduction

Power and morality both involve desirable resources. Power is defined as having asymmetric control over desirable resources (e.g., money; Emerson, 1962; Magee & Galinsky, 2008), and morality often involves the allocation of desirable resources to the self or others (e.g., be selfish or fair; Haidt & Kesebir, 2010). In the current chapter, I discuss how having a position of power changes people—the intrapersonal effects of power—and focus on how power changes individuals' judgments of others' morality. The chapter is structured as follows. I first outline what moral judgment is and isn't. I then discuss the state of the current literature on power and moral judgment and highlight how considering the social context can help resolve outstanding theoretical inconsistencies. I lastly lay out a roadmap for future research on the topic.

Research to date suggests that power makes individuals view others as lacking moral character. That is, as selfish, uncompassionate, and unethical. Nevertheless, there are also reasons to assume that power can have positive effects on moral judgments (e.g., greater optimism causing people to see others as allies; Anderson & Galinsky, 2006; Brion & Anderson, 2013). Here, I suggest that power can have both positive and negative effects on moral judgments of others, depending on whether the social context emphasizes cooperation or competition (see Figure 9.1). I propose that power makes individuals view others' moral character more positively when cooperation is the perceived norm, whereas power makes individuals view others' moral character more negatively when competition is the perceived norm.

Understanding how social power shapes estimates of others' moral character is important for several reasons. There is an abundance of research on the effects of power on an individual's own moral decisions and moral behaviors (e.g., lying, cheating, hypocrisy; Lammers et al., 2008; Dubois et al., 2015), attesting to the relation between people's control over desirable resources and how they act to accumulate or retain such resources. However, far fewer studies have examined how power changes an individual's judgment of others' moral character. The dominant theories on power (e.g., approach-inhibition theory, Keltner et al., 2003) seem ill-suited to explain the current findings on moral judgments of others, making theoretical expansion prudent. Individuals in positions of power also frequently decide on who receives resources (reward) and who does not (punish), and their evaluations of others' moral character and perceived deservingness are instrumental in guiding these decisions (Mooijman et al, 2015; van Prooijen & van den Bos, 2014; Wiltermuth & Flynn, 2013). Understanding how power shapes the evaluation of others' moral character, then, helps us understand how resource inequalities are created and perpetuated by power holders. Since people's perception of what is fair depends in part on whether they think others appropriately reward them (Mooijman et al., 2017; Tyler & Lind, 1992), this analysis also helps us understand how power holders create and perpetuate a sense of fairness amongst those subject to their decisions (e.g., subordinates, citizens).

Moral judgment

Moral judgments involve evaluations of someone's moral character—their perceived inclination to think, feel, and act in a way that is consistent with prevailing norms of right and wrong (Cohen et al., 2014). Right and wrong in this context refers to social norms indicating how people ought to behave and how they ought not to behave in a certain situation (Ellemers & Van den Bos, 2012). Accurately estimating the likelihood that others will act in line with important norms or guidelines is particularly consequential for those controlling the outcomes of others—i.e., power holders. For instance, when managers decide whether to monitor subordinates' workplace behaviors, they are likely to estimate whether subordinates will comply with organizational rules and regulations. Are they seen as tempted to free ride, cut corners, or cheat? Or comply with rules and norms? What managers think the answer to this question is determines whether they will install systems that monitor subordinates' actions in the workplace (e.g., monitor the amount of time they are actively working versus surfing the internet; Schweitzer et al., 2018). Similarly, government officials might base their decisions on how they judge the moral character of citizens: for instance, they are more likely to fine citizens for incorrectly filling out tax forms when they judge this behavior to be the result of cheating rather than incompetence. When this judgment is erroneous, governments criminalize innocent citizens. Power holders' moral judgments, then, can have far-reaching implications for themselves as well as others depending on them.

The current chapter focuses on judgments of other people's morality rather than their competence, a distinction that is analogous to what trust scholars call "integrity-based trust" as compared to "ability-based trust." Integrity-based trust refers to the judgment that someone can be trusted to comply with ethical rules and regulations (e.g., be fair, do not lie or steal), whereas ability-based trust refers to the judgment that someone can be trusted to have adequate skills and abilities to achieve certain goals (e.g., to do their job; Mayer et al., 1995; see also Leach et al., 2007). In principle, these two types of judgments are independent. It is possible to view someone as inclined to cheat on their taxes and competent at doing so. It is also possible to perceive someone as incompetent but inclined to pay their fair share of taxes (e.g., make a mistake and unintentionally underreport income to the authorities). The intrapersonal process of moral judgment, then, revolves about estimating someone's integrity rather than their competence (for work on how power shapes perceptions of others' competence, see Georgeson & Harris, 1998).

Power often elicits negative moral judgments

Although power and the impact of power differences between individuals have garnered a tremendous amount of research attention over the last decades, relatively few studies have been devoted to understanding how positions of power shape people's judgments of others' moral character (Fleischmann & Lammers, 2020). The studies that do exist suggest that having high power makes individuals view others as lacking moral character. For instance, Mooijman et al. (2015) showed that being placed in a position of power increases the extent to which individuals believe others are selfish and inclined to break norms, rules, and regulations. The authors demonstrated this by asking participants to recall a time in their life when they had held a position of power or lacked such power. This autobiographical recall assignment is commonly used and tends to make participants feel temporarily powerful or powerless (Galinsky et al., 2003). After being primed in this way, participants were confronted with various scenarios.

One of these scenarios asked participants whether citizens are inclined to commit tax fraud (e.g., "When it really comes down to it, most taxpayers will be tempted to commit tax fraud"). Participants who felt powerful were more likely to believe that citizens are tempted to commit tax fraud than participants who felt powerless. Further, these moral judgments were consequential, as they made high-power participants more supportive of punishments aimed at deterring citizens from committing tax fraud (e.g., install mandatory minimums, use public punishments). Similar effects were observed when examining the impact of power differences on moral judgments in other contexts. In a follow-up paper, Mooijman et al. (2019) demonstrated that high-power managers were more likely to think that their subordinates are tempted to come late to work, slack off, or steal office-supplies than low-power managers. They found that these moral judgments related to intrapersonal concerns held by the manager, rather than being prompted by specific behaviors of their subordinates. That is, the suspicion that subordinates lacked moral character was explained by power holders' own desire to maintain their power. Accordingly, viewing others as lacking moral character made managers more inclined to take actions to protect their power position (e.g., prevent others from breaking rules; instill fear; monitor their actions).

Besides the studies summarized above, there is additional empirical evidence suggesting that having or acquiring a position of power makes individuals more likely to view others as lacking moral character. Brion et al. (2019) showed a negative association between momentary changes in power and changes in the perception that others are trustworthy. Likewise, Schilke et al. (2015)

provided empirical evidence for the notion that power makes people more likely to believe that others will exploit them in contexts where exchanging resources is risky. More generally, Du Plessis et al. (2023) showed that power holders tend to see others competing with them over who controls valuable resources. This expectation in itself fosters the perception that others are selfish, and even malicious, rather than benevolent (for similar findings, see Feenstra et al., 2020; Inesi et al., 2012; Weber et al., 2004).

A slightly different, but informative, perspective was taken by Wiltermuth and Flynn (2013). They refer to the notion that power holders view the world with more certainty, and accordingly suggest that power increases morality clarity, which refers to the phenomenon of seeing transgressions as unambiguously morally wrong. They demonstrated this by asking participants to recall a time in their life when they either had or lacked power. After this high vs. low power prime was induced, participants were confronted with the following scenario, highlighting competing loyalties in a moral dilemma:

> Your colleague, whom you consider to be a friend, is looking to hire a new manager in her department. She has identified an external candidate she would like to hire, but company rules require her to consider internal candidates first. She has asked you not to disclose to people within the company that she has already picked out an external candidate for the position. However, you know two employees in your area who would like to have this job, and each has asked you directly if your colleague has already picked someone for this position. You decide to tell them that she has not picked anyone yet.

Wiltermuth and Flynn demonstrated that high-power participants considered this behavior more unambiguously wrong than low-power participants and also recommended harsher punishments for this behavior. Similarly, van Prooijen et al. (2014) found that participants who were primed with power recommended harsher punishments and longer sentences for offenders of various crimes (e.g., knowingly selling a broken car that ends up severely injuring the buyer). Power increased punishment severity because participants were more likely to view the offender as possessing negative character traits (e.g., evil, cruel). Taken together, this body of research suggests that considering social situations from a position of high power makes it more likely that people view others as lacking moral character.

Power may also induce positive moral judgments

Notably, there is a relative absence of research demonstrating that power makes individuals view others' moral character more positively. Nevertheless, there are reasons to assume that power can also increase positive moral judgments. For instance, Brion and Anderson (2013) demonstrated that high-power individuals are more likely than low-power individuals to view others as their allies, to which they attribute positive features. They argue that this is caused by power leading individuals to be more optimistic about opportunities offered by their position, and to focus more on the rewarding aspects of their social environment. This idea is consistent with the approach-inhibition theory of power that postulates that power is associated with the behavioral activation system (BAS; Keltner et al., 2003; Cho & Keltner, 2020). According to this reasoning, power holders are more likely to act and view their social environment as filled with rewards rather than threats. It makes sense, then, to assume that if power holders hold positive world views and underestimate risks, that they might also view the moral character of those around them more positively. By comparison, those lacking such power are more vulnerable and should be more careful in trusting the good intentions and moral character of others. Thus, having power may induce relatively positive moral judgments.

This raises an interesting question: *when* does power lead individuals to view others' moral character more positively or more negatively? I argue that prior research highlighting the negative implications of power for moral judgment has addressed the impact of power too narrowly and did not consider the larger social context. As a result, this prior work has not systematically examined relevant boundary conditions. I propose that power can have positive and negative effects on moral judgments of others, depending on whether the social context emphasizes cooperation or competition. Power makes individuals view others' moral character more positively when cooperation is the perceived norm, whereas power makes individuals view others' moral character more negatively when competition is the perceived norm.

The social context of moral judgment

Most theories on power highlight the position of the power holder but do not explicitly take into account the larger social context in which power holders make their moral judgments of others. Consequently, it is unclear how power impacts moral judgments, depending on when cooperative or selfish behavior is perceived as the norm. For instance, some situations are perceived as governed by norms of cooperation whereas others are perceived as governed by norms of competition. In many business settings, where relationships are transactional and involve resources exchange, people expect others to compete with them for resources and bend the rules in their favor (Tenbrunsel & Smith-Crowe, 2008). In fact, merely reminding people of business-related concepts, such as sanctions and money, already makes them view others as competitors (Tenbrunsel & Messick, 1999). These findings align with prior research on power that shows the negative implications of power for moral judgment: that is, having power, which reminds individuals of their resources, money, and ability to sanction (Tost, 2015), may act as a signal that relationships with others are transactional and based on resource exchange. This may foster the perception that others lack moral character and are selfish and unethical.

However, power holders do not solely act in settings where competition is the perceived norm. They also operate in settings where cooperation is perceived to be prevalent. For instance, although managers and subordinates do not have equal access to resources, they often strive to achieve the same goals. Workplace projects with tight deadlines, collective sales goals, and competition from other firms require managers and subordinates to coordinate and cooperate effectively within their teams, organizations, and institutions (Tjosvold, 1989). Similarly, members of military teams must anticipate each other's needs, work towards team-level goals, and help each other in case of life and death (Stanton, 2011). Likewise, citizens and their governments must cooperate when faced with significant external threats such as pandemics, wars, and financial crises. Without the cooperation of most citizens, societies are unable to solve collective-action problems (Barclay & Benard, 2020). In these situations, cooperation rather than competition between high-power and low-power individuals is the norm and high- and low-power individuals may perceive to share common goals, identities, and relevant group memberships. How does this shape the relationship between power and moral judgment?

Power, moral judgments, and social norms

The situated focus theory of power postulates that power directs people's attention to the actions they must take in each situation to achieve important goals (Guinote, 2017). The powerful will prioritize the dominant needs of a given situation, whereas the powerless are more easily distracted by situational difficulties and momentary concerns (e.g., thoughts and feelings irrelevant to situational needs). Indeed, research has shown that power makes individuals better at pursuing situationally relevant goals (e.g., persist at boring tasks; Guinote, 2007), inhibiting goal-irrelevant distractions (e.g., suppress intruding thoughts; Smith et al., 2008), and understanding what goals they should prioritize (e.g., the core parts of the task; Magee & Smith, 2013). Research has also shown that power increases self-interested behavior for people who have the goal to pursue their own self-interest, whereas power increases prosocial behavior for people who have the goal to be attentive and take into account others' views and needs (Chen, Lee-Chai, & Bargh, 2001; see also Galinsky et al., 2003). This means that instead of focusing on the main effects of high vs low power on moral judgments, we should understand the interactive effects of power and the dominant needs of a given social situation on moral judgment.

Prior research on power and moral judgment, for instance, has typically placed participants in settings where their interests *conflicted* with the interests of others. Mooijman et al. (2015, 2019), Du Plessis et al. (2022), and Schilke et al. (2015) used some version of a social dilemma game where participants' interests misaligned with the interests of others (e.g., participants could maximize their return by taking money out of a common good). Participants were then asked to what extent others were trustworthy and would cooperate, or whether others were untrustworthy and would be selfish at participants' expense. This means that participants were made to understand the social context as one where others might be inclined to be selfish and display exploitative behaviors. In a similar vein, Wiltermuth and Flynn (2013), and van Prooijen et al. (2014), elicited responses to scenarios where others broke the rules. This means that the social context presented to participants was one where others had already broken rules, displayed a questionable moral character, and had to be punished. Most studies to date on the impact of power on moral judgments, in other words, examined contexts that can be characterized in retrospect as settings where cooperation is not a given, selfish behavior can be expected, and others' moral character is questionable. It is therefore no surprise that these studies showed that power made individuals view others' moral character more negatively.

Indeed, these contexts induced goals that high-power were more likely to focus on than low-power individuals. When social contexts emphasize that people's interests are misaligned, and desirable resources might be taken from you, power focuses individuals' attention on the goal to protect their resources from others and prevent exploitation. In fact, research has shown that people can view others' moral character negatively as a resource-protection-strategy (Feenstra et al., 2020). When people are motivated to protect their resources, they assume that others are selfish, uncompassionate, and unethical because doing so allows them to take the appropriate actions to avoid being exploited (e.g., not share resources with others; use sanctioning and monitoring systems; Mooijman et al., 2019). In addition, when the social context emphasizes that others have already broken rules, power focuses people on the goal to prevent them from breaking more rules (Mooijman et al, 2015). It also focuses attention on offenders' negative characteristics, as viewing offenders positively might mean erroneously assuming that they will not break any future rules (van Prooijen et al., 2014). Thus, the reason why prior research has found that power induces negative moral judgments may be due to the usage of social contexts that emphasized competition and rule-breaking behavior over cooperation.

Consistent with the notion that social contexts matter for understanding the relationship between power and the moral judgment of others, Brion et al (2013) found that people primed with high power, compared to low power, *over*estimated the extent to which their team members were willing to cooperate with them. This study was conducted with college students who worked on

Intrapersonal level: intrapersonal effects of power

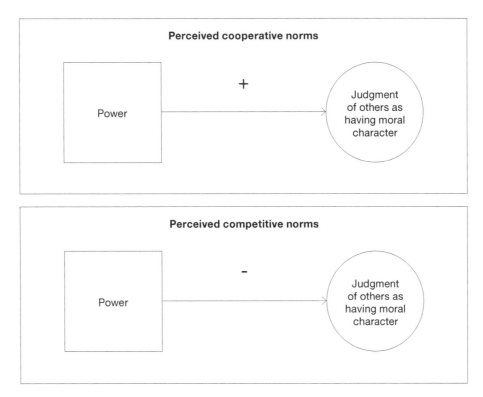

Figure 9.1 Perceived cooperative and perceived competitive norms.

team projects together and were asked whether their fellow students were allies who were inclined to help them with task-related problems. This finding aligns with the notion that power makes individuals view others' moral character more positively when cooperation is perceived as the norm. Indeed, cooperation tends to be the perceived norm in student teams, as students typically share both an identity as students at their respective university and the goal to bring their team's project to a successful end. Brion and Anderson's (2013), then, studied social settings with perceived cooperative norms. This made powerful individuals view others' moral character more positively. Taken together, the current body of work on power and moral judgment suggests that power makes individuals view others' moral character more positively when cooperation is the perceived norm, whereas power makes individuals view others' moral character more negatively when competition and rule breaking is the perceived norm.

Future research directions

If social context moderates the relationship between power and moral judgment, then researchers of moral judgment need to take this into account in their theorizing and their research designs. Exclusively focusing on settings where rule-breaking behavior is common, interests are misaligned, or ethically dubious behaviors are salient, increase the odds that power makes individuals view others' moral character more negatively. It also increases the odds that a literature draws erroneous conclusions on how power shapes moral judgment. Of course, some strands of research might specifically want to address those settings and exclusively focus on research paradigms that highlight these aspects of social interactions (e.g., trust games; public goods games; crime). Nevertheless, when interpreting results from such studies it is important to take into account that their conclusions on the role of power are bounded by this specific choice of social context. Indeed, because the current analysis suggests that the impact of power on the moral judgment of others is bounded by social context, it provides implications for integrating research on power and moral judgment with other theoretical perspectives.

For instance, a subset of research on power has focused on integrity-based trust and drawn the conclusion that power decreases trust in others (e.g., Mooijman & Graham, 2018). Although there is empirical evidence that supports this conclusion, the notion that power amplifies dominant situational goals suggests that perceived interpersonal similarity and joint group membership may change the relationship between power and trust. Research on social identity has demonstrated that people trust others more when these others are similar (vs. dissimilar) to them and share (vs. do not share) a group membership with them (Tanis & Postmes, 2005). Within groups, cooperation tends to be the norm, whereas between groups, competition tends to be more prevalent (Wildschut et al., 2003). It is possible, then, that high-power individuals trust similar others more, but dissimilar others less, than low-power individuals. It is also possible that how people construe power (as a personal opportunity or as responsibility for others; see Scholl et al., 2022 for a detailed discussion on this) changes the relationship between power and moral judgment. When people see their power as an opportunity to advance their own interests at the expense of others, this highlights conflicting interests. In contrast, when people see their power as a responsibility for others' needs and interests, this highlights mutual, cooperative interests. A responsibility construal of power may make high-power individuals view others' moral character more positively than low-power individuals; whereas an opportunity construal of power may make high-power individuals view others' moral character more negatively than low-power individuals. The current chapter, then, provides a way of thinking about the relationship between power, moral judgment, and social context that connects to other theoretical perspectives and provides concrete and useful future research directions.

Conclusion

In this chapter, I considered how people's high vs low power positions impact upon their moral judgments of others. I reviewed the state of the current literature on power and moral judgment, highlighted how considering the social context in which power holders make moral judgments can help resolve outstanding theoretical inconsistencies, and made suggestions for future research on the topic. As such, I focused on how having a position of power changes the way individuals evaluate the moral character of others—the intrapersonal effects of power. Given the omnipresence of power and the far-reaching consequences of judging others as having or lacking moral character, future research should integrate research on power and moral judgment with social identity theory and the construal of power as an opportunity or responsibility. Doing so could provide a more nuanced, dynamic, and complete picture of the relationship between power, social context, and the judgment of others' moral character.

References

Anderson, C., & Galinsky, A. D. (2006). Power, optimism, and risk-taking. *European Journal of Social Psychology, 36*, 511–536.

Barclay, P., & Benard, S. (2020). The effects of social versus asocial threats on group cooperation and manipulation of perceived threats. *Evolutionary Human Sciences, 2*, e54.

Brion, S., & Anderson, C. (2013). The loss of power: How illusions of alliance contribute to powerholders' downfall. *Organizational Behavior and Human Decision Processes, 121*, 129–139.

Brion, S., Mo, R., & Lount, R. B. (2019). Dynamic influences of power on trust: Changes in power affects trust in others. *Journal of Trust Research, 9*, 6–27.

Chen, S., Lee-Chai, A. Y., & Bargh, J. A. (2001). Relationship orientation as a moderator of the effects of social power. *Journal of Personality and Social Psychology, 80*, 173–187.

Cho, M., & Keltner, D. (2020). Power, approach, and inhibition: Empirical advances of a theory. *Curr. Opin. Psychol., 33*, 196–200. doi: 10.1016/j.copsyc.2019.08.013

Cohen, T. R., Panter, A. T., Turan, N., Morse, L., & Kim, Y. (2014). Moral character in the workplace. *Journal of Personality and Social Psychology, 107*, 943–963.

Dubois, D., Rucker, D. D., & Galinsky, A. D. (2015). Social class, power, and selfishness: When and why upper and lower class individuals behave unethically. *Journal of Personality and Social Psychology, 108*, 436–449.

du Plessis, C., Nguyen, M. H. B., Foulk, T. A., & Schaerer, M. (2023). Relative power and interpersonal trust. *Journal of Personality and Social Psychology, 124*(3), 567–592. https://doi.org/10.1037/pspi0000401

Ellemers, N., & van den Bos, K. (2012). Morality in groups: On the social-regulatory functions of right and wrong. *Social and Personality Psychology Compass, 6*, 878–889.

Emerson, R. M. (1962). Power-dependence relations. *American Sociological Review, 27*, 31–41.

Feenstra, S., Jordan, J., Walter, F., & Stoker, J. I. (2020). Antecedents of leaders' power sharing: The roles of power instability and distrust. *Organizational Behavior and Human Decision Processes, 157*, 115–128.

Fleischmann, A., & Lammers, J. (2020). Power and moral thinking. *Current Opinion in Psychology, 33*, 23–27.

Galinsky, A. D., Gruenfeld, D. H., & Magee, J. C. (2003). From power to action. *Journal of Personality and Social Psychology, 85*, 453–466.

Georgesen, J., & Harris, M. J. (1998). Why's my boss always holding me down? A meta-analysis of power effects on performance evaluations. *Personality and Social Psychology Review, 3*, 184–195.

Guinote, A. (2007). Behavior variability and the Situated Focus Theory of Power. *European Review of Social Psychology, 18*, 256–295.

Guinote, A. (2017). How power affects people: Activating, wanting, and goal seeking. *Annual Review of Psychology, 68*, 353–381.

Haidt, J., & Kesebir, S. (2010). Morality. In S. Fiske, D. Gilbert, & G. Lindzey (Eds.) *Handbook of Social Psychology*, 5th Edition. Hobeken, NJ: Wiley. Pp. 797–832.

Inesi, E. M., Gruenfeld, D. H., & Galinsky, A. D. (2012). How power corrupts relationships: Cynical attributions for others' generous acts. *Journal of Experimental Social Psychology, 48*, 795–803.

Keltner, D., Gruenfeld, D. H., & Anderson, C. (2003). Power, approach, and inhibition. *Psychological Review, 110*, 265–284.

Lammers, J., Gordijn, E. H., & Otten, S. (2008). Looking through the eyes of the powerful. *Journal of Experimental Social Psychology, 44*, 1229–1238.

Leach, C. W., Ellemers, N., & Barreto, M. (2007). Group virtue: The importance of morality (vs. competence and sociability) in the positive evaluation of in-groups. *Journal of Personality and Social Psychology, 93*, 234–249.

Magee, J. C, & Galinsky, A. D. (2008). Social hierarchy: The self-reinforcing nature of power and status. *Academy of Management Annals, 2*, 351–398.

Magee, J. C., & Smith, P. K. (2013). The social distance theory of power. *Personality and Social Psychology Review, 17*, 158–186.

Mayer, R. C., Davis, J. H., & Schoorman, F. D. (1995). An integrative model of organizational trust. *Academy of Management Review, 20*, 709–734.

Mooijman, M., & Graham, J. (2018). Unjust punishments in organizations. *Research in Organizational Behavior, 38*, 95–106.

Mooijman, M., Van Dijk, W. W., Ellemers, N., & Van Dijk, E. (2015). Why leaders punish: A power perspective. *Journal of Personality and Social Psychology, 109*, 75–89.

Mooijman, M., Van Dijk, W. W., Van Dijk, E., & Ellemers, N. (2017). On sanction-goal justifications: How and why deterrence justifications undermine rule compliance. *Journal of Personality and Social Psychology, 112*(4), 577–588. https://doi.org/10.1037/pspi0000084

Mooijman, M., Van Dijk, W. W, Van Dijk, E., & Ellemers, N. (2019). Leader power, power stability, and interpersonal trust. *Organizational Behavior and Human Decision Processes, 152*, 1–10.

Scholl, A., Ellemers, N., Scheepers, D., & Sassenberg, K. (2022). Construal of power as opportunity or responsibility. *Advances in Experimental Social Psychology, 65,* 57–107.

Schilke, O., Reimann, M., & Cooke, S. (2015). Power decreases trust in social exchange. *Proceedings of the National Academy of Sciences, 112,* 12950–12955.

Schweitzer, M. E., Ho, T-H., & Zhang, X. (2018). How monitoring influences trust: A tale of two faces. *Management Science, 64,* 253–270.

Smith, P. K., Jostmann, N. B., Galinsky, A. D., & van Dijk, W. (2008). Lacking power impairs executive functions. *Psychological Science, 19,* 441–447.

Stanton, N. E. (2011). *Trust in military teams.* Boca Raton FL: CRC Press.

Tanis, M., & Postmes, T. (2005). Short communication: A social identity approach to trust: Interpersonal perception, group membership and trusting behavior. *European Journal of Social Psychology, 35,* 413–424.

Tenbrunsel, A. E., & Messick, D. M. (1999). Sanctioning systems, decision frames, and cooperation. *Administrative Science Quarterly, 44,* 684–707.

Tenbrunsel, A., & Smith-Crowe, K. (2008). Ethical decision making: Where we've been and where we're going. *The Academy of Management Annals, 2,* 545–607.

Tjosvold, D. (1989). Interdependence and power between managers and employees: A study of the leader relationship. *Journal of Management, 15,* 49–62

Tost, L. (2015). When, why, and how do powerholders "feel the power"? Examining the links between structural and psychological power and reviving the connection between power and responsibility. *Research in Organizational Behavior, 35,* 29–56.

Tyler, T. R., & Lind, E. A. (1992). A relational model of authority in groups. In J. M. Olson & M. P. Zanna (Eds.), *Advances in experimental social psychology* (Vol. 25, pp. 115–191). New York, NY: Oxford University Press.

van Prooijen, J. W., Coffeng, J., & Vermeer, M. (2014). Power and retributive justice: How trait information influences the fairness of punishment among power holders. *Journal of Experimental Social Psychology, 50,* 190–201.

van Prooijen, J. W., & van den Bos, K. (2009). We blame innocent victims more than I do: Self-construal level moderates responses to just-world threats. *Personality and Social Psychology Bulletin, 35*(11), 1528–1539.

Weber, J. M., Malhotra, D., & Murnighan, J. K. (2004). Normal acts of irrational trust: Motivated attributions and the trust development process. *Research in Organizational Behavior, 26,* 75–101.

Wildschut, T., Pinter, B., Vevea, J. L., Insko, C. A., & Schopler, J. (2003). Beyond the group mind: A quantitative review of the interindividual-intergroup discontinuity effect. *Psychological Bulletin, 129,* 698–722.

Wiltermuth, S. S., & Flynn, F. J. (2013). Power, moral clarity, and punishment in the workplace. *Academy of Management Journal, 56*(4), 1002–1023.

10
THE INTERPERSONAL LEVEL
Interpersonal consequences of moral judgments about others

Christopher W. Bauman and Erik G. Helzer

Abstract

Perceived moral similarity or dissimilarity has profound effects on interpersonal judgment and relationships. People are apt to avoid or withdraw from relationships with those who hold divergent moral beliefs or transgress moral rules. This tendency to distance oneself from perceived moral deviants exists, in part, because morality is the primary dimension on which people evaluate others when forming impressions of them. Moreover, when people perceive a situation to involve morality, they are especially prone to attributing differences in beliefs and perceived transgressions to dispositional traits and defects of character.

- People's global judgments about the extent to which others have good or bad moral character are a core aspect of person perception.
- People draw inferences about others' character traits based on the moral judgments others make, and these inferences affect relationships and interpersonal behavior.
- Perceptions of morality also shape the way individuals interact with one another.
- Violations of morality prompt person-focused attributions that may be difficult to overcome.

Introduction

In a laboratory study reported by Skitka, Bauman, and Sargis (2005), student participants expected to interact with another student as part of a study ostensibly about how people get to know one another. Prior to meeting this other student, participants were told that they were randomly selected to receive "inside information" about the other student and learned the other student held a strong pro-choice attitude about abortion. The experimenter then escorted participants to another room to meet and converse with the other student. Upon entering the room, participants could see a chair near the center of the room with a book bag and jacket on it, and a stack of chairs against the far wall. The experimenter acted surprised that the other student was not in the room and asked the participant to take down a chair from the stack and get settled while he looked for the other student. After giving the participant enough time to get settled, the experimenter returned, measured the distance the participant left between their chair and the one they expected the other participant to use. Analysis indicated that after controlling for multiple measures of attitude strength recorded in class at the beginning of the semester, the extent to which participants associated their attitude about abortion with their moral beliefs (i.e., their moral conviction about the issue) predicted how much physical distance they created between themselves and where they expected the other student to sit. Greater moral conviction expressed by pro-choice participants was associated with less distance between the chairs, and greater moral conviction expressed by pro-life participants was associated with more distance between the chairs. Other researchers have since replicated this finding and observed similar effects with a pro-life target and using other commonly moralized issues (Wright et al., 2008).

Arguably, the tendency to distance oneself from those who do not share one's moral beliefs has become more pronounced in recent years. Throughout much of the world, people have become more polarized in their moral beliefs (Finkel et al., 2020; Gidron et al., 2019). Technology has provided the means to distance oneself more effectively from those who do not share one's moral beliefs and to align oneself more closely with those who do (Dylko, 2016; Merten, 2021). During the COVID-19 pandemic, we witnessed the moralization of face mask mandates, compulsory vaccination, and other public health initiatives (e.g., Prosser et al., 2020). These issues sparked moral outrage among individuals on one side against the other and prompted interpersonal divides (e.g., Chen & Rohla, 2018). In recent years, we also saw entire social media platforms created to support a particular set of moral and political beliefs over another set, creating the ultimate means of social distancing (through self-selection) by enabling people to avoid others who do not share their moral convictions. From a societal perspective, understanding the domain of interpersonal moral judgment is both timely and essential.

This chapter focuses on the way that moral judgments shape interpersonal processes and relationships. For the purposes of this chapter, we define *morality* as individuals' beliefs about fundamental standards for how people ought to conduct themselves, and we define *moral judgment* as the evaluations people formulate about the extent to which people and actions do or do not conform to their sense of morality. We adopt definitions that are psychological and descriptive, focusing on individuals' subjective determinations of morality, rather than an approach in which situations, people, or actions are assumed to possess certain inherent moral characteristics. In short, this chapter approaches morality as a phenomenon that occurs in the mind of perceivers, and one that is fundamentally attuned to interpersonal interactions (see Bauman & Skitka, 2009).

In what follows, we first discuss how morality affects person-perception, the basic foundation of interpersonal interactions. We then discuss the body of evidence documenting the effect of morality on individuals' willingness to form interpersonal relationships and on the interpersonal dynamics that shape interactions. In the second half of the chapter, we examine why morality exhibits such profound effects on interpersonal processes, exploring how the phenomenology of moral beliefs and judgments contribute to strong inferences about the character and identity of others who do or do not act in accordance with one's sense of morality. We close by considering the implications of this analysis for understanding moral processes in social discourse. A conceptual model of the processes outlined in this chapter is provided in Figure 10.1.

Morality and interpersonal perception

Morality comprises a yet unspecifiable number of basic concerns that underlie the standards for conduct that people endorse (see Sinnott-Armstrong & Wheatley, 2013). However, we identify two rough clusters of concerns that tend to emerge across different moral frameworks developed in the literature. One identifiable cluster of concerns involves social interdependence or responsibilities

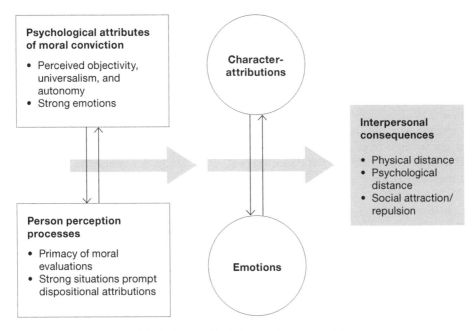

Figure 10.1 A conceptual model of why morality influences interpersonal interactions.

people have to others. The other cluster involves individual independence or autonomy. For example, domain theory differentiates between the moral and personal domains (e.g., Turiel, 1983), moral foundations theory differentiates between binding and individuating foundations (e.g., Graham et al., 2013; Haidt, 2008), and the model of moral motives differentiates between other- or group-focused motives and self-focused motives (Janoff-Bulman & Carnes, 2013). Thus, morality is primarily concerned with governing interpersonal interactions by prescribing and proscribing responsibilities and rights.

Because morality is fundamentally associated with governing interpersonal interactions, it is perhaps not surprising that people's global judgments about the extent to which others have good or bad moral character are a core aspect of person perception, or how individuals form impressions of others. We view person-perception processes as the foundation for interpersonal relations because initial and ongoing person perceptions are the basis on which people make decisions about whether and how much to invest in interpersonal relationships. Abele and Wojciszke (2014) note that research on impression formation commonly differentiates between traits that relate to social orientation (i.e., communion, warmth) and traits related to individual efficacy (i.e., ability, competence), and that this distinction mirrors the fundamental challenges humans face: (1) to be accepted as a member of important groups, and (2) to pursue individual goals (see Lind, 2001). When evaluating others, people weigh information about social orientation more heavily than information about individual efficacy because whether a person's intentions are benevolent or malicious dramatically changes the potential consequences of how effectively a person can pursue their intentions (e.g., Bauman & Skitka, 2012; Cottrell et al., 2007). Information related to social orientation has as much as twice the impact on people's interpersonal judgments as traits related to individual efficacy (e.g., Abele & Wojciszke, 2007; Brambilla et al., 2019; De Bruin & Van Lange, 2000).

In recent years, general models of person perception processes have been adapted and extended to explain how moral information affects global impressions of individuals. Research shows that morality is a distinguishable and particularly impactful part of social orientation (e.g., Brambilla et al., 2019; Brambilla et al., 2011; Goodwin et al., 2014; Leach et al., 2007). For example, Goodwin and colleagues (2014) report several studies showing that people differentiate between moral traits (e.g., honest, loyal, fair) and other prosocial traits (e.g., friendly, warm, sociable), and base their global impressions of others more on moral information than other prosocial traits. They find that morality dominates people's judgments about the suitability of others for important social relationships (e.g., close friends, romantic partners, and coworkers), whereas other prosocial traits have little added effect (Goodwin et al., 2014, Study 5). Furthermore, morality is the most important factor in determining whether people like, respect, and feel they know others, relative to information about other prosocial traits or traits related to individual efficacy (Hartley et al., 2016). People also expect that changes to their own or others' moral beliefs would fundamentally change the essence of that person's identity, in part because these changes would alter their relationships with others (Heiphetz et al., 2017). In short, individuals' moral characteristics play a major role in others' general impressions of who they are and the degree to which they are seen as good candidates for investing interpersonal resources (Helzer & Critcher, 2018).

Morality can unite and divide

Several lines of research demonstrate that morality is not just important to person perception but also consequential to interpersonal judgment and behavior. A large body of research shows that, across several contexts, moral conviction consistently affects interpersonal interactions by prompting people to distance themselves from morally dissimilar others (e.g., Skitka et al., 2005; Wright et al., 2008; Zaal et al., 2017). In particular, Skitka and colleagues' program of research explores the antecedents and consequences of individuals' subjective assessment that a particular issue or situation is connected to their fundamental sense of right and wrong and illustrates the effects of moral discord on interpersonal moral judgment (for a review, see Skitka et al., 2021). This work isolates the unique contribution of moral conviction to people's attitudes and behavior by measuring and controlling for attitude strength (e.g., attitude extremity, importance, and centrality) and a variety of other factors as well (e.g., religiosity, political orientation). For example, survey studies that ask participants to report their attitudes about self-nominated or researcher-provided contemporary issues (e.g., abortion, capital punishment, legalization of marijuana, and nuclear power) find that higher levels of moral conviction are associated with lower levels of comfort interacting with people who hold different attitudes about the issue. After controlling for multiple indicators of attitude strength and several individual differences, greater moral conviction predicts a stronger desire to avoid attitudinally dissimilar others in both more intimate and more distant relationships (e.g., close friends, romantic partners, and coworkers, but also shop keepers and personal physicians; Skitka et al., 2005).

Interpersonal consequences associated with morality can also stem from global judgments about individuals, not just differences of opinions on individual issues. Barranti, Carlson, and Furr (2016) find that discrepancies between the way individuals assess their own moral character and how acquaintances rate the individuals' moral character are associated with reduced liking and respect on the part of acquaintances. These interpersonal costs are stronger for disagreements about moral character traits than disagreements about other facets of individuals' personalities, indicating that moral impressions are a particularly influential component of interpersonal judgment.

Moreover, people are apt to draw inferences about others' traits based on the moral judgments others make, and these inferences, in turn, are likely to affect relationships and interpersonal behavior (Everett et al., 2016; Rom et al., 2017; Uhlmann et al., 2013). For example, Uhlmann and colleagues (2013) find that people perceive decision makers as lower in empathy and integrity when they choose options in moral dilemmas that are consistent with utilitarian concerns (e.g., throwing a dying man overboard to prevent a lifeboat from sinking and killing everyone on board) compared to when they choose options that are consistent with deontological concerns (e.g., refusing to throw the dying man off the lifeboat), even though, on average, people report that the utilitarian choices these situations are more moral. Similarly, people perceive others as more moral but less competent when they choose options in moral dilemmas that are consistent with deontological concerns compared to when they choose options that are consistent with utilitarian concerns (Rom et al., 2017). Even the length of time people take to decide what to do in moral situations can have interpersonal consequences. For example, people are less critical of others who pause to deliberate rather than immediately choose an immoral course of action, such as pocketing a lost wallet (Critcher et al., 2013; see also Critcher et al., 2020). Importantly, these effects go beyond impression formation. People perceive others who make decisions about moral dilemmas that are consistent with deontological concerns as more trustworthy and find them to be more attractive social partners than those who make decisions that are consistent with utilitarian concerns (Everett et al., 2016). Moreover, people may even change their self-presentation strategies to help mitigate potential backlash they expect to face from others based on their choices (Rom & Conway, 2018). Taken together, these studies clearly indicate that people make consequential inferences about others based on their choices in moral situations.

Perceptions of morality also shape the way individuals interact with one another. When speaking with someone they perceive as immoral rather than moral, people are less likely to display nonverbal behaviors that facilitate interpersonal liking and rapport, including mimicry and synchrony (Brambilla et al., 2016; Menegatti et al., 2020). For example, Menegatti and colleagues (2020) manipulated impressions of an interaction partner to seem moral vs. immoral, sociable vs. unsociable, or competent vs. incompetent, and assessed participants' nonverbal behavior in a conversation with the interaction partner. Participants engaged in less mimicry and took a more closed off posture when interacting with partners portrayed as immoral compared to when interacting with partners who were portrayed as unsociable or incompetent. Moreover, third party observers rated the interactions as less smooth in the immoral than unsociable or incompetent conditions, indicating the friction that moral judgments can create in interpersonal interactions.

Although the bulk of research has focused on the power of moral disagreement or moral violations to harm interpersonal processes, there is evidence that moral agreement (i.e., convergence between people on moral beliefs) facilitates interpersonal coordination. People are drawn to morally similar others, not just repelled by morally dissimilar others (e.g., Skitka et al., 2005; Wright et al., 2008). Also, moral conviction prompts others to initiate contact with others to garner social support for their beliefs; for example, activists often seek to form new relationships with likeminded others through door-to-door canvassing and hosting meetings in their homes (e.g., Skitka et al., 2017).

We also note that links between moral judgment and interpersonal processes can operate in the opposite direction, such that interpersonal closeness or warmth toward individuals can bias judgments of others' morality. The *mere liking effect* describes a tendency for people to attribute moral attributes to individuals they like versus do not like, even when the reasons for liking are unrelated to or at odds with common sense morality (Bocian et al., 2018; Bocian, & Wojciszke, 2014). Similarly, when leaders in good standing break rules, people are less apt to blame and punish others who subsequently commit similar transgressions because leaders' (bad) behavior influences observers' perceptions of relevant norms (Bauman et al., 2016). When paired with the research reviewed above, these studies suggest a self-reinforcing cycle of interpersonal moral judgment, such that esteemed (vs. scorned) others may be judged as more moral, which reinforces liking, subsequent interpersonal behaviors, and even moral judgments themselves.

Why morality affects interpersonal judgment and behavior

In this section, we consider why morality exerts such profound effects on interpersonal processes. We focus on the phenomenology of moral judgments—the way individuals experience their moral beliefs and judgments—to explain the interpersonal costs associated with moral disagreement. Deviations from what perceivers judge to be the morally correct course of action are not easily explained away by situational or other transitory forces. Instead, the indelible mark of a perceived moral transgression tends to come in the form of judgments of an individual's character, which carries long term consequences for interpersonal relations.

Characteristics of moral judgments and beliefs

Moral beliefs and judgments tend to differ psychologically from mere preferences or opinions in several important ways (Skitka et al., 2021). For example, people tend to experience their moral beliefs as objective—more like scientific facts than personal points of view (Goodwin & Darley 2008; Skitka et al., 2005). People also perceive their moral beliefs to be universally applicable in the sense that everyone, regardless of status or culture, should endorse and abide by them (Skitka et al., 2005; Turiel, 1983; Van Bavel et al., 2012). Moreover, people perceive morality to compel people to act on their own accord and supersede any mandates set by authorities (Skitka et al., 2009). Taken together, the sense of objectivity, universalism, and autonomy that accompanies moral beliefs carries distinct interpersonal consequences: Because people are responsible for their moral beliefs and actions, those who share one's moral beliefs are readily judged as correct and good, and those who diverge from one's moral beliefs are readily judged as incorrect and bad. In short, the psychology of moral conviction prompts people to attribute others' similarities and differences to deep-seeded strengths or flaws of character, respectively. Although there are no doubt exceptions and moderators to this overarching picture, this account provides a fairly accurate description of the interpersonal gridlock that can occur when individuals differ from one another on issues held with strong moral conviction.

Violations of morality prompt person-focused attributions

Because moral beliefs are imbued with the properties described above, morality may trigger attributional processes that crystallize perceived interpersonal differences. To understand why, consider the possibility that people perceive situations and issues concerning morality as "strong situations." Strong situations are contexts that provide clear behavioral norms that typically constrain individual variability in behavior, resulting in behavioral conformity with relevant norms (Mischel, 1977). From an attributional perspective (e.g., Kelley, 1973), knowing that an individual acted in accordance with relevant norms in a strong situation may tell you very little about who the person is and how they differ from others; however, knowing that an individual violated relevant norms and acted contrary to the behavioral expectations set by a strong situation may prompt attributional processes aimed at trying to understand why *this* person acted in *this* way despite the demands of the situation. The most readily available explanation is that some stable characteristic of the person caused them to act contrary to the clear prescriptive norms of the situation.

Based on this analysis, we would expect that the interpersonal costs associated with disagreements about morality (in the form of attitudes, judgments, and interpersonal behaviors) will be stronger than the interpersonal benefits associated with agreements about morality. Some support for this claim comes from recent research by Guglielmo and Malle (2019), who find that interpersonal blame is both more amplified and more differentiated than interpersonal praise, holding constant the degree of the praise- or blame-eliciting behavior. This is consistent with the *negativity effect*, which has been shown to impact interpersonal processes in close relationships and social interaction more generally (De Bruin & Van Lange, 2000; Fiske, 1980; for a review, see Baumeister et al., 2001).

Moral emotions promote attributional certainty and inhibit revision

Despite the cognitive connotation of judgment, moral judgments are widely recognized as possessing strong emotional components (e.g., Haidt, 2001; Prinz & Nichols, 2010). Perceived moral transgressions and transgressors trigger strong emotions, especially anger (e.g., Haidt, 2003; Skitka et al., 2004; 2006; Tetlock et al., 2000). Anger is associated with greater certainty, which can affect information processing in several ways, such as preempting further processing of stimuli in the manner required to revise initial impressions (e.g., Tiedens & Linton, 2001; for a review see Lerner, et al., 2015). Moreover, people who are angry are more likely to presume that harm has occurred (Gutierrez & Giner-Sorolla, 2007), which can reinforce people's perception that a moral violation has occurred and should be punished (e.g., Malle et al., 2014; Smith & Lazarus, 1993). Thus, the emotions prompted by spontaneous moral judgments of acts or actors who violate one's moral standards can reinforce and amplify initial interpersonal impressions and perceptions. Of course, emotions involve appraisals and action tendencies that also have direct effects on judgment and behavior, independent of their effects on moral attributions (Frijda, 2007).

Future directions for research

Privileged status of moral beliefs

One question for future research is whether one's meta-ethical belief system impacts the tendency to assign privileged status to one's own moral commitments, and thus moderates the interpersonal consequences associated with moral disagreement. A meta-ethical belief system refers to one's beliefs about the nature of morality, such as whether morality is believed to be objective or absolute vs. relative and subjective (e.g., Forsyth, 1980). For example, one form of moral relativism is rooted in the belief that morality cannot be objectively determined because it is rooted in culturally variable social practices. This perspective prompts some to adopt the normative position that others' views ought to be tolerated. Alternatively, some may simply view tolerance as a virtue in and of itself, regardless of their meta-ethical commitments. In either case, people who espouse these views may be less likely to associate their moral beliefs with objectivity, universalism, and autonomy and may therefore be less likely to exhibit differences in how they interact with others depending on moral similarity or dissimilarity. In short, future research could seek to identify boundary conditions of the interpersonal consequences of morality, especially as a means toward understanding when and how differently minded people can get along.

Attributional processes

According to our analysis, many of the detrimental interpersonal effects of moral disagreement stem from the tendency to make negative attributions about others' character. Future research should seek to identify factors that moderate this tendency as a means to mitigate interpersonal conflict.

The tendency to form dispositional attributions on the basis of limited behavioral information is recognized as automatic and fundamental (Gilbert & Malone, 1995; Jones, 1979; Uleman et al., 1996), but the trait inference process is subject to moderating factors. For example, research indicates that engaging in elaborate, in-depth, or systematic processing can subdue dispositional attributions in favor of more complex, enriched causal explanation (D'Agostino & Fincher-Kiefer, 1992; Fletcher et al., 1990; Forgas, 1998). Relatedly, research on construal level theory suggests that psychological proximity (versus distance) to a target can reduce the tendency to form spontaneous trait inferences based on limited behavioral information (Rim et al., 2009). The challenge is that in cases of moral disagreement, individuals' motivations to engage in systematic, elaborative processing or to attain psychological proximity with dissimilar others may be weak or non-existent.

Additional research is needed to understand how to disrupt strong dispositional attributions in cases of moral disagreement. One promising finding from the stereotyping literature is that training individuals to consider situational explanations for behavior can diminish the tendency to engage in outgroup derogation (Stewart et al., 2009). Similarly, encouraging a growth or "incremental" mindset—seeing others as works in progress rather than fixed entities—has been shown to increase tolerance and willingness to compromise with outgroup members by reducing harmful dispositional attributions (Levontin et al., 2013). Thus, where practical, structured interventions targeting unhelpful attributions be a useful means of upsetting the processes depicted in Figure 10.1.

Unitary or foundation-specific consequences

Many contemporary theories of morality can be classified as pluralistic views; they maintain that people apply multiple, distinct moral values or foundations when making moral judgments or deciding on moral courses of action (e.g., Graham et al., 2013; Janoff-Bulman & Carnes, 2013; Rai & Fiske, 2011). These theories suggest that morality itself has distinct dimensions that jointly influence people's judgment. However, other research on the psychological experience of morality suggests that, irrespective of the particular values or foundations upon which one's moral judgments are based, morality generates a common experience (e.g., Skitka & Bauman, 2008; Skitka et al., 2015). That is, the way people feel and act when confronting moral issues is largely the same, irrespective of what values or foundation of morality underpins their concern (see also Gray et al., 2012). Therefore, there is an opportunity to better understand the link between the structure of morality and the psychology of how people experience morality. Future research could systematically examine people's reactions to moral violations of different values or foundations and test whether they have different interpersonal consequences. For example, violations of moral purity may be especially likely to elicit disgust and prompt people to disengage with transgressors whereas acts that cause unjustified harm to others may be especially likely to elicit anger and prompt people to engage and punish transgressors.

Conclusion

Moral judgments affect interpersonal processes ranging from basic elements of person perception to decisions about with whom to engage and how to engage with people. These effects, and the mechanisms that underpin them, can easily increase polarization along moral lines: Initial moral disagreement between individuals triggers judgments, attributions, emotions, and behaviors that increase interpersonal distance and degrade or diminish subsequent interactions (Figure 10.1). In a pluralistic society, engagement with individuals who do not share one's moral views is unavoidable and potentially beneficial, so what are we to do? One option is to follow our intuitive psychology, which results in deeper entrenchment and greater polarization. This tendency may be exacerbated by leaders who seek to energize supporters and demonize critics by framing issues as threats to the moral order. Another option is to make deliberate attempts to understand divergent perspectives, resist the temptation to attribute moral differences to fundamental deficits in character, engage in collective sensemaking, and approach moral disagreements as pragmatic problems that may have mutually acceptable solutions.

References

Abele, A. E., & Wojciszke, B. (2007). Agency and communion from the perspective of self and others. *Journal of Personality and Social Psychology, 93*, 751–763.

Abele, A., & Wojciszke, B. (2014). Communal and agentic content in social cognition: A dual perspective model. *Advances in Experimental Social Psychology, 50*, 195–255.

Barranti, M., Carlson, E. N., & Furr, R. M. (2016). Disagreement about moral character is linked to interpersonal costs. *Social Psychological and Personality Science, 7*(8), 806–817.

Bauman, C. W., & Skitka, L. J. (2009). In the mind of the perceiver: Psychological implications of moral conviction. In D. Bartels, C. W. Bauman, L. J. Skitka, & D. Medin (Eds.), *Moral judgment and decision making: Psychology of learning and motivation* (pp. 341–364). San Diego, CA: Academic Press.

Bauman, C. W., & Skitka, L. J. (2012). Corporate social responsibility as a source of employee satisfaction. *Research in Organizational Behavior, 32*, 63–86.

Bauman, C. W., Tost, L. P., & Ong, M. (2016). Blame the shepherd not the sheep: Imitating higher-ranking transgressors mitigates punishment for unethical behavior. *Organizational Behavioral and Human Decision Processes, 137*, 123–141.

Baumeister, R. F., Bratslavsky, E., Finkenauer, C., & Vohs, K. D. (2001). Bad is stronger than good. *Review of General Psychology, 5*, 323–370.

Bocian, K., Baryla, W., Kulesza, W. M., Schnall, S., Wojciszke, B. (2018). The mere liking effect: Attitudinal influences on judgments of moral character. *Journal Experimental Social Psychology, 79*, 9–20.

Bocian, K., Wojciszke, B. (2014). Self-interest bias in moral judgments of others' actions. *Personality and Social Psychology Bulletin, 40*, 898–909.

Brambilla, M., Carraro, L. Castelli, L., & Sacchi, S. (2019). Changing impressions: Moral character dominates impression updating. *Journal of Experimental Social Psychology, 82*, 64–73.

Brambilla, M., Rusconi, P., Sacchi, S., & Cherubini, P. (2011). Looking for honesty: The primary role of morality (vs. sociability and competence) in information gathering. *European Journal of Social Psychology, 41*, 135–143.

Brambilla, M., Sacchi, S., Menegatti, M., Moscatelli, S. (2016). Honesty and dishonesty don't move together: Trait content information influences behavioral synchrony. *Journal of Nonverbal Behavior, 40*, 171–186.

Cottrell, C. A., Neuberg, S. L., & Li, N. P. (2007). What do people desire in others? A sociofunctional perspective on the importance of different valued characteristics. *Journal of Personality and Social Psychology, 92*, 208–231.

Chen M. K, & Rohla R. (2018). The effect of partisanship and political advertising on close family ties. *Science, 360*(6392), 1020–1024.

Critcher, C. R., Helzer, E. G., & Tannenbaum, D. (2020). Moral character evaluation: Testing another's moral-cognitive machinery. *Journal of Experimental Social Psychology, 87*, 103906.

Critcher, C. R., Inbar, Y., & Pizarro, D. A. (2013). How quick decisions illuminate moral character. *Social Psychological and Personality Science, 4*, 308–315.

D'Agostino, P. R., & Fincher-Kiefer, R. (1992). Need for cognition and the correspondence bias. *Social Cognition, 10*, 151–163. doi:https://doi.org/10.1521/soco.1992.10.2.151

De Bruin, E. N. M. & Van Lange, P. A. M. (2000). What people look for in others: Influences of the perceiver and the perceived on information selection. *Personality and Social Psychology Bulletin, 26*, 206–219.

Dylko, I. B. (2016). How technology encourages political selective exposure. *Communication Theory, 26*, 389–409.

Everett, J. A., Pizarro, D. A., & Crockett, M. J. (2016). Inference of trustworthiness from intuitive moral judgments. *Journal of Experimental Psychology: General, 145*, 772–787

Finkel, E. J., Bail, C. A., Cikara, M., Ditto, P.H., Iyengar, S., Klar, S., Mason, L., McGrath, M.C., Nyhan, B., Rand, D. G., Skitka, L. J., Tucker, J. A., Van Bavel, J. J., Wang, C. S., & Druckman, J. N. (2020). Political sectarianism in America: A poisonous cocktail of othering, aversion, and moralization. *Science, 370*(6561), 533–536.

Fiske, S. T. (1980). Attention and weight in person perception: The impact of negative and extreme behavior. *Journal of Personality and Social Psychology, 38*, 889–906.

Fletcher, G. J., Reeder, G. D., & Bull, V. (1990). Bias and accuracy in attitude attribution: The role of attributional complexity. *Journal of Experimental Social Psychology, 26*, 275–288.

Forgas, J. P. (1998). On being happy and mistaken: Mood effects on the fundamental attribution error. *Journal of Personality and Social Psychology, 75*, 318–331.

Forsyth, D. R. (1980). A taxonomy of ethical ideologies. *Journal of Personality and Social Psychology, 39*, 175–184.

Frijda, N. H. (2007). *The laws of emotion*. Mahwah, NJ: Erlbaum.

Gidron, N., Adams, J., & Horne, W. (2019). Toward a comparative research agenda on affective polarization in mass publics. *APSA Comparative Politics Newsletter, 29*, 30–36.

Gilbert, D. T., & Malone, P. S. (1995). The correspondence bias. *Psychological Bulletin, 117*(1), 21.

Goodwin, G. P., & Darley, J. M. (2008). The psychology of meta-ethics: Exploring objectivism. *Cognition, 106*, 1339–1366.

Goodwin, G.P., Piazza, J. & Rozin, P. (2014). Moral character predominates in person perception and evaluation. *Journal of Personality and Social Psychology, 106*, 148–168.

Graham, J., Haidt, J., Koleva, S., Motyl, M., Iyer, R., Wojcik, S. P., & Ditto, P. H. (2013). Moral foundations theory: The pragmatic validity of moral pluralism. *Advances in Experimental Social Psychology, 47*, 55–130.

Gray, K., Young, L., Waytz, A. (2012). Mind perception is the essence of morality. *Psychological Inquiry, 23*, 101–124.

Guglielmo, S., & Malle, B. F. (2019). Asymmetric morality: Blame is more differentiated and more extreme than praise. *PLoS ONE, 14*(3), Article e0213544.

Gutierrez, R., & Giner-Sorolla, R. (2007). Anger, disgust, and presumption of harm as reactions to taboo-breaking behaviors. *Emotion, 74*, 853–868

Haidt, J. (2003). The moral emotions. In R. J. Davidson, K. R. Scherer, & H. H. Goldsmith (Eds.), *Handbook of affective sciences* (pp. 852–870). Oxford, England: Oxford University Press.

Haidt, J. (2001). The emotional dog and its rational tail: a social intuitionist approach to moral judgment. *Psychological Review, 108*(4), 814.

Haidt, J. (2008). Morality. *Perspectives on Psychological Science, 3*, 65–72.

Hartley, A. G., Furr, R. M., Helzer, E. G., Jayawickreme, E., Velasquez, K. R., & Fleeson, W. (2016). Morality's centrality to liking, respecting, and understanding others. *Social Psychological and Personality Science, 7*, 648–657.

Heiphetz, L., Strohminger, N., & Young, L. L. (2017). The role of moral beliefs, memories, and preferences in representations of identity. *Cognitive Science, 41*, 744–767.

Helzer, E. G., & Critcher, C. R. (2018). What do we evaluate when we evaluate moral character. *Atlas of Moral Psychology*, 99–107.

Janoff-Bulman, R. & Carnes, N. C. (2013). Surveying the moral landscape: Moral motives and group-based moralities. *Personality and Social Psychology Review, 17*, 219–236.

Jones, E. (1979). The rocky road from acts to dispositions. *American Psychologist, 34*, 107–117.

Kelley, H. H. (1973). The process of causal attribution. *American Psychologist, 28*, 107–128.

Leach, C., Ellemers, N., & Barreto, M. (2007). Group virtue: The importance of morality (vs. competence and sociability) in the positive evaluation of in-groups. *Journal of Personality and Social Psychology, 93*, 234–249.

Lerner, J.S., Li, Y., Valdesolo, P., Kassam, K. (2015). Emotion and decision making. *Annual Review of Psychology, 66*, 799–823.

Levontin, L., Halperin, E., & Dweck, C. S. (2013). Implicit theories block negative attributions about a longstanding adversary: The case of Israelis and Arabs. *Journal of Experimental Social Psychology, 49*, 670–675.

Lind, E. A. (2001). Fairness heuristic theory: Justice judgments as pivotal cognitions in organizational relations. In J. Greenberg, & R. Cropanzano (Eds.), *Advances in organizational justice* (pp. 56–88). Stanford, CA: Stanford University Press.

Malle, B. F., Guglielmo, S., & Monroe, A. E. (2014). A theory of blame. *Psychological Inquiry, 25*, 147–186.

Menegatti, M., Moscatelli, S., Brambilla, M., Sacchi, S. (2020). The honest mirror: Morality as a moderator of spontaneous behavioral mimicry. *European Journal of Social Psychology, 50*, 1394–1405.

Merten, L. (2021). Block, hide or follow: Personal news curation practices on social media. *Digital Journalism, 9*(8), 1018–1039.

Mischel, W. (1977). On the future of personality measurement. *American Psychologist, 32*, 246–254.

Prinz, J. J., & Nichols, S. (2010). Moral emotions. In J. M. Doris, & The Moral Psychology Research Group (Eds.), *The moral psychology handbook* (pp. 111–146). Oxford: Oxford University Press.

Prosser, A. M. B., Judge, M., Bolderdijk, J. W., Blackwood, L., & Kurz, T. (2020). "Distancers" and "non-distancers"? The potential social psychological impact of moralizing COVID-19 mitigating practices on sustained behaviour change. *British Journal of Social Psychology, 59*, 653–662.

Rai, T. S., & Fiske, A. P. (2011). Moral psychology is relationship regulation: moral motives for unity, hierarchy, equality, and proportionality. *Psychological Review, 118*, 57–75.

Rim S., Uleman J. S., Trope Y. (2009). Spontaneous trait inference and construal level theory: Psychological distance increases nonconscious trait thinking. *Journal of Experimental Social Psychology, 45*, 1088–1097. doi: 10.1016/j.jesp.2009.06.015. PMID: 21822331; PMCID: PMC3150821.

Rom, S. C., & Conway, P. (2018). The strategic moral self: Self-presentation shapes moral dilemma judgments. *Journal of Experimental Social Psychology, 74*, 24–37.

Rom, S. C., Weiss, A. & Conway, P. (2017). Judging those who judge: Perceivers infer the roles of affect and cognition underpinning others' moral dilemma responses. *Journal of Experimental Social Psychology, 69*, 44–58.

Sinnott-Armstrong, W., & Wheatley, T. (2013). Are moral judgments unified? *Philosophical Psychology, 27*, 451–474.

Skitka, L. J., Bauman, C. W. (2008). Moral conviction and political engagement. *Political Psychology, 29*, 29–54

Skitka, L. J., Bauman, C. W., Aramovich, N. P., & Morgan, G. C. (2006). Confrontational and preventative policy responses to terrorism: Anger wants a fight and fear wants "them" to go away. *Basic and Applied Social Psychology, 28*, 375–384.

Skitka, L. J., Bauman, C.W., & Lytle, B. L. (2009). The limits of legitimacy: moral and religious convictions as constraints on deference to authority. *Journal of Personality and Social Psychology, 97*, 567–578.

Skitka, L. J., Bauman, C. W., & Mullen, E. (2004). Political tolerance and coming to psychological closure following September 11, 2001: An integrative approach. *Personality and Social Psychology Bulletin, 30*, 743–756.

Skitka, L. J., Bauman, C. W., Sargis, E. G. (2005). Moral conviction: Another contributor to attitude strength or something more? *Journal of Personality and Social Psychology, 88*, 895–917.

Skitka, L. J., Hanson, B. E., & Wisneski, D. C. (2017). Utopian hopes or dystopian fears? Understanding the motivational underpinnings of morally motivated political engagement. *Personality and Social Psychology Bulletin, 43*, 177–190.

Skitka, L. J., Hanson, B. E., Morgan, G. S., & Wisneski, D. C. (2021). The psychology of moral conviction. *Annual Review of Psychology, 72*, 347–366.

Skitka, L. J., Morgan, G. S., Wisneski, D. C. (2015). Political orientation and moral conviction: a conservative advantage or an equal opportunity motivator of political engagement? In J. Forgas, W. Crano, & K. Fiedler (Eds.), *Social psychology and politics* (pp. 57–74). New York, NY: Routledge.

Smith, C. A., & Lazarus, R. S. (1993). Appraisal components, core relational themes, and the emotions. *Cognition and Emotion, 7*, 233269.

Stewart, T. L., Latu, I. M., Kawakami, K., & Myers, A. C. (2010). Consider the situation: Reducing automatic stereotyping through situational attribution training. *Journal of Experimental Social Psychology, 46*, 221–225.

Tetlock, P. E., Kirstel, O. V., Elson, B., Green, M., & Lerner, J. (2000). The psychology of the unthinkable: Taboo trade-offs, forbidden base rates, and heretical counterfactuals. *Journal of Personality and Social Psychology, 78*, 853–970.

Tiedens, L.Z., & Linton, S. (2001). Judgment under emotional certainty and uncertainty: The effects of specific emotions on information processing. *Journal of Personality and Social Psychology, 81*, 973–988.

Turiel, E. (1983). *The development of social knowledge*. Cambridge, UK: Cambridge University press.

Uhlmann, E. L., Zhu, L. L., & Tannenbaum, D. (2013). When it takes a bad person to do the right thing. *Cognition, 126*, 326–334.

Uleman, J. S., Newman, L. S., & Moskowitz, G. B. (1996). People as flexible interpreters: Evidence and issues from spontaneous trait inference. In M. P. Zanna (Ed.), *Advances in experimental social psychology* (Vol. *28*, pp. 211–279). New York: Academic Press.

Van Bavel, J. J., Packer, D. J., Johnson Haas, I., & Cunningham, W. C. (2012). The importance of moral construal: Moral versus non-moral construal elicits faster, more extreme, universal evaluations of the same actions. *PLOS ONE, 7*(11), e48693

Wright, J. C., Cullum, J., & Schwab, N. (2008). The cognitive and affective dimensions of moral conviction: implications for attitudinal and behavioral measures of interpersonal tolerance. *Personality and Social Psychology Bulletin, 34*, 1461–1476.

Zaal, M. P., Saab, R., O'Brien, K., Jeffries, C., Barreto, M., & van Laar, C. (2017). You're either with us or against us! Moral conviction determines how the politicized distinguish friend from foe. *Group Processes and Intergroup Relations, 20*, 519–539.

11
THE INTRAGROUP LEVEL
Moral character in group perception

Marco Brambilla and Simona Sacchi

Abstract

Although the role of morality in social life has been at the center of the psychological investigation from the discipline origins, the importance of moral character in shaping group perception has received less attention. This chapter reviews recent research showing the dominant role of moral contents in group evaluation. Thus, moral traits are more relevant than non-moral traits (i.e., sociability and competence) when people gather information and form global impressions of ingroup and outgroup targets. Such a primacy relates to the link between morality and the perception of threat. Indeed, moral information is key to establishing whether the group members have beneficial or harmful intentions and whether they pose a threat to the individual and the group's life. The chapter also reviews work showing that morality is key in shaping the group self-concept and self-enchantment. We conclude by outlining a trajectory for future research.

- Morality drives the impressions that we form and the evaluations that we make of group members.
- Morality is the most important quality for feeling good about one's ingroup.
- Given that morality is a central part of the self-concept and ingroup image, people are very sensitive to moral threats and reproach.
- Morality is key in group perception because it establishes whether ingroup and outgroup members are beneficial or harmful.

Introduction

The study of morality and its role in social life permeates the history of human thought since its origins. Indeed, scholars dating back to Aristotle have argued that morality should be placed at the top of the virtues' hierarchy as a good to which everyone must aspire. Extant work on moral psychology has been concerned with morality, especially when analyzing thinking, reasoning, and social development (for a review, Ellemers et al., 2019). Yet, compared to these strands of research, the relevance of morality in shaping impressions of individuals and groups has received less attention. One reason that could explain such a gap is the widespread reliance on a traditional view that people form impressions by combining only two fundamental dimensions: Warmth and competence (Abele et al., 2021; Fiske et al., 2002). However, in the last decade, a newly emerging perspective has shown that morality is not only a critical and separable dimension of social evaluation but that it may even be the primary dimension when people are asked to form impressions of individuals and groups (Brambilla & Leach, 2014; Brambilla et al., 2021; Ellemers & Van den Bos, 2012; Goodwin, 2015). Thus, this chapter reviews work illustrating the distinctiveness and primacy of morality in social evaluation, focusing on group perception in particular. More specifically, we review insights that demonstrate that morality has a primary role in guiding the impressions that we form and the evaluations that we make of group members, and this can be seen at early and more mature stages of impression formation. We also review works showing the importance of morality for group self-concept and intra-group behavioural regulation. After briefly describing the two-factor models of social perception, we first consider work showing the primary role of moral categories at different stages of group impression formation. We discuss findings showing that people gather information on others' morality and that information concerning morality has a greater impact on the global impressions of group members than information concerning non-moral characteristics. We then consider work on the validation of the group morality and its impact on self and group image.

Two-dimensional models of impression formation: theoretical bases

People continuously evaluate themselves, other individuals, their own groups, and other groups in society. Most of these evaluations are based on two broad dimensions (for reviews, see Abele et al., 2021; Abele & Wojciszke, 2014; Fiske et al., 2007; Wojciszke, 2005) that are warmth and competence (also referred to as communion and agency or horizontal and vertical dimensions). While warmth refers to benevolence in social relations and captures traits such as friendliness, kindness, and trustworthiness, competence relates to the power to achieve one's goals effectively and captures qualities such as efficiency, intelligence, and capability (Asch, 1946; Rosenberg et al., 1968). These dimensions are relevant to our impressions of people because they signal whether someone's intentions towards us are beneficial or harmful (i.e., warmth) and whether they have the ability to fulfill their intentions (i.e., competence).

The warmth by competence framework has been extensively employed to understand interpersonal (Abele & Wojciszke, 2014; Rosenberg et al., 1968; Wojciszke 2005) and group evaluations (Fiske et al., 2002). At the interpersonal level, the influential Dual Perspective Model (DPM; Abele & Wojciszke, 2014) reveals that warmth and competence account for most of the variance in global impressions of other individuals and that most of the experienced past events with other people are framed in terms of either warmth or competence. Although both dimensions are important, the DPM also shows that in social interaction warmth information receives higher weight in forming an overall impression of another individual than competence information. Such a priority reflects the functional necessity to find out the benevolent or malevolent intentions of other individuals.

At the group level, the relevance of warmth and competence has been mainly shown by the impressive work on the Stereotype Content Model (SCM; Fiske et al., 2002). Findings across 50 countries show that stereotypes are not uniformly positive or negative, but rather can be simultaneously positive on warmth and negative on competence, or vice versa (Fiske, 2018). The studies in this area have also argued that perceivers prioritize warmth information when evaluating ingroup and outgroup members because warmth information is functional in revealing others' intentions.

Despite the relevance of the two-dimensional models of social evaluation, there has been recent debate surrounding alternative models of person and group perception (Brambilla et al., 2021; Ellemers & Van den Bos, 2012; Koch et al., 2016). Indeed, an important conceptual ambiguity suffuses the notion of warmth. It conflates aspects of sociability, such as friendliness, with aspects of morality, such as honesty (for a discussion, Brambilla & Leach, 2014; Goodwin, 2015). However, a person can be honest, but not necessarily sociable and friendly, or vice versa. In a similar vein, while some groups have been stereotyped as honest but not especially sociable (e.g., Japanese; Katz & Braly, 1933) some other groups are viewed as social but immoral (e.g., homosexuals; Brambilla & Butz, 2013; Madon, 1997). While sociability refers to an orientation to affiliate with and form connections with others, morality relates to the perceived correctness and virtue of our interaction partners (Brambilla & Leach, 2014). In light of this distinction, recent research reveals that distinguishing the sociability and morality components of warmth can enrich the examination of social evaluation. For instance, the Moral Primacy Model of Impression Development (MPM; Brambilla et al., 2021) has been recently developed as a framework to understanding social perception. It centers around the assumptions that morality, sociability, and competence are conceptually distinct characteristics that make unique contributions to impression formation.

At the interpersonal level, evaluations of other individuals are reliably factored into three relevant trait dimensions that can be interpretable as morality, sociability, and competence (Goodwin et al., 2014). Moreover, across study designs, contexts, or measurement techniques, moral traits are stronger determinants of overall impressions than non-moral traits. Thus, it appears that morality is central to judgements and evaluations we form of other individuals. The distinction between sociability, competence, and morality is not confined to interpersonal perception; it also enriches the examination of group perception, as shown in the work reviewed in the following paragraphs.

Evaluating ingroup and outgroup members: morality dominates group impressions

In the attempt of studying group's virtue, Leach and colleagues (2007) found that traits indicating morality (e.g., sincere, trustworthy) were distinguishable from traits indicating sociability (e.g., friendly, kind) and competence (e.g., intelligent, skilled). Their work further showed that people consider morality as the most important quality for feeling good about one's ingroup. By manipulating morality, sociability, and competence qualities, the authors highlighted that perceived ingroup morality was the strongest predictor of pride in the group. These early findings inspired several lines of research on the primacy of morality in group life (Ellemers et al., 2019). For instance, a substantial amount of research on the regulation of individual behavior within groups revealed that shared moral standards play a critical role in defining people's social identities and behavioral coordination within their ingroup (Ellemers et al., 2013). Indeed, these studies consistently showed that group members are particularly concerned about the group's evaluation of their morality rather than non-moral characteristics and are more inclined to behave in line with morality-based ingroup norms (Ellemers et al., 2008; Ellemers & Van den Bos, 2012; Pagliaro et al., 2011). Furthermore, shared moral values within the group function to define a distinct and positive social identity (Ellemers et al., 2013).

If on one side, morality regulates the group life and group members' behaviors, on the other side, it critically forges social evaluation and the stages of impression formation. Impression formation is a multi-componential process, starting with either a search or with a selection of the information useful to make a judgment of a social target, and ending with a global evaluation of that target (Carlston, 2013). Empirical work has shown the key role of moral qualities at early stages of impression formation, that is when individuals select informative evidence. For instance, one work tested how people search for information to form impressions of group members (Brambilla et al., 2011). Specifically, Italian participants were asked to evaluate the relevance of 15 positive traits balanced for favorability and evaluative extremity (five for each dimension of morality, sociability, and competence) for judging an ingroup (Italian guy) or an outgroup target (Indian guy) with reference to different goals: morality-relevant (revealing a secret to the target), sociability-relevant (inviting the target to a party), competence relevant (hiring the target for a research project), and global (forming an impression of the target) goals. Moral qualities were rated as the most informative cues regardless of the goal type and the target group. Moreover, in the global goal condition, when participants were asked to form a global impression of the target, they indicated greater interest in obtaining information about morality-related traits, thus attesting to morality's primary role in information gathering. Importantly, morality-related and sociability-related traits were differentially selected in all four goal conditions, suggesting that they may represent two distinct evaluative contents. Besides fitting with prior findings documenting that people highly value trustworthiness in others (Cottrell et al., 2007), this work further reveals that morality was highly valued for both ingroup and outgroup targets.

These findings were confirmed by a second study, in which participants were asked to select three questions to investigate ingroup's (vs. outgroup) morality, sociability, and competence from a defined pool of queries varied by hypothesis confirming power. Participants were more interested in posing questions about the target's morality than sociability or competence. Furthermore, participants searched for more diagnostic negative information when inquiring about ingroup's and outgroup's morality than when inquiring about their sociability (or competence). Indeed, individuals are motivated to question and falsify others' morality to detect threatening behaviors and protect themselves (Rusconi et al., 2020; Skowronski & Carlston, 1987).

Taken together, the empirical work reviewed suggests that information about morality is preferentially selected over sociability and competence information when people aim to form global impressions of others. Such a primacy of morality fits with a functionalist perspective discussed in the introduction. Indeed, knowing another's intentions for good or ill is more essential for survival and group life than knowing whether a person can fulfil those intentions (Fiske et al., 2007). In social interactions, people are primarily interested in discovering whether fellow group members' intentions are beneficial or harmful, that is, whether they represent an opportunity or a threat. Given that morality captures the perceived correctness of social targets, it makes sense that we are oriented to others' morality as moral qualities would be more essential to establish the extent to which someone poses a threat.

Inspired by these findings, more recent work on the MPM investigated whether the leading role of morality goes beyond information seeking and affects first impressions (Brambilla et al., 2012). Specifically, participants were asked to provide their impression of an unfamiliar immigrant group (i.e., the Ortandesi), depicted as high (vs. low) in morality, sociability, or competence. Supporting the primacy of morality, results showed that participants reported a more positive impression of the social target when the group was described as highly moral rather than lacking morality. By contrast, sociability and competence information did not play any meaningful role in predicting impressions. One study tested the socio-functionalist view of morality in first impressions of groups and showed that the morality of the group had such a large effect on global impressions because the outgroup's morality was closely linked to the perception of threat. Thus, when an outgroup was presented as immoral it was not liked because it was seen as highly threatening. Thus, moral information appears more relevant when forming a global evaluative judgement of social groups than information about sociability and competence. Moreover, these findings empirically supported the general idea that morality is fundamental in social judgment because it prefigures whether another party is beneficial or harmful.

The empirical work reviewed shows that moral content is prioritized for both ingroup and outgroup members. Thus, the irrelevance of the target membership suggests that the primacy of morality is a stable effect, unaffected by the intergroup context. Nevertheless, different mechanisms might explain the same relevance of moral-related traits in forming impressions of ingroup an outgroup members. To investigate these underlying processes, a new set of experiments asked participants to rate either an outgroup or an ingroup member differently described in terms of morality, sociability, and competence (Brambilla et al., 2013). The findings consistently supported the primacy of morality in shaping group evaluations and behavioral intentions. Indeed, both the outgroup and the ingroup target were liked when described as moral and disliked and kept at distance when described as lacking morality; by contrast, competence- and sociability-related cues had no significant impact on evaluations and behavioral intentions. Furthermore, when both the ingroup and the outgroup target were presented as immoral, they were disliked because perceived as highly threatening. Importantly, going beyond a general perception of threat, this set of studies explored how specific profiles of threat affect the relationship between moral traits and ingroup/outgroup impressions. The findings showed that morality is key in shaping outgroup evaluations because the immoral outgroup is perceived as a real and concrete threat to the ingroup's survival possibilities and safety. On the opposite side, ingroup morality had a primary role in predicting ingroup impressions because the ingroup member's immorality threatens group-image and integrity. Thus, moral characteristics have a primary role (over non-moral characteristics) in shaping impressions and behavioral intentions towards ingroup and outgroup members. Moreover, although the perception of threat is the key underlying mechanism, different and complementary profiles of social menace explain the primacy of ingroup's and outgroup's morality. Monitoring the outgroup morality may be functional for defending the ingroup from an immoral outgroup member who is potentially harmful to the individual and group survival. Conversely, scrutinizing the morality of ingroup members may be functional to the punishment of members' selfishness and unfair behavior, and the preservation of group reputation and internal cooperation (Ellemers & Van den Bos, 2012).

The importance of being (perceived) moral: morality as group validation

Given that morality is a central part of the self-concept and ingroup image (Leach et al., 2007), people are very sensitive to moral threats and reproach. Indeed, given the primacy of moral information in defining group image, people anticipate receiving ingroup respect when adhering to morality-related norms (Pagliaro et al., 2011). In the same vein, an ingroup member's immorality fosters a sense of threat to the ingroup integrity and leads to negative behavioral intentions towards the moral transgressor (Brambilla et al., 2013).

However, witnessing immoral actions and transgression of moral norms is not likely to elicit a sense of threat exclusively. When the social perceivers do not share group membership with the wrongdoer, the immoral act might also enhance the perception of ingroup moral superiority (Epley & Dunning, 2000), foster a sense of doing comparatively well through downward social comparison (Suls & Wheeler, 2013), and reduce the sense of threat to the ingroup and personal moral identity (Minson & Monin, 2012). In line with this reasoning, recent work within the frame of the MPM explored the effects of participants' exposure to an immoral (vs. moral) behavior on self-view and sense of self-satisfaction (Sacchi et al, 2021). This work reveals an enhancement of self-representation when participants were presented with an immoral behavior performed by an outgroup member. Moreover, this effect was moderated by the level of participants' identification: The stronger the identification with their own group, the more positive their self-view in the face of an outsider's moral wrongdoing. Importantly, this self-view enhancement is not due to a generic influence of an external negative behavior but to a specific effect of a moral violation. Indeed, the negative (vs. positive) behavior concerning a different dimension (i.e., competence) did not affect participants' self-views at any level of ingroup identification.

As shown by this line of research, the sense of group moral superiority promotes pride to be in, a sense of belonging and positive self-perceptions. From a complementary perspective, several studies revealed that threats to the moral status of the ingroup might generate defensive responses rather than strivings to improve in the moral domain (Minson & Monin, 2012). In stark contrast, acknowledging the moral status of the ingroup, as remembering the group moral actions, is likely to reduce self-protective reactions and promote prosocial orientations and willingness to help disadvantaged groups (van Leeuwen et al., 2013). Consistent with this idea, a set of three experimental studies showed that positive feedback about ingroup morality improves attitudes towards immigrants and increases anger over their predicament. Moreover, this benevolent standpoint towards the underprivileged group promoted by the ingroup moral validation is likely to encourage collective action on its behalf, as the defence of the immigrants' rights (Vázquez et al., 2022).

Therefore, as detailed in this paragraph, the dominant role of moral qualities in forging threat perception and impression formation on ingroup and outgroup members might have some relevant effects. Since morality is a key driver of social evaluation, it is not surprising that people strive to affirm themselves and their groups as moral, as well as being perceived as moral by others. Indeed, anticipating reproach on the moral domain or seeing the ingroup as less moral than other groups might be perceived as threatening for the individual and the group.

Conclusion

The work we have reviewed here shows that morality has a primary role in guiding the impressions that we form and the evaluations that we make of group members. Thus, when collecting information about group members to form an impression, morality is preferentially selected over non moral characteristics (sociability and competence). Moreover, once information is available to make judgments about a group member, morality plays a primary and distinct role compared to other dimensions. The work reviewed in this chapter has not only shown the primacy of morality in impressions of both ingroup and outgroup members, but it has also cast light on the mechanisms underlying such a primary role. Morality is critical to establishing whether ingroup and outgroup members have harmful or beneficial intentions, and thus whether they can be friends or foes. In other words, morality drives group perception because morality and the perception of threat are inherently linked. Concerns around the image of one's own group explain the relationship between the perceived (im)morality of one's own group and reactions to the (im)moral ingroup. Conversely, safety threat, explains the relationship between the perceived (im)morality of an unknown individual that does not belong to our group and reactions to that (im)moral target individual. In sum, our judgments of another party's morality are more important to the essential decision we must make about whether they represent an opportunity or a threat. And, our judgments of our own morality are an important basis for feeling good about ourselves as individuals or as group members (Figure 11.1).

Intragroup level: moral character in group perception

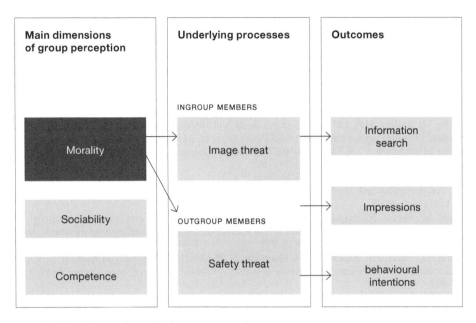

Figure 11.1 The primacy of morality in group perception.

The works reviewed across the chapter revealed that judging a group as moral does not have the same implications as judging them as sociable. By showing that morality and sociability make unique contributions to impression formation, the work reviewed in the chapter suggests the importance of distinguishing the sociability and morality components of warmth (Brambilla et al., 2021; see also Abele et al., 2021).

The research evidence presented in this chapter also raises several future research possibilities. An important direction for further research would be to broaden the notion of morality. Indeed, most studies reviewed in the chapter conceived morality mainly in terms of trustworthiness and honesty. However, morality might be conceived more broadly than this definition implies (Gray & Graham, 2019). For instance, Moral Foundations Theory (see Graham et al., 2011) suggests that morality encompasses aspects connected to harm, fairness, loyalty, authority, and purity. Thus, one direction that would be interesting to take in further research is to investigate how different moral characteristics affect impression formation and group-based identities and intragroup behavioural regulation. Pursuing the goal of extending this narrow definition of morality, future studies might also explore the role of rule-based morality (deontology) vs. outcome-based morality (utilitarianism) in forging group life and social perception (Sacchi et al., 2014). Although the lines of research on moral reasoning and social perception of morality have developed in a completely independent way, it has been recently shown that agents who express deontological moral judgments are preferred as social partners and perceived as more trustworthy than agents who express consequentialist preferences (Crockett et al., 2021). Building on these findings and bridging these two theoretical traditions, future studies could compare the social perception of social targets that act according to moral rules (deontology) with that of targets who follow sociability- or competence-related norms. Moreover, the social perceiver's impressions derived from rule-based vs. outcome-based behaviours in different domains might be explored.

References

Abele, A. E., Ellemers, N., Fiske, S. T., Koch, A., & Yzerbyt, V. (2021). Navigating the social world: Toward an integrated framework for evaluating self, individuals, and groups. *Psychological Review, 128*, 290.

Abele, A.E. & Wojciszke, B. (2014). Communal and agentic content in social cognition: A Dual Perspective Model. *Advances in Experimental Social Psychology, 50*, 195–255.

Asch, S. (1946). Forming impressions of personality. *Journal of Abnormal and Social Psychology, 41*, 1230–1240.

Brambilla, M., & Butz, D.A. (2013). Intergroup threat and outgroup attitudes: Macro-level symbolic threat increases prejudice against gay men. *Social Psychology, 44*, 311–319.

Brambilla, M., & Leach, C. W. (2014). On the Importance of being moral: The distinctive role of morality in social judgment. *Social Cognition, 32*, 397–408.

Brambilla, M., Rusconi, P., Sacchi, S., & Cherubini, P. (2011). Looking for honesty: The primary role of morality (vs. sociability and competence) in information gathering. *European Journal of Social Psychology, 41*, 135–143.

Brambilla, M., Sacchi, S., Pagliaro, S., & Ellemers, N. (2013). Morality and intergroup relations: Threats to safety and group image predict the desire to interact with outgroup and ingroup members. *Journal of Experimental Social Psychology, 49*, 811–821.

Brambilla, M., Sacchi, S., Rusconi, P., & Goodwin, G. P. (2021). The primacy of morality in impression development: Theory, research, and future directions. *Advances in Experimental Social Psychology, 64*, 187–262.

Brambilla, M., Sacchi, S., Rusconi, P., Cherubini, P., & Yzerbyt, V. Y. (2012). You want to give a good impression? Be honest! Moral traits dominate group impression formation. *British Journal of Social Psychology, 51*, 149–166.

Carlston, D. E. (Ed.). (2013). *The Oxford handbook of social cognition*. New York, NY: Oxford University Press.

Cottrell, C. A., Neuberg, S. L., & Li, N. P. (2007). What do people desire in others? A sociofunctional perspective on the importance of different valued characteristics. *Journal of Personality and Social Psychology, 92*, 208–231.

Crockett, M. J., Everett, J. A., Gill, M., & Siegel, J. Z. (2021). The relational logic of moral inference. *Advances in Experimental Social Psychology, 64*, 1–64.

Ellemers, N., Pagliaro, S., & Barreto, M. (2013). Morality and behavioural regulation in groups: A social identity approach. *European Review of Social Psychology, 24*, 160–193.

Ellemers, N., Pagliaro, S., Barreto, M., & Leach, C. W. (2008). Is it better to be moral than smart? The effects of morality and competence norms on the decision to work at group status improvement. *Journal of Personality and Social Psychology, 95*, 1397–1410.

Ellemers, N., & Van den Bos, K. (2012). Morality in groups: On the social-regulatory functions of right and wrong. *Social and Personality Psychology Compass, 6*, 878–889.

Ellemers, N., Van Der Toorn, J., Paunov, Y., & Van Leeuwen, T. (2019). The psychology of morality: A review and analysis of empirical studies published from 1940 through 2017. *Personality and Social Psychology Review, 23*, 332–366.

Epley, N., & Dunning, D. (2000). Feeling "holier than thou": Are self-serving assessments produced by errors in self- or social prediction? *Journal of Personality and Social Psychology, 79*, 861–875.

Fiske, S. T. (2018). Stereotype content: Warmth and competence endure. *Current Directions in Psychological Science, 27*, 67–73.

Fiske, S. T., Cuddy, A. J. C., Glick, P., & Xu, J. (2002). A model of (often mixed) stereotype content: Competence and warmth respectively follow from perceived status and competition. *Journal of Personality and Social Psychology, 82*, 878–902.

Fiske, S.T., Cuddy, A.J.C., & Glick, P. (2007). Universal dimensions of social cognition: Warmth and competence. *Trends in Cognitive Sciences, 11*, 77–83.

Goodwin, G. P. (2015). Moral character in person perception. *Current Directions in Psychological Science, 24*, 38–44.

Goodwin, G. P., Piazza, J., & Rozin, P. (2014). Moral character predominates in person perception and evaluation. *Journal of Personality and Social Psychology, 106*, 148–168

Gray, K., & Graham, J. (Eds.). (2019). *Atlas of moral psychology*. New York: Guilford Publications.

Graham, J., Nosek, B. A., Haidt, J., Iyer, R., Koleva, S., & Ditto, P. H. (2011). Mapping the moral domain. *Journal of Personality and Social Psychology, 101*, 366–385.

Katz, D., & Braly, K. (1933). Racial stereotypes of one hundred college students. *The Journal of Abnormal and Social Psychology, 28*, 280–290.

Koch, A., Imhoff, R., Dotsch, R., Unkelbach, C., & Alves, H. (2016). The ABC of stereotypes about groups: Agency/socioeconomic success, conservative–progressive beliefs, and communion. *Journal of Personality and Social Psychology, 110*, 675–709

Leach, C. W., Ellemers, N., & Barreto, M. (2007). Group virtue: The importance of morality (vs. competence and sociability) in the positive evaluation of in-groups. *Journal of Personality and Social Psychology, 93*, 234–249.

Madon, S. (1997). What do people believe about gay males? A study of stereotype content and strength. *Sex Roles, 37*, 663–685.

Minson, J. A., & Monin, B. (2012). Do-gooder derogation: Disparaging morally motivated minorities to defuse anticipated reproach. *Social Psychological and Personality Science, 3*, 200–207.

Pagliaro, S., Ellemers, N., & Barreto, M. (2011). Sharing moral values: Anticipated ingroup respect as a determinant of adherence to morality-based (but not competence-based) group norms. *Personality and Social Psychology Bulletin, 37*, 1117–1129.

Rosenberg, S., Nelson, C., & Vivekananthan, P.S. (1968). A multidimensional approach to the structure of personality impressions. *Journal of Personality and Social Psychology, 9*, 283–294.

Rusconi, P., Sacchi, S., Brambilla, M., Capellini, R., & Cherubini, P. (2020). Being honest and acting consistently: Boundary conditions of the negativity effect in the attribution of morality. *Social Cognition, 38*, 146–178.

Sacchi, S., Brambilla, M., & Graupmann, V. (2021). Basking in detected vice: Outgroup immorality enhances self-view. *Group Processes & Intergroup Relations, 24*, 371–387.

Sacchi, S., Riva, P., Brambilla, M., & Grasso, M. (2014). Moral reasoning and climate change mitigation: The deontological reaction towards the market-based approach. *Journal of Environmental Psychology, 38*, 252–261.

Skowronski, J. J., & Carlston, D. E. (1987). Social judgement and social memory: The role of cue diagnosticity in negativity, positivity, and extremity biases. *Journal of Personality and Social Psychology, 52*, 689–699.

Suls, J., & Wheeler, L. (Eds.). (2013). *Handbook of social comparison: Theory and research.* New York, NY: Kluwer Academic/Plenum Press.

Van Leeuwen, E., van Dijk, W. W., & Kaynak, Ü (2013). Of saints and sinners: How collective pride and guilt affect outgroup helping. *Group Processes & Intergroup Relations, 16*, 781–796.

Vázquez, A., López-Rodríguez, L., Gómez, Á., & Brambilla, M. (2022). Verification of ingroup morality promotes willingness to participate in collective action for immigrants' rights. *Group Processes & Intergroup Relations, 25*, 174–192.

Wojciszke, B. (2005). Morality and competence in person- and self-perception. *European Review of Social Psychology, 16*, 155–188.

12
THE INTERGROUP LEVEL
Social neuroscience of intergroup decision-making

Jennifer Kubota, Richa Gautam, and Jasmin Cloutier

Abstract

Burdens and rewards are inequitably distributed across various social group memberships (e.g., by race, gender, ethnicity, SES). While considerable research has examined the processes underlying intergroup cognition, relatively less research has considered how these mechanisms contribute to bias in morally-relevant intergroup decisions. This chapter reviews the limited behavioral and neuroscientific research on intergroup decision-making related to trust, cooperation, and fairness. This review shows that group membership affects these decisions and often contains moral dilemmas. The overlap in the neural antecedents implicated in intergroup impression formation, moral reasoning, and decision-making is also reviewed to derive a new Intergroup Moral Value Computation Model. Together the reviewed research highlights the importance of considering the flexible integration of ingroup vs. outgroup partner characteristics and social norms to understand moral judgments and decisions. We conclude by discussing remaining questions and future directions for intergroup moral decision-making research.

- Ingroup favoritism impacts decisions to trust and cooperate with others as well as assessments of fairness in intergroup contexts.
- Context, motivation, goals, reputation, and social norms can enhance or reduce ingroup favoritism in trust, cooperation, and fairness.
- Social neuroscience and computational modeling allow researchers to better understand and predict the role of ingroup favoritism in moral intergroup decisions.

Introduction

Morality allows us to live cooperatively in groups, and deciding whom to trust, cooperate with, and who is just is the backbone of social living. In this way, trust, cooperation, and fairness considerations are morally relevant decisions. Throughout history, countless examples of moral principles have been applied to some but not all members of society, with certain groups relegated to unjust and inequitable treatment. Humans are more likely to trust, cooperate, and judge someone's actions as fair if they are similar in their characteristics (e.g., age, gender, status, race, culture, language, sexual orientation, political ideology, etc.). To better understand how and why biases occur in intergroup moral decisions and what may be done to combat these biases, this chapter reviews the small but growing social neuroscience literature on the morally relevant decisions of trust, cooperation, and fairness. Predicting the intentions of others helps us efficiently navigate our social world. When encountering another person, we rapidly evaluate whether they are likely to help or harm us, which in turn can influence our decisions to trust and cooperate with them and assess their actions as fair or just. Social evaluations scaffold impressions and moral judgments, helping perceivers rapidly differentiate fair from unfair, cooperators from competitors, and friend from foe. For most of scholarly history, an assumption of rationality informed theories of human decision-making (Camerer, 2003). These theories typically assume that actors weigh and apply information in an unbiased manner, and that strictly rational humans would seek to maximize gains and reduce costs regardless of the group membership of their interaction partner or team. But moral reasoning, judgements, and decisions are not always rational. Examples of this irrationality may occur when individuals consider the social group of belonging of victims of moral transgressions. If someone does not share the same language, racialized background, socioeconomic status, nationality, gender, or age, others may not come to their aid to the same extent as those who share these characteristics. Furthermore, they may not trust them, cooperate with them, and view their actions as fair as they would for ingroup members.

Decades of research reveals that people prefer their ingroup and compete more with their outgroup. These decision biases stem in part from the spontaneous categorization and evaluation of others based on their social identity. In an intergroup context, our decisions are skewed by the familiarity and esteem we have for our ingroup, and by our outgroup prejudices, stereotypes, and conflicts. Threats to the ingroup can become personal (Tajfel et al., 1979), even when ingroup–outgroup boundaries are minimal (Tajfel et al., 1971). Therefore, decision-making can differ, both in its process or outcome, for ingroup and outgroup members. Unsurprisingly, intergroup decision-making is riddled with moral dilemmas. Differential treatment of others based on their group affiliations is considered prima facie immoral (Brenick & Killen, 2014; Møller & Tenenbaum, 2011). And yet, we engage in it often when making intergroup decisions. For this reason, almost every intergroup decision involves moral considerations.

Trust and cooperation are the foundation of social relationships. Trustworthiness, cooperation, and fairness are typically valued principles and often described as the right thing to do when a partner has "good" qualities. Not trusting or cooperating with a kind and just person can cast doubt on the individual's morals. Trust has been described as a moral value (Uslaner, 2008), and is more likely to occur when one believes a partner or group will act benevolently and justly. Untrustworthy individuals are often described in moral terms as dishonest, self-interested, and unjust. In addition, cooperation has been described as a moral imperative (morality-as-cooperation model; Curry, 2016). Many forms of cooperation, such as reciprocation, equal distribution of resources, being brave, and helping groups or kin, are often valued moral principles cross-culturally (Curry et al., 2019). Both trust and cooperation are critical to facilitate social relations, but as we describe in this chapter, these moral decisions (to trust, to cooperate, to assess an action as just or fair) are not always rendered similarly when the partner is an ingroup versus an outgroup member.

In this chapter, we provide an overview of the growing body of research on intergroup decision-making. Because existing work on this topic is broad and spans multiple identity domains including race, gender, age, sexual orientation, status, political ideology, etc., we will only provide a snapshot of the exciting work being done. Before reviewing some of the current research, we will first briefly summarize behavioral and neuroscientific methods used in decision-making research on trust, cooperation, and fairness. We will conclude by proposing an intergroup value computation model we hope can be generative for future intergroup decision-making research.

Decision-Making Methods Relevant to Moral Psychology

Behavioral Decision-Making Paradigms

How might researchers examine and model the psychological and neural processes underlying intergroup trust, cooperation, and fairness? To do so, researchers often ask participants to make explicit decisions about or on behalf of ingroup and/or outgroup members. Decision-making tasks typically assess our actions in material interactions and are performed under a variety of conditions (e.g., in dyads or groups, when interactions are iterative or single, with certain or uncertain outcomes, during stressful or calm conditions, or even when individuals in a group must make their choice sequentially versus simultaneously). There are a variety of decision tasks relevant to moral psychology that can be broadly organized into two categories: positive decision domains (e.g., trust games [TG], stag hunt, public goods games [PGG]; fairness assessments; justice game [JG]), and negative decision domains (e.g., ultimatum games [UG], dictator game [DG], lottery choice task [LCT]). Several features of these tasks are well suited for probing intergroup moral decision-making. For one, these tasks provide more generalizable insights into everyday decision processes. These games are played with partners, allowing researchers to examine how group membership influences moral decisions systematically. Additionally, because some tasks are incentivized, a participant's choice may represent their genuine preference for the ingroup versus the outgroup. We focus our review on the positive decision domains but remind readers that the negative decision domains have consequential outcomes, such as punishment.

Neuroscientific and Computational Methods

Increased interest in social and affective neuroscience and neuroeconomics has led to greater enthusiasm for the use of neuroscientific, physiological, and computational methods to understand human decision-making. When applying decision-tasks to morally relevant intergroup decisions, researchers have primarily relied on temporally sensitive measures, such as event-related brain potentials (ERPs) from electroencephalograms (EEG), and spatially sensitive measures, such as functional magnetic resonance imaging (fMRI). Because neural measures can assess real-time processes that are insensitive to purposeful misrepresentation, they are useful in situations with social desirability concerns. This is critical when examining intergroup decision-making because social norms frequently impact how individuals respond when making explicit decisions. Moreover, the mechanisms guiding decision-making can be inaccessible to the decision-makers and therefore difficult to characterize and change. Neural and physiological measures can assess the spontaneous processes that occur prior to the explicit decision. This is useful to assess when, for example, cognitive control is enacted to override a prepotent response (e.g., a stereotype or prejudice) based on self-presentation or norm concerns (e.g., a goal to be equitable).

Computational modelling is also an important analytical tool to study decision-making. Computational models can mathematically outline an individual's valuation of a stimulus, action, or outcome. Measured and modelled as value signal, it is a type of reward signal that indicates the subjective experience of the reward. It can be augmented with additional parameters—for example, estimating an individual's value of perceived loss and risk, or their attitudes about outgroups, etc. One of the advantages of decision-making tasks mentioned above is that they are amenable to formalizing the choice process to derive parameters indicative of individual differences during decision-making. By estimating parameters trial by trial, computational models map out their relative roles during decision-making. In combination with neuroimaging efforts, researchers can identify distinct neural regions and processes that are associated with parameters relevant to moral decisions identified through computational modelling. Together, these approaches can lead to a better understanding of the mechanisms that give rise to intergroup decision biases. Therefore, computational methods can lead to theoretically informed formal models. Additionally, these models can be used algorithmically to discover the proportional impact of each mechanistic parameter (Suzuki & O'Doherty, 2020).

Intergroup Decision-Making

To better understand social neurosciences contributions to intergroup moral decision making, we will first briefly discuss existing behavioral research on trust, cooperation, and fairness.

Tajfel extended decision-making to an intergroup context, finding that individuals allocate more resources to their ingroup than outgroup (Billig & Tajfel, 1973; Tajfel et al., 1971). From this early research it became clear that in some contexts humans can be more sensitive to maximizing differences in intergroup rewards rather than maximizing ingroup gains. However, this was an oversimplification, as ingroup favoritism is a strong factor impacting decision-making. Much of this initial decision-making research was based on arbitrary groups (minimal groups). Billig and Tajfel (1973) found that arbitrarily dividing people into groups lead to monetary discrimination against the outgroup. Tajfel and colleagues (1971) also found individuals allocated more money to ingroups when groups are determined by task performance or preference. Over time, however, it became clear that this bias extends beyond minimal groups to groups based on their members' social identity (e.g., Kubota et al., 2013). Individuals expect ingroup members to reciprocate and consider receiving future rewards more likely from them (e.g., Misch et al., 2021), trust them more (e.g., McAuliffe & Dunham, 2016; Rotella et al., 2013), and cooperate with them more (Brewer & Kramer, 1986; McAuliffe & Dunham, 2016). In fact, not only do we expect ingroup members to favor us, but we also expect people in general to favor their ingroup. Termed parochial altruism, this preference for altruistic behavior towards ingroup members and mistrust or hostility towards outgroup members is a pervasive feature of intergroup moral decision-making. Consequently, we find negative behavior towards ingroup members to be less just (Tajfel, 1982).

As aforementioned, these judgments are inherently moral. Intergroup biases may be justified by individuals with the help of more complicated (and contradictory) moral conventions (e.g., "one should help their community"; Miller & Bersoff, 1992). Accordingly, researchers use paradigms with additional moral considerations (e.g., deciding if an action is just) to make the morality inherent and salient in intergroup decisions. Thanks to such paradigms, we now know that humans find ingroup members to be fairer (e.g., Mattan et al., 2020); especially under scarcity, (Chae et al., 2022) while judging moral transgressions of outgroup members as more unjust than those of ingroup members (Chapman et al., 2020), judging their unfair offers to be more acceptable (Kubota et al., 2013), and imitating their immoral behaviors (Vives et al., 2022).

However, discrimination against outgroup members can be mitigated. For example, in the United States where conversations of injustice in policing are now widespread, individuals may perceive White police officers as more unjust and aggressive towards Black civilians than White civilians (Dang et al., 2022), which in turn shapes their assessment of the fairness of an officer's behavior. The culture signals that injustice is likely to occur in certain situations and consequently individuals aligned with those cultural values are more likely to be on guard for injustice during these interactions. Evidence of outgroup members' generosity towards the ingroup (Chiang, 2021) and reputational concerns about seeming biased or racist also increase outgroup trust, cooperation (Romano et al., 2017), and helping behavior (Zhan et al., 2019). This suggests that cultural norms, partner behavior, and motivations are important factors in decreasing the likelihood of discrimination in moral intergroup decisions.

Altogether, these studies indicate that people typically favor ingroup members but also highly value their personal social outcomes. These outcomes are dependent upon the decision-making context—ingroup favoritism is stronger in interdependent contexts (e.g., in PGG or TG), but subsides when decisions are independent (e.g., DG; Balliet et al., 2014). In independent contexts, individuals act more consistently with Group Bounded Reciprocity Theory (GBRT; Yamagishi & Mifune, 2016), which posits that humans titrate their cooperation based on the known or assumed trustworthiness of others. Therefore, social norms and context play an important role in intergroup moral decision-making.

Social Neuroscience of Intergroup Categorization and Evaluation

Brief Introduction to the Social Neuroscience of Intergroup Bias

Social neuroscience has sought to understand how, when, and why we form and express intergroup bias. Some of the first investigations focused on categorization and evaluative associations of social groups using ERPs (e.g., Kubota & Ito, 2007). Research has found that people process visible group membership (e.g., assumed race, gender, age) fast and efficiently (Kubota & Ito, 2017). Humans can also process social group membership based on knowledge (e.g., social status, sexual orientation, political ideology) relatively fast and efficiently (e.g., Mattan et al., 2018). Therefore, whether we make inferences based on perceptual information or knowledge based on reported information or interactions, partner identity can have an almost-immediate impact on our impressions and subsequent decisions.

Intergroup Perception and Categorization

Cues to others' social identity are efficiently gleaned from perceivable information and are then used to form impressions and evaluations which can subsequently impact decision-making (Brambilla et al., 2013; Ellemers & van Nunspeet, 2020). So far, psychological research on intergroup perception has focused largely on the use of visual cues, specifically from faces (although the little research that exists on intergroup perception from auditory cues is in line with findings from visual perception studies; Formanowicz & Suitner, 2020; Latinus & Belin, 2011). Signs of outgroup membership are attended to rapidly, leading to faster social categorization for outgroup members compared to ingroup members (Stroessner, 1996; Woo et al., 2020). These signs are processed within milliseconds (ms), with assumed race processed within approximately 122 ms of an encounter (Ito & Urland, 2003). When considering that moral decisions are often made with this information available (i.e., when individuals can readily see or hear another), this fast and efficient processing of social categories sets the stage for unfolding biases in the perceiver's thoughts, feelings, and subsequent behavior.

Cultural associations can facilitate social categorization. When the perceived belongs to categories that are assumed to be more compatible (e.g., Black men, Asian women), they are processed faster than categories that are assumed to be less compatible (e.g., Black women, Asian men; Johnson et al., 2012). Moreover, individuals can be guarded about who to let into their ingroup. As such when cues are ambiguous, the influence of context (Brielmann et al., 2015; Huart et al., 2005) and of the perceiver's motivations (Gaither et al., 2016; Hackel et al., 2017; Mattan et al., 2018) creep in to shape categorization in a manner functionally beneficial to the perceiver.

Once cues of outgroup membership have been perceived, attention to outgroup members wanes. Outgroup faces tend to be processed in a more featural than configural manner, which impedes individuation (Cloutier et al., 2005; Cloutier & Macrae, 2007). This reduction in configural face processing is marked by a lowered negative ERP around 170 ms (the N170) after face onset (Ratner & Amodio, 2013). Soon after, an increased negative ERP around 200 ms (the N200) marks deeper processing of ingroup faces (Kubota & Ito, 2007). This lowered attentional processing leads to deficits in remembering outgroup faces (known as the other race effect [ORE] or the cross-race deficit [CRD]; Correll et al., 2021). Notably, the ORE is absent when perceivers have been socialized to see the group as their ingroup or when individuals have more contact with the outgroup. For example, children adopted into families belonging to races different than theirs do not show ORE for faces belonging to their parents' racial groups (de Heering et al., 2010; Sangrigoli et al., 2005). Intergroup contact also decreases the ORE (Meissner & Brigham, 2001) with the greatest impact of contact on memory occurring for childhood interactions (Singh et al., 2022). Therefore, the ORE is limited to groups one has not been socialized into or had childhood or extended exposure.

The difference in perceptual processing for ingroup and outgroup faces also has consequences for moral perception (Cassidy et al., 2017). Faces that are not perceptually individuated may be more likely to be dehumanized, or deprived of human qualities (Hugenberg et al., 2016), and even more so when the faces belong to outgroups that are culturally dehumanized (Goff et al., 2008). Once social group membership has been categorized, our evaluative biases towards those affiliations are activated.

Intergroup and Moral Evaluation

Ingroup members are often associated with positive evaluations while outgroup members are associated with negative evaluations (Tajfel, 1974). These evaluations can be based solely on assumptions derived from culturally prescribed prejudices and stereotypes, but nonetheless rapidly and spontaneously influence our thoughts, feelings, and behaviors (Fiske & Neuberg, 1990). The perception, storage, and expression of social group evaluations share neural circuits with other emotionally and socially relevant information (see Kubota et al., 2012; Mattan, Wei, et al., 2018). These regions include those that support the identification of faces (fusiform face area [FFA]); the evaluation of individuals based on perceptual characteristics or personal knowledge of group identity (amygdala, ventral striatum [VS], and ventromedial prefrontal cortex [VMPFC]); inferences of mental states (dorsomedial prefrontal cortex [DMPFC], temporoparietal junction [TPJ], superior temporal sulcus [STS]); and the regulation of intergroup bias, which is often driven by the perceiver's goals and motivations, (anterior cingulate cortex [ACC], and dorsolateral prefrontal cortex [DLPFC]). The individual's prejudices, stereotypes, motivations to avoid bias, and internalization of social norms impact the recruitment of these brain networks when perceiving and responding to others based on their identity.

By the age of four, we may acquire enough cultural prejudices and stereotypes to have negative evaluative associations with outgroup members (Dunham et al., 2008), and by age seven we often consider outgroup members to be more likely to commit immoral acts (Liberman et al., 2018). These associations are swift. Within 200 ms outgroup members are attended to like other threatening categories (e.g., spiders, angry faces; the P200; Kubota & Ito, 2017, 2007). Slightly later, at 300 ms (the P300), individuals evaluate others and differentiate the moral status of social targets (Gyurovski et al., 2018). Therefore, social categorization can dominate early impressions by directing attention to threatening others (for some outgroup members) and subsequently shape evaluative processing. In this way, the path to moral decisions often starts with social categorization.

As expected, the neural substrates of moral evaluation overlap with the neural circuit supporting social evaluation. Moral evaluation often elicits affective responses indexed by amygdala activity and frequently involve increased connectivity between the amygdala and the VMPFC (Shenhav & Greene, 2014). Social evaluation recruits the ventromedial prefrontal cortex (VMPFC), a region shown to evoke greater responses associated with positive evaluation of others during impression formation (Dang et al., 2019). For example, increased VMPFC activity when viewing moral compared to immoral others has been found (Cloutier et al., 2012; Cloutier & Gyurovski, 2014). The role of the VMPFC in moral judgments has also been observed in lesion studies, with a documented reduction in judgment of harmful intent in patients with VMPFC lesions (Young et al., 2010). Furthermore, moral conflict monitoring, like other forms of conflict monitoring between prepotent responses and actual responses, has been found to recruit the anterior cingulate cortex (Cui et al., 2016, 2021; Greene et al., 2004), which is part of the salience and cognitive control networks. The ACC may index if an individual is morally conflicted—for example when their moral evaluations differ from their decisions. This conflict, as reflected in ACC activity, is also found when individuals respond with stereotypes even though they espouse egalitarian ideals (Amodio et al., 2006). Therefore, individuals have prepotent moral evaluative responses that allow them to swiftly identify a person or action as good or bad, but those associations may conflict with how they behave. Individuals may have positive associations with an ingroup member but decide not to trust them because they have a bad reputation. Not only can evaluations be regulated via motivation (Krosch et al., 2017; Mattan, Kubota, et al., 2018) but also individuation (Brauer & Er-Rafiy, 2011; Kubota & Ito, 2017), familiarity (Lowe, 2021; Mousa, 2019), social norms (De Franca & Monteiro, 2013), and a sense of belonging to the same superordinate group (Gaertner et al., 1993). Therefore, evaluations do not always directly predict intergroup decisions, including moral decision-making.

Social Neuroscience of Intergroup Decision-making

Because the outcomes of decisions are typically observable, decision-making may be especially sensitive to self-presentational concerns. Moreover, the mechanisms guiding decisions can be inaccessible to the decision-makers and therefore difficult to characterize and change. Social neuroscience is an excellent toolkit for mapping the mechanisms that guide intergroup moral decision-making. Researchers can quantify ongoing psychological processes without an overt response and without subjects' self-reflection on the psychological operations. Social neuroscience has provided important theoretical and methodological advancements to the study of intergroup trust, cooperation, and fairness. Below we provide a brief introduction to social neuroscience of decision-making and then review the existing literature.

Brief Introduction to the Social Neuroscience of Decision-making

Trust, cooperation, and fairness all rely on interactions among psychological systems (e.g., motivation, affect, cognition, executive control) that engage key brain regions also anchored in domain-general neural networks. Since domain-general processes are also recruited in response to various social stimuli, these networks largely overlap with the networks involved in intergroup processing.

The key brain regions involved in decision-making, including moral decisions, are part of the reward network, salience network, executive control network, and social cognition network (Krueger & Meyer-Lindenberg, 2019). The reward network facilitates the value computations (i.e., how important or rewarding is this stimuli) of social and non-social stimuli. VMPFC is proposed to be the central hub of this circuit. It receives inputs from the striatum, orbitofrontal cortex (OFC), substantia nigra (SN), and ventral tegmental area (VTA; (Bartra et al., 2013; Levy & Glimcher, 2012). The salience network is sensitive to the aversiveness of a stimulus—including its relative risk and uncertainty. It includes the amygdala, the dorsal ACC (DACC), and anterior insula (AI). The executive control network mobilizes regulation and facilitates the integration of goal and motivation dependent strategies. It includes the DLPFC, ventrolateral prefrontal cortex (VLPFC), and the ACC. Finally, the social cognition system, also referred to as the mentalizing or "theory of mind" network, is used to evaluate relational inferences and predict the intentions and likely behaviors of others. It includes the temporoparietal junction (TPJ), dorsomedial prefrontal cortex (DMPFC), and superior temporal sulcus (STS). Involvement of these networks can be modulated by the group membership of decision partners. Below we provide a brief description of how these brain networks are involved in trust, cooperation, and fairness in an intergroup context.

Intergroup Trust and Cooperation

Positive evaluations, as indexed by greater activity in the reward system, lead to greater trust and more cooperative decisions. Trustful decisions typically result from inferences of a partner's good intentions and a history of positive outcomes with the partner. However, trust can be hard to achieve in intergroup contexts that are perceived to be zero-sum and/or competitive. Baseline ingroup trust is often extended to unfamiliar ingroup members, but not to outgroup members. The existence of additional negative stereotypes and prejudices towards outgroups coupled with baseline mistrust can make it even harder to achieve intergroup cooperation at the outset. But over time, evidence of an outgroup individual's trustworthiness and cooperativeness can increase trust.

Individuals are often self- and close-other-interested. As such, rewards given to ingroup members activate the reward network, leading to greater VS activity (Hackel et al., 2017). Therefore, ingroup "love" may be a stronger predictor of intergroup bias, especially following ingroup bonding (Yang et al., 2020). For example, Telzer and colleagues (2015) found that greater reward signals in the VS in response to ingroup members predicted donations to ingroup members during a prosocial giving task. Moreover, when donating to outgroup members, participants with a stronger ingroup identity showed heightened activation in the cognitive control network (VLPFC, ACC) and the social cognition network (TPJ, DMPFC; Telzer et al., 2015). Similarly, Hughes et al. (2017) found that ingroup trust was unaffected when individuals were given more time to deliberate. In comparison, outgroup trust increased when individuals had time to deliberate about their trust decisions and engaged cognitive control (Hughes et al., 2017). This indicates that overcoming self- and close-other-interest can occur when individuals engage in greater mentalizing of outgroup members and greater self-regulatory cognitive control to overcome ingroup favoritism.

Moral behavior during an interaction with ingroup members or when group membership is unknown elicits greater trust, which persists even in light of explicit trust violations. For example, individuals make riskier decisions to share during a TG with individuals described as morally good based on their previous actions (Delgado et al., 2005). The VS (part of the reward network) differentiated between positive and negative feedback but only for partners described as morally neutral. However, VS activity did not differentiate feedback, winning money or losing money, for morally good partners or morally bad partners. This suggests that moral impressions can diminish reliance on feedback that indicates a partner's risk, biasing risk assessments for moral individuals (Delgado et al., 2005).

Trust is the backbone of cooperation. Just as we trust ingroup members more, we also cooperate more with ingroup than outgroup members (Balliet et al., 2014). Because many cooperative decisions require thinking about the intentions of the partner(s), they often involve brain regions from the social cognition network working in collaboration with the salience and reward networks (Tsoi et al., 2016). Individuals often engage mentalizing regions more for ingroup members (Merritt et al., 2021). Like trust, cooperation with the outgroup increases as mentalizing about outgroup members' intentions increases (Tsoi et al., 2016). Individuals are also especially likely to engage in mentalizing when their expectations are violated, for example, when receiving unexpected negative feedback from ingroup members or unexpected positive rewards from outgroup members. Individuals may engage in mentalizing in these situations to try to make sense of what happened. However, research has yet to connect violations of expectations and engagement of mentalizing networks with changes in cooperation. This is an important avenue for future research.

We are more likely to help ingroup members, even when such help incurs us personal harms (Hein et al., 2010). We may even find the pain of outgroup members rewarding, and the more rewarding we find it (as indexed by VS activity), the less likely we are to help outgroup members (Hein et al., 2010). However, when at risk of social harm (e.g., negative reputation), we help ingroup and outgroup members equally (Zhan et al., 2019). Therefore, individuals are more likely to help or withdraw from prosocial behavior depending on the social characteristics of the partner—i.e., whether they share group membership—supporting an account of ingroup favoritism in prosocial behavior, but also the social consequences of such behavior.

Intergroup Fairness

Perceptions of fairness also affect our likelihood to trust and cooperate (Balliet et al., 2014). The reward network (specifically the VS and VMPFC) are more active when assessing fair offers than unfair offers (Kable & Glimcher, 2007), especially when individuals identify more strongly with the ingroup (Apps et al., 2018). A growing body of research finds that VMPFC activity reliably differentiates between fair and unfair offers (Gabay et al., 2014), with greater VMPFC activity to fair offers. Lesions to VMPFC reduce sensitivity to the fairness of offers (Gu et al., 2015), which may lead to difficulty adhering to social and group norms (Anderson et al., 1999).

Fair offers may represent greater reward value because of our aversion to inequity (Apps et al., 2018). Rejecting unfair offers reflects prosociality (when it involves sacrifice of self and ingroup resources) and promotes cooperation and enforcement of a fairness norm (Kaltwasser et al., 2016). Hence, accepting unfair offers associated with resource gains may require effort. Supporting this assumption, disruption of DLPFC, which is part of the cognitive control network, using transcranial magnetic stimulation (TMS) is associated with decreased rejection rates of unfair offers during a UG (Knoch et al., 2008). DLPFC may also support norm compliance that can lead to economic loss. For example, Baumgartner and colleagues (2011) found that disrupting the DLPFC using TMS during a UG led to a decrease in normative behavior (i.e., rejection of unfair offers that violate the norm of fairness). Participants who made more frequent costly normative decisions displayed significantly greater activity in, and connectivity between, DLPFC and VMPFC (Baumgartner et al., 2011; see also Crockett et al., 2017).

Ingroup members are assumed to be more moral (Liberman et al., 2018). In fact, when ingroup members engage in unfair behavior, activity in the social cognition network (DMPFC, TPJ) increases as individuals try to understand egregious ingroup behavior (Baumgartner et al., 2012). Therefore, group norms that dictate supporting the ingroup may override our judgement of fair behavior. Engaging in immoral behavior (hostility, harm) for the benefit of the ingroup recruits the cognitive control network (specifically the DLPFC) and the social cognition network (specifically the TPJ; Yang et al., 2020) to override the reduced activity in the reward network (specifically the VMPFC), as immoral behaviors tend to elicit less reward value (Han et al., 2021). In some cases, we may even disassociate our selves from our morality (marked by reduced activation of the DMPFC in the social cognitive network) in order to enact immoral behaviors for the ingroup's benefit (Cikara et al., 2014).

These findings suggest that activity in social cognitive and cognitive control networks, and the functional connectivity between them, may index willingness to incur cost in favor of ingroup members when assessing fairness during decision-making. This aligns with the possibility that the reason that application of costly normative moral decisions is rare is that self- and ingroup-interests frequently runs counter to fairness.

Intergroup Moral Value Computation Model

Intergroup decision-making is marked by a strong ingroup bias that can be mitigated by multiple contextual and motivational factors. Integrating across existing behavioral and neuroscientific research, we propose an Intergroup Moral Value Computation Model positing that the computation of the value of social decisions is modulated by top-down influences such as group affiliation(s), moral considerations, and social norms. In this model, reinforcement learning (RL) computations are derived from the reward and salience neural networks based on (assumed and learned) predictions about the intentions of our partners and our own motives, morals, and/or social norms that are derived from the social cognition network. The executive control network then regulates prepotent responses bringing them in line with our intentions. Therefore, to arrive at an intergroup value computation, individuals derive a utility function that weighs five parameters: *who is the partner* (which involves activation of prior beliefs and knowledge, e.g., stereotypes, prejudices, or available person-knowledge), *the agent's moral preferences* (e.g., concerns for others' outcomes, concerns about justice and fairness, etc.); *the value of the outcome* (i.e., extent it will benefit or hurt them, sully their reputation or by extension their ingroup); *the outcome's probability given an action* (e.g., certainty of reward, the partner's predicted intentions, etc.); and *the social norms surrounding an action* (e.g., possible sanctions or reputational damage).[1] This value function is updated as more information is gathered. Over iterative interactions, decisions to cooperate with an outgroup member, for example, can change as the outgroup member's reputation evolves. If we return to the basic conceptual model of decision value, we can derive predictions for how partner and decision maker identity influence stimulus value and the subsequent action (Figure 12.1).

The Intergroup Value Computation Model incorporates both positive and negative representations and is repeatedly updated based on each action's outcome. The reward network

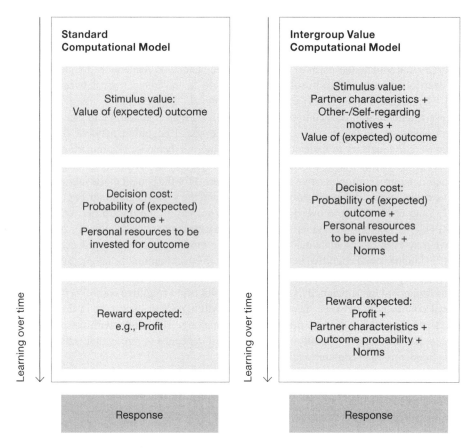

Figure 12.1 Standard computational model vs intergroup value computational model.

(VMPFC, VS and DS, OFC, SN, and VTA), salience network (amygdala, DACC, and AI) and social cognition network (TPJ, DMPFC, and STS) modulate both the stimulus value and the decision cost (Figure 12.2). During first encounters or single interactions, expectations and norms largely drive these computations. Over multiple encounters, decision value and decision cost are modulated by prediction and action errors learned from repeated interactions. This allows for the titration of decisions across time, with VMPFC acting as a hub integrating information from these networks. The cognitive control network (DLPFC, VLPFC, DACC) mobilizes executive control and facilitates the integration of context to bring in line actions with value. This model is distinct from previous RL value computational frameworks because it includes information about partner's and perceiver's group membership, as well as social norms and allows for novel predictions to further explain seemingly irrational decisions that may be made during intergroup interactions.

Unresolved Questions and Future Directions

The research on intergroup moral decision-making is growing, but much is left to consider. Group membership affects decisions in part by shifting value computations, impacting whom we

Intergroup level: social neuroscience of decision-making

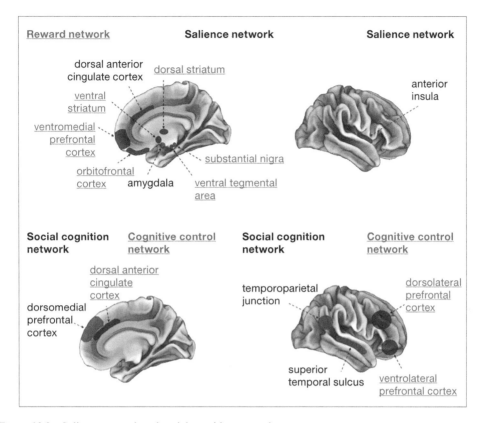

Figure 12.2 Salience network and social cognition network.

trust, how we cooperate, and tolerance of unfairness. Alarmingly, group membership can factor into decisions to trust or punish others even when it comes at a personal cost. This perspective highlights that "gains" in a given scenario are not limited to material gains—we highly value abstract "gains" that come from maintaining good group reputations, from being adored by our fellow ingroup members, and from following social norms. These findings reintroduce the "human" into human decision-making—our social tendencies, concerns, and fears may be "irrational," but are just as important as more "rational" gains in determining action. The contribution of context in our decisions is a cause for optimism – intergroup dynamics can be reframed to reduce ingroup favoritism and improve relations. Therefore, intergroup discrimination can be regulated. Future research should consider how regulation fails when it is difficult to rapidly update group associations (e.g., under stress or threat).

To improve applicability, decision-making research on morality should expand the external validity of experimental paradigms to better reflect how decisions occur in real life. For example, in intergroup situations, individuals may make egalitarian decisions under optimal or observed conditions, but discriminatory ones under pressure or uncertainty, both features of many everyday situations. Additionally, many of our paradigms tend to measure dyadic behavior when many decisions happen in groups. We need to generate and utilize paradigms that put the "group" back in "intergroup" and move beyond dyadic interactions.

Future research should aim to fill a current gap in neuroscientific investigations of intergroup decision making. For example, there is no research on how available knowledge about a specific outgroup member may alter moral decisions towards the whole outgroup. Additionally, investigations typically focus on a single social identity when we inhabit multiple social identities at any given time. To ensure that results are generalizable, researchers must take an intersectional approach and consider how multiple social identities and their power dynamics shape decision-making, improving our understanding of how participant characteristics and culture impact decisions.

Finally, as it becomes increasingly common for humans to interact with artificial intelligence (A.I.), research should also push the boundaries of how we define intergroup relations and moral decisions by examining trust and cooperation between humans and A.I. In our changing world, it is becoming critical to understand how to minimize algorithmic bias. This includes not just bias in the development of A.I. but also in interactions with A.I., which can vary in social characteristics, such as competence and human likeness.

Given the prevalence of intergroup inequity in decision-making (i.e., not all social groups have the power or the opportunity to make decisions), an important future frontier is to address what we can do about discriminatory decisions. Our inequitable division of burdens and rewards based on social group membership can only be made equitable by identifying factors that reduce discrimination in intergroup moral decisions.

Note

1 Note that the agent's moral preferences and norms surrounding an action are specified as two distinct parameters to separate personal stances from conventional expectations.

References

Amodio, D. M., Kubota, J. T., Harmon-Jones, E., & Devine, P. G. (2006). Alternative mechanisms for regulating racial responses according to internal vs external cues. *Social Cognitive and Affective Neuroscience*, *1*(1), 26–36.

Anderson, S. W., Bechara, A., Damasio, H., Tranel, D., & Damasio, A. R. (1999). Impairment of social and moral behavior related to early damage in human prefrontal cortex. *Nature Neuroscience*, *2*(11), 1032–1037.

Apps, M. A., McKay, R., Azevedo, R. T., Whitehouse, H., & Tsakiris, M. (2018). Not on my team: Medial prefrontal cortex responses to ingroup fusion and unfair monetary divisions. *Brain and Behavior*, *8*(8), e01030.

Balliet, D., Wu, J., & De Dreu, C. K. (2014). Ingroup favoritism in cooperation: A meta-analysis. *Psychological Bulletin*, *140*(6), 1556.

Bartra, O., McGuire, J. T., & Kable, J. W. (2013). The valuation system: A coordinate-based meta-analysis of BOLD fMRI experiments examining neural correlates of subjective value. *Neuroimage*, *76*, 412–427.

Baumgartner, T., Götte, L., Gügler, R., & Fehr, E. (2012). The mentalizing network orchestrates the impact of parochial altruism on social norm enforcement. *Human Brain Mapping*, *33*(6), 1452–1469.

Baumgartner, T., Knoch, D., Hotz, P., Eisenegger, C., & Fehr, E. (2011). Dorsolateral and ventromedial prefrontal cortex orchestrate normative choice. *Nature Neuroscience*, *14*(11), 1468–1474.

Billig, M., & Tajfel, H. (1973). Social categorization and similarity in intergroup behaviour. *European Journal of Social Psychology*, *3*(1), 27–52.

Brambilla, M., Sacchi, S., Pagliaro, S., & Ellemers, N. (2013). Morality and intergroup relations: Threats to safety and group image predict the desire to interact with outgroup and ingroup members. *Journal of Experimental Social Psychology*, *49*(5), 811–821.

Brauer, M., & Er-Rafiy, A. (2011). Increasing perceived variability reduces prejudice and discrimination. *Journal of Experimental Social Psychology*, *47*(5), 871–881.

Brenick, A., & Killen, M. (2014). Moral judgments about Jewish–Arab intergroup exclusion: The role of cultural identity and contact. *Developmental Psychology*, *50*(1), 86.

Brewer, M. B., & Kramer, R. M. (1986). Choice behavior in social dilemmas: Effects of social identity, group size, and decision framing. *Journal of Personality and Social Psychology*, *50*(3), 543.

Brielmann, A. A., Gaetano, J., & Stolarova, M. (2015). Man, You Might Look Like a Woman—If a Child Is Next to You. *Advances in Cognitive Psychology*, *11*(3), 84.

Camerer, C. F. (2003). Strategizing in the brain. *Science*, *300*(5626), 1673–1675.

Cassidy, B. S., Krendl, A. C., Stanko, K. A., Rydell, R. J., Young, S. G., & Hugenberg, K. (2017). Configural face processing impacts race disparities in humanization and trust. *Journal of Experimental Social Psychology, 73*, 111–124.

Chae, J., Kim, K., Kim, Y., Lim, G., Kim, D., & Kim, H. (2022). Ingroup favoritism overrides fairness when resources are limited. *Scientific Reports*, *12*(1), 1–11.

Chapman, M. S., May, K. E., Scofield, J., DeCoster, J., & Bui, C. (2020). Does group membership affect children's judgments of social transgressions? *Journal of Experimental Child Psychology, 189*, 104695.

Chiang, Y.-S. (2021). Indirect reciprocity for mitigating intergroup hostility: A vignette experiment and an agent-based model on intergroup relations between mainland Chinese and Taiwanese. *Journal of Conflict Resolution*, *65*(2–3), 403–426.

Cikara, M., Jenkins, A. C., Dufour, N., & Saxe, R. (2014). Reduced self-referential neural response during intergroup competition predicts competitor harm. *NeuroImage, 96*, 36–43.

Cloutier, J., Ambady, N., Meagher, T., & Gabrieli, J. (2012). The neural substrates of person perception: Spontaneous use of financial and moral status knowledge. *Neuropsychologia*, *50*(9), 2371–2376.

Cloutier, J., & Gyurovski, I. (2014). Ventral medial prefrontal cortex and person evaluation: Forming impressions of others varying in financial and moral status. *Neuroimage, 100*, 535–543.

Cloutier, J., & Macrae, C. N. (2007). Who or what are you?: Facial orientation and person construal. *European Journal of Social Psychology*, *37*(6), 1298–1309.

Cloutier, J., Mason, M. F., & Macrae, C. N. (2005). The perceptual determinants of person construal: Reopening the social-cognitive toolbox. *Journal of Personality and Social Psychology*, *88*(6), 885.

Correll, J., Ma, D. S., & Davis, J. P. (2021). Perceptual tuning through contact? Contact interacts with perceptual (not memory-based) face-processing ability to predict cross-race recognition. *Journal of Experimental Social Psychology*, *92*, 104058.

Crockett, M. J., Siegel, J. Z., Kurth-Nelson, Z., Dayan, P., & Dolan, R. J. (2017). Moral transgressions corrupt neural representations of value. *Nature Neuroscience*, *20*(6), 879–885.

Cui, F., Huang, X., Li, X., Liao, C., Liu, J., & Luo, Y. (2021). Moral conflict in economic decision making: The role of the anterior cingulate cortex—striatum pathway. *Cerebral Cortex*, *31*(11), 5121–5130.

Cui, F., Ma, N., & Luo, Y. (2016). Moral judgment modulates neural responses to the perception of other's pain: An ERP study. *Scientific Reports*, *6*(1), 1–8.

Curry, O. S. (2016). Morality as cooperation: A problem-centred approach. In *The evolution of morality* (pp. 27–51). Springer.

Curry, O. S., Mullins, D. A., & Whitehouse, H. (2019). Is it good to cooperate? Testing the theory of morality-as-cooperation in 60 societies. *Current Anthropology*, *60*(1), 47–69.

Dang, T. P., Mattan, B. D., Barth, D. M., Handley, G., Cloutier, J., & Kubota, J. T. (2022). Perceiving social injustice during arrests of Black and White civilians by White police officers: An fMRI investigation. *NeuroImage, 119153*.

Dang, T. P., Mattan, B. D., Kubota, J. T., & Cloutier, J. (2019). The ventromedial prefrontal cortex is particularly responsive to social evaluations requiring the use of person-knowledge. *Scientific Reports*, *9*(1), 1–11.

De Franca, D. X., & Monteiro, M. B. (2013). Social norms and the expression of prejudice: The development of aversive racism in childhood. *European Journal of Social Psychology*, *43*(4), 263–271.

De Heering, A., De Liedekerke, C., Deboni, M., & Rossion, B. (2010). The role of experience during childhood in shaping the other-race effect. *Developmental Science*, *13*(1), 181–187.

Delgado, M. R., Frank, R. H., & Phelps, E. A. (2005). Perceptions of moral character modulate the neural systems of reward during the trust game. *Nature Neuroscience*, *8*(11), 1611–1618.

Dunham, Y., Baron, A. S., & Banaji, M. R. (2008). The development of implicit intergroup cognition. *Trends in Cognitive Sciences*, *12*(7), 248–253.

Ellemers, N., & van Nunspeet, F. (2020). Neuroscience and the social origins of moral behavior: How neural underpinnings of social categorization and conformity affect everyday moral and immoral behavior. *Current Directions in Psychological Science*, *29*(5), 513–520.

Fiske, S. T., & Neuberg, S. L. (1990). A continuum of impression formation, from category-based to individuating processes: Influences of information and motivation on attention and interpretation. In *Advances in experimental social psychology* (Vol. 23, pp. 1–74). Elsevier.

Formanowicz, M., & Suitner, C. (2020). Sounding strange (r): Origins, consequences, and boundary conditions of sociophonetic discrimination. *Journal of Language and Social Psychology*, *39*(1), 4–21.

Gabay, A. S., Radua, J., Kempton, M. J., & Mehta, M. A. (2014). The Ultimatum Game and the brain: A meta-analysis of neuroimaging studies. *Neuroscience & Biobehavioral Reviews, 47*, 549–558.

Gaertner, S. L., Dovidio, J. F., Anastasio, P. A., Bachman, B. A., & Rust, M. C. (1993). The common ingroup identity model: Recategorization and the reduction of intergroup bias. *European Review of Social Psychology*, *4*(1), 1–26.

Gaither, S. E., Pauker, K., Slepian, M. L., & Sommers, S. R. (2016). Social belonging motivates categorization of racially ambiguous faces. *Social Cognition*, *34*(2), 97.

Goff, P. A., Eberhardt, J. L., Williams, M. J., & Jackson, M. C. (2008). Not yet human: Implicit knowledge, historical dehumanization, and contemporary consequences. *Journal of Personality and Social Psychology*, *94*(2), 292.

Greene, J. D., Nystrom, L. E., Engell, A. D., Darley, J. M., & Cohen, J. D. (2004). The neural bases of cognitive conflict and control in moral judgment. *Neuron*, *44*(2), 389–400.

Gu, X., Wang, X., Hula, A., Wang, S., Xu, S., Lohrenz, T. M., Knight, R. T., Gao, Z., Dayan, P., & Montague, P. R. (2015). Necessary, yet dissociable contributions of the insular and ventromedial prefrontal cortices to norm adaptation: Computational and lesion evidence in humans. *Journal of Neuroscience*, *35*(2), 467–473.

Gyurovski, I., Kubota, J., Cardenas-Iniguez, C., & Cloutier, J. (2018). Social status level and dimension interactively influence person evaluations indexed by P300s. *Social Neuroscience*, *13*(3), 333–345.

Hackel, L. M., Zaki, J., & Van Bavel, J. J. (2017). Social identity shapes social valuation: Evidence from prosocial behavior and vicarious reward. *Social Cognitive and Affective Neuroscience*, *12*(8), 1219–1228.

Han, X., Zhou, S., Fahoum, N., Wu, T., Gao, T., Shamay-Tsoory, S., Gelfand, M. J., Wu, X., & Han, S. (2021). Cognitive and neural bases of decision-making causing civilian casualties during intergroup conflict. *Nature Human Behaviour*, *5*(9), 1214–1225.

Hein, G., Silani, G., Preuschoff, K., Batson, C. D., & Singer, T. (2010). Neural responses to ingroup and outgroup members' suffering predict individual differences in costly helping. *Neuron*, *68*(1), 149–160.

Huart, J., Corneille, O., & Becquart, E. (2005). Face-based categorization, context-based categorization, and distortions in the recollection of gender ambiguous faces. *Journal of Experimental Social Psychology*, *41*(6), 598–608.

Hugenberg, K., Young, S., Rydell, R. J., Almaraz, S., Stanko, K. A., See, P. E., & Wilson, J. P. (2016). The face of humanity: Configural face processing influences ascriptions of humanness. *Social Psychological and Personality Science*, *7*(2), 167–175.

Hughes, B. L., Ambady, N., & Zaki, J. (2017). Trusting outgroup, but not ingroup members, requires control: Neural and behavioral evidence. *Social Cognitive and Affective Neuroscience*, *12*(3), 372–381.

Ito, T. A., & Urland, G. R. (2003). Race and gender on the brain: Electrocortical measures of attention to the race and gender of multiply categorizable individuals. *Journal of Personality and Social Psychology*, *85*(4), 616.

Johnson, K. L., Freeman, J. B., & Pauker, K. (2012). Race is gendered: How covarying phenotypes and stereotypes bias sex categorization. *Journal of Personality and Social Psychology*, *102*(1), 116.

Kable, J. W., & Glimcher, P. W. (2007). The neural correlates of subjective value during intertemporal choice. *Nature Neuroscience*, *10*(12), 1625–1633.

Kaltwasser, L., Hildebrandt, A., Wilhelm, O., & Sommer, W. (2016). Behavioral and neuronal determinants of negative reciprocity in the ultimatum game. *Social Cognitive and Affective Neuroscience*, *11*(10), 1608–1617.

Knoch, D., Nitsche, M. A., Fischbacher, U., Eisenegger, C., Pascual-Leone, A., & Fehr, E. (2008). Studying the neurobiology of social interaction with transcranial direct current stimulation—The example of punishing unfairness. *Cerebral Cortex*, *18*(9), 1987–1990.

Krosch, A. R., Tyler, T. R., & Amodio, D. M. (2017). Race and recession: Effects of economic scarcity on racial discrimination. *Journal of Personality and Social Psychology*, *113*(6), 892.

Krueger, F., & Meyer-Lindenberg, A. (2019). Toward a model of interpersonal trust drawn from neuroscience, psychology, and economics. *Trends in Neurosciences, 42*(2), 92–101.

Kubota, J. T., Banaji, M. R., & Phelps, E. A. (2012). The neuroscience of race. *Nature Neuroscience*, *15*(7), 940–948.

Kubota, J. T., & Ito, T. A. (2007). Multiple cues in social perception: The time course of processing race and facial expression. *Journal of Experimental Social Psychology*, *43*(5), 738–752.

Kubota, J. T., & Ito, T. (2017). Rapid race perception despite individuation and accuracy goals. *Social Neuroscience*, *12*(4), 468–478.

Kubota, J. T., Li, J., Bar-David, E., Banaji, M. R., & Phelps, E. A. (2013). The price of racial bias: Intergroup negotiations in the ultimatum game. *Psychological Science*, *24*(12), 2498–2504.

Latinus, M., & Belin, P. (2011). Human voice perception. *Current Biology*, *21*(4), R143–R145.

Levy, D. J., & Glimcher, P. W. (2012). The root of all value: A neural common currency for choice. *Current Opinion in Neurobiology*, *22*(6), 1027–1038.

Liberman, Z., Howard, L. H., Vasquez, N. M., & Woodward, A. L. (2018). Children's expectations about conventional and moral behaviors of ingroup and outgroup members. *Journal of Experimental Child Psychology*, *165*, 7–18.

Lowe, M. (2021). Types of contact: A field experiment on collaborative and adversarial caste integration. *American Economic Review*, *111*(6), 1807–1844.

Mattan, B. D., Barth, D. M., Thompson, A., FeldmanHall, O., Cloutier, J., & Kubota, J. T. (2020). Punishing the privileged: Selfish offers from high-status allocators elicit greater punishment from third-party arbitrators. *PloS One*, *15*(5), e0232369.

Mattan, B. D., Kubota, J. T., Dang, T. P., & Cloutier, J. (2018). External motivation to avoid prejudice alters neural responses to targets varying in race and status. *Social Cognitive and Affective Neuroscience*, *13*(1), 22–31.

Mattan, B. D., Wei, K. Y., Cloutier, J., & Kubota, J. T. (2018). The social neuroscience of race-based and status-based prejudice. *Current Opinion in Psychology*, *24*, 27–34.

McAuliffe, K., & Dunham, Y. (2016). Group bias in cooperative norm enforcement. *Philosophical Transactions of the Royal Society B: Biological Sciences*, *371*(1686), 20150073.

Meissner, C. A., & Brigham, J. C. (2001). Thirty years of investigating the own-race bias in memory for faces: A meta-analytic review. *Psychology, Public Policy, and Law*, *7*(1), 3.

Merritt, C. C., MacCormack, J. K., Stein, A. G., Lindquist, K. A., & Muscatell, K. A. (2021). The neural underpinnings of intergroup social cognition: An fMRI meta-analysis. *Social Cognitive and Affective Neuroscience*, *16*(9), 903–914.

Miller, J. G., & Bersoff, D. M. (1992). Culture and moral judgment: How are conflicts between justice and interpersonal responsibilities resolved? *Journal of Personality and Social Psychology*, *62*(4), 541.

Misch, A., Paulus, M., & Dunham, Y. (2021). Anticipation of future cooperation eliminates minimal ingroup bias in children and adults. *Journal of Experimental Psychology: General*, *50*(10), 2036–2056.

Møller, S. J., & Tenenbaum, H. R. (2011). Danish majority children's reasoning about exclusion based on gender and ethnicity. *Child Development*, *82*(2), 520–532.

Mousa, S. (2019). Building tolerance: Intergroup contact and soccer in post-ISIS Iraq. *Program on Governance and Local Development Working Paper*, *26*.

Ratner, K. G., & Amodio, D. M. (2013). Seeing "us vs. them": Minimal group effects on the neural encoding of faces. *Journal of Experimental Social Psychology*, *49*(2), 298–301.

Romano, A., Balliet, D., Yamagishi, T., & Liu, J. H. (2017). Parochial trust and cooperation across 17 societies. *Proceedings of the National Academy of Sciences*, *114*(48), 12702–12707.

Rotella, K. N., Richeson, J. A., Chiao, J. Y., & Bean, M. G. (2013). Blinding trust: The effect of perceived group victimhood on intergroup trust. *Personality and Social Psychology Bulletin*, *39*(1), 115–127.

Sangrigoli, S., Pallier, C., Argenti, A. M., Ventureyra, V. A., & de Schonen, S. (2005). Reversibility of the other-race effect in face recognition during childhood. *Psychological Science*, *16*(6), 440–444.

Shenhav, A., & Greene, J. D. (2014). Integrative moral judgment: Dissociating the roles of the amygdala and ventromedial prefrontal cortex. *Journal of Neuroscience*, *34*(13), 4741–4749.

Singh, B., Mellinger, C., Earls, H. A., Tran, J., Bardsley, B., & Correll, J. (2022). Does cross-race contact improve cross-race face perception? A meta-analysis of the cross-race deficit and contact. *Personality and Social Psychology Bulletin*, *48*(6), 865–887.

Stroessner, S. J. (1996). Social categorization by race or sex: Effects of perceived non-normalcy on response times. *Social Cognition*, *14*(3), 247.

Suzuki, S., & O'Doherty, J. P. (2020). Breaking human social decision making into multiple components and then putting them together again. *Cortex*, *127*, 221–230.

Tajfel, H. (1974). Social identity and intergroup behaviour. *Social Science Information*, *13*(2), 65–93.
Tajfel, H. (1982). Social psychology of intergroup relations. *Annual Review of Psychology*, *33*(1), 1–39.
Tajfel, H., Billig, M. G., Bundy, R. P., & Flament, C. (1971). Social categorization and intergroup behaviour. *European Journal of Social Psychology*, *1*(2), 149–178.
Tajfel, H., Turner, J. C., Austin, W. G., & Worchel, S. (1979). An integrative theory of intergroup conflict. *Organizational Identity: A Reader*, *56*(65), 9780203505984–16.
Telzer, E. H., Ichien, N., & Qu, Y. (2015). The ties that bind: Group membership shapes the neural correlates of in-group favoritism. *NeuroImage*, *115*, 42–51.
Tsoi, L., Dungan, J., Waytz, A., & Young, L. (2016). Distinct neural patterns of social cognition for cooperation versus competition. *NeuroImage*, *137*, 86–96.
Uslaner, E. M. (2008). Trust as a moral value. *The Handbook of Social Capital*, 101–121.
Vives, M.-L., Cikara, M., & FeldmanHall, O. (2022). Following your group or your morals? The in-group promotes immoral behavior while the out-group buffers against it. *Social Psychological and Personality Science*, *13*(1), 139–149.
Woo, P. J., Quinn, P. C., Méary, D., Lee, K., & Pascalis, O. (2020). A developmental investigation of the other-race categorization advantage in a multiracial population: Contrasting social categorization and perceptual expertise accounts. *Journal of Experimental Child Psychology*, *197*, 104870.
Yamagishi, T., & Mifune, N. (2016). Parochial altruism: Does it explain modern human group psychology? *Current Opinion in Psychology*, *7*, 39–43.
Yang, J., Zhang, H., Ni, J., De Dreu, C. K., & Ma, Y. (2020). Within-group synchronization in the prefrontal cortex associates with intergroup conflict. *Nature Neuroscience*, *23*(6), 754–760.
Young, L., Bechara, A., Tranel, D., Damasio, H., Hauser, M., & Damasio, A. (2010). Damage to ventromedial prefrontal cortex impairs judgment of harmful intent. *Neuron*, *65*(6), 845–851.
Zhan, Y., Xiao, X., Tan, Q., Zhang, S., Ou, Y., Zhou, H., Li, J., & Zhong, Y. (2019). Influence of self-relevance and reputational concerns on altruistic moral decision making. *Frontiers in Psychology*, *10*. www.frontiersin.org/articles/10.3389/fpsyg.2019.02194

PART IV

Moral emotions

PART IVA

A vision on moral emotions

13
A VISION (AND DEFINITION) OF MORAL EMOTIONS

Roger Giner-Sorolla

Psychological research on moral emotions has increased dramatically in the past 20 years. A recent Google Scholar search of sources with "psychology" or "psychological" in the title showed 14 uses of "moral emotions" in 2000 and 297 in 2020, an over twentyfold increase. This trend outstrips the near-fourfold rise in total articles in such outlets (from 16,170 in 2000 to 58,280 in 2020). More systematic bibliometry also confirms a 20-year rise in moral emotion themes, although other fields of moral psychology have risen even more dramatically (Ellemers et al., 2019).

My own research program bears witness to the transformative effect of the "moral emotions" Zeitgeist. After joining my first permanent position at the University of Kent, my research, inspired by many conversations with Jonathan Haidt during a postdoc at the University of Virginia, went in all directions: guilt and shame in self-control of personal habits and prejudice; expressions of guilt and shame in national-level apologies; the role of anger and disgust in reactions to seemingly harmless moral transgressions. Only a sudden insight in the mid-2000s, that these interests fell under the umbrella of moral emotions, allowed me to claim a coherent "branding" and move ahead with such projects as a book on moral emotions (Giner-Sorolla, 2013).

But what are these so-called moral emotions? Of course, "emotion" is a common term in psychology, but it has for decades resisted a single, agreed-upon definition (e.g., Russell, 2012 and others in that Special Issue). The term "morality" also covers some phenomena which are not universally agreed to be moral in nature: for example, moral domains such as authority or violations of norms that do not involve interpersonal harm. Indeed, the definition of morality is as much a problem in psychology as it is in philosophy (Schein & Gray, 2018; Gert & Gert, 2020). And the two can link up in many ways.

Most generally, any interface of emotions with morality might be labelled as moral emotion – effects on happy mood on fairness judgments, for example, or effects of moral character on anxiety. But such a broad scope does not define "moral emotion," any more than the existence of people in France who eat Swiss cheese help us define a "French cheese".

More narrowly, we might insist that the label cover any kind of emotion that only functions morally: that is, toward the good of other individuals, society, or the future self. However, few emotions fit this profile. Ellemers et al. (2019), for example, found the most studied moral emotions in psychology to be guilt, shame, and disgust. Of these, only guilt is purely moral, but arguably so: some self-control contexts of guilt are not morally relevant (Hofmann et al., 2018).

Shame can be felt about a failure of competence or social stigma, neither of which is a moral concern. Disgust can protect the self from disease, and anger and contempt can also be used for selfish reasons.

Some positive emotions do seem purely moral: sympathy involves caring for another's suffering (Stellar & Keltner, 2014); elevation involves observing a moral exemplar (Thomson & Siegel, 2017); and gratitude responds to feeling helped by promoting help for others (McCullough et al., 2001). But in my view, a definition of moral emotions that leaves out anger, disgust, and shame, would not fit present-day usage.

I prefer that "moral emotions" simply show major adaptations that **functionally support moral processes**. This definition is consistent with Haidt's (2003) influential analysis of moral emotions. Functions include upholding norms through action against those who break them (Haidt's "other-condemning" emotions: anger, disgust, contempt); inhibiting or punishing one's own misbehavior (Haidt's self-condemning emotions: guilt, shame, embarrassment); positively rewarding praise-worthy actions (Haidt's "other-praising" emotions: elevation, gratitude); and helping people in need (Haidt's "other-suffering" emotion, compassion).

Haidt (2003) proposed two criteria for a moral emotion: disinterested elicitor, and prosocial outcome. **Disinterest** derives from Haidt's expansive definition of morality: to count as moral, a concern should only extend beyond individual self-interest. It need not concern interpersonal harm, or follow Kantian rules such as being applied universally. Thus, getting angry about harm to the self is not moral, any more than being afraid is; but getting angry about harm to another person is.

Disinterest is particularly useful in answering how a moral emotion is different from a merely social emotion. For example, love involves another person. But as Haidt (2003) observes, love is less moral if contingent on mutual benefit, and more moral if it benefits the other at the expense of the self.

Disinterest also might explain why an obvious gap exists in the taxonomy of moral emotions: positive self-evaluative emotions such as pride. Sometimes, moral behavior might be reinforced by an entirely sincere self-congratulation. But the very concept is so suspiciously self-interested that we almost lack the language to speak of "moral pride" – only "authentic" as opposed to "hubristic" pride (Mercadante et al., 2021) which applies alike to moral and personal achievements.

The flexible nature of identification, however, challenges the criterion of disinterest. Witness the exchange between Cialdini (e.g., 1991) and Batson (e.g., Batson & Shaw, 1991) respectively doubting and upholding the disinterestedness of helping. Batson himself later turned this logic around to question the altruism of anger (Batson et al., 2007) – if we are most angry about wrongs to people we feel close to, is this disinterest? In social relations, identification with another includes them in the self (Aron et al., 1991). Thus, even emotions that benefit others do so by tying their interests to the joy or pain of the self. A functionally focused definition bypasses these paradoxes by hinging upon the outcome rather than process of an emotion. It is perfectly "moral" to adapt a self-interested process to a goal that ultimately benefits others.

Haidt's second criterion, **prosocial outcome**, also should be looked at functionally. As defined in Haidt (2003) these outcomes are action tendencies, chiefly helping and punishing. They are presented as collectively rational responses to appraisals that other people need help or punishment, respectively. However, my own integrative functional theory (IFT; Giner-Sorolla, 2013) builds on this insight but expands beyond it. IFT recognizes that appraisal-to-action sequences are only one function out of four that emotions serve. The others are association (of the emotion, directly to a stimulus); self-regulation (responding to the outcome of one's own action); and communication (signaling to others).

Of these, communication is perhaps the most important to understanding the full range of prosocial outcomes. Specifically, some emotions in Haidt's (2003) review, such as shame and contempt, lack dominant moral action outcomes. Rather, their moral function is to send a message. Shame's actions of self-abasement and avoidance, as well as its nonverbal signal, communicate a loss of social rank and desire for appeasement (Keltner & Harker, 1998), often in response to moral failings. Contempt likewise sends signals of disapproval about people who show negative character, including but not limited to moral character (Fischer & Giner-Sorolla, 2016).

As a whole, research on moral emotions is hard to survey, because it may not declare itself as "moral". Rather, it often arrives under the name of the emotion itself, connecting it to topics of moral interest such as prosocial acts, punishment, or social judgment. Studies, in fact, may encompass moral and non-moral contexts of the same emotion, which is perfectly legitimate by our expanded definition. However, I want to highlight two themes in research which are strongly worth following.

First, following on the important communication function, some scholars are investigating how expressions of moral emotions create an environment that upholds and enforces moral norms, even outside of cases where emotions directly provoke helping or punitive action. For example, emotions such as disgust or contempt can create indirect consequences for norm violators, where third parties are called upon to act, and more generally to spread the low reputation of the violator (e.g., Molho et al., 2017). At the same time, expressions of moral emotions can also enhance the reputation of the expresser, whether through outrage and disgust (Brady et al, 2020; Kupfer & Giner-Sorolla, 2017) or shame and guilt (Stearns & Parrott, 2012; Halmesvaara et al., 2020). Indeed, many functional theories of emotion expression highlight the management of reputation as an important goal (e.g., Morris & Keltner, 2001; Ross & Dumouchel, 2004; P. K. Smith & Magee, 2015).

Second, research on group-based moral emotions is of particular interest, although not always advertised with the "moral" label (Mackie & E. R. Smith, 2018). The group is relevant to moral emotions in at least two senses. Most obviously, members of a group such as a nation respond to moral emotions in relations with other groups, much as individuals use moral emotions in relations with other individuals. Thus, guilt, shame, morally motivated hostility, and positive moral emotions are all increasingly studied in response to the threats and opportunities for moral goals that other groups and one's own group present.

However, there is also a sense in which all group-based emotions are moral, in Haidt's expansive sense, because they bind group members together beyond individual self-interest. For example, even if existential threat to an individual is not moral, existential threat to a group raises intensely moral questions of how the group should act in response, not least with the protection of its future generations in mind (Hirschberger et al., 2016). Likewise, group-based pride may be judged as inappropriate when it takes a hubristic form (Salmela & Sullivan, 2022). But arguably, even when it leads to hostility toward other groups (e.g., de Figueiredo & Elkins, 2003), collective pride belongs to the moral realm, to the extent that such hostility is seen as protecting the interests of other ingroup members in a zero-sum situation (Amira et al., 2021).

To conclude, the scope of moral emotions ensures that they will continue to drive ideas and evidence on social relations, whether or not any scholars have the epiphany that they have become moral emotions experts. An implication of functional theory, too, is that the multiple functions and levels of moral emotions will continue to generate conflicts and raise provocative questions (Giner-Sorolla, 2013). For instance, the need to communicate a particular emotion toward a social goal can conflict with appraisals of what is actually going on; or well-established associations between sexual behaviors and disgust might be challenged by new appraisals. It is these conflicts between functions and a different social levels that have the most potential to generate thought-provoking explanations of many social dilemmas.

In closing, it is notable that the recent wave of moral psychology has been going strong for 20 years. However, much of this progress has been achieved within specific frameworks agreed upon as morally relevant, such as life-or-death dilemmas, prosocial economic decision-making, or punitive moral judgments. Moral psychology also needs to consider the philosophical scope of the field as a whole (e.g. Beal, 2020; and for a review of the interactions between philosophical and psychological definitions in historical and contemporary scholarship, see Stich, 2018). I hope that my above attempt to provide a pragmatic working definition of moral emotions will prove a useful contribution to this reconsideration.

References

Amira, K., Wright, J. C., & Goya-Tocchetto, D. (2021). In-group love versus out-group hate: Which is more important to partisans and when? *Political Behavior*, *43*(2), 473–494.

Aron, A., Aron, E. N., Tudor, M., & Nelson, G. (1991). Close relationships as including other in the self. *Journal of Personality and Social Psychology*, *60*(2), 241.

Batson, C. D., & Shaw, L. L. (1991). Evidence for altruism: Toward a pluralism of prosocial motives. *Psychological Inquiry*, *2*(2), 107–122.

Batson, C. D., Kennedy, C. L., Nord, L. A., Stocks, E. L., Fleming, D. Y. A., Marzette, C. M., ... & Zerger, T. (2007). Anger at unfairness: Is it moral outrage?. *European Journal of Social Psychology*, *37*(6), 1272–1285.

Beal, B. (2020). What are the irreducible basic elements of morality? A critique of the debate over monism and pluralism in moral psychology. *Perspectives on Psychological Science*, *15*(2), 273–290.

Brady, W. J., Crockett, M. J., & Van Bavel, J. J. (2020). The MAD model of moral contagion: The role of motivation, attention, and design in the spread of moralized content online. *Perspectives on Psychological Science*, *15*(4), 978–1010.

Cialdini, R. B. (1991). Altruism or egoism? That is (still) the question. *Psychological Inquiry*, *2*(2), 124–126.

de Figueiredo Jr, R. J., & Elkins, Z. (2003). Are patriots bigots? An inquiry into the vices of in-group pride. *American Journal of Political Science*, *47*(1), 171–188.

Ellemers, N., van der Toorn, J., Paunov, Y., & van Leeuwen, T. (2019). The psychology of morality: A review and analysis of empirical studies published from 1940 Through 2017. *Personality and Social Psychology Review*, *23*(4), 332–366. https://doi.org/10.1177/1088868318811759

Fischer, A., & Giner-Sorolla, R. (2016). Contempt: Derogating others while keeping calm. *Emotion Review*, *8*(4), 346–357.

Gert, B., & Gert, J. (2020). The definition of morality. Stanford Encyclopaedia of Philosophy, Fall 2020 edition. Retrieved from https://plato.stanford.edu/entries/morality-definition/

Giner-Sorolla, R. (2013). *Judging passions: Moral emotions in persons and groups*. Psychology Press.

Haidt, J. (2003). The moral emotions. In Davidson, R. J., Scherer, K. R., & Goldsmith, H. H., *Handbook of affective sciences* (pp. 852–870). Oxford University Press.

Halmesvaara, O., Harjunen, V. J., Aulbach, M. B., & Ravaja, N. (2020). How bodily expressions of emotion after norm violation influence perceivers' moral judgments and prevent social exclusion: A socio-functional approach to nonverbal shame display. *PloS One*, *15*(4), e0232298.

Hirschberger, G., Ein-Dor, T., Leidner, B. and Saguy, T. (2016). How is existential threat related to intergroup conflict? Introducing the Multidimensional Existential Threat (MET) Model. *Frontiers in Psychology*, *7*, 1877.

Hofmann, W., Meindl, P., Mooijman, M., & Graham, J. (2018). Morality and self-control: How they are intertwined and where they differ. *Current Directions in Psychological Science*, *27*(4), 286–291.

Keltner, D., & Harker, L. (1998). The forms and functions of the nonverbal signal of shame. In P. Gilbert & B. Andrews (Eds.), *Shame: Interpersonal behavior, psychopathology, and culture* (pp. 78–98). Oxford University Press.

Kupfer, T. R., & Giner-Sorolla, R. (2017). Communicating moral motives: The social signaling function of disgust. *Social Psychological and Personality Science*, *8*(6), 632–640.

Mackie, D. M., & Smith, E. R. (2018). Intergroup emotions theory: Production, regulation, and modification of group-based emotions. In *Advances in Experimental Social Psychology* (Vol. *58*, pp. 1–69). Academic Press.

McCullough, M. E., Kilpatrick, S. D., Emmons, R. A., & Larson, D. B. (2001). Is gratitude a moral affect?. *Psychological Bulletin*, *127*(2), 249–266.

Mercadante, E., Witkower, Z., & Tracy, J. L. (2021). The psychological structure, social consequences, function, and expression of pride experiences. *Current Opinion in Behavioral Sciences, 39*, 130–135.

Molho, C., Tybur, J. M., Güler, E., Balliet, D., & Hofmann, W. (2017). Disgust and anger relate to different aggressive responses to moral violations. *Psychological Science*, *28*(5), 609–619.

Morris, M. W., & Keltner, D. (2000). How emotions work: The social functions of emotional expression in negotiations. *Research in Organizational Behavior, 22*, 1–50.

Ross, D., & Dumouchel, P. (2004). Emotions as strategic signals. *Rationality and Society*, *16*(3), 251–286.

Russell, J. A. (2012). Introduction to special section: On defining emotion. *Emotion Review*, *4*(4), 337–337.

Salmela, M., & Sullivan, G. B. (2022). The rational appropriateness of group-based pride. *Frontiers in Psychology, 13:* 848644.

Schein, C., & Gray, K. (2018). The theory of dyadic morality: Reinventing moral judgment by redefining harm. *Personality and Social Psychology Review*, *22*(1), 32–70.

Smith, P. K., & Magee, J. C. (2015). The interpersonal nature of power and status. *Current Opinion in Behavioral Sciences, 3*, 152–156.

Stearns, D. C., & Parrott, W. G. (2012). When feeling bad makes you look good: Guilt, shame, and person perception. *Cognition & Emotion*, *26*(3), 407–430.

Stich, S. (2018). The quest for the boundaries of morality. In A. Zimmerman, K. Jones & M. Timmons (Eds.), *The Routledge handbook of moral epistemology* (pp. 15–37). Routledge.

Stellar, J. E., & Keltner, D. (2014). Compassion. In M. M. Tugade, M. N. Shiota, & L. D. Kirby (Eds.), *Handbook of positive emotions* (pp. 329–341). The Guilford Press.

Thomson, A. L., & Siegel, J. T. (2017). Elevation: A review of scholarship on a moral and other-praising emotion. *The Journal of Positive Psychology*, *12*(6), 628–638.

PART IVB

Empirical review chapters on moral emotions

14

THE INTRAPERSONAL LEVEL

Beyond contamination and disgust—the role of moral emotion in threat monitoring and moral judgment

Simone Schnall and Robert K. Henderson

Abstract

Accumulating evidence indicates that intrapersonal feelings and intuitions can causally influence moral condemnation of certain acts. The role of disgust has received a lot of research attention as a moral emotion related to physical wellbeing and disease avoidance. However, research has revealed a somewhat complex pattern of findings, which may be due to the methodological challenges of testing this link. Here we propose that the estimated (lack of) resources and capabilities to cope with immoral actions generally raises feelings of threat and anxiety. This results from an intrapersonal process of threat monitoring that takes stock of the social threats of immoral acts in the light of individual coping resources. When deficits are found, the threat experienced leads to greater condemnation of acts that are morally wrong. In other words, we suggest that emotions signaling high estimated cost of exposing themselves to moral harm make people especially intolerant of immoral actions.

- Judgments of right vs wrong not only result from rational deliberation: intrapersonal feelings and intuitions can causally influence moral condemnation of certain acts.
- Research has addressed the role of disgust as a moral emotion in relation to physical wellbeing and disease avoidance, as part of the Behavioural Immune System.
- The desire to avoid harm resulting in moral condemnation can be extended to the social domain.
- Harsh evaluations of moral transgressions in different domains relate to perceived risks due to old age and social exclusion.

Introduction

An extensive literature, by now spanning several decades and thousands of published articles, has demonstrated that a wide range of cognitive processes takes place in a relatively automatic, effortless and unconscious manner (for a review, see de Neys, 2021). Nevertheless, morality has long been treated as if it were exempt from such "irrational" forces (see also Conway, this volume; Everett, this volume). With moral judgments often being considered the pinnacle of human rationality, it is disconcerting to entertain the possibility that people might in fact rely on their feelings and intuitions when deciding between right and wrong. Indeed, for any legal system to work properly, assessments of wrongdoing and attributions of culpability need to follow from factual evidence, rather than being swayed by subjective concerns. The recognition that moral judgments and decisions may also occur on an automatic, effortless level, and therefore be guided by emotional responses that emerge outside of focal awareness, has become popular only fairly recently.

Moral emotions can be grouped into those that are focused on the self, and those that are focused on others (Tangney, Stuewig, & Mashek, 2007). The former include *shame*, *guilt* and *embarrassment*, and are experienced when people realise they violated a moral norm, and therefore feel bad about themselves (see Gausel, this volume). As a result, they are likely to modify their behaviour, in order to avoid experiencing those aversive emotions in the future. Other-focused emotions are elicited when evaluating the moral actions of others. They are positive when observing acts that are rule-abiding, prosocial and generally put the need of others before one's own (Algoe & Haidt, 2009). In particular, *gratitude* results from receiving a personal benefit from another person (e.g., Algoe, Haidt & Gable, 2008), while *moral elevation* results from witnessing someone act in a morally praiseworthy, selfless way toward someone else (e.g., Schnall, Fessler & Roper, 2010). On the negative side, other-focused moral emotions include *anger* and *disgust* when concluding that another person's actions are morally reprehensible because they violate societal norms. Here, we focus on the latter emotion, because it has been studied extensively, but the findings emerging in the literature are somewhat complex. We propose that while disgust can be central in judging which acts are right or wrong, other concerns about one's health and safety can equally influence moral judgments even if they do not involve feelings of disgust as such.

Research on moral disgust has grown out of attempts to delineate the role of quick intuition versus deliberative reason, which has been called a "turning point" in research in moral psychology (Ellemers, van der Toorn, Paunov, & van Leeuwen, 2019). This started with a seminal paper by Haidt (2001) outlining the *Social Intuitionist Model*, based on the primacy of automatic intuitions in shaping moral considerations. This view has its roots in moral philosophy, exemplified by the eighteenth-century philosopher David Hume, who famously proposed that reason plays a subordinate role to "the passions" (1739/1985). According to this idea, moral evaluations arise from quick emotional reactions, followed by rationalizations that involve generating reasons for that evaluation, even when such reasons may not be entirely plausible – or were not consciously deliberated ahead of time.

Going beyond views of morality as a set of abstract principles that philosophers can discern by theoretical analysis, intuition-based approaches suggest that morality deals with concrete concerns involving harm, exploitation, subversion, and betrayal, among other challenges to survival. That is, people are first and foremost interested in determining whether engaging with someone might constitute an opportunity for potential cooperation, or instead, a threat to one's physical safety. More specifically, people judge right and wrong relative to a core set of moral domains (Graham, Haidt, & Nosek, 2009): *Care* expects people to act on feelings of compassion and empathy, while condemning those who inflict harm or pain on others. *Fairness* promotes the goal of sharing resources equally among group members, and rejecting those who take more than they deserve, or cheat others. *Loyalty* grows out of the recognition that belonging to a community requires shared responsibility for joint outcomes, and not betraying the group's values. *Authority* concerns respect for hierarchies, and for one's own place in the social order of a community. Finally, *Purity* (also called *Sanctity*) suggests that the human body has immaterial and sacred value (e.g., the "body as a temple" in a God-given natural order). Thus, it needs to be safeguarded from physical and spiritual contamination, to avoid debasing or degrading the self. Central to the notion that there is a fixed set of moral foundations (whether those five, or others; for a recent update, see Atari et al., 2022), is the claim that there are a number of profound moral dimensions that go beyond the conscious reasoning processes that were long considered to form the basis of moral understanding (Kohlberg, 1970).

The Purity foundation, and related feelings of repulsion and disgust, has received considerable research attention. Due to its evolutionary function related to disease avoidance (Rozin, Haidt, & McCauley, 2008; Tybur, Lieberman, Kurzban, & DiScioli, 2013), disgust forms part of the so-called "Behavioural Immune System" (Murray & Schaller, 2016; Schaller, 2006). It is part of a constellation of cognitions, emotions, and behaviors that prompts the avoidance of contact with pathogens, parasites, and other forms of contamination that could compromise health and survival. For instance, the strongest disgust elicitors tend to be those that suggest that another person might be seriously ill (Curtis, de Barra, & Aunger, 2011). Indeed, one of the most critical risks involves the possibility of being in close contact with someone who may carry a communicable disease. Feeling disgusted therefore indicates to the person who is experiencing it that there is danger in the environment, with the relevant action tendency being avoiding, or withdrawing from the stimulus that elicits disgust: It is adaptive to stay away from things that could make you sick, or in an extreme case, could kill you.

Going beyond the concrete threat of contagious disease, it is also adaptive to stay away from someone who may be likely to violate social norms and act in ways that many people would agree to be immoral. Thus, it has been proposed that the scope of disgust, originally a basic emotion related to physical health, can be extended to the social domain. The experience of disgust might thus help to avert potential harm originating from other people's bad intentions, making moral transgressions emotionally repulsive (Rozin et al., 2008). In other words, feeling disgusted indicates that something, or someone, could pose a threat to key values in society. As the most direct test of the notion that feelings of physical disgust play a role in moral evaluations, research has experimentally manipulated disgust and asked participants to judge moral transgressions. This work will be reviewed next.

Disease threat, and inducing and reducing disgust

Early experimental procedures to elicit the experience of disgust included learned associations during hypnosis (Wheatley & Haidt, 2005), exposure to an offensive smell, a dirty work environment, a disgusting film clip, or recollection of a past event involving physical disgust (Schnall, Haidt, Clore, & Jordan, 2008), reading a disgusting sentence (e.g., biting into an apple with a worm inside; van Dillen, van der Waal, van den Bos, 2012), or the sound of someone vomiting (Seidel & Prinz, 2013). This and other work, has produced more and more evidence that physical disgust can also be applied to the social domain (Rozin et al., 2008).

However, it has become increasingly clear that the nature of this link is complex (for reviews, see Inbar & Pizarro, 2022; Schnall, 2017). Furthermore, it is not so easy to develop appropriate manipulations and measures, and the presence of moderating factors can make it difficult to draw unambiguous conclusions. First, disgust manipulations suffer from the same complications as any experimental mood induction: The affect needs to be strong enough to create the desired state, but also subtle enough to not make the true source of their feeling obvious to participants (Schnall, Haidt, Clore, & Jordan, 2015). Disgust, however, by its very nature, is an intense emotion that compels immediate action. An experimental induction that produces a very strong state of disgust increases the risk that participants become aware of the manipulation and discount its affective influence (Schwarz & Clore, 1983). One paper found evidence for precisely such a process (Kugler, Ye, Motro, & Noussair, 2020). Using virtual reality, participants were induced to feel either disgust, sadness or a neutral state. Disgusted participants reported less trust toward others and, as a behavioural measure, sent fewer funds in a trust game than those in the control conditions. These findings support the notion that disgust makes individuals more cautious about other people. Importantly, however, the effect of the disgust manipulation disappeared once participants' attention was drawn to the correct source of their disgust. Similarly, it makes sense that effects of disgust have only been observed when participants who had been administered a disgust manipulation actually reported feeling disgusted (Białek, Muda, Fugelsang, & Friedman, 2021). Thus, whether participants in fact experience disgust makes a difference. However, a subtle background state is required for effective mood manipulations (Schwarz & Clore, 1983), which may not be sufficient to elicit the strong, powerful emotion that characterizes disgust.

As an added complication, vignettes of moral transgressions, especially those violating the Purity dimension (e.g., eating a dead dog after it got hit by a car and died), often elicit very strong condemnation in and of themselves. This not only means that participants in ostensibly neutral conditions are also exposed to a description of a situation that induces disgust, but it is difficult to increase the level of disgust in the experimental condition above and beyond the state that the stimuli are already producing under control conditions. Resulting ceiling effects make it impossible to test mean differences between conditions (Schnall, 2014; Chapman & Anderson, 2014). In our work we found ceiling effects on several occasions for Purity assessments (Henderson & Schnall, 2021b). This happened even when we drew them from a set that was standardised to elicit responses in the mid-range of the scale (Clifford, Iyengar, Cabeza, & Sinnott-Armstrong, 2015). Similarly, when examining the raw data (osf.io/4kz32) of a replication attempt (Johnson et al., 2016) of Study 3 reported in Schnall et al. (2008), an excessive number of extreme scores (i.e., 7 on a scale from 1 to 7) is apparent, which suggests a ceiling effect that makes the replication inconclusive. Equally problematic, however, is to use stimuli involving morally neutral actions (e.g., reading a magazine belonging to someone else before returning it to them) (Jylkkä, Härkönen, & Hyönä, 2021). A disgust induction did not show an effect here, presumably because the stimulus had no moral valence to begin with. Finally, while most studies used moral transgressions (i.e., judging whether an action is wrong), some used sacrificial moral dilemmas involving a trade-off between utilitarian vs. deontological moral reasoning. In recent research (Białek et al., 2021) the moral condemnation effects relating to disgust were observed with the former, but not always with the latter stimuli. Thus, the choice of appropriate methods to operationalize the role of disgust can be quite challenging.

Recent research has made substantial progress in addressing some of the problems outlined above. Most importantly, to circumvent the possibility of ceiling effects, rather than attempting to experimentally *increase* disgust, Tracy, Steckler and Heltzel (2019) developed a manipulation to *decrease* it. To achieve this, they administered pills containing ginger, an antiemetic known to reduce nausea. Their logic was that a reduced gut feeling of disgust might attenuate moral condemnation. A first study established that ingestion of ginger had the intended effect, in that it reduced disgust reported in response to images of spoilt food, mutilated bodies and other elicitors of physical repulsion. Further studies were conducted to test the key hypothesis that reducing the experience of disgust would influence moral condemnation. These studies showed that compared to participants who had received a placebo pill, those who had ingested a ginger pill showed less strict moral judgments toward Purity violations, provided these were of moderate, rather than high severity.

Finally, a range of moderating variables have been identified, which complicates the interpretation of prior findings. These have included private body consciousness (Schnall et al., 2008; Tracy et al., 2019), attentional control (Van Dillen, van der Waal, van den Bos, 2012), emotional differentiation (Cameron, Payne, & Doris, 2013), mindfulness (Sato & Sugiura, 2014), disgust sensitivity (Ong, Mullette-Gillman, Kwok, & Lim, 2014) and psychological distance (van Dijke, van Houwelingen, De Cremer, & De Schutter, 2018). Unfortunately, a meta-analysis of studies on the role of disgust on moral judgments (Landy & Goodwin, 2015) only examined main effects. Thus, it disregarded the moderators that had been documented in the literature up until that point, which makes it difficult to draw conclusions about the true magnitude of hypothesized effects.

In an attempt to get around the complexities of experimental disgust inductions, we made concerns about contamination and physical threat salient without inducing disgust itself. This work investigated whether subjectively perceived danger related to the novel coronavirus (SARS-CoV-2) in the early days of the COVID-19 pandemic would be associated with condemnation of immoral acts. We examined this in US samples, recruited during the first wave of the pandemic. Here, individuals who were highly worried about catching COVID-19 delivered harsher moral judgements than those who were less worried. This was the case for transgressions covering all five moral foundations, all of which were unrelated to COVID-19 itself. This included Harm (e.g., laughing at a friend's dad being the janitor), Fairness (e.g., bribing a landlord to get one's apartment repainted), Loyalty (e.g., leaving the family business to go work for the main competitor), Authority (e.g., a star player ignoring her coach's order during a game), and Purity (e.g., urinating in the pool at an amusement park). Importantly, this finding remained robust when controlling for political orientation, a relevant confound given that in the US in 2020 there was a growing partisan divide regarding level of worry about the ongoing pandemic (Conway, Woodard, Zubrod, & Chan, 2021). We interpret this to suggest that raising concerns about physical health and safety renders moral infractions to appear more threatening than they would be otherwise. As such this is a real-life confirmation of experimental findings showing that when threat of disease is made salient, participants subsequently deliver harsher moral judgments relative to participants in a neutral condition (Murray, Kerry, & Gervais, 2019).

Beyond disgust and the behavioral immune system: threat monitoring

So far we have argued that disgust functions as an aspect of the Behavioral Immune System that is geared toward preventing contamination and contagious disease, and can exert a causal influence on abstract moral judgments relating to a range of moral concerns. Even though research to examine this reasoning has been subject to various methodological challenges, it has yielded some supporting evidence. Extending the link between the Behavioral Immune System and morality, we suggest that in making moral judgments, people not only are influenced by concerns about their physical health but other challenges as well. That is, when in a position where coping resources are relatively low, it is prudent to be highly sensitive to any potential wrongdoers because they would constitute a further threat. Indeed, anticipated moral condemnation—negative affective judgment of a conspecific's behavior—serves a crucial role in inhibiting unethical behaviour because people care deeply about maintaining positive moral reputations, and are responsive to expressions of disapproval and reputation devaluation (Fehr, 2004; Vonasch et al., 2018; Wu, Balliet, & Van Lange, 2016). We therefore suggest people condemn potential transgressors all the more harshly when they feel ill-equipped to protect themselves against them (see Figure 14.1).

Supporting this idea, research we conducted showed that moral condemnation is amplified in response to threats beyond the concerns covered by the Behavioural Immune System, or feelings of disgust. So far we found evidence for this conjecture with respect to old age and its accompanying risks (Henderson & Schnall, in preparation), and thwarted fundamental social needs as a consequence of social exclusion (Henderson & Schnall, 2021a, 2021b). Overall we propose that people constantly evaluate the extent to which threats across a range of domains are present, not just regarding physical contamination. When in doubt about their ability to expose themselves to such threat, people err on the side of condemning action that may reflect an individual's harmful intentions. Importantly, we propose that this is a *domain-general* process, such that a threat in a given domain (e.g., social exclusion) increases condemnation not only of transgressions related to that domain (e.g., someone being mean to another person) but also transgressions covering the entire spectrum of the moral foundations described above.

To further test this general idea, we assessed people's propensity to take into account their coping resources in the face of a different type of threat to their physical health. For this purpose, we focused on participants' biological age as an indicator of threat/coping resources, and related this to their evaluations of moral wrongdoers. We did so on the assumption that old age coincides with a decrease in physical strength, and older adults are generally more vulnerable and thus face greater risks in their environment. Therefore they should condemn moral transgressors more harshly than younger adults because they would be ill-equipped to guard themselves against such individuals. We presume the underlying variable to be people's subjective perception of their own preparedness to deal with moral transgressors.

To test the hypothesis that older adults would deliver harsher moral verdicts, as well as a potential mechanism for this effect, an online study indicated that the relationship between age and moral disapproval across the five moral foundations was mediated by risk perception: Older adults were more sensitive to physical risks than younger adults, which in turn was associated with stricter moral judgments. Indeed, moral wrongdoers pose a potential physical risk, and thus older adults may be motivated to condemn them more harshly in order to deter potential danger. The process of threat monitoring therefore is broader than the concerns covered by the Behavioural Immune System, and resulting feelings of disgust.

We also examined the age-morality hypothesis in two large different datasets: the European Social Survey (ESS) and the World Values Survey (WVS). The ESS contains representative samples from 30 European countries, surveyed biannually between 2002 to 2018. For each of the nine rounds, age was associated with stricter moral views about Authority—we tested this foundation specifically because relevant items were included in the ESS. Importantly, we controlled for political orientation, alongside other demographic variables, and the effect remained robust. Going beyond WEIRD countries, we found a similar effect for Fairness—the items available in the dataset—when analyzing the WVS, comprising data from more than 100 countries around the world, collected between 1981 and 2019. Because the latest wave of the WVS (2017–2019) included additional questions involving Harm and Purity concerns, we examined this specific wave in more detail. Again we replicated the earlier finding, with older adults judging those transgressions to be less acceptable than younger adults. Because the pattern was the same across different waves covering many years we can rule out the presence of a generational effect, i.e., effects being due to differences across different birth cohorts.

In addition to physical challenges such as disgust and old age, we expanded our investigation to a threat that does not fall directly into the domain of physical health, namely a lack of social connection. Indeed, social relationships are so crucial for survival that the pain of having been rejected by others activates the same neural substrates as physical pain (Eisenberger & Lieberman, 2003). Moreover, physical self-preservation and social belonging have been characterized as "central goals" for human survival (Dickerson & Kemeny, 2004). Because of the critical importance of having close social relationships (as opposed to being left out), we hypothesized that challenges to social acceptance in the form of social exclusion would strengthen disapproval of moral wrongdoers. In two studies we found an indirect effect, such that participants who had been

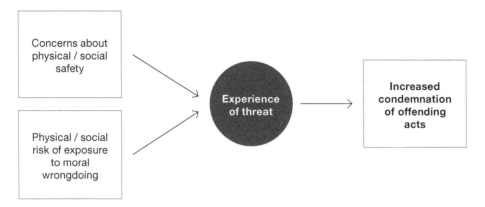

Figure 14.1 Experience of threat.

excluded while playing an interactive game reported a reduced sense of their fundamental social needs being met, which in turn was associated with stricter judgements toward moral wrongdoers. Furthermore, in a correlational study, we found that social anxiety, which is typically thought to be a warning signal of threat that can potentially undermine one's social relationships, showed a substantial relationship with moral condemnation ($r = .43$). This finding suggest that a perceived threat to the extent to which one can rely on a social network, can fortify judgements of moral wrongdoing. In sum, individuals who acutely experience, or are chronically attuned to having their social needs unmet, are more sensitive to potential moral transgressions.

These findings extend theoretical contributions concerning influences on moral considerations beyond disgust as a consequence of physiological challenges to health. That is, beyond infections and illnesses, other risk including aging and senescence as well as thwarted fundamental social needs likewise fortify moral judgements. In short, threats to crucial resources of various kinds appear to activate stricter assessments of moral wrongdoing.

Better safe than sorry

The Behavioural Immune System has been proposed to follow what has been termed the "smoke detector principle" (Nesse, 2005): A false positive error (e.g., alarm in response to burnt toast) is far less serious than a false negative error (failing to activate in response to a severe fire). In the latter case as a negative consequence some mental and physical effort might have been expended unnecessarily, while in the latter case one's very survival could be at stake. Many bodily and behavioral responses adhere to this pattern, such as pronounced pain, inflammation, nausea, anxiety, and fear in response to the uncertain possibility of challenges to health and safety (Nesse & Schulkin, 2019). Thus, if an individual has contact with a potentially dangerous predator, a possibly deadly toxin, or a moral transgressor, then fleeing from the animal, avoiding contact with the contaminant, or expressing disapproval toward the offense is more adaptive than failing to execute those actions. In other words, natural selection shaped mechanisms that regulate defensive systems on the principle of "better safe than sorry", which means the organism is more likely to overreact than to underreact in response to even the slightest possibility of physical or social danger. Feelings of disgust (as a consequence of exposure to contaminants), anxiety (as a consequence of thwarted social needs), and other emotions that arise as a consequence of potential threats instill increased moral vigilance to avoid additional dangers from wrongdoers.

We similarly propose that in the process of threat monitoring, an implicit mental accounting of the relative costs and benefits of overestimating the dangers posed by a moral wrongdoer, versus underestimating, the costs of the former greatly outweigh the costs of the latter when one's ability to cope is already compromised. This, however, is an assumption that awaits empirical testing. To confirm our notion of threat monitoring in the context of making moral judgments, it will be important for future research to ask participants to report on their cost-benefit analysis involving subjectively perceived risks relative to available coping resources. Similarly, it will be useful to directly measure feelings beyond disgust that might reflect a threat response, in particular anxiety. Individual differences with respect to coping resources are likely to also be relevant, with some participants considering the same situation a threat, while others consider it a challenge (Blascovich & Mendes, 2010). Overall, just as has been shown with effects of disgust on moral judgment, it is likely that the precise process of threat monitoring will turn out to be complex.

References

Algoe, S. B., & Haidt, J. (2009). Witnessing excellence in action: The 'other-praising' emotions of elevation, gratitude, and admiration. *The Journal of Positive Psychology, 4*(2), 105–127.

Algoe, S. B., Haidt, J., & Gable, S. L. (2008). Beyond reciprocity: gratitude and relationships in everyday life. *Emotion, 8*(3), 425–429.

Atari, M., Haidt, J., Graham, J., Koleva, S., Stevens, S. T., & Dehghani, M. (2022, March 4). Morality beyond the WEIRD: How the nomological network of morality varies across cultures. https://doi.org/10.31234/osf.io/q6c9r

Białek, M., Muda, R., Fugelsang, J., & Friedman, O. (2021). Disgust and moral judgment: Distinguishing between elicitors and feelings matters. *Social Psychological and Personality Science, 12,* 304–313.

Blascovich, J., & Mendes, W. B. (2001). Challenge and threat appraisals. In *Feeling and thinking: The role of affect in social contagion* (pp. 59–82). Cambridge: Cambridge University Press.

Cameron, C. D., Payne, B. K., & Doris, J. M. (2013). Morality in high definition: Emotion differentiation calibrates the influence of incidental disgust on moral judgments. *Journal of Experimental Social Psychology, 49,* 719–725.

Chapman, H. A., & Anderson, A. K. (2014). Trait physical disgust is related to moral judgments outside of the purity domain. *Emotion, 14,* 341–348.

Clifford, S., Iyengar, V., Cabeza, R., & Sinnott-Armstrong, W. (2015). Moral foundations vignettes: A standardized stimulus database of scenarios based on moral foundations theory. *Behavior Research Methods, 47,* 1178–1198.

Conway, L. G., Woodard, S. R., Zubrod, A., & Chan, L. (2021). Why are conservatives less concerned about the coronavirus (COVID-19) than liberals? Comparing political, experiential, and partisan messaging explanations. *Personality and Individual Differences, 183,* 111–124.

Curtis, V., de Barra, M., & Aunger, R. (2011). Disgust as an adaptive system for disease avoidance behaviour. *Philosophical Transactions of the Royal Society of London. Series B, Biological Sciences, 366,* 389–401.

De Neys, W. (2021). On dual- and single-process models of thinking. *Perspectives on Psychological Science, 16,* 1412–1427.

Dickerson, S. S., & Kemeny, M. E. (2004). Acute stressors and cortisol responses: a theoretical integration and synthesis of laboratory research. *Psychological Bulletin, 130,* 355–391.

Eisenberger, N. I., Lieberman, M. D., & Williams, K. D. (2003). Does rejection hurt? An fMRI study of social exclusion. *Science, 302*(5643), 290–292.

Ellemers, N., van der Toorn, J., Paunov, Y., & van Leeuwen, T. (2019). The psychology of morality: A review and analysis of empirical studies published from 1940 through 2017. *Personality and Social Psychology Review, 23,* 332–366.

Fehr, E. (2004). Don't lose your reputation. *Nature, 432,* 449–450.

Graham, J., Haidt, J., & Nosek, B. A. (2009). Liberals and conservatives rely on different sets of moral foundations. *Journal of Personality and Social Psychology, 82,* 1029–1046.

Haidt, J. (2001). The emotional dog and its rational tail: A social intuitionist approach to moral judgment. *Psychological Review, 108,* 814–834.

Henderson, R. K., & Schnall, S. (in preparation). Older age is associated with fortified moral judgments.
Henderson, R. K., & Schnall, S. (2021a). Disease and disapproval: COVID-19 concern is related to greater moral condemnation. *Evolutionary Psychology, 19*, 14747049211021524.
Henderson, R. K., & Schnall, S. (2021b). Social threat indirectly increases moral condemnation via thwarting fundamental social needs. *Scientific Reports, 11*, 1–11.
Hume, D. (1739/1985). *A treatise of human nature*. London: Penguin Classics.
Inbar, Y., & Pizarro, D. A. (2022). How disgust affects social judgments. *Advances in Experimental Social Psychology, 65*, 109–166.
Johnson, D. J., Wortman, J., Cheung, F., Hein, M., Lucas, R. E., Donnellan, M. B., Ebersole, C. R., & Narr, R. K. (2016). The effects of disgust on moral judgments: Testing moderators. *Social Psychological and Personality Science, 7*, 640–647.
Jylkkä, J., Härkönen, J., & Hyönä, J. (2021) Incidental disgust does not cause moral condemnation of neutral actions. *Cognition and Emotion, 35*, 96–109.
Kohlberg, L. (1970). Education for justice: A modern statement of the Platonic view. In T.R. Sizer and N.F. Sizer (Eds.), *Moral education: Five lectures* (pp. 56–83). Cambridge, MA: Harvard University Press.
Kugler, T., Ye, B., Motro, D., & Noussair, C. N., (2020). On trust and disgust: Evidence from face reading and virtual reality. *Social Psychological and Personality Science, 11*, 317–325.
Landy, J. F., & Goodwin, G. P. (2015). Does incidental disgust amplify moral judgment? A meta-analytic review of experimental evidence. *Perspectives on Psychological Science, 10*, 518–536.
Murray, D. R., Kerry, N., & Gervais, W. M. (2019). On disease and deontology: Multiple tests of the influence of disease threat on moral vigilance. *Social Psychological and Personality Science, 10*, 44–52.
Murray, D. R., & Schaller, M. (2016). The behavioural immune system: Implications for social cognition, social interaction and social influence. *Advances in Experimental Social Psychology, 53*, 75–129.
Nesse, R. M. (2005). Natural selection and the regulation of defenses: A signal detection analysis of the smoke detector principle. *Evolution and Human Behavior, 26*, 88–105.
Nesse, R. M., & Schulkin, J. (2019). An evolutionary medicine perspective on pain and its disorders. *Philosophical Transactions of the Royal Society B, 374*, 20190288.
Ong, H. H., Mullette-Gillman, O. A., Kwok, K., & Lim, J. (2014). Moral judgment modulation by disgust is bi-directionally moderated by individual sensitivity. *Frontiers in Psychology, 5*, 194.
Rozin, P., Haidt, J., & McCauley, C. R. (2008). Disgust. In M. Lewis & J. M. Haviland (Eds.), *Handbook of emotions* (3rd ed., pp. 757–776). New York: Guilford Press.
Sato, A., & Sugiura, Y. (2014). [Dispositional mindfulness modulates automatic transference of disgust into moral judgment]. *Shinrigaku Kenkyu: The Japanese Journal of Psychology, 84*, 605–611.
Schaller, M. (2006). Parasites, behavioral defenses, and the social psychological mechanisms through which cultures are evoked. *Psychological Inquiry, 17*, 96–101.
Schnall, S. (2014). Clean data: Statistical artifacts wash out replication efforts. *Social Psychology, 45*, 315–317
Schnall, S. (2017). Disgust as embodied loss aversion. *European Review of Social Psychology, 28*, 50–94.
Schnall, S., Haidt, J., Clore, G. L., & Jordan, A. H. (2008). Disgust as embodied moral judgment. *Personality and Social Psychology Bulletin, 34*, 1096–1109.
Schnall, S., Haidt, J., Clore, G. L., & Jordan, A. H. (2015). Landy and Goodwin (2015) confirmed most of our findings, then drew the wrong conclusions. *Perspectives on Psychological Science, 10*, 537–538.
Schnall, S., Roper, J., & Fessler, D. M. (2010). Elevation leads to altruistic behavior. *Psychological Science, 21*(3), 315–320.
Schwarz, N., & Clore, G. L. (1983). Mood, misattribution, and judgments of well-being: Informative and directive functions of affective states. *Journal of Personality and Social Psychology, 45*, 513–523.
Seidel, A., & Prinz, J. (2013). Sound morality: Irritating and icky noises amplify judgments in divergent moral domains. *Cognition, 127*, 1–5.
Tangney, J. P., Stuewig, J., & Mashek, D. J. (2007). Moral emotions and moral behavior. *Annual Review of Psychology, 58*, 345–372.
Tracy, J. L., Steckler, C. M., & Heltzel, G. (2019). The physiological basis of psychological disgust and moral judgments. *Journal of Personality and Social Psychology, 116*, 15–32.
Tybur, J. M., Lieberman, D. Kurzban, R., & DiScioli. P. (2013). Disgust: Evolved function and structure. *Psychological Review, 120*, 65–84.

van Dijke, M., van Houwelingen, G., De Cremer, D., & De Schutter, L. (2018). So gross and yet so far away: Psychological distance moderates the effect of disgust on moral judgment. *Social Psychological and Personality Science, 9*, 689–701.

van Dillen, L. F., van der Wal, R. C., & van den Bos, K. (2012). On the role of attention and emotion in morality: Attentional control modulates unrelated disgust in moral judgments. *Personality and Social Psychology Bulletin, 38*, 1222–1231.

Vonasch, A. J., Reynolds, T., Winegard, B. M., & Baumeister, R. F. (2018). Death before dishonor: Incurring costs to protect moral reputation. *Social Psychological and Personality Science, 9*, 604–613.

Wheatley, T., & Haidt, J. (2005). Hypnotic disgust makes moral judgments more severe. *Psychological Science, 16*, 780–784.

Wu, J., Balliet, D. & Van Lange, P. A. (2016) Gossip versus punishment: The efficiency of reputation to promote and maintain cooperation. *Scientific Reports 6*, 23919.

15
THE INTERPERSONAL LEVEL
What is shame? Shame as a relational network of emotion-experience

Nicolay Gausel

Abstract

Shame is a complex emotion. It involves an activation of the self through violation of internalized moral norm. It also involves criticism of self by the self and the risk of criticism of the self by imagined or real others – in addition to be a motivator for action. In this chapter, I will discuss the combination of these elements while addressing issues currently debated within shame literature, such as 'guilt versus shame', how to understand 'shaming' and 'moral failure versus competence failure'. I will discuss a growing controversy on whether shame promotes defensive, anti-social motivations or pro-social, approach motivations. I will discuss if shame can be defined, and how it can be measured. This is followed by some practical implications. Finally, I will suggest directions ahead for shame researchers and encourage a view of moral emotions as an integrated process where appraisals, feelings and responses interact in a relational network.

- The subjective experience of shame should be understood within a combined relational network of appraisals, feelings and responses.
- Shame cannot be experienced if the self is not activated, or if there is no self.
- In the shame experience, the activated self will take action to cope with the violation of internalized moral norm and the criticism that follow from it.
- Individuals reporting shame for apparently non-moral reasons (e.g., competence failure) describe the failure in moral terms when encouraged to explain why it was a failure.
- Understanding the dynamics of the shame experience can have profound practical implications, since it can have pro-social, self-reformatory potential.

Introduction

As 2009 begun, I was finalizing my PhD thesis on shame and how to best understand its pro-social potential, when an Austrian court case received attention of international media. An elderly man had imprisoned his daughter for 24 years, raped and enslaved her, murdering seven infants he had fathered with her. Concurrently, he maintained his social image or façade as a moral person. Expert psychiatrists following the court case argued 'people like him' could not experience moral emotions, such as shame. And indeed, they appeared to be right as the elderly man would enter court holding up a blue folder covering his face, remaining silent throughout the court hearings except from when he refused to plead guilty. However, approaching the end of court hearings they played the videotape of his daughter's testimony. The court then noticed the elderly man was crying and in a low tone asking for permission to address the court. To everyone's surprise (including the expert psychiatrists) he admitted that he felt *shameful* for his misdeeds. Realizing his failures could not be undone, he reassured the court he could only look for ways to make amends and offer restitution. He then declared he would unconditionally accept the verdict. The following day he entered court *without* hiding his face.

I will return to this example later in this chapter when I address a core controversy in shame research, but before I can get to that, I will address five shared agreements within the literature on shame. Following this, I will highlight some current issues with shame research. Then, I will address some controversies in shame research using the example above. Towards the end, I will discuss whether shame can be defined, and how it can be measured, followed by some practical suggestions. Finally, I will suggest some directions ahead for shame researchers.

Shame and shared agreements

Shame and the activation of the self. It's been known for more than hundred years that the self is the acting agent in the shame-experience (e.g., Smith, 1915). One can now say with confidence that the shame experience is *about* the self (e.g., Tangney & Dearing, 2002) and *cannot be experienced* if the person does not appraise the self as being activated (Gausel & Leach, 2011; Lewis, 1971). Consequently, whatever leads to shame being felt, *the self must somehow be implicated*, whether this is on an intrapersonal level (Lewis, 1971; Lickel et al., 2014; Tangney, 1991), interpersonal level (Gausel et al., 2016; Løkkeberg et al., 2021) or group-level (Gausel et al., 2012; Gausel & Brown, 2012; Lickel et al., 2005). Said easily, and this is important to understand; *there can be no shame if the self is not activated or if there is no self.* By such, there is agreement that shame is a *self-related* emotion that is experienced when the self is activated (see Figure 15.1).

Shame and violation of internalized, moral norms. What activates the self in response to shame? The most straightforward answer is appraised violation of an *internalized* moral norm (Lewis, 1971). I underline internalized, as the norm must be an integrated part of the self for the self to appraise it has violated something (Gausel, 2013). Naturally, if the individual is unaware of the norm, or is aware but has not internalized it, the individual cannot be expected to feel ashamed for violating it. This is likely the reason for why someone is 'shameless'; they have not internalized the norm that others think should have been internalized. Someone experiencing shame therefore report they have failed to live up to internalized moral norm or have violated such a norm (e.g., Ferguson et al., 2007; Gausel & Leach, 2011). Consequently, as shame is felt due to the self being activated by the failure to live up to internalized moral norms (see Figure 15.1), shame is seen as belonging to the group of *moral* emotions.

Shame and unpleasant criticism. There is great consensus that the word 'shame' is used to verbalize an unpleasant emotional experience (Smith, 1915; Levin, 1971; for a review, see Gausel & Leach, 2011; Tangney & Dearing, 2002). It can vary in intensity, but mainly, the experience of unpleasantness manifest itself via two forms of criticism: Either in terms of *self-criticism* or in terms of *social-criticism* (see Figure 15.1 for an illustration of how criticism fuels back into the activated self).

Interpersonal level: what is shame?

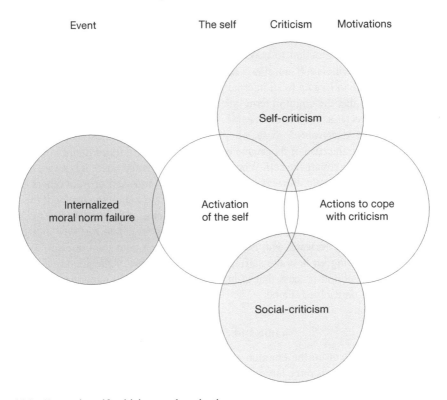

Figure 15.1 Event, the self, criticisms and motivations.

In regard of *self-criticism*, shame can involve milder forms of self-criticism (Gausel et al., 2016), more serious forms of self-directed anger (Smith et al., 2002; Tangney, 1991; Tangney et al., 1992), to the most intense forms of self-directed hostility (Lewis, 1971) and disgust (Giner-Sorolla & Espinosa, 2011) making it so severe it becomes unbearable (Rustomjee, 2009). Whatever the intensity of the criticism, the common agreement is that shame involves an inner judgemental verdict criticizing one's self and its integrity (Gausel & Leach, 2011). Thus, shame belongs to the group of *self-critical* emotions.

The other form of criticism involved with shame is *social-criticism*. This is the subjective concern that others might find out about the moral failure and thus condemn (Gausel & Leach, 2011) and criticize one for it (Tangney et al., 1996; Eriksson et al., 2021). The condemning others can be an imagined other (Lewis, 1971) or an imagined internal audience made up of unspecified others, specified others or oneself (Gausel, 2013). It can also be anticipated condemnation from real others (Gausel & Leach, 2011). Whatever the source of condemnation, the failure of the shameful individual is publicly exposed (Smith et al., 2002) inviting social aversion (Van Kleef, et al., 2015) and social criticism (Gausel & Leach, 2011) effectively barring the violator from continued belongingness with others (Gausel, 2013). Depending on the degree of norm violation, anger (Gausel et al., 2018; Van Kleef et al., 2015), violence (Retzinger, 1991) and murder (Rustomjee, 2009) might be inflicted upon the violator, in addition to more formalized social criticism such as physical exclusion through imprisonment (Tangney et al., 2014). Due to the severe implications of being socially criticized, shame is sometimes referred to as a *social* emotion.

Shame as a motivator for action. There is shared agreement across the emotion literature that shame is a self-related, moral emotion that is closely associated with criticism motivating the shameful individual to take action to cope with the criticism they experience, whether this is self-criticism or social-criticism (Gausel & Leach, 2011; Tangney & Dearing, 2002). Figure 15.1 illustrates how a failure to live up to an internalized moral norm activates the self in a directional network. You can see that the emotion term 'shame' is not present in the model. This is because *the model is 'shame'* as far as the literature agree. Therefore, I call this model *'The agreed network of the relational shame-experience'*. As seen in this visual representation, something self-relevant must have happened. In the case of the shame experience, an internalized moral norm must have been violated in order to activate the self. When the self has been activated, it is aware of what has happened. At this exact moment, the self receives criticism from it-self or from others (imagined or real) for having violated a norm. Following this, the self takes action to cope with the criticism (note; inaction is also action). You can see the different elements of the model overlap each other in a directional pattern. This is because the different elements operate *together* in a combined relational network moving forward with actions meant to cope with the criticism, followed by renewed actions depending on how the self appraises the success of the action taken. It is this renewed network of emotion-process that is the continued emotional experience of shame that does not go away: the unresolved shame.

Shame and current issues

Having a shared agreement on the emotion-experience of shame has helped the field of moral emotions to embark on at least three larger issues.

Is shame only about failure of morality? There is increasing empirical support to argue shame can be felt in the aftermath of non-moral failures in addition to moral ones. For instance, already in 2002, Smith et al. found incompetence to be strongly linked with shame, and shame to be more associated with non-moral experiences than moral. Somewhat similar to this, de Hooge et al. have repeatedly demonstrated that competence-related failures elicit shame (e.g., 2008, 2010, 2018), and Løkkeberg et al. (2021) recently demonstrated how shame arose from failure in interpersonal communication. That non-moral failures are associated with the experience of shame is drawing increased attention from scholars within the shame-literature. Due to this current issue, one might ask if non-moral failures make shame a non-moral emotion? It is valuable to remember that we have known for more than 50 years that individuals reporting shame for apparently non-moral reasons (such as failing on a practical task) describe the failure in moral terms when encouraged to explain *why* it was a failure (Lewis, 1971). Thus, I personally try focus not so much on the act of failure, but more on how the failure is appraised (Gausel & Leach, 2011).

Shaming? Another topic addressed in the literature on moral emotions is the process of being humiliated and shamed, and whether this can be used as a tool to prevent individuals within a society from violating morality (Braithwaite, 1989). Shaming is typically understood as a *social process* where someone who are higher in status and power inflict psychological pain upon a norm-violator through social humiliation (Braithwaite, 1989). The common argument is that shaming done 'properly' will get people 'back in line' so to speak (Ahmed et al., 2001) and thus, encourage the norm-violator to start feeling the shame they seemed to lack in the first place (Taylor, 2013). However, this reasoning has little empirical support (Harris, 2006) leading to exhortations against shaming as it seems to motivate aggression, not shame (Gausel, 2013; Åslund et al., 2009). Instead of shaming, it is encouraged to forgive (Ahmed & Braithwaite, 2005) and reassure the transgressor of acceptance and belongingness (Gausel, 2013); elements that are a key in making people want to change who they are (Rogers, 1961).

Shame and guilt: Two different emotion processes, or the same thing? Shame and guilt have received the attention of scholars in moral emotions for decades (Jones, 1910; Leach, 2017). Personally, I find it hard to understand why these two emotions weighted up against each other have received so much attention. If I should guess why, I would say that the debate has evolved out of a function of living and doing research within a cultural, religious context while ignoring the impact of this cultural, religious context. One might notice that most researchers focusing on guilt belong to the catholic culture where guilt is key emotion to be expressed after failure and repair come in the form of making amends through acts of moral repair-behaviour (these same researchers typically advocate that one should separate the self from its behaviour so the behaviour can be condemned[1]). In contrast, most researchers focusing on shame belong to the protestant culture where shame is key emotion to be expressed after failure and repair comes in the form of – not acts of moral repair-behaviour – but in repairing the defective self through psychological self-reform.

Nevertheless, various (sometimes conflicting) understandings of the differences (and similarities) between the two emotions have been proposed. For instance, Lewis (1971) proposed a difference in the intrapsychological positioning of the self in response to guilt and shame-experiences, while Tangney and Dearing (2002) proposed a difference based on foci. Others point to a possible difference based on private versus public awareness of failure (Smith et al., 2002). However, despite all attempts to disentangle the two, shame and guilt seems to be resisting a definitive separation in empirical investigations (Gausel & Leach, 2011; Leach, 2017) – even though there are indications that the self is *less active* in guilt than in shame (Gausel & Leach, 2011; Tangney & Dearing, 2002) and that correlations between the two seems to diminish on a group-level making an empirical disentanglement of the two more outspoken (e.g., Gausel & Brown, 2012, Gausel et al., 2012). Taken together, the topic of shame and guilt as different or not welcomes great debate in the current literature on moral emotions.

Shame and controversies

Even though there are agreements within shame research, work on shame is not without controversies. As theorizing and research move forward new understandings will surface causing controversy when they challenge the 'zeitgeist'. Typically, advocates of 'zeitgeist' will accept alterations to established knowledge but resist and even warn a set-back if these new views are adopted.

Shame: Anti-social or pro-social? Perhaps the greatest controversy per now is the theoretical view originating around 2006–2011 explaining *why* shame is an unpleasant, yet adaptive emotion promoting *self-reform* through pro-social approach and contrite repair motivations (e.g., Gausel 2006, 2009; Gausel & Leach, 2011; for an alternative approach based on *maintenance* of positive self-view see; de Hooge et al., 2008, 2010). This self-reformatory, adaptive view contrasts the prevailing understanding of shame as a maladaptive, self-defensive emotion. That shame was theorized to be a maladaptive, self-defensive emotion gained popularity around late 1980s to mid-1990s, and grew out of a clinical-social movement where shame was understood as a responsible for considerable intrapersonal and interpersonal tumult due to an array of self-defensive and anti-social motivations (e.g., Lewis, 1992; Tangney, 1991; Tomkins, 1987; Retzinger, 1991; Scheff, 1994).

In introductory example, both views are in play. *In support of the maladaptive, self-defensive view* the elderly man engages in at least three different defensive strategies: First, he literally covers his face with a folder. Second, he refuses to accept responsibility for immorality. Third, he remains muted. *In support of the adaptive, pro-social view*, we can observe at least four different pro-social strategies: First, there is admittance of responsibility. Second, there is admittance of immorality. Third, there is expressions of contrition. Fourth, there are declarations of wanting to make amends and restitution. As the example provides both self-defence *and* pro-sociality, the question arise: Which is caused by shame? The answer is evident. When self-defence is used there is no expression of 'shame' or any other emotions. However, when 'shame' *is* expressed, pro-sociality *is* expressed. In fact, the following day after expressing 'shame' he no longer covered his face.

This example, which is not unusual, challenge the view of shame as a maladaptive, self-defensive emotion. Currently, the theoretical view of shame as a maladaptive, anti-social emotion cannot explain the pro-sociality following the expression of shame in this example – even though some might say that the elderly man is using the wrong term to express his feelings and had he known the 'correct' emotion term he would have used 'guilt' (or 'regret' for that matter). Alternatively, some would say shame in this example is muddled with guilt, and had it been a 'guilt-free shame' there would be only self-defence in this example. In contrast, advocates of shame as an adaptive emotion promoting pro-social approach and contrite repair motivations (e.g., Gausel & Leach, 2011) would say these words *would typically* be spoken by a shameful individual following acceptance of a self-related moral failure. Moreover, they would provide empirical support to back it up (e.g., Berndsen & Gausel, 2015; de Hooge et al., 2008, 2010; 2018; Gausel & Brown, 2012; Gausel et al., 2012, 2016, 2018; Leach & Cidam, 2015; Lickel et al., 2014; Løkkeberg et al., 2021; Shepherd et al., 2013; Tangney et al., 2014).

There is reason to believe the controversy of shame being either an anti-social or a pro-social emotion is likely to continue, but it is worth observing that a long-standing and influential scholar on moral emotions has begun debating the pro-social, self-reformatory potential of shame (Tangney et al., 2014). That said, what view will prevail in this controversy is for the future to unveil.

Shame and unresolved questions

Shame is an unusually complex emotional experience that carries with it many unresolved questions in which I will address two of them in this chapter: Can shame be defined? How can shame be measured?

Can shame be defined? If the answer is 'yes' to this question one would find oneself in good company. There are plenty of theorists on shame offering their definition. Depending on who one consult one is likely to find something that will fit one's taste (Gausel, 2014). The reason for the various definitions is likely due to limitations in fully understanding what an emotion is (Russel & Barrett, 1999; Frijda, 1986) not to say what shame is (Gausel & Leach, 2011). That said, we know something about shame after more than 100 years of research: As shown in this chapter there is agreement that when people report they feel 'shame' they *typically also* report their self being activated, that they have violated an internalized moral norm, and they experience unpleasantness due to self-criticism, and they are motivated to do something (even inaction is action as something is likely going on inside the person, see Lewis, 1971). Other than this there is little agreement (Gausel, 2014).

Contrasting the tendency to define 'shame' as having a singular, consistent and uniform meaning, shame researchers (and emotion-oriented researchers alike) can approach the shame-experience as a relational network of appraisals, feelings and responses (Gausel, 2014; Gausel & Leach, 2011; Gausel et al., 2012, 2016, 2018, Løkkeberg et al., 2021). This basically means opening boundaries between different scientific fields to draw from each other's knowledge to better understand the complexity of the shame-experience. With this network approach one can synthesize relational patterns (Smith & Kirby, 2009) in structural models (e.g., Gausel et al., 2012, 2016; 2018; Løkkeberg et al., 2021) to investigate how individuals activate their self (or 'ego') to appraise a self-relevant situation involving goal relevance (Lazarus, 1991), such a failing to live up to a moral norm. Depending on how the self is activated through appraisals of a situation and goal relevance, one is far better equipped to understand people's subjective use of emotion words (Foucault, 1982; Siemer et al., 2007) and subsequent motivations (Gausel & Leach, 2011; Gausel, 2014). Naturally, this relational network approach is more complex than believing emotions to have a singular, consistent and uniform meaning, but the up-side is that one can actually start to understand what people mean when they decide to use an emotion term such as 'shame' (Gausel & Leach, 2011; Gausel, 2014).

How to measure shame? The above discussion paves way to a related unresolved question: How should we measure shame? If we leave the topic of definition aside, one might notice that almost all research on shame relies on *acknowledged* and *verbalized* shame; whether this is investigated with qualitative or quantitative methods. It is important to account for acknowledged, verbalized shame and I too use this approach (after all, it is the verbalization of 'shame' that appear in the introductory example and by such help us identify a shame-experience). However, I must admit that I am not so impressed by myself that I can identify an acknowledged, verbalized emotion term within its semantic context (Davidson, 1967).

In recent years, I have therefore come to believe that verbalized shame is just the tip of the iceberg in the shame-experience; the final stage when the cat is out of the bag so to speak. I firmly believe that *much* is going on inside of us before we reach the level of processing where we can identify and verbalize emotional distress with a specific emotion-term. Actually, Helen Block Lewis (1971) focused more on this level of internal processing than she did on acknowledged, verbalized shame (or guilt), labelling the internal non-verbalized processual emotion operation as 'unidentified shame' and 'bypassed shame' (and so does Retzinger, 1991 and Scheff, 1994). Personally, I believe June Tangney's influential research on shame with the TOSCA (Tangney et al., 1991) to be somehow tapping into these unacknowledged, non-verbalized aspects of shame. I have noted that Tangney's research relies on scenarios and various descriptions of oneself in meeting with these scenarios (but not using acknowledged emotion terms such as 'shameful'). I sometimes wonder if this is one possible path ahead *if* one avoids the temptation to pre-define shame (and guilt), rather utilizing a relational network approach to the *whole* emotion-experience of the shame-process. In this way, one can track so much more than just acknowledged, verbalized emotion terms, and perhaps open up Lewis' (1971) approach to the processual experience of shame? At least, that would be an attempt to have a look underwater to see what's under the verbalized tip of the 'shame-berg'.

Shame: important practical implications

Can there be a practical application of the knowledge we have of moral emotions, such as shame? Yes. One application is to understand how failures of the self gradually influence the individual as unrepaired failures accumulate over time. Another application is to understand how moral norms are internalized on a subjective level.

Failures of the self. If there is an *acknowledged* violation of a moral norm (e.g., lying), then the norm has already been internalized. This will activate the self. The activated self will appraise the moral failure as a specific failure of the self (Gausel & Leach, 2011). Since a *specific* failure moral failure does not pose an overwhelming threat to one's self-image (one is still helpful, generous, funny etc.,) the failure of the self can be repaired (Leach & Cidam, 2015). The self-criticism of shame will therefore motivate the norm-violator to address the failure and repair it (e.g., apologize and start telling the truth from now on) (Gausel & Leach, 2011). If this is achieved, the self is reformed as the failure is mended. Naturally, some failures are graver than others and will more heavily impact the self-image but it is still a specific failure. This experience of specific moral failure and shame is equivalent to what we can term 'non-clinical shame' (or 'everyday-shame', some might also call it; 'having a bad conscience').

However, people can violate *additional* moral norms before they have managed to repair the previous failure. They have now two (or more) specific failures threating their self-image as a moral person. Two or more failures can be dealt with, but it's harder to reform and repair than only one. Moreover, the self-criticism of shame is still active from previous failure. Accumulating amounts of unrepaired failures will likely move the shameful individual towards more intense forms of self-criticism. This emotion-experience of accumulating unrepaired moral failures and shame is equivalent to what we can term 'borderline-clinical shame' where a growing feeling of inferiority begin to appear.

If there are too many moral failures to handle, the individual appraises their self-image as a total failure, as globally defective (Gausel & Leach, 2011). At this stage, self-reform and repair is believed to be impossible. Overwhelmed by the sheer number of failures (and the criticism that goes with each one of these failures), the previously active self becomes inactive. As the self is no longer active, the emotional experience of shame vanish, and with it, the motivation to address failures vanish. This leaves the individual with little less option than to withdraw (Leach & Cidam, 2015). It is in this stage that the feeling of inferiority will dominate instead of shame (Gausel & Leach, 2011), and with it, self-directed hostility and disgust will hammer the person to the ground. This emotion-experience of overwhelming amounts of unrepaired moral failures and a globally defective, inactive self with a dominating feeling of inferiority is equivalent to what many will recognize as 'clinical shame'.

Internalized moral norms. Norms and moral norms exist. But so does people and cultures. As people travel to other cultures or meet other cultures online, their understanding of norms will begin to change. Some people will internalize new norms or they will alter existing norms. Others will not yet know of a norm or they feel it doesn't apply to them and their culture. Through this interactive norm exchange, the norm-based self will start to change. Some norms will be internalized, some will be abandoned, while others will not even exist. This is normal. Hence, a helper may be advised to remember that norms change over time and across cultures (Sandholtz, 2007), and that our own moral standards count only for ourselves, not for others, and not for our clients.

It is therefore wise to understand that people will *only* think there has been a norm violation *if* they have internalized the moral norm (Gausel, 2013). There can be many reasons for a norm not to be internalized, but it is good to remember that some people will appraise a norm-violation whereas others will not. Consequently, a professional helper should resist the temptation to transfer their own moral norms onto their clients or judge moral transgressors. Instead, helpers should try to create an environment of trust where their clients can express their emotion-experience without the risk of condemnation (e.g., Rogers, 1961) as condemning or shaming someone for norm violations *will not help*. Shaming people does not lead to the internalization of norms and it does not lead to a perpetrator feeling ashamed. If anything, it leads to social pleasing due to fears of rejection (Gausel, 2013), and rejection is the motivator behind all sorts of anti-social responses, including violence and murder (Gausel & Leach, 2011).

Conclusion

Where do we go from now? My answer is that researchers on shame and other moral emotions join efforts and rest disagreements. Where we disagree, we disagree but we should continue to pursue the emotion-experience of shame together not against one another. We have shared agreements that should unite us. It is my hope that we may start view moral emotions, such as 'shame', as an integrated, cognition-emotion process where appraisals, feelings and responses interact in a relational network. This calls for an acknowledgment of shame (and other emotions) as a complex emotion-experience where definitions become obsolete, where emotions words are not detached from the semantic context providing it with meaning (Davidson, 1967), where we address shame as being more than just an acknowledged, verbalized tip of the iceberg, and where we finally remove boundaries between different scientific fields so we can start draw from a pool of accumulated knowledge to better understand the complexity of moral emotions.

Note

1 In my eyes, this is an invention coming from psychological therapy that does not correspond with reality. That is, reality in the sense of how a society operate. A society would see a failure as belonging to the individual and not as separated from the individual. This is why people are sentenced to prison for their actions (i.e., their failures). It is not their actions being sentenced to prison; it is the person itself, the self. Personally, I think it is misleading to try to separate the self from its action. This is because our actions are ours. If I try to condemn the action pretending the self is not producing the action, I will not only do the person wrong by releasing them from their responsibility, but the self will be affected regardless as the self has in fact produced the action which is being condemned.

References

Ahmed, E., & Braithwaite, J. (2005). Forgiveness, shaming, shame and bullying. *Australian & New Zealand Journal of Criminology*, *38*(3), 298–323.
Ahmed, E., Harris, N., Braithwaite, J., & Braithwaite, V. (2001). *Shame management through reintegration*. Cambridge, UK: Cambridge University Press.
Åslund, C., Starrin, B., Leppert, J., & Nilsson, K. W. (2009). Social status and shaming experiences related to adolescent overt aggression at school. *Aggressive Behavior: Official Journal of the International Society for Research on Aggression*, *35*(1), 1–13.
Berndsen, M & Gausel, N. (2015). When majority members exclude ethnic minorities: The impact of shame on the desire to object to immoral acts. *European Journal of Social Psychology. 45*, 728–741. doi: 10.1002/ejsp.2127
Braithwaite, J. (1989). *Crime, shame and reintegration*. Cambridge, UK: Cambridge University Press.
Davidson, D. (1967). Truth and Meaning, *Synthese*, *17*, 304–323. doi: 10.1007/BF00485035
De Hooge, I. E., Breugelmans, S. M., & Zeelenberg, M. (2008). Not so ugly after all: when shame acts as a commitment device. *Journal of Personality and Social Psychology*, *95*(4), 933.
De Hooge, I. E., Breugelmans, S. M., Wagemans, F. M., & Zeelenberg, M. (2018). The social side of shame: Approach versus withdrawal. *Cognition and Emotion*, *32*(8), 1671–1677.

De Hooge, I. E., Zeelenberg, M., & Breugelmans, S. M. (2010). Restore and protect motivations following shame. *Cognition and Emotion*, *24*(1), 111–127.

Eriksson, K., Strimling, P., Gelfand, M., Wu, J., Abernathy, J., Akotia, C. S., ... & Van Lange, P. A. (2021). Perceptions of the appropriate response to norm violation in 57 societies. *Nature Communications*, *12*(1), 1–11.

Ferguson, T. J., Brugman, D., White, J., & Eyre, H. L. (2007). Shame and guilt as morally warranted experiences. In: J.L. Tracy, R.W., Robins and J.P. Tangney (Eds) *The self-conscious emotions: Theory and research*, 330–348.

Foucault, M. (1982). The subject and power. *Critical Inquiry*, *8*, 777–795.

Frijda, N. H. (1986). *The emotions*. Cambridge, UK: Cambridge University Press

Gausel, N. (2006). *Gravity keeps my head down, or is it maybe shame? The effects of Essence and Reputation in Shame on defensive responses, blame and pro-social emotions*. MSc in Psychology Thesis, University of Sussex

Gausel, N. (2009). *Uncovering the pro-social potential of shame with a differentiated model of shame-related appraisals and feeling"*. DPhil in Psychology Thesis, University of Sussex, ID: 506802.

Gausel, N. (2013). Self-reform or self-defense? Understanding how people cope with their moral failures by understanding how they appraise and feel about their moral failures. In M. Moshe & N. Corbu. (Eds.), *Walk of shame*. (pp. 191–208). Hauppauge, NY, USA: Nova Publishers

Gausel, N. (2014). What does "I feel ashamed" mean? avoiding the pitfall of definition by understanding subjective emotion language. In K. G. Lockhart (Ed.) *Psychology of Shame: New Research*. (pp. 157–166). Hauppauge, NY: Nova Publishers

Gausel, N., & Brown, R. (2012). Shame and guilt—Do they really differ in their focus of evaluation? wanting to change the self and behavior in response to ingroup immorality. *Journal of Social Psychology, 152*, 547–567. https://doi.org/10.1080/00224545.2012.657265

Gausel, N., & Leach, C. (2011). Concern for self-image and social image in the management of moral failure: Rethinking shame. *European Journal of Social Psychology, 41*, 468–478. https://doi.org/10.1002/ejsp.803

Gausel, N., Leach, C. W. Mazziotta, A., & Feuchte, F. (2018). Seeking revenge or seeking reconciliation? How concern for social-image and felt shame helps explain responses in reciprocal intergroup conflict. *European Journal of Social Psychology, 48*, 62–72. doi: 10.1002/ejsp.2295

Gausel, N., Leach, C., Vignoles, V., & Brown, R. (2012). Defend or repair? Explaining responses to in-group moral failure by disentangling feelings of shame, rejection, and inferiority. *Journal of Personality and Social Psychology, 102*, 941–960. https://doi.org/10.1037/a0027233

Gausel, N., Vignoles, V. L., & Leach, C. W. (2016). Resolving the paradox of shame: Differentiating among specific appraisal-feeling combinations explain pro-social and self-defensive motivation. *Motivation and Emotion, 40*, 118–139. https://doi.org/10.1007/s11031-015-9513-y

Giner-Sorolla, R., & Espinosa, P. (2011). Social cuing of guilt by anger and of shame by disgust. *Psychological Science, 22(1)*, 49–53. https://doi.org/10.1177/0956797610392925

Harris, N., (2006). Reintegrative shaming, shame, and criminal justice. *Journal of Social Issues, 62*, 327—346.

Jones, E. (1910). Psycho-analysis and education. *Journal of Educational Psychology, 1*(9), 497.

Lazarus, R. S. (1991). *Emotion and adaption*. New York: Oxford University Press.

Leach, C. W. (2017). Understanding shame and guilt. In *Handbook of the psychology of self-forgiveness* (pp. 17–28). Cham: Springer.

Leach, C.W., & Cidam, A. (2015). When is shame linked to constructive approach orientation? *Journal of Personality and Social Psychology, 109* (983–1002), https://doi.org/10.1037/psps0000037983

Levin, S. (1971). The psychoanalysis of shame. *International Journal of Psycho-Analysis, 52*, 355–362.

Lewis, H. B. (1971). *Shame and guilt in neurosis*. New York: International Universities Press

Lewis, M. (1992). *Shame. The exposed self*. New York: The Free Press.

Lickel, B., Kushlev, K., Savalei, V., Matta, S., Schmader, T., & Desteno, D. (2014). Shame and the motivation to change the self. *Emotion, 14(6)*, 1049–1061. https://doi.org/10.1037/a0038235.

Lickel, B., Schmader, T., Curtis,M., Scarnier,M.,& Ames, D. R. (2005).Vicarious shame and guilt. *Group Processes and Intergroup Relations, 8*, 145–157. https://doi.org/10.1177/1368430205051064.

Løkkeberg, S.T, Gausel, N., Giner-Sorolla, R., & Leach, C.W. (2021). Risking the social bond: Motivations to defend or to repair when dealing with displeasing information. *Current Psychology*. doi: https://doi.org/10.1007/s12144-021-01678-8

Retzinger, S. M. (1991). *Violent emotions: Shame and rage in marital quarrels*. Thousand Oaks, CA:Sage Publications.

Rogers, C. R. (1961). The process equation of psychotherapy. *American Journal of Psychotherapy, 15*(1), 27–45.

Russell, J. A., & Barrett, L. F. (1999). Core affect, prototypical emotional episodes, and other things called emotion: Dissecting the elephant. *Journal of Personality and Social Psychology, 76*(5), 805–819. https://doi.org/10.1037/0022-3514.76.5.805

Rustomjee, S. (2009). The solitude and agony of unbearable shame. *Group Analysis, 42*(2), 143–155.

Sandholtz, W. (2007). *Prohibiting plunder: How norms change*. New York: Oxford University Press.

Scheff, T. J. (1994). *Microsociology. Discourse, emotion, and social structure*. Chicago, London: The University of Chicago Press.

Shepherd, L., Spears, R., & Manstead, A. S. (2013). The self-regulatory role of anticipated group-based shame and guilt in inhibiting in-group favoritism. *European Journal of Social Psychology, 43*(6), 493. https://doi.org/10.1002/ejsp.1971

Siemer, M., Mauss, I., & Gross, J. J. (2007). Same situation – Different emotions: How appraisals shape our emotions. *Emotion, 7*(3), 592–600. https://doi.org/10.1037/1528-3542.7.3.592

Smith, C. A., & Kirby, L. D. (2009). Putting appraisal in context: Toward a relational model of appraisal and emotion. *Cognition and Emotion, 23*(7), 1352–1372.

Smith, R. H., Webster, J. M., Parrott, W. G., & Eyre, H. L. (2002). The role of public exposure in moral and nonmoral shame and guilt. *Journal of Personality and Social Psychology, 83*(1), 138.

Smith, T. L. (1915). Note on the psychology of shame. *The American Journal of Psychology, 26*(2), 229–235. https://www.jstor.org/stable/1413252

Tangney, J. P. (1991). Moral affect: The good, the bad, and the ugly. *Journal of Personality and Social Psychology, 61*, 598–607. doi: 10.1037/0022-3514.61.4.598.

Tangney, J. P. & Dearing, R. L. (2002). *Shame and guilt*. New York: Guildford.

Tangney, J. P., Stuewig, J., & Martinez, A. G. (2014). Two faces of shame: The roles of shame and guilt in predicting recidivism. *Psychological Science, 25*(3), 799–805.

Tangney, J. P., Wagner, P., Fletcher, C., & Gramzow, R. (1992). Shamed into anger? The relation of shame and guilt to anger and self-reported aggression. *Journal of Personality and Social Psychology, 62*(4), 669.

Tangney, J. P., Wagner, P. E., Gavlas, J., & Gramzow, R. (1991). *The test of self-conscious affect for adolescents (TOSCA-A)*. Fairfax, VA: George Mason University.

Tangney, J. P., Wagner, P. E., Hill-Barlow, D., Marschall, D. E., & Gramzow, R. (1996). Relation of shame and guilt to constructive versus destructive responses to anger across the lifespan. *Journal of Personality and Social Psychology, 70*(4), 797.

Taylor, G. (2013). Shame, integrity, and self-respect. In Dignity, character, and self-respect (pp. 157–178). New York: Routledge.

Tomkins, S. S. (1987). *Shame*. New York: The Guilford Press.

Van Kleef, G. A., Wanders, F., Stamkou, E., & Homan, A. C. (2015). The social dynamics of breaking the rules: Antecedents and consequences of norm-violating behavior. *Current Opinion in Psychology, 6*, 25–31.

16
THE INTRAGROUP LEVEL
Moral emotions, empathy, and acceptance of others as ingroup members—a social neuroscience perspective

Eric J. Vanman

Abstract

Emotions that we associate with morality appear to become more intractable when groups are involved. Guilt, shame, and disgust can impede acceptance of others as part of our group. I review three research projects that used social neuroscience methods to investigate group moral emotions. The first investigated disgust's role when people become stigmatized because of their weight. A second line of research examined collective guilt in both a minimal group paradigm and a context with historical transgressions, and demonstrated how guilt and shame about an ingroup's actions can be quickly learned but also varied across people. A third line of research examined schadenfreude and counter-empathy, showing increased empathy for group members' actions but also retaliatory responses to expressions of glee from an outgroup. In all three cases, our research focused on the intragroup level—how group members respond to others who ostensibly should be part of the collective "we."

- Moral emotions (guilt, shame, disgust, schadenfreude) are critical drivers of intragroup processes, such as acceptance and inclusion.
- Neuroscientific and physiological methods (i.e., ERPs, fMRI, EMG) have been used to detect reactions to moral emotions, over and beyond the classical self-report.
- Moral disgust is often accompanied by the idea that the person eliciting the emotion is not worthy of consideration as fully human.
- P300 can reliably index collective guilt, even though this may not be a very intense emotion.
- Expressions of schadenfreude, typically investigated at the interpersonal and intergroup level, might also be informative of intragroup processes since they affect ingroup identification and intragroup responses.
- Moral group responses affect how we perceive our group members, including processes that increase group cohesion and others that reduce it. In this way, they are fundamentally connected to the problem of accepting people into society.

Intragroup level: moral emotions, empathy, and acceptance

Introduction

Just like every other facet of our social lives, emotions play a crucial role in our interactions with others who are group members. Whether it is the shared joy of our team's success in the championship game, the shared sadness when members of our community are afflicted with a debilitating virus, or pride when a member of the group succeeds beyond our wildest dreams, our connections to others as group members yield the same sorts of emotional reactions that occur when such events happen to us as individuals. Likewise, emotions associated with morality, such as guilt, shame, and disgust, can be elicited by others because of their group memberships. In this chapter, I review research from my laboratory investigating such group moral emotions using self-report and social neuroscience methods. Specifically, I discuss the roles of moral disgust, collective guilt and anger, and schadenfreude in group contexts, which largely examine these responses at the intragroup level. Figure 16.1 provides an overall representation of the eliciting conditions, moral

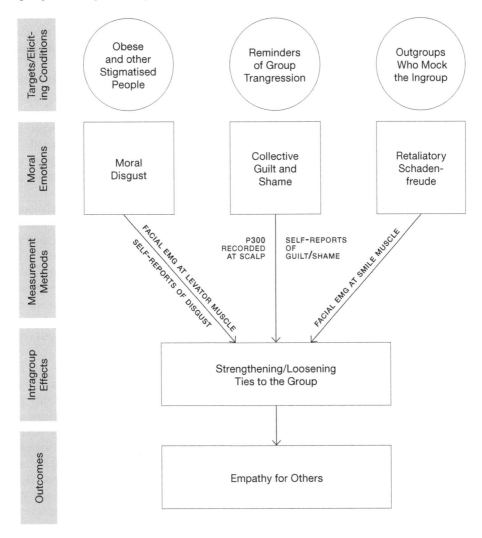

Figure 16.1 Moral group responses.

emotions, and effects on the group that my research group has investigated. As I will argue, moral emotions may impede our acceptance of others as part of our group. I thus also argue for an essential remedy to accepting others based on their group memberships—empathy.

Disgust

In the past two decades, researchers have found that the emotion of disgust appears to be associated with specific groups and group members (Hodson et al., 2013; Taylor, 2007). Although disgust likely has its functional origins in distaste (i.e., the avoidance of toxins in food), for many animals, including humans, disgust evolved to help defend organisms from bacteria and viruses (Curtis et al., 2011). Yet, for humans, disgust is also associated with avoiding people who violate social and moral norms (Giner-Sorolla et al., 2018; Tybur et al., 2009). Those people who intentionally harm children, for example, will often be viewed as disgusting and will be avoided by others and perhaps sanctioned with ostracism or even criminal charges. Other members of society who reliably elicit disgust include drug addicts, smokers, politicians, and homeless people (Vartanian, 2010). Such moral disgust is often accompanied by thoughts that the person eliciting the emotion is not worthy of consideration as fully human (Vartanian et al., 2021).

Obesity is another common elicitor of disgust because it involves impurity and moral violations (Lieberman et al., 2012). Notably, efforts to reduce prejudice toward obese people by changing cognitive beliefs (e.g., about the controllability of body weight) tend to be ineffective in reducing negative attitudes and stereotypes (Daníelsdóttir et al., 2010) because the obesity stigma is rooted in emotional reactions to obese people. Indeed, across several studies, Vartanian and his colleagues have demonstrated that self-reports of disgust elicited by obesity predict negative attitudes, negative stereotypes, and greater social distance toward obese people (Vartanian, 2010; Vartanian et al., 2013, 2016).

Most of the research on the role of moral disgust in interpersonal and intergroup relations has relied on self-reports. For example, across three studies, Watanabe and Laurent (2021) found that some people reported feeling disgusted when viewing images of interracial couples in the United States. Although such self-reports, which measure one's subjective feelings, are an important component of the emotional response, they can also provide an incomplete picture. Self-reports may reflect concerns about social desirability and the motivation to comply with social norms. For example, society might regularly describe and depict certain people as "disgusting," so one could feel compelled to agree with that assessment, even though the sight of such people does not actually elicit a disgust response. Social neuroscience methods can provide alternatives to self-reports that offer additional insights into complex emotional reactions.

For example, testing hypotheses derived from the Stereotype Content Model (Fiske et al., 2002), Harris and Fiske (2006) found that when viewing two particular social groups, homeless people and drug addicts, participants reported feeling more disgust than they did for other social groups, which did not elicit disgust. Moreover, fMRI bold activity in the amygdala and insula, two brain regions typically activated when people experience fear and disgust, respectively, increased when participants viewed the images of the homeless and drug addicts. The authors interpreted this finding as evidence that stigmatized groups regarded as low in warmth and competence are dehumanized. Similarly, EEG recorded at the scalp in the form of event-related potentials (ERPs) demonstrated that signals originating from the insula were greater when both Black and White participants viewed pictures of Black–White interracial couples, which were consistent with self-reports of disgust and dehumanization (Skinner & Hudac, 2017).

In my laboratory, we have used facial electromyography (EMG; see Tassinary et al., 2016, for an overview) to measure affective responses when people view others' faces. Notably, one of the emotional expressions that facial EMG can readily measure is disgust, which is characterized by pulling the upper lip in a way that creates wrinkles on both sides of the nose using the levator labii superior muscles (Rymarczyk et al., 2019; Philipp et al., 2012; Vrana, 1993). Thus, we used the facial EMG approach to investigate the link between disgust and reactions to obese people (Vartanian et al., 2018). Across four studies, participants viewed a series of images while facial EMG was recorded from the levator labii and corrugator (i.e., used to furrow the brows in negative expressions) muscle sites. Although, in all studies, participants reported greater disgust for obese images, we found no evidence that the target's body size or other factors that typically influence evaluations of obese people (e.g., their effort to lead a healthy lifestyle) affected the levator response.

Admittedly, we were surprised by our findings at first. As mentioned above, a substantial literature already existed that suggested obesity was associated with disgust reactions. Why would we not get a similar association between self-reports and physiological indicators of disgust here? One possible explanation is that pathogen-evoked disgust—the "core" disgust response humans share with other animals—is distinct from socio-moral disgust (Simpson et al., 2006). Biologically threatening disgust may evoke an immediate physiological response with little cognitive elaboration, whereas socio-moral stimuli may elicit more elaborated disgust appraisals that come from experience. People may be taught during development which behaviors and groups do morally wrong, "disgusting" things. People who are obese but otherwise share our group identity don't appear to elicit this type of biological disgust, at least as measured by facial EMG. Thus, people's reactions to obese people and other specific stereotyped groups appear to be culturally learned. Even so, learning to associate obese or homeless people with a verbal label of disgust can lead to dehumanization and avoidance. Our evidence suggesting that it is not pathogen-evoked disgust, however, suggests that the disgust response here might be more amenable to interventions that promote acceptance of these groups into the larger ingroup.

Collective guilt

Schlink's (2010) essays in *Guilt about the Past* are about the generations of Germans since the Third Reich who have had to grapple with the guilt for acts for which they had no direct responsibility. History is full of other groups that have suffered similar guilt by association. In such situations, collective emotions like guilt, shame, or ingroup-directed anger result when one makes an appraisal that the ingroup has violated some standard of behavior of the group (Doosje et al., 1998; Iyer et al., 2003; Vollberg & Cikara, 2018). These group-based emotions can, in turn, facilitate the reparation of historical transgressions such as slavery, genocide, and other human rights violations (for a review, see Wohl et al., 2006). Like research on moral disgust, however, most research on these emotions of collective responsibility has relied solely on self-report questionnaires. This reliance on self-reports becomes problematic in situations where social norms dictate that group members should feel guilt about the wrongdoings of the group's ancestors, so, due to self-presentational concerns, self-reports of collective guilt may not reflect whether one actually feels guilt. Thus, in research with my students (Vanman et al., 2014), we examined the potential for a psychophysiological marker of collective guilt, the P300 component of event-related potentials (ERPs), that might not be as susceptible to social desirability concerns. The P300 is typically elicited in experimental paradigms when a low-probability target (e.g., a "boop" sound or a red circle) is mixed in with high-probability non-target items (e.g., "a beep" sound or blue circles). The less frequent the low-probability target is presented, the larger the amplitude of the resulting P300 amplitude is. Importantly, if the target item is perceived as being like the non-target stimuli (e.g., a woman is smiling slightly among a set of smiling women targets), it will not be processed as being a low-probability event; therefore, the resulting P300 will be smaller in amplitude (Ito, 2013). Thus, the P300 can serve as a marker of guilt because stimuli associated with guilt or shame (i.e., a stolen apple or a picture of someone you have bullied) will elicit a large P300 than stimuli that are not associated with these emotions.

To investigate whether the P300 can serve as a marker of collective guilt, we presented potentially guilt-laden stimuli compared to control stimuli that were associated with the actions of an ingroup member. If the ingroup member had done something that the participant viewed as shameful or guilt-inducing for the group, then the presentation of a stimulus associated with that act should elicit a large P300 that would be correlated with the participant's collective guilt or shame. We conducted two experiments—one involving artificial groups and the other involving a real group associated with a past intergroup transgression. In the first experiment, a confederate acting as another team member did harm to one of the groups—the "accidental" destruction of the other team's flag—so that the ingroup became the perpetrators and the other group the victims. This design allowed us to examine the responses of people not involved in the specific act but who were members of the same group (i.e., the perpetrators).

All participants were then tested individually a few days later when they were presented images pertaining to the first session while ERPs were recorded. The images included pictures of flags drawn by (apparently) different teams in the experiment or faces of participants wearing the red or blue team t-shirts. The target stimuli were the victim team's flag or the confederate's face, presented in a sequence of non-target stimuli. We hypothesized that the P300 amplitude would be larger for the target stimuli if the participant had a collective emotional response to the first session. Participants who were part of the perpetrator group (i.e., the one to whom the confederate belonged) also rated their collective guilt, collective shame, and anger towards the ingroup. Analyses revealed that those who reported more collective guilt in the perpetrator group had larger P300s when viewing task-relevant stimuli.

In Experiment 2, White Australian participants viewed stimuli associated with the Stolen Generations, an actual historical event in which Aboriginal children were forcibly removed from their homes. P300 amplitudes to Aboriginal images were correlated with self-reports of collective guilt and anger about the Stolen Generations. Moreover, participants who said they felt no collective guilt showed greater P300s when the experimenter reminded them about White Australians' responsibility. Thus, across two studies, we found that the P300 can serve as a marker of collective emotions that arise from intergroup transgressions. In both experiments, those participants in the perpetrator group who reported more collective guilt or intergroup-directed anger about the transgression, whether created in a laboratory or one that occurred decades before, manifested greater P300 amplitudes when a significant probe stimulus was presented among a sequence of other task-related images. Although collective guilt may not be a very intense emotion (Gunn & Wilson, 2011; Swim & Miller, 1999), our findings indicate that the P300 can reliably index it. In addition, our research identified the importance of other group-based emotions and guilt in predicting participants' P300 amplitudes. Research on intragroup emotions will benefit from using the ERP methodology. ERPs have already been used in several investigations of group phenomena, including social categorization effects, stereotyping, and the regulation of prejudiced responses (Amodio & Cikara, 2021; Ito, 2013).

Since conducting this research, another team of social neuroscientists has investigated collective guilt in the brain using fMRI (Li et al., 2020). Research in the previous decade has demonstrated the cingulate cortex and the insula are activated during interpersonal interactions that elicit guilt (Radke et al., 2011; Yu et al., 2014). Like Experiment 1 in our 2014 study, Li et al. (2020) assigned participants to artificial groups, and a confederate would commit a transgression (i.e., "mistakenly" apply a shock) against members of the other group who were confederates. All of this occurred while an individual participant ostensibly interacted with others via computer while lying in the fMRI scanner. As predicted, cingulate and insula activity was greater when participants viewed their group members than the outgroup. Although they had not contributed to the transgressions against the outgroup, their sense of shared responsibility for what happened was related to the same areas that are activated when a person feels guilty for a personal transgression they committed.

This research using brain measures in investigations of collective emotions shows their potential in gaining new insights into the role of collective guilt (and related moral emotions) in group outcomes. For example, self-reports of collective guilt have already been demonstrated to predict intergroup behavior, such as political action (Leach et al., 2006) and group apologies for past atrocities (McGarty et al., 2005). Future research should investigate the use of P300 or fMRI activation in a collective guilt situation to predict a person's support for similar actions.

Schadenfreude

Typically, when something unfortunate happens to another person that causes them distress or pain, people respond with some degree of empathy and perhaps even compassion. Such empathic responses can lead to helping the person in distress. This appears to be the "moral" thing to do—if someone needing our help elicits our attention, we help. What happens if, instead of eliciting empathy when we see someone in need, we experience the opposite—counter-empathy? A more commonly used term now, even in the English language—is the German word *schadenfreude*, which connotes a positive response to someone else's pain. The emotion of schadenfreude has been examined at both the interpersonal and intergroup levels and appears to be a "multi-determined" emotion (van Dijk et al., 2011). Factors that have been found to promote and facilitate the experience of schadenfreude include: (1) a threat to one's self-view (van Dijk et al., 2012); (2) the pain of one's group being inferior (Leach & Spears, 2009); (3) dislike and envy of the target (Smith et al., 1996); (4) the target's deservingness of the misfortune (Feather & Sherman, 2002); (5) when one gains from the misfortune (Combs et al., 2009); and (6) when groups are set in direct competition (Cikara & Fiske, 2012).

Most of these factors involve some degree of comparing the relative state of oneself to others. For example, in the case of envy, a misfortune befalling an envied person is pleasing as it may transform an unpleasant comparison into a downward comparison (Smith et al., 1996). Focusing on this link between social comparison and schadenfreude, schadenfreude may have evolved as a reaction to inequity aversion—that is, the dislike of unfairness or inequality (Shamay-Tsoory et al., 2014). According to this perspective, schadenfreude is the positive response to the cessation of an aversive unequal situation. In support of this hypothesis, Shamay-Tsoory et al. found that children as young as 24 months showed greater pleasure following the termination of an unequal situation compared to an equal situation, even when both conditions resulted in a potential gain for the child.

However, schadenfreude does not always arise from the termination of an unfair situation. At the group level, two main factors appear to most strongly facilitate the experience of schadenfreude: group identification and a competitive context. The mere presence of competition is sufficient to incite schadenfreude at an outgroup's misfortune. In addition, the strength of identification with one's group that often occurs alongside competition further facilitates the experience of schadenfreude (Cikara et al., 2011). So, whereas researchers have mainly examined schadenfreude at the interpersonal and intergroup levels, our interest here is on how expressions of schadenfreude further affect identification with one's own group.

Engaging in schadenfreude expressions has important intragroup benefits for the ingroup. There is consistent evidence that sharing emotions in group settings can strengthen bonds between group members, increase group cohesion and identification, and enhance loyalty towards the ingroup (Kessler & Hollbach, 2005; Spoor & Kelly, 2004). Similarly, laughter theorists have argued that sharing laughter or humor in a group encourages group solidarity and morale and unites group members (Gervais & Wilson, 2005; Mazzocconi et al., 2020; Panksepp, 2000). Thus, collectively enjoying the misfortunes of an outgroup and showing dominance towards that group may lead members to feel even more identified with their group and willing to act on behalf of the group. If the groups are involved in direct competition when this occurs, the increases in group cohesion brought about by engaging in schadenfreude expressions may result in tangible group benefits, such as enhanced performance and cooperation abilities.

Although this chapter is focused on the intragroup level, it is important to remember that intragroup processes are influenced by the relationship of one's group to another. A person's perceptions of their own group members can be affected by how outsiders respond to them. In my laboratory, we investigated such effects using artificial groups where participants were assigned to be a red or blue team member. They individually viewed a series of misfortune scenarios involving other red and blue team members in one experiment. Participants were also shown how other ostensible participants had responded to each misfortune scenario. Participants who became the target of intergroup schadenfreude saw outgroup members continually smiling at their ingroup members' misfortunes. Participants who did not become the target of intergroup schadenfreude also saw others smiling at misfortunes; however, these were not systematically from or directed to either group. Implicit measures of participants' affect were obtained using facial EMG, as detecting schadenfreude can be difficult through explicit measures (Cikara & Fiske, 2012). We recorded facial muscle activity from the zygomaticus major (cheek muscle) and orbicularis oculi (lower eyelid). Both muscles are involved in expressions of positive affect, particularly at more intense levels, but activation of orbicularis oculi doesn't always accompany zygomaticus activity.

Across two studies, and in line with predictions, participants who became the target of schadenfreude retaliated by demonstrating greater smiling responses (zygomaticus major activity) toward outgroup misfortunes compared to ingroup misfortunes. Given the speed of these responses (less than one second), these smiling responses suggest an implicit expression of retaliatory schadenfreude to the misfortunes of outgroup members. These preliminary findings build upon the work of Szameitat et al. (2009), who found that schadenfreude laughter was perceived as high in arousal and dominance, and, therefore, may function to assert dominance in a less hostile manner. We speculate that repeatedly being subjected to others' schadenfreude responses to the ingroup may cause a person to feel negative about their own group. Retaliatory schadenfreude may therefore function to reassert feelings of dominance about one's ingroup and the person thus disparages the outgroup in return. Thus, at the intragroup level, although it may be morally reprehensible to display glee at others' pains and losses, this collective schadenfreude may increase group solidarity and strengthen the group overall. Studies are underway in our laboratory to investigate further such ingroup dynamics in retaliatory schadenfreude. For example, we are interested in whether expressing retaliatory schadenfreude increases group identification across time.

Implications of moral emotions for people in groups

As I have indicated in Figure 16.1, moral group responses have effects on how we perceive the members of our group, including processes that increase group cohesion (e.g., during retaliatory schadenfreude) and others that reduce it (e.g., collective guilt). These emotional responses, whether learned or not, can also dictate if we will include stigmatized others in our circle. Judging others as morally disgusting, for example, seems comparatively easy to overcome, once we might learn that a person's plight is beyond their control. More importantly, however, the ability to expand or contract our group memberships will also have downstream effects on our ability to have empathy for others outside our group.

Our capacity to empathize—to share and understand the emotions of others—is a crucial component of human sociality. However, one's emotional response to the suffering or misfortune of another person also appears strongly dependent on the groups—social, cultural, racial, political, or otherwise—to which we belong (Eres & Molenberghs, 2013). As such, issues of morality also come into play that determine our emotions. From an early age, we may have been taught that some members of society, such as homeless or obese people, have deviated from social norms of conduct and thus deserve our disgust and subsequent dehumanization. Others remind us of our collective guilt in the way members of our ingroup have treated them, whether in the past or present. Still, others may laugh at our misfortunes as we thus feel an urge to retaliate, not with kindness, but with retaliatory schadenfreude that builds up those who are already in our group and further alienates us from those who are not. Such moral responses do not bode well for a more accepting society, as people readily demonstrate increased empathy towards their own groups and attenuated empathy for members of the outgroup (Vanman, 2016).

Emotional responses to people in groups have played a critical role in understanding prejudice. Using a media campaign to change beliefs about others (e.g., "immigrants create more jobs than they destroy") will be ineffective if people are still considered a threat based on their other defining characteristics. People appear to have developed a "behavioral immune system," prompting avoidance of potentially harmful objects. This system is thought to be hypersensitive, erring on the side of false positives rather than false negatives (Schaller & Neuberg, 2008). Thus, automatic emotional responses are not deterred by changes in people's beliefs about others. It is notable, in this context, that the most effective approaches for reducing prejudice towards a range of different human outgroups have been to induce empathy (a positive intergroup emotion) in perceivers (Cuddy et al., 2007; Vanman, 2016). Moreover, reminding people about their ingroup members' role in committing transgressions to others may also serve to repair long-damaged relationships.

References

Amodio, D. M., & Cikara, M. (2021). The social neuroscience of prejudice. *Annual Review of Psychology*, 72(1), 439–469. https://doi.org/10.1146/annurev-psych-010419-050928

Cikara, M., Bruneau, E. G., & Saxe, R. R. (2011). Us and them: Intergroup failures of empathy. *Current Directions in Psychological Science*, 20(3), 149–153. https://doi.org/10.1177/0963721411408713

Cikara, M., & Fiske, S. T. (2012). Stereotypes and schadenfreude. *Social Psychological and Personality Science*, 3(1), 63–71. https://doi.org/10.1177/1948550611409245

Combs, D. J. Y., Powell, C. A. J., Schurtz, D. R., & Smith, R. H. (2009). Politics, schadenfreude, and ingroup identification: The sometimes happy thing about a poor economy and death. *Journal of Experimental Social Psychology*, 45(4), 635–646. https://doi.org/10.1016/j.jesp.2009.02.009

Cuddy, A. J. C., Rock, M. S., & Norton, M. I. (2007). Aid in the aftermath of Hurricane Katrina: Inferences of secondary emotions and intergroup helping. *Group Processes & Intergroup Relations*, 10(1), 107–118. https://doi.org/10.1177/1368430207071344

Curtis, V., de Barra, M., & Aunger, R. (2011). Disgust as an adaptive system for disease avoidance behaviour. *Philosophical Transactions of the Royal Society B: Biological Sciences*, *366*(1563), 389–401. https://doi.org/10.1098/rstb.2010.0117

Daníelsdóttir, S., O'Brien, K. S., & Ciao, A. (2010). Anti-fat prejudice reduction: A review of published studies. *Obesity Facts*, *3*(1), 47–58. https://doi.org/10.1159/000277067

Doosje, B., Branscombe, N. R., Spears, R., & Manstead, A. S. R. (1998). Guilty by association: When one's group has a negative history. *Journal of Personality and Social Psychology*, *75*(4), 872–886. https://doi.org/10.1037/0022-3514.75.4.872

Eres, R., & Molenberghs, P. (2013). The influence of group membership on the neural correlates involved in empathy. *Frontiers in Human Neuroscience*, *7*. https://doi.org/10.3389/fnhum.2013.00176

Feather, N. T., & Sherman, R. (2002). Envy, resentment, schadenfreude, and sympathy: Reactions to deserved and undeserved achievement and subsequent failure. *Personality and Social Psychology Bulletin*, *28*(7), 953–961. https://doi.org/10.1177/014616720202800708

Fiske, S. T., Cuddy, A. J. C., Glick, P., & Xu, J. (2002). A model of (often mixed) stereotype content: Competence and warmth respectively follow from perceived status and competition. *Journal of Personality and Social Psychology*, *82*(6), 878–902. https://doi.org/10.1037/0022-3514.82.6.878

Gervais, M., & Wilson, D. S. (2005). The evolution and functions of laughter and humor: A synthetic approach. *The Quarterly Review of Biology*, *80*(4), 395–430. https://doi.org/10.1086/498281

Giner-Sorolla, R., Kupfer, T., & Sabo, J. (2018). What makes moral disgust special? An integrative functional review. In J. M. Olson (Ed.), Advances in experimental social psychology (Vol. 57, pp. 223–289). Academic Press. https://doi.org/10.1016/bs.aesp.2017.10.001

Gunn, G. R., & Wilson, A. E. (2011). Acknowledging the skeletons in our closet. *Personality and Social Psychology Bulletin*, *37*(11), 1474–1487. https://doi.org/10.1177/0146167211413607

Harris, L. T., & Fiske, S. T. (2006). Dehumanizing the lowest of the low. *Psychological Science*, *17*(10), 847–853. https://doi.org/10.1111/j.1467-9280.2006.01793.x

Hodson, G., Choma, B. L., Boisvert, J., Hafer, C. L., MacInnis, C. C., & Costello, K. (2013). The role of intergroup disgust in predicting negative outgroup evaluations. *Journal of Experimental Social Psychology*, *49*(2), 195–205. https://doi.org/10.1016/j.jesp.2012.11.002

Ito, T. A. (2013). Imaging the pictures in our heads: Using ERPs to inform our understanding of social categorization. In B. Derks, D. Scheepers, & N. Ellemers (Eds.), *Neuroscience of prejudice and intergroup relations* (pp. 25–44). Psychology Press.

Iyer, A., Leach, C. W., & Crosby, F. J. (2003). White guilt and racial compensation: The benefits and limits of self-focus. *Personality and Social Psychology Bulletin*, *29*(1), 117–129. https://doi.org/10.1177/0146167202238377

Kessler, T., & Hollbach, S. (2005). Group-based emotions as determinants of ingroup identification. *Journal of Experimental Social Psychology*, *41*(6), 677–685. https://doi.org/10.1016/j.jesp.2005.01.001

Leach, C. W., Iyer, A., & Pedersen, A. (2006). Anger and guilt about ingroup advantage explain the willingness for political action. *Personality and Social Psychology Bulletin*, *32*(9), 1232–1245. https://doi.org/10.1177/0146167206289729

Leach, C. W., & Spears, R. (2009). Dejection at in-group defeat and schadenfreude toward second- and third-party out-groups. *Emotion*, *9*(5), 659–665. https://doi.org/10.1037/a0016815

Li, Z., Yu, H., Zhou, Y., Kalenscher, T., & Zhou, X. (2020). Guilty by association: How group-based (collective) guilt arises in the brain. *NeuroImage*, *209*, 116488. https://doi.org/10.1016/j.neuroimage.2019.116488

Lieberman, D. L., Tybur, J. M., & Latner, J. D. (2012). Disgust sensitivity, obesity stigma, and gender: Contamination psychology predicts weight bias for women, not men. *Obesity*, *20*(9), 1803–1814. https://doi.org/10.1038/oby.2011.247

Mazzocconi, C., Tian, Y., & Ginzburg, J. (2020). What's your laughter doing there? A taxonomy of the pragmatic functions of laughter. *IEEE Transactions on Affective Computing*, 1–1. https://doi.org/10.1109/TAFFC.2020.2994533

McGarty, C., Pedersen, A., Wayne Leach, C., Mansell, T., Waller, J., & Bliuc, A.-M. (2005). Group-based guilt as a predictor of commitment to apology. *British Journal of Social Psychology*, *44*(4), 659–680. https://doi.org/10.1348/014466604X18974

Panksepp, J. (2000). The riddle of laughter. *Current Directions in Psychological Science*, *9*(6), 183–186. https://doi.org/10.1111/1467-8721.00090

Philipp, M. C., Storrs, K. R., & Vanman, E. J. (2012). Sociality of facial expressions in immersive virtual environments: A facial EMG study. *Biological Psychology*, *91*(1). https://doi.org/10.1016/j.biopsycho.2012.05.008

Radke, S., de Lange, F. P., Ullsperger, M., & de Bruijn, E. R. A. (2011). Mistakes that affect others: An fMRI study on processing of own errors in a social context. *Experimental Brain Research*, *211*(3–4), 405–413. https://doi.org/10.1007/s00221-011-2677-0

Rymarczyk, K., Żurawski, Ł., Jankowiak-Siuda, K., & Szatkowska, I. (2019). Empathy in facial mimicry of fear and disgust: Simultaneous EMG-fMRI recordings during observation of static and dynamic facial expressions. *Frontiers in Psychology*, *10*. https://doi.org/10.3389/fpsyg.2019.00701

Schaller, M., & Neuberg, S. L. (2008). Intergroup prejudices and intergroup conflict. In C. Crawford & D. Kerbs (Eds.), *Foundations of evolutionary psychology* (pp. 404–414). Erlbaum.

Schlink, B. (2010). *Guilt about the past*. Anansi.

Shamay-Tsoory, S. G., Ahronberg-Kirschenbaum, D., & Bauminger-Zviely, N. (2014). There is no joy like malicious joy: Schadenfreude in young children. *PLoS ONE*, *9*(7), e100233. https://doi.org/10.1371/journal.pone.0100233

Simpson, J., Carter, S., Anthony, S. H., & Overton, P. G. (2006). Is disgust a homogeneous emotion? *Motivation and Emotion*, *30*(1), 31–41. https://doi.org/10.1007/s11031-006-9005-1

Skinner, A. L., & Hudac, C. M. (2017). "Yuck, you disgust me!" Affective bias against interracial couples. *Journal of Experimental Social Psychology*, *68*, 68–77. https://doi.org/10.1016/j.jesp.2016.05.008

Smith, R. H., Turner, T. J., Garonzik, R., Leach, C. W., Urch-Druskat, V., & Weston, C. M. (1996). Envy and schadenfreude. *Personality and Social Psychology Bulletin*, *22*(2), 158–168. https://doi.org/10.1177/0146167296222005

Spoor, J. R., & Kelly, J. R. (2004). The evolutionary significance of affect in groups: Communication and group bonding. *Group Processes & Intergroup Relations*, *7*(4), 398–412. https://doi.org/10.1177/1368430204046145

Swim, J. K., & Miller, D. L. (1999). White guilt: Its antecedents and consequences for attitudes toward affirmative action. *Personality and Social Psychology Bulletin*, *25*(4), 500–514. https://doi.org/10.1177/0146167299025004008

Szameitat, D. P., Alter, K., Szameitat, A. J., Darwin, C. J., Wildgruber, D., Dietrich, S., & Sterr, A. (2009). Differentiation of emotions in laughter at the behavioral level. *Emotion*, *9*(3), 397–405. https://doi.org/10.1037/a0015692

Tassinary, L. G., Cacioppo, J. T., & Vanman, E. J. (2016). The somatic system. In J. T. Cacioppo, L. G. Tassinary, & G. G. Berntson (Eds.), *Handbook of psychophysiology* (4th Ed., pp. 151–182). Cambridge University Press.

Taylor, K. (2007). Disgust is a factor in extreme prejudice. *British Journal of Social Psychology*, *46*(3), 597–617. https://doi.org/10.1348/014466606X156546

Tybur, J. M., Lieberman, D., & Griskevicius, V. (2009). Microbes, mating, and morality: Individual differences in three functional domains of disgust. *Journal of Personality and Social Psychology*, *97*(1), 103–122. https://doi.org/10.1037/a0015474

van Dijk, W. W., Ouwerkerk, J. W., van Koningsbruggen, G. M., & Wesseling, Y. M. (2012). "So you wanna be a pop star?": Schadenfreude Following another's misfortune on TV. *Basic and Applied Social Psychology*, *34*(2), 168–174. https://doi.org/10.1080/01973533.2012.656606

van Dijk, W. W., Ouwerkerk, J. W., Wesseling, Y. M., & van Koningsbruggen, G. M. (2011). Towards understanding pleasure at the misfortunes of others: The impact of self-evaluation threat on schadenfreude. *Cognition & Emotion*, *25*(2), 360–368. https://doi.org/10.1080/02699931.2010.487365

Vanman, E. J. (2016). The role of empathy in intergroup relations. *Current Opinion in Psychology*, *11*, 59–63. https://doi.org/10.1016/j.copsyc.2016.06.007

Vanman, E.J., Henrion, M.G., Berndt, S.L., & Iyer, A. (2014). Collective emotions on the brain: Towards a social neuroscience of intergroup transgressions. Unpublished manuscript.

Vartanian, L. R. (2010). Disgust and perceived control in attitudes toward obese people. *International Journal of Obesity*, *34*(8), 1302–1307. https://doi.org/10.1038/ijo.2010.45

Vartanian, L. R., McCutcheon, T. B., & Rubenstein, S. A. (2021). Disgust, prejudice, and stigma. In *The Handbook of Disgust Research* (pp. 173–190). Springer International Publishing. https://doi.org/10.1007/978-3-030-84486-8_10

Vartanian, L. R., Thomas, M. A., & Vanman, E. J. (2013). Disgust, contempt, and anger and the stereotypes of obese people. *Eating and Weight Disorders*, *18*(4). https://doi.org/10.1007/s40519-013-0067-2

Vartanian, L. R., Trewartha, T., Beames, J. R., Azevedo, S. M., & Vanman, E. J. (2018). Physiological and self-reported disgust reactions to obesity. *Cognition and Emotion*, *32*(3), 579–592. https://doi.org/10.1080/02699931.2017.1325728

Vartanian, L. R., Trewartha, T., & Vanman, E. J. (2016). Disgust predicts prejudice and discrimination toward individuals with obesity. *Journal of Applied Social Psychology*, *46*(6). https://doi.org/10.1111/jasp.12370

Vollberg, M. C., & Cikara, M. (2018). The neuroscience of intergroup emotion. *Current Opinion in Psychology*, *24*, 48–52. https://doi.org/10.1016/j.copsyc.2018.05.003

Vrana, S. R. (1993). The psychophysiology of disgust: Differentiating negative emotional contexts with facial EMG. *Psychophysiology*, *30*(3), 279–286.

Watanabe, S., & Laurent, S. M. (2021). Disgust toward interracial couples: Mixed feelings about Black–White race mixing. *Social Psychological and Personality Science*, *12*(5), 769–779. https://doi.org/10.1177/1948550620939411

Wohl, M. J. A., Branscombe, N. R., & Klar, Y. (2006). Collective guilt: Emotional reactions when one's group has done wrong or been wronged. *European Review of Social Psychology*, *17*(1), 1–37. https://doi.org/10.1080/10463280600574815

Yu, H., Hu, J., Hu, L., & Zhou, X. (2014). The voice of conscience: Neural bases of interpersonal guilt and compensation. *Social Cognitive and Affective Neuroscience*, *9*(8), 1150–1158. https://doi.org/10.1093/scan/nst090

17
THE INTERGROUP LEVEL

Moral emotions in intergroup relations—the motivations and consequences of advantaged group members' aims to challenge the intergroup inequality

Bertjan Doosje, Hanna Szekeres, Enzo Cáceres Quezada, Michael Boiger and Judit Kende

Abstract

In this chapter, we focus on the role of moral emotions in intergroup contexts. Specifically, we address the question which members of advantaged groups will engage in collective actions to challenge the unequal intergroup configuration (question 1) and how are such actions by potential allies perceived by members of disadvantaged groups (question 2)? Among members of advantaged groups, we distinguish between prideful identifiers (associated with pride), power-cognizant identifiers (related to guilt/shame) and weakly identifiers (linked to neutrality), and argue that power-cognizant identifiers are most likely to engage in collective actions for disadvantaged groups. Such potential allies are most likely accepted by members of disadvantaged groups when they display an altruistic motivation (making them being trusted), show a high level of awareness of power dynamics (that creates hope), and, finally, offer autonomy-oriented help (related to feelings of empowerment and being respected). Future directions and practical implications are presented.

- In intergroup context, group members experience moral emotions when a particular intergroup inequality is made salient.
- When members of advantaged groups experience group-based guilt due to their awareness of the illegitimacy of the intergroup power dynamics, they are more likely to challenge the intergroup inequality.
- Members of disadvantaged groups are more likely to trust and accept potential allies from advantaged groups to the extent that these allies appear to hold altruistic motivations for challenging the intergroup inequality.
- Examining both the level and content of in-group identification creates a more complex, but fuller picture of offering and acceptance of challenges to the intergroup inequality.

Introduction

This chapter focuses on the role of moral emotions in intergroup relations. Oftentimes, group members experience these moral emotions when a particular intergroup inequality is made salient. For example, when the issue of slavery is made salient, descendants of enslaved people might experience group-based moral outrage, while descendants of slave holders might experience group-based shame. A central argument in our chapter, however, is that not all group members will appraise contexts of intergroup inequality in the same manner. Consequently, we aim to understand the differences in the experience of moral emotions in contexts of intergroup inequality.

In the next Section, we describe three types of emotional and behavioral orientations to intergroup inequality by both disadvantaged and advantaged group members. Then, we focus on the emotions and motivations by members of *advantaged* group members to challenge the intergroup inequality, and to become a potential ally in the fight against inequality. In the subsequent Section, we focus on the emotional, attitudinal and behavioral reactions by members of *disadvantaged* groups to such potential allies. We then describe the main controversies, unresolved questions and future directions. In the final section, we describe practical implications of our analysis.

We use the example of Black Lives Matter to specify our aims. According to a PEW research center survey in the US in September 2021, the Black Lives Matter movement is supported by 83% of Black Americans (Horowitz, 2021), likely driven by moral outrage. There is more diversity in support among White adults in the US: the percentage of support (47%) is about the same as (or slightly lower than) the percentage of those who do not support the movement (53%).

The divergent stand points to BLM is an example illustrating that not every member of an advantaged group reacts in the same manner to intergroup inequalities. In this chapter, we aim to address the following questions related to this issue: How can we explain this diversity in reactions to (past or present) intergroup inequalities by members of advantaged groups? Why do some members of advantaged groups join actions to challenge the intergroup inequality that might be perceived as going against the interest of their own group? Which moral emotions play a role here? In addition, we aim to examine the reception of these potential allies. Specifically, how do members of disadvantaged groups perceive these potential allies? Are they welcomed wholeheartedly as genuine allies? Or might they be perceived with some suspicion about their motives of supporting the disadvantaged group's cause? Again, we examine the role of moral emotions in this context.

Three types of emotional and behavioral orientations to intergroup inequality by disadvantaged and advantaged group members

Before diving into the answers to these questions, we aim to present the broader context in which we place them. Specifically, we propose three types of emotional, attitudinal and behavioral orientations to intergroup inequality by members of disadvantaged and advantaged groups. We aim to specify which moral emotions, attitudes and behavioral reactions are associated with the three orientations in a context of intergroup inequality, as described in Figure 17.1.

First, for *prideful* members of advantaged groups, we argue that the most dominant emotions are (obviously) pride towards the in-group but also fear of losing group status. These members are motivated to defend the inequality, for example by negating the historical path that might be associated with their advantaged position (see next section for a more extensive argument of the role of history in the appraisals of intergroup inequality). Second, and most relevant for the current chapter, a power-cognizant orientation among members of an advantaged group is characterized

Intergroup level: moral emotions in intergroup relations

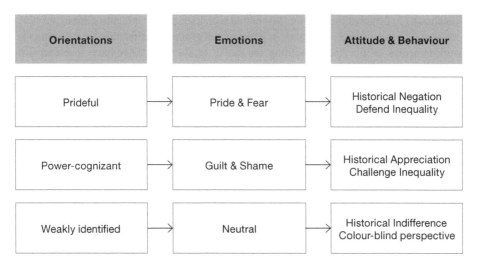

Figure 17.1 Orientations, emotions, attitudes and behavior.

by the experience of group-based guilt and shame. Guilt and shame as moral emotions make them likely to critically appreciate the historical dimension of the intergroup inequality by connecting the dots between current out-group disadvantage and historical oppression. In addition, they are likely to challenge the intergroup inequality, arguably at the expense of their own group's position. The most dominant associated behaviors include reparations or support for more structural changes in the intergroup configuration. As such, they are more prone to become allies in the fight against inequality. Third, we distinguish a weakly identified orientation, which is associated with emotional detachment to the intergroup inequality, distancing that is analogue to their low ingroup identification as advantaged group members. Such in-group detachment underpins a more individual-focused psychological orientation, which enables meritocratic attitudes in tandem with glossing over group-based aspects of intergroup inequality such as its history.

In the remainder of this chapter, we address two questions: (1) Which emotions are associated with the likelihood that members of *advantaged* groups challenge the intergroup inequality (even at the expense of the in-group's position)? (2) How do members of *disadvantaged* groups respond emotionally to such potential allies? Together, the answers to these questions provide insight into the most fruitful manners in which members of disadvantaged and advantaged group may work together to reduce intergroup inequality.

Which emotions are associated with the likelihood for members of advantaged group to challenge the intergroup inequality?

In this section, we address the first central question, namely: which emotions are associated with the likelihood for members of advantaged groups to challenge the intergroup inequality? We use the three different orientations to examine which emotions, attitudes and actions are most likely to be present among such members.

In their review, Radke et al. (2020) specify four motivations of members of an advantaged group to challenge the intergroup inequality: (1) out-group focused motivation (associated with low in-group identification), (2) in-group focused motivation (associated with high in-group identification), (3) personal motivation (associated with high personal identification), and (4) morality motivation (associated with high superordinate group identification, e.g., humanity). In our work (Cáceres et al., 2022), building on Radke et al., we further have specified different types of orientations based on a combination of both *level* and *content* of identification among advantaged group members in the context of Dutch racial and ethnic intergroup relationships. In the Netherlands, white people typically hold the advantaged group position being the heirs of the colonial quests undertaken since the 16th century by the Dutch empire. In contrast, non-white Dutch people are often descendants of colonized people (e.g., with Antillean, Surinamese, and Indonesian backgrounds), but not always (e.g., Dutch people with a Moroccan and Turkish background have never been colonized by the Dutch).

In our framework, we argue that moral emotions play an important role. Thus, we discuss the three different forms of identification among white people and how they are related to emotions and attitudes regarding group-based inequality. Subsequently, we relate these three identity types to color-blindness literature as contemporaneous repertoire towards racial and ethnic inequality.

Advantaged group members' identity forms and their association with emotions and attitudes towards intergroup inequality

As indicated, we argue that both *level* and *content* of identification are relevant to distinguish identity forms among members of advantaged groups. First, we argue that feelings of pride coupled with relatively high ingroup identification in their ethnic heritage will be associated with prideful orientation, which is characterized by a denial or defense of intergroup inequality. For them, being Dutch describes their ethnic identity. In contrast, some white people are likely to experience negative emotions such as group-based guilt and shame when thinking about intergroup inequality and still holding a relatively high ingroup identification. They are power-cognizant people, which means that they are aware of the power dynamics in their society. They recognize their ethnic/racial group membership (Goren & Plaut, 2012), and refer to themselves in those identity terms (i.e., "I am a white Dutch person"). Finally, we argue that a weakly identified white identity will be related to a more muted and neutral emotional state regarding group-based intergroup inequality. They may opt for a color-blind perspective. Their low in-group attachment as advantaged group members allows them to not fully accept a critical historical appreciation of intergroup inequality in comparison to power-cognizants. At the same time, they do not feel the need to defend their in-group's position as much as prideful people tend to do. Interestingly, in terms of describing their ethnic identity, they use the Dutch word "*blank*" instead of "*wit*", because they associate *blank* with positive traits such as cleanliness and transparency, whereas they associate *wit* only with their skin-color. In this sense, lower identification among advantaged group members was associated to group-distancing strategies aimed to prevent the threat of being perceived as racially and ethnically marked and thereby privileged (Knowles et al., 2014).

Relations to color-blindness versus color-cognizance

Furthermore, these three identity forms can be mapped into contemporaneous attitudinal repertoires towards racial inequalities, namely color-blindness and color-cognizance (or color-consciousness). Color-blindness as intergroup outlook stresses that race and skin color should not influence people's lives, abhorring the effects that group membership might have on social life (Leslie et al., 2020). As a result, individuals tend to be emphasized at expense of their group-based features for the sake of inclusivity (Knowles et al., 2009; Neville et al., 2013). This intergroup process is underpinned by two interrelated forms of evasion: color-evasion and power-evasion. Color-evasion emphasizes sameness, rejecting the idea of white racial superiority but also evading the difference made by race and ethnicity in social life. Power evasion circumvents the acknowledgement of intergroup power imbalances (Awad & Jackson, 2016). In this way, color-blindness tends to obscure the marks of group-based inequalities among disadvantaged group members but also the signs of group-based privilege among the advantaged ones.

In terms of our three identity forms, a weakly white identity should correspond with both color and power-evasion: they tend to not see color as a consequence of their own ingroup detachment. Such an outlook allows them to get rid of the burden of acknowledging their advantaged identity in tandem with the historical roots of their privilege and outgroups' disadvantage. As a consequence, group-based features such as emotions are deemed as bias, ending up in muting moral emotions. Instead, allegedly neutral meritocratic attitudes may be upheld that allocates dignity and worth to individuals instead of groups. They advocate a color-blind perspective.

Prideful identity, on the other hand, is expected to be especially related to a high level of power-evasion: they defend or deny the power dynamics by means of ingroup pride as moral emotion. In contrast to weak identifiers, their prideful and high in-group identification would not allow them to evade color to the extent in which weak identifiers do.

Finally, we argue that power-cognizant identity form should be associated with color-cognizance: they are prone to see color and acknowledge the role of it in society in terms of power dynamics in accordance with their ingroup identity configuration as advantaged group members. They are the ones that aim to challenge the imbalance in intergroup status by engaging in collective actions in support of the disadvantaged group

To conclude, we illustrate in Figure 17.1 how the above mentioned psychological features are related. In explaining the reason why some members of advantaged groups engage in collective action aimed at improving the disadvantaged group's position, we argue it is important to distinguish among three advantaged forms of identity. Some of the highly identified members of an advantaged group are likely to experience pride due to their group's position and they are likely to defend or deny the intergroup inequality. Weakly identified people might mute their moral emotions, disassociating from their group and circumventing the group-based dynamics of advantage and disadvantage. Finally, power-cognizant people, also highly identified group members, are more prone to experience group-based guilt and shame by accepting the illegitimately received historical advantages, and aim to challenge the imbalance in intergroup status by engaging in collective actions to support the disadvantaged group.

Even when individual members of advantaged groups embrace these three interrelated psychological features of high ingroup privilege acknowledgment, historical acknowledgment of intergroup inequality, and color-cognizance, will that always work? In the next section, we outline how members of disadvantaged groups may experience such efforts of members of advantaged groups to challenge the intergroup inequality. When will they be perceived as trustworthy allies and when as a "devil in disguise"? And which emotions play a role here?

How do members of disadvantaged groups perceive members of advantaged groups who aim to challenge the intergroup inequality?

In the previous section, we have examined the likelihood of members of advantaged groups to engage in actions on behalf of the disadvantaged group. In this section, we focus on the second central question of this chapter, namely how do members of disadvantaged groups perceive

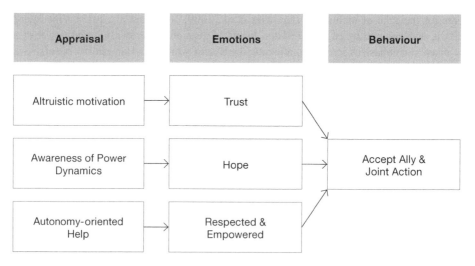

Figure 17.2 Appraisal, emotions, behavior.

members of advantaged group that aim to challenge inequality? Will they be perceived as "allies" or as "disguised enemies" (as they are members of the advantaged out-group)? And what is the role of emotions in this context?

We argue that, again, emotions play an important role in this context. In general, members of disadvantaged groups are expected to avoid the experience of feelings of dependence or inferiority. On the other hand, feelings of hope for a better future and trust of such out-group members' allyship might be ignited among disadvantaged group members, which would predict acceptance of such challenges to inequality by members of advantaged groups. More specifically, we claim that important appraisals of the intergroup context are associated with specific emotions, which are related to behavior in terms of acceptance vs. rejection of potential allies and of welcomed joint collective action (see Figure 17.2). After introducing the topic more broadly, we will discuss three appraisals that we argue will predict emotions and subsequent behavior in terms of acceptance: Altruistic motivation and trust, awareness of power dynamics and hope and autonomy-oriented help and empowerment.

Further introduction

As argued in the Introduction, collective action to reduce intergroup inequality is often performed by individuals who are targets of discrimination but not exclusively. BlackLivesMatter and HeForShe are just some of many examples where advantaged group members joined the social movement (hereby "allies"). Such allyship can instigate different reactions. On the one hand, it is often perceived quite positively, because it is seen as benevolent and instrumental. Indeed, when allies join a movement, the cause and the movement become more accepted by the majority society, influence public opinion more positively, and therefore more likely lead to social change (Kutlaca et al., 2022).

On the other hand, there are many conditions in allyship that could negatively affect disadvantaged group's motivation and effectiveness of allyship. For example, positive intergroup contact can demobilize the disadvantaged group; their distinct group identity can be compromised in the process of establishing a common identity with allies; and allies may dominate or take over the movement while being unaware of their own privileges (Droogendyk et al., 2016). Such critical effects are often voiced by disadvantaged group activists.

Indeed, a study conducted among African-Americans in US and Palestinians in Israel-Palestine, respectively, showed that "joint collective action" (action performed together with allies) poses a dilemma for the disadvantaged group between its instrumentality and its potential to normalize power relations between the groups (for example, by derailing the issue—Hasan-Aslih et al., 2022). Thus, disadvantaged group members see strategic benefits to joint action, but they are also concerned with potential co-option of the movement, which decreases their overall openness to allies.

Meanwhile other studies indicate less conditional acceptance of challenge to inequality from allies. For example, refugees not only considered "autonomy-oriented challenge to inequality" (which offers inequality-recipients the tools to challenge inequality themselves) as relatively helpful in achieving social change—they also evaluated "dependency-oriented challenge to inequality" (which gives the recipients the full solution to a problem) as positive (Becker et al., 2019). Furthermore, in another study conducted among African-Americans in the US and women in Germany, disadvantaged group participants evaluated an advantaged group ally who confronted prejudice more positively, or at least equally well as an in-group member who confronted prejudice (Kutlaca et al., 2020).

Thus, there seems to be an inconsistency in the literature about the reception of allyship. We argue and discuss how these differences in reactions are likely to be explained by the conditions present in given contexts.

Perceived motivation of allies and trust

One such condition is the *(perceived) motivation of allies* (see Figure 17.2). To what extent does the observed act in that context hold personal cost or risks to the ally, or moreover, personal benefits? Indeed, activists sometimes feel that allies show solidarity for egoistic reasons, such as bolstering their self-image, gaining social belonging to an "activist" group, or relinquishing in-group responsibility (Droogendyk et al., 2016)—and advantaged group allies sometimes indeed hold such motivations (e.g., Knowles et al., 2014; Radke et al., 2020). For example, women were less likely to accept a man's (compared to a woman's) help, because they attributed less empathy and altruistic motives to the man vs. the woman (Borinca et al., 2020). Thus, the perceived cost-benefit signals allies' egoistic–altruistic motivation. While appraisal of egoistic motivation would elicit feelings of distrust, disadvantaged group members would attribute altruistic reasons to allies given that their actions involve high personal costs and low personal benefit. These altruistic appraisals would elicit feelings of trust in allies and in turn increase acceptance of allyship.

Awareness of power dynamics and hope

Beyond evaluations of cost-benefit, another condition that can determine perceived motivation is perceived *awareness of power dynamics* (see Figure 17.2). The more allies communicate genuine understanding and acknowledgement of power inequality, the more selfless their action is perceived (Iyer & Achia, 2021), likely because that awareness provides a selfless explanation and more structural understanding for their help in challenging to inequality. This aspect is critical to disentangle allyship behavior led by weakly identified advantaged group members from power-cognizant ones, whose relatively higher in-group identification among the latter precludes individualistic understanding of inequality that is more prevalent among the formers. Moreover, when allies who are social justice organization leaders (which otherwise is demobilizing for the disadvantaged group) communicate awareness of inequality, it increases disadvantaged group's *hope* in that leadership and increases their willingness for joint action (Iyer & Achia, 2021). In contrast, when disadvantaged group members appraise low level of power awareness in allies, they would likely experience disappointment in and despair for allyship. Therefore perceived awareness of power dynamics can instill hope for improvement in the intergroup situation, and in turn increases acceptance of allyship.

Autonomy- versus dependency-oriented help, feeling respected and empowerment

However, even given perceived selfless motivation, there is still concern on how allies treat disadvantaged group within the movement. For example, allies may behave paternalistically and make them feel inferior. Certainly, disadvantaged group activists have voiced concern that allies can act as "saviors" ("White savior complex"; Droogendyk et al., 2016). In the previously mentioned study with refugees, the majority of Germans' paternalistic beliefs were positively related to offering dependency-oriented challenge to inequality and negatively related to offering autonomy-oriented challenge to inequality, and the latter was also driven by perceived high competence of refugees (Becker et al., 2019). While refugees might have perceived both forms of challenges as selfless, sensing paternalism could partially explain why they were more favorable to autonomy-oriented than dependency-oriented help to challenge inequality.

Considering these findings and often voiced concern about allies dominating the movement (Droogendyk et al., 2016), we argue that another key factor that would affect openness to allyship is *type of help* to challenge to inequality offered by the ally and corresponding sense of *paternalism*. While autonomy-oriented challenge to inequality would elicit feelings of empowerment and feeling respected, dependency-oriented challenge to inequality may elicit a sense of inferiority and feeling disrespected.

As an initial investigation of the factors that affect openness to allyship, we interviewed Roma activists ($N=6$) in Hungary (which will be followed up with a survey research). In semi-structured interviews, we asked about their experiences with allies from the majority society. The main concerns that were raised and that mitigate openness to allyship are in line with our assumptions. Specifically, allies were perceived as tending to (a) reap personal benefits of allyship (e.g., advancing their career or boosting self-image), (b) to be less aware of the severity of Roma people's disadvantage and less willing to acknowledge their own personal privileges, (c) prefer to provide dependency-oriented help (vs. autonomy) and (d) tend to dominate or take over the movement. These are concerns that all are associated with less trust in allies and less hope in improvement of the situation of Roma people in society.

Interestingly, while all activists interviewed have reoccurring negative experiences with paternalism, it does not necessarily affect their acceptance of allyship. They explained that their group is so marginalized in society that even paternalistic challenges to inequality may be welcomed, especially because Roma people do not have the resources (time and energy) to engage in collective action.

To summarize, we argue that the extent to which potential allies from advantaged groups and joint action will be welcomed (or not) by members of disadvantaged groups depends on appraisals and associated emotions. First, a potential ally perceived as highly altruistically motivated will be highly trusted and accepted. Second, when allies are perceived as highly aware of the intergroup power dynamics, they are relatively likely to instigate hope and be accepted. Finally, when the help is appraised as autonomy-oriented, this is associated with feelings of being respected and empowerment, which makes acceptance relatively likely. Overall, it is important to investigate disadvantaged group's perceptions, because it can provide insight and guide for allies in their communication and attitude in joint collective action efforts.

Controversies, unresolved questions and future directions

Having discussed how some members of advantaged group may be motivated to engage in collective action aimed at improving the position of the disadvantaged group and how such actions may be perceived by members of disadvantaged groups, we identify three interesting unresolved questions. The first question is: Does it make sense to consider both level and content of in-group identification? Are they always separate entities or not? We believe that our work shows that it is crucial to integrate level and content of in-group identification to better predict group-based emotions in unequal intergroup contexts among advantaged group members. Future work could fruitfully explore the interaction between level and content of in-group identification in explaining group-based emotions such as anger or moral outrage by members of disadvantaged groups in unequal intergroup settings. For example, do highly identified members of disadvantaged group with a high power-cognizant identity form experience group-based anger most strongly?

A second question that is unresolved: Are perceptions of intergroup inequality relatively fixed or is it possible to manipulate these? Which manipulations seem most promising, also in the long run? There is evidence that presenting large-scale data to illustrate inequality might work better than presenting a single strong case of inequality to change people's perceptions of inequality (Callaghan et al., 2021). We argue that in order to manipulate such perceptions, one needs to carefully balance the need to feel positive about one's group and the willingness to acknowledge that intergroup inequality is indeed present and needs to be addressed. In this context, furthering knowledge about power-cognizance among advantaged group members is crucial. How to convey intergroup power imbalances and the group-based differences that signal such inequality as a source of intergroup appreciation circumventing the temptation of group-blindness?

A third and final unresolved question is how allies' challenge to inequality and beneficiaries' reaction to such behavior by allies might interact with each other. For example, how might meta-perceptions (how do the beneficiaries perceive me, my intentions?) motivate allies? To give a specific example: What happens when potential allies think that members of the disadvantaged groups think: "Oh, they are only in it to make them feel proud of themselves"? Does that make potential allies act in a more modest manner than they would have done under other circumstances (e.g., downplaying their potential impact in the public debate)? Alternatively, it could be possible that allyship by influential members of advantaged groups might stimulate members of disadvantaged groups to experience hope and enthusiasm, to "get up and stand up", because they can envision social change.

Practical implications

In this chapter, we have offered insights into which people from advantaged groups under what conditions will be motivated to engage in collective actions on behalf of disadvantaged groups. In addition, we have tackled the question about the reception of such help to challenge inequality: Under what conditions is such help to challenge inequality welcomed by members of disadvantaged groups?

When we combine the insights we gained by addressing these questions, we can formulate practical implications. First of all, in order to avoid misunderstanding and disappointment, it is important to take into account an interactive perspective in which members of both disadvantaged and advantaged groups are encouraged to address and acknowledge each other's needs and expectations quite openly. From our analysis, it seems that the members of advantaged groups that are most likely to engage in collective action, because they are aware of the intergroup power dynamics and their positionality, precisely are the ones that are most likely to be accepted by members of the disadvantages groups. But this power-awareness has to be discussed openly first rather than to be taken for granted. Second, engagement in joint collective action may work best if people are willing and motivated to take each other's perspective. This means for a member of an advantaged group to carefully listen to and act upon the point of view of the disadvantaged group (and not to dominate the discussion). For members of disadvantaged groups, perspective taking might imply trying to really understand the motivation of a person from an advantaged group, without automatically assuming self-serving motivations of this person. Only then, in the spirit of *true collective* action that harnesses the most from the virtuous effects of both advantaged group members and disadvantaged group members joining social struggles, it might be possible to overcome the potential hurdles of such a joint venture.

References

Awad, & Jackson, K. M. (2016). The measurement of color-blind racial ideology. In H. A. Neville, M. E. Gallardo, & D. W. Sue (Eds.), *The myth of racial color blindness: Manifestations, dynamics, and impact* (pp. 141–156). American Psychological Association. https://doi.org/10.1037/14754-009

Becker, J. C., Ksenofontov, I., Siem, B., & Love, A. (2019). Antecedents and consequences of autonomy-and dependency-oriented help toward refugees. *European Journal of Social Psychology, 49*, 831–838. https://doi.org/10.1002/ejsp.2554

Borinca, I., Falomir-Pichastor, J. M., & Andrighetto, L. (2020). "How can you help me if you are not from here?" Helper's familiarity with the context shapes interpretations of prosocial intergroup behaviors. *Journal of Experimental Social Psychology, 87*, 103944. https://doi.org/10.1016/j.jesp.2019.103944

Cáceres, E., Kende, J., Boiger, M., Hitschfel, C., Hickson, H., & Doosje, B. (2022). When White people gauge the weight of the past: The role of identity strategies in linking colonialism to current inequalities. Unpublished manuscript.

Callaghan, B., Harouni, L., Dupree, C. H., Kraus, M. W., & Richeson, J. A. (2021). Testing the efficacy of three informational interventions for reducing misperceptions of the Black–White wealth gap. *Proceedings of the National Academy of Sciences, 118*, e2108875118. https://doi.org/10.1073/pnas.2108875118

Droogendyk, L., Wright, S. C., Lubensky, M., & Louis, W. R. (2016). Acting in solidarity: Cross-group contact between disadvantaged group members and advantaged group allies. *Journal of Social Issues, 72*, 315–334. https://doi.org/10.1111/josi.12168

Goren, M. J., & Plaut, V. C. (2012). Identity form matters: White racial identity and attitudes toward diversity. *Self and Identity, 11*, 237–254. https://doi.org/10.1080/15298868.2011.556804

Hasan-Aslih, S., Pliskin, R., Shuman, E., Van Zomeren, M., Saguy, T., & Halperin, E. (2022). *The dilemma of "Sleeping with the Enemy": A first examination of what (de)motivates disadvantaged group members to partake in joint collective action.* [Manuscript submitted for publication]. Department of Psychology, Hebrew University, Jerusalem, Israel.

Horowitz, J. M. (2021). Support for Black Lives Matter declined after George Floyd protests, but has remained unchanged since. www.pewresearch.org/fact-tank/2021/09/27/support-for-black-lives-matter-declined-after-george-floyd-protests-but-has-remained-unchanged-since/

Iyer, A., & Achia, T. (2021). Mobilized or marginalized? Understanding low-status groups' responses to social justice efforts led by high-status groups. *Journal of Personality and Social Psychology, 120*, 1287–1316. https://doi.org/10.1037/pspi0000325

Knowles, E. D., Lowery, B. S., Chow, R. M., & Unzueta, M. M. (2014). Deny, distance, or dismantle? How white Americans manage a privileged identity. *Perspectives on Psychological Science, 9*, 594–609. https://doi.org/10.1177/1745691614554658

Knowles, Lowery, B. S., Hogan, C. M., & Chow, R. M. (2009). On the malleability of ideology: Motivated construals of color blindness. *Journal of Personality and Social Psychology, 96*, 857–869. https://doi.org/10.1037/a0013595

Kutlaca, M., Becker, J., & Radke, H. (2020). A hero for the outgroup, a black sheep for the ingroup: Societal perceptions of those who confront discrimination. *Journal of Experimental Social Psychology, 88*, 103832. https://doi.org/10.1016/j.jesp.2019.103832

Kutlaca, M., Radke, H. R., & Becker, J. C. (2022). The impact of including advantaged groups in collective action against social inequality on politicized identification of observers from disadvantaged and advantaged groups. *Political Psychology, 43*, 297–314. https://doi.org/10.1111/pops.12755

Leslie, L. M., Bono, J. E., Kim, Y. (S.), & Beaver, G. R. (2020). On melting pots and salad bowls: A meta-analysis of the effects of identity-blind and identity-conscious diversity ideologies. *Journal of Applied Psychology, 105*, 453–471. https://doi.org/10.1037/apl0000446

Neville, H. A., Awad, G. H., Brooks, J. E., Flores, M. P., & Bluemel, J. (2013). Color-blind racial ideology: Theory, training, and measurement implications in psychology. *The American Psychologist, 68*, 455–466. https://doi.org/10.1037/a0033282

Radke, H. R., Kutlaca, M., Siem, B., Wright, S. C., & Becker, J. C. (2020). Beyond allyship: Motivations for advantaged group members to engage in action for disadvantaged groups. *Personality and Social Psychology Review, 24*, 291–315. https://doi.org/10.1177/1088868320918698

PART V

Moral behaviour

PART VA

A vision on moral behaviour

18
BEHAVIOURAL ETHICS
A retrospective reflection and prospective prescription

Ann E. Tenbrunsel

As an entering doctoral student at the Kellogg Graduate School of Management in the fall of 1991, I was intrigued by the questions that were being asked (and answered) by the faculty, particularly by Max Bazerman and Maggie Neale who would eventually become two of my advisors. Their research focused on why people made suboptimal decisions as measured by a rationality benchmark, particularly in the negotiation context. This fascinated me but I found myself interested in a slightly different question, namely why do people make submoral decisions? Or as I said then, "Why do good people behave badly and not realize that they are doing so?" It's a question that seems obvious now and, is evidenced by this handbook, a topic that is voluminous enough to generate significant research. But in 1991, the idea that a faculty member in business school would do research on ethics was completely foreign, and I am forever grateful to my dissertation advisor, Max Bazerman, and my committee advisors, Dave Messick, Maggie Neale and Dawn Iacobucci, for encouraging me to pursue my interests as strange as they seemed at the time. Linda Trevino of course had blazed the way almost a decade earlier by studying the role of individual variables and culture on ethical and unethical behaviour (Trevino, 1986). My interests took a slightly different tact, pursuing the impact of cognitive and decision-making processes on unethical behaviour, and later on, the influence of the context on those processes. While there was a curiosity in the topic, the path was a rocky one with one well-known researcher commenting after a job talk, "This is interesting but what are you going to study when this is no longer a fad?" and faculty from another well-known university stating, "We love your research but we just don't know what to do with it in a business school." I was thankful that a few schools could see the light and that Notre Dame has never been anything but supportive as I have pursued this topic.

The field of course has blossomed since those early days and it was a joy to see that happen. Countless new insights have been identified, too many to detail here (and apologies in advance for not citing papers I should have and citing some of my own papers out of ease). But let me focus on a few that were particularly exciting and relevant to me, beginning with research at the individual level. I am of course partial to decision frames (insert smiley emoji here), or the way in which a decision is categorized into sub-types (i.e., business decision, ethics decision, finance decision, legal decision), and their explanatory value in predicting ethical fading and unethical behaviour (Tenbrunsel & Messick, 1999; Kern & Chugh, 2009; Rees et al., 2021). Beyond the fact that it was something I worked on in collaboration with the late and beloved Dave Messick, it applied Goffman's work on framing (1974) to the field of ethics, and in doing so, helps to explain the variability in individual responses to a contextual stimulus in a moral context. There have been many other exciting developments at the individual level, including but not limited to, foundational work on moral identity (Aquino & Reed, 2002), moral character (Cohen et al., 2014), moral disengagement (Moore, 2015), moral emotions (Haidt, 2003; Tangney et al., 2007) and moral foundations (Graham et al., 2012). One of the studies on intrapersonal processes I talk about most when presenting my research is that done by Woodzicka and LaFrance (2001), who provide a compelling example of forecasting errors, demonstrating that women overpredict the extent to which they would stand up to sexually harassing questions in an interview. This and other findings on the same phenomenon suggest, among other things, that training focused on hypothetical predictions may leave individuals ill-prepared to face ethical dilemmas.

Research has also looked beyond the individual decision maker, examining the impact of others on our own unethical behaviour. This research has identified numerous effects, from those not only above us in the organizational hierarchy (Mayer et al., 2012) but also those below us (Ahmad et al., 2020) and those around us (John et al., 2014). Given the importance ascribed to observers of unethical behaviour for reducing destructive actions, work on motivated blindness has been particularly crucial. Gino and Bazerman (2009), for example, demonstrated this is more likely to occur when the unethical behaviour of others is gradual. The practical import of this research is significant, particularly in the accounting industry where the dangers of motivated blindness have been voiced for decades (Bazerman et al., 1997), and for understanding the prevalence of sexual harassment and the contributing role of inaction by observers and institutions (Tenbrunsel et al., 2019).

Aggregating up a level to the organization, there have been numerous investigating how structural features of the organization impact unethical behaviour, including the role of organizational culture and climate (Trevino et al., 1998; Tenbrunsel et al., 2003) and the impact of reward systems (Jansen & Von Glinow, 1985; Schweitzer et al., 2004; Welsh & Ordonez, 2014) and sanctions (Tenbrunsel & Messick, 1999; Balliet et al., 2011). An examination at the organizational level also introduces hierarchy and sources of power, which have in turn been linked to unethical and ethical behaviour (see Lammers et al., 2015 for a review). Two papers that I think about and mention quite frequently in class and with corporate audiences address the interaction of individual and corporate influences. Desai et al. (2014) provide a compelling demonstration of gender bias in the workplace as a function of marital status outside of the organization, demonstrating that men in traditional marriages have less positive views of women in the workplace and are more likely to prevent advancement of qualified women. Particularly compelling is the finding that single men who marry women who are not employed become less positive about women in the workplace than they were before they were married, which helps eliminate any confounds with partner selection and attitudes. The impact of political ideologies on a firm's corporate social responsibility (CSR) is also significant. Unveiled in research conducted by Chin et al. (2013), results demonstrated that liberal CEOs were more likely to support CSR, even during times of low performance. In doing so, this research highlights the organizational implications of a relatively new but understudied executive attribute.

There have also been exciting methodological developments over the last few decades that have expanded our insights into moral behaviour. Advances in neuroscience have enabled confirmation of empirical claims, particularly those made by researchers in the cognitive arena who often have to make assumptions about the "black box." Greene et al. (2004), for example, argued that different cortices (different areas of the brain) were dominant in moral decisions involving emotional versus cognitive processes. This type of research was particularly comforting to those speculating on the two-selves problems in ethical decisions (Schelling, 1984), supporting theoretical arguments on the "want self" and "should self" that we made in the earlier work on behavioural ethics (Bazerman et al., 1998) and, truth be told, making us feel less crazy for proposing this. Methodologically, the push to move beyond laboratory and survey-based methods and incorporate field research is critical if, as noted below, the field is to rise to the challenge of producing relevant research (Larkin et al., 2021).

Examining the path forward, it is essential that behavioural ethics research is increasing relevant. There are several paths that we can and should take to ensure this occurs. First, it is important that the field continues to expand the list of relevant, dependent variables that are examined. Lying and misrepresentation have been the primary dependent variables of choice of such research given the clear-cut connection to unethical behaviour. While it is critical to mitigate these actions, it is also important to continue to expand the list of behaviours that are studied in order to increase the impact of the field. Fulmer, Barry and Long (2009), for example, highlight the importance of moving beyond informational deception to also incorporate emotional deception. O'Leary-Kelly and Bowes-Sperry (2001) have long argued for sexual harassment to be seen as an ethical issue, a proposition that was recently re-visited from a behavioural ethics lens (Tenbrunsel et al., 2019). Moral values have been linked to vaccine hesitancy (Amin et al., 2017), which has been identified as a moral issue given the designation of vaccines as a common good (Borges & Dos Santos, 2021). Economic inequality, central in public policy, has recently been linked to an increase in the acceptance of others' unethical behaviour (To et al., 2021). Knocking down the boundaries between work and non-work will also be fruitful in creating new paths for behavioural ethicists. Hardin et al. (2020) found, for example, that displaying family photos reduces financial transgressions.

Perhaps one of the more exciting and critical issues facing the field of behavioural ethics revolves around technology. Increasingly part of the workplace (Standage, 2016; Stone et al., 2016), significant attention is given to the impact of AI on ethical behaviour (Agrawal et al., 2017; Dignum, 2018). The range of issues to be studied is vast. Perhaps one of the most pressing issue is whether behavioural ethics, and its focus on unintentional behaviour (Bazerman & Gino, 2012), is applicable to AI-made decisions, given that all decisions made by an AI could be argued to be intentional. Additionally, the burden of codifying ethics rests on the shoulders of AI system developers, and it has been argued that, because they tend to be most familiar with consequentialists theories, they will be more likely to use them in designing AI decision making structures (Yu et al., 2018). Thus, researchers in the behavioural ethics domain should explore how intrapersonal attributes affect the programming of an AI's ethical decision-making process, particularly given that this impact could be long-lasting and ill-understood. Attention should also be directed to whether the notion of "blind spots" apply to AI-based decisions. Can AI fall prey to slippery slope behaviour, such that it accepts incremental deviations from ethical behaviour which increase over time? Conversely, does AI "balance out" its ethical decisions, engaging in a form of moral licensing that produces an ethical-unethical repeat pattern of behaviour?

Technology also introduces exciting methodological possibilities that can offer realism, allowing not only for the study of new mediators but also an opportunity to study contexts in which it is difficult to get field data. Virtual reality (VR) technology, for example, can overcome the limitations of written scenarios and other typical methodologies, with sexual harassment research being one of those most likely to benefit (Zyda, 2005). Additionally, VR has been used to study bystander empathy, and, in doing so, it is argued to be a good compromise between the control offered by experiments and the ecological validity of field studies (Kozlov and Johansen, 2010).

As excited as I was to begin research in what is now known as behavioural ethics, I am even more inspired looking at the field it has become and the field it can be. Fortunately, we have moved beyond the need to justify this field of study. It is now time to continue to pursue relevant, rigorous science that makes a marked difference for organizations and society.

References

Agrawal, A., Gans, J., & Goldfarb, A. (2017). How AI will change the way we make decisions. *Harvard Business Review*, July 26.

Ahmad M.G., Klotz A.C., & Bolino MC. (2020). Can good followers create unethical leaders? How follower citizenship leads to leader moral licensing and unethical behavior. *Journal of Applied Psychology, 106*(9), 1374–1390. doi: 10.1037/apl0000839

Amin, A.B., Bednarczyk, R.A., Ray, C.E., Melchiori, K. J., Graham, J., Huntsinger, J. R., & Omer, S. B. (2017). Association of moral values with vaccine hesitancy. *Nature Human Behavior 1*, 873–880 https://doi.org/10.1038/s41562-017-0256-5

Aquino, K. & Reed, A. (2002). The self-importance of moral identity. *Journal of Personality and Social Psychology, 83(6)*, 1423–1440.

Balliet, D., Mulder, L. B., & Van Lange, P. A. M. (2011). Reward, punishment, and cooperation: A meta-analysis. *Psychological Bulletin, 137(4)*, 594–615. https://doi.org/10.1037/a0023489

Bazerman, M.H., & Gino, F. (2012). Behavioral ethics: Toward a deeper understanding of moral judgment and dishonesty. *Annual Review of Law and Social Science, 8,* 85–104.

Bazerman, M.H., Morgan, K.P. & Loewenstein, G.F. (1997). The impossibility of auditor independence. *Sloan Management Review, 38*(4), 89–94.

Bazerman, M., Tenbrunsel, A. & Wade-Benzoni, K. (1998). Negotiating with yourself and lLosing: Making decisions with competing internal preferences. *The Academy of Management Review, 23(2)*, 225–241.

Borges, G. S., & Dos Santos, B. F. (2021). COVID-19 vaccine as a common good. *Journal of Global Health, 11*, 03109. https://doi.org/10.7189/jogh.11.03109

Chin, M. K., Hambrick, D. C., & Trevino, L. K. (2013). Political ideologies of CEOs: The influence of executives' values on corporate social responsibility. *Administrative Science Quarterly, 58(2)*, 197–232. https://doi.org/10.1177/0001839213486984

Cohen T.R., Panter A.T., Turan N., Morse L., & Kim Y. (2014). Moral character in the workplace. *Journal of Personality and Social Psychology, 107*, 943–63.

Desai, S. D., Chugh, D., & Brief, A. P. (2014). The implications of marriage structure for men's workplace attitudes, beliefs, and behaviors toward women. *Administrative Science Quarterly, 59(2)*, 330–365. https://doi.org/10.1177/0001839214528704

Dignum, V. (2018). Ethics in artificial intelligence: Introduction to the special issue. *Ethics and Information Technology, 20*, 1–3. http://doi.org/10.1007/s10676-018-9450-z

Fulmer, I. S., Barry, B., & Long, D. A. (2009). Lying and smiling: Informational and emotional deception in negotiation. *Journal of Business Ethics, 88(4)*, 691–709. www.jstor.org/stable/40295027

Gino, F., & Bazerman, M.H. (2009). When misconduct goes unnoticed: The acceptability of gradual erosion in others' unethical behavior. *Journal of Experimental Social Psychology, 45*, 708–719.

Goffman, E. (1974). *Frame analysis: An essay on the organization of experience*. Harvard University Press.

Graham, J., Haidt, J., Koleva, S., Motyl, M., Iyer, R., Wojcik, S., & Ditto, P. H. (2012). Moral foundations theory: The pragmatic validity of moral pluralism. *Advances in Experimental Social Psychology, 47*, 55–130.

Greene, J. D., Nystrom, L. E., Engell, A. D., Darley, J. M., & Cohen, J. D. (2004). The neural bases of cognitive conflict and control in moral judgment. *Neuron, 44(2)*, 389–400. https://doi.org/10.1016/j.neuron.2004.09.027

Haidt, J. (2003). The Moral Emotions. In Davidson, R.; Scherer, Klaus; Goldsmith, H. (eds*.). Handbook of affective sciences*. Oxford: Oxford University Press. pp. 855. ISBN 978-0-19-512601-3.

Hardin, A.E., Bauman, C. W., & Mayer, D.M. (2020). Show me the … family: How photos of meaningful relationship reduce unethical behavior at work. *Organizational Behavior and Human Decision Processes, 161*, 93–108.

Jansen, E. & Von Glinow, M.A. (1985). Ethical ambivalence and organizational reward systems. *Academy of Management Review, 10(4)*, 814–822.

John, L.K., Loewenstein, G., & Rick, S.I. (2014). Cheating more for less: Upward social comparisons motivate the poorly compensated to cheat. *Organizational Behavior and Human Decision Processes, 123*(2), 101–109.

Kern, M. C., & Chugh, D. (2009). Bounded ethicality: The perils of loss framing. *Psychological Science, 20*(3), 378–384. https://doi.org/10.1111/j.1467-9280.2009.02296.x

Kozlov, M. D., & Johansen, M. K. (2010). Real behavior in virtual environments: psychology experiments in a simple virtual-reality paradigm using video games. *Cyberpsychology, Behavior and Social Networking, 13*(6), 711–714. https://doi.org/10.1089/cyber.2009.0310

Lammers, J. Galinsky, A.D., Dubois, D. & Rucker, D.D. (2015). Power and morality. *Current Opinion in Psychology, 6*, 15–19.

Larkin, I., Pierce, L., Shalvi, S., & Tenbrunsel, A. (2021). The opportunities and challenges of behavioral field research on misconduct. *Organizational Behavior and Human Decision Processes, 166*, 1–8. https://doi.org/10.1016/j.obhdp.2021.06.004

Mayer, D. M., Aquino, K., Greenbaum, R. L., & Kuenzi, M. (2012). Who displays ethical leadership, and why does it matter? An examination of antecedents and consequences of ethical leadership. *Academy of Management Journal, 55*(1), 151–171.

Moore C. (2015). Moral disengagement. *Current Opinion in Psychology, 6*, 199–204

O'Leary-Kelly, A. M., & Bowes-Sperry, L. (2001). Sexual harassment as unethical behavior: The role of moral intensity. *Human Resource Management Review, 11*(1–2), 73–92. https://doi.org/10.1016/S1053-4822(00)00041-3

Rees, M.R., Tenbrunsel, A.E., & Diekmann, K.A. (2021). It's just business: understanding how business frames differ from ethical frames and the effect on unethical behavior. *Journal of Business Ethics, 176*, 429–449 https://doi.org/10.1007/s10551-020-04729-5

Schelling, T.C. (1984). *Choice and consequences: Perspectives of an errant economist.* Cambridge, MA: Harvard University Press.

Schweitzer, M.E., Ordóñez, L. & Douma, B. (2004). Goal setting as a motivator of unethical behavior. *Academy of Management Journal, 47 (3)*, 422–432

Standage, T. (2016). The return of the machinery question. *The Economist.* Retrieved from www.economist.com/news/special-report/21700761-after-many-false-starts-artificial-intelligence-has-taken-will-it-cause-mass

Stone, P., Brooks, R., Brynjolfsson, E., Calo, R., Etzioni, O., Hager, G., … Teller, A. (2016). Artificial intelligence and life in 2030. One hundred year study on artificial intelligence: Report of the 2015–2016 study panel. Stanford, CA. Retrieved from http://ai100.stanford.edu/2016-report

Tangney, J.P., Stuewig, J., & Mashek, D.J. (2007). Moral emotions and moral behavior. *Annual Review of Psychology, 58*(1), 345–372.

Tenbrunsel, A. E., & Messick, D. M. (1999). Sanctioning systems, decision frames, and cooperation. *Administrative Science Quarterly, 44*(4), 684–707. https://doi.org/10.2307/2667052

Tenbrunsel, A. E., Rees, M. R., & Diekmann, K. A. (2019). Sexual harassment in academia: Ethical climates and bounded ethicality. *Annual Review of Psychology, 70*, 245–270. https://doi.org/10.1146/annurev-psych-010418-102945

Tenbrunsel, A. E., Smith-Crowe, K., & Umphress, E. E. (2003). Building houses on rocks: The role of the ethical infrastructure in organizations. *Social Justice Research, 16(3)*, 285–307. https://doi.org/10.1023/A:1025992813613

To, C., Wiwad, D, & Kouchaki, M. (2021). Economic inequality increases the acceptability of others' unethical behavior. *Academy of Management Proceedings,* https://doi.org/10.5465/AMBPP.2021.12392symposium

Trevino, L. K. (1986). Ethical decision making in organizations: A person-situation interactionist model. *The Academy of Management Review, 11*(3), 601–617. https://doi.org/10.2307/258313

Treviño L.K., Butterfield K.D. & McCabe D.L. (1998) The ethical context in organizations: Influences on employee attitudes and behaviors. *Business Ethics Quarterly, 8(3)*: 447–476.

Welsh, D.T., & Ordonez, L.D. (2014). The dark side of consecutive high performance goals: Linking goal setting, depletion and unethical behavior. *Organizational Behavior and Human Decision Processes, 123*(2), 79–89.

Woodzicka, J. A., & LaFrance, M. (2001). Real versus imagined gender harassment. *Journal of Social Issues, 57(1)*, 15–30. https://doi.org/10.1111/0022-4537.00199

Yu, H., Shen, Z., Miao, C., Leung, C., Lesser, V. R., & Yang, Q. (2018). Building ethics into artificial intelligence. IJCAI'18: Proceedings of the 27th International Joint Conference on Artificial Intelligence, 5527-5533.

Zyda, M. (2005). From visual simulation to virtual reality to games. *Computer, 38(9)*, 25–32. 10.1109/MC.2005.297.

PART VB

Empirical review chapters on moral behavior

19
THE INTRAPERSONAL LEVEL

From feelings to moral actions—a working memory model of emotional influences on people's own moral behaviours

Lotte F. van Dillen

Abstract

People's moral choices and actions are greatly influenced by their emotional states and dispositions. Whereas these influences have typically been described as automatic and involuntary, here I will argue that they rely on general-purpose working memory mechanisms and are therefore restricted by capacity limitations. I will discuss a variety of empirical findings that illustrate this point across both positive and negative emotional influences, and for various moral behaviours. The findings show that when cognitive load increases—due to a competing task—emotional processing in working memory decreases, and as a result, influences moral choices and actions. Additionally, these findings emphasize the importance of individual differences in working memory functioning, such as attentional control skills, that allow for more flexible regulation of emotional influences on behaviour. I will end my overview with some unresolved questions and practical implications.

- Whether a person's moral behaviour is affected by the emotions they experience, depends on their mental capacity.
- Working memory functions as a central hub for affective processing and behavioural regulation.
- Working memory load can decrease both the effects of negative emotions on punitive moral behaviour, as well as the effects of positive emotions on prosocial moral behaviour.
- Future research might reveal conditions under which feelings benefit or undermine moral behaviour, and how working memory resources can thus be strategically employed.

Introduction

It is now well established in psychological science that people's own moral behaviour is shaped by emotions or affective processes more broadly. As noted in Ellemers et al. (2019, p.335) an important principle that connects different theoretical perspectives on human morality is 'the

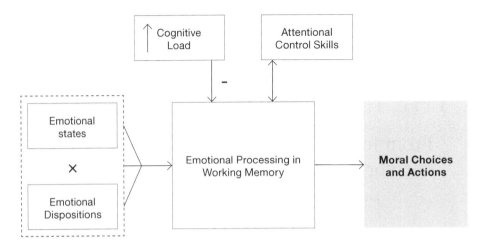

Figure 19.1 Working memory as a central hub for affective processing and for the regulation of affective influences on people's moral choices and actions. People's emotional states and dispositions shape their moral choices and actions, in so far as these are elaborated upon in working memory. When cognitive load of a competing task increases, emotional processing in working memory decreases, and as a result, it influences moral choices and actions. Individual differences in working memory functioning, such as attentional control skills, allow for more flexible regulation of such emotional influences.

realization that this involves deliberate thoughts and ideals about right and wrong, as well as behavioural realities and emotional experiences people have…'. This realization, although prevalent for some time in the philosophical tradition, gained momentum in experimental psychology following Haidt's influential paper 'The emotional dog and its rational tail' (Haidt, 2001) that pointed towards the emotional basis of moral intuitions about for instance harm and care. This paper led to a surge in research aimed at identifying which specific emotions lead to which specific moral tendencies but also whether certain affective dispositions shape people's behavioural choices and decisions in the moral domain in certain ways.

This chapter will not focus on the specifics of the various emotion effects but rather on the strong emphasis that theoretical models have typically placed on the automatic nature of emotional influences on people's own moral behaviour (i.e. Haidt, 2001; Paxton & Greene, 2010), and the idea that, once aroused, the impact of emotions is difficult to constrain (although emotions can both inform and result from more deliberate thinking; e.g., Cushman, 2013). Here, I propose that whereas emotional responses indeed typically arise quickly and effortlessly (Bradley, 2009), and commonly influence people's moral behaviour outside awareness (Haidt, 2001), these need not always shape people's behavioural choices and decisions in the moral domain. This, I argue, depends on people's mental capacity to processes emotional information. To illustrate this point, I will elaborate on a previously developed theoretical framework (depicted in Figure 19.1.; Van Dillen & Koole, 2007; Hofmann & Van Dillen, 2012; Van Dillen & Hofmann, 2023). This framework identifies working memory as a central hub for affective processing and for the regulation of affective influences on people's choices and actions. Whereas the original framework is aimed at explaining these influences across various behavioural domains, here, I focus on how it can be applied to the moral domain.

Working memory as a central hub for affective processing

The human working memory system is often described as a system for integrating and manipulating different information inputs as to generate a coherent (behavioural) output in line with the current task context (D'Esposito & Postle, 2015). It has been well established that working memory capacity is limited (Miller, 1956), such that when cognitive load increases, processing of certain information is prioritized at the cost of other information. This prioritization typically occurs in accordance with our focal goals (Knudsen, 2007). A compelling illustration of this notion is the finding that when asked to perform complex mental calculations, people tend to focus their gaze upwards or even close their eyes, as to minimize potentially disruptive visual input (Glenberg et al., 1998).

Over the past few decades, evidence has accumulated that affective processing is bounded by the same general principles of cognition as any type of information processing (e.g., Erber & Tesser, 1992; Hur, Iordan, Dolcos, & Berenbaum, 2017; Barley, Bauer, Wilson, & MacNamara, 2021; Van Dillen & Koole, 2007). Erber and Tesser (1992) were among the first to systematically explore capacity constraints on affective processing. They showed that negative moods decreased due to increasing task load, a phenomenon which they labelled 'task absorption'. In a first experiment, they found that participants reported less intense negative moods in response to an emotionally arousing film clip when they subsequently solved complex rather than simple math equations for ten minutes. In a second experiment, they observed similar absorption effects for participants who were told that investing effort in the math task was instrumental for their performance (rather than unrelated). Hence, the more effort participants invested in the math task, the more their performance neutralized the previously induced negative mood.

The findings described above suggest that task-related and affective information compete over the same limited working memory resources (Van Dillen & Koole, 2007). Due to its high motivational relevance, affective information is typically prioritized (Bradley, 2009), and may accordingly impact people's mental states and behaviour when working memory demands of other activities are low. After all, the capacity to screen the environment quickly and effectively for potential threats and incentives has high adaptive value (Bradley, 2009). However, when a focal task demands more mental resources, for example, because of its high complexity, fewer resources will be available for processing affective information (Knudsen, 2007). Indeed, a large body of evidence now supports this notion across various types of negative and positive affective stimuli, such as faces (Van Dillen & Derks, 2012), visual scenes (Barley et al. 2021; Cohen, Moyal, & Henik, 2015), pain stimuli (Buhle & Wager, 2010), and even pleasant and aversive tastes and smells (Hoffmann-Hensel et al., 2017; Liang et al., 2018). The suppressive effects have also been demonstrated for a diverse range of working memory tasks, such as memorizing digits or characters (Van der Wal & Van Dillen, 2013), playing demanding visuo-spatial games like Tetris (Gummerum et al., 2016), or performing complex arithmetic (Erber & Tesser, 1992).

The idea that affective processing and cognitive function engage an overlapping set of domain-general, capacity-limited mental resources has been corroborated by neuropsychological research. Under more demanding task conditions, such studies observed an inverse coupling between neural responses in affect-related brain networks on the one hand, and networks involved in working memory on the other hand. Typically, affective brain responses were down-regulated whereas working memory-related activity was upregulated when task demands increased (Buhle & Wager, 2010; Erk, Kleczar, & Walter, 2007; Van Dillen, Heslenfeld & Koole, 2009; Van Dillen & Van Steenbergen, 2018), although the reverse pattern has also been observed, for example when, orthogonally, the intensity of affective stimulation was increased (Buhle & Wager, 2010).

From feelings to moral actions: a brief overview of state and dispositional emotional influences on moral behaviour

As already noted, both state and dispositional emotional influences on people's own moral behaviour have been widely documented in recent years. Disgust and anger have been found to drive people's rejection and punishment of others' moral transgressions (Harle & Sanfey, 2007; Moretti & di Pellegrino, 2010), whereas other-praising emotions such as gratitude and elevation have typically been observed to facilitate people's prosocial behaviour and caring responses (Algoe & Haidt, 2009).

Feelings of disgust motivate the rejection of people violating our key values (Rozin, Haidt, & McCauley, 2000), even when these feelings are irrelevant for the judgment at hand (e.g., Schnall et al., 2008). And more grateful individuals express greater moral outrage about harms perpetrated against others (Keefer et al., 2020). Feelings of disgust (Moretti & di Pellegrino, 2010) and sad moods (Harle & Sanfey; 2007) also increase the tendency to reject unfair offers in an ultimatum game (where the recipient can only accept or reject), compared to happy or neutral moods. Interestingly, third-party punishment of unfair distributions is increased in individuals experiencing anger (Gummerum et al., 2016) compassion (Pfattheicher, Sassenrath & Keller, 2019) and gratitude (Vayness, Duong, & DeSteno, 2020). Insights from these experimental games suggest that a variety of both positive and negative emotions shape people's responses to fairness violations by others, even when they themselves are not affected, and even when their response incurs personal costs, pointing again to emotions' powerful reach.

Much like emotional states, emotional dispositions have been found to shape moral behaviour in distinct ways. A large body of studies has demonstrated a positive association between dispositional disgust sensitivity and rejective tendencies towards moral transgressions (see also Harris & Mungur, this volume; Schnall, this volume). The emotion specificity or domain dependence of such dispositional effects is still under debate (e.g., Landy & Piazza, 2019; Van Leeuwen et al., 2017). However, most important for this analysis, the overall association between greater negative affective sensitivity and harsher moral condemnations has been firmly established. Moreover, emotional dispositions have been linked to sensitivity to moral rejection. For instance, eye tracking research showed that greater trait social anxiety is associated with greater selective avoidance of facial cues of social rejection, in particular after one's moral identity has been threatened (Van Dillen et al., 2017). Similarly, individual differences in negative and positive affectivity (e.g., trait anger, disgust, and sympathy) have been differently associated with more utilitarian versus deontological moral preferences (Baron, Gürçay, & Luce, 2018). Trait gratitude (Ma, Tunney, & Ferguson, 2017), moreover, has consistently been associated with prosociality—in particular, in social situations with salient reciprocity norms.

In sum, and as depicted in the first box of Figure 19.1, a rich collection of findings suggest that both context-specific emotional states as well as more dispositional emotional tendencies shape people's own moral behaviour. Emotions shape people's moral choices and actions, even when they bear no relevance to the actual situation, illustrating their potent reach. However, like any type of information, the effects of emotional information on our choices and actions are restrained by the boundaries of working memory functioning, as I will propose next.

Working memory constrains of emotional influences on moral behaviour

Several extensions of earlier work on emotional influences on moral behaviour have shown that when people's working memory capacity is taxed by a demanding task, both stimulus-induced and dispositional emotion influences on moral behaviour are suppressed (Van Dillen et al, 2012; Wang et al., 2011; Gummerum et al., 2016). This has been demonstrated for a variety of distracter tasks that induce cognitive load. For instance, performing a cognitively engaging—yet neutral—writing task (e.g., about the layout of the local post office, or a double decker driving down the streets) decreased the displacement of anger, and the associated aggressive behaviour, in response to an initial provocation (Bushman et al., 2005). Similarly, playing Tetris for three minutes following an autobiographical anger induction, reduced participants' decisions to punish others for their unfair distributions in an economic game—to levels compared to people in a neutral state (Gummerum et al., 2016; see also: Wang et al. 2011). Furthermore, in a series of three studies in which incidental disgust resulted in harsher rejections of moral transgressions compared to a neutral affective state, this effect greatly diminished following a similar three-minute Tetris intervention (Van Dillen et al, 2012).

Findings further showed that individual differences in attentional control, an important working memory-related skill (Derryberry, 2002), mediated the positive relation between participants' disgust intensity and the severity of their moral rejections—but only in the absence of the Tetris intervention. That is, cognitive load induced by playing Tetris overruled these individual differences: When instructed to focus on their feelings in the absence of external demands, participants with strong attentional control reported equally intense disgust, and judged the moral transgression equally severe, as participants with weak attentional control. This suggests that people with strong attentional control skills are not merely inhibiting any disgust feelings but can more flexibly tune emotional processing up or down depending on what the specific task calls for (see Figure 19.1).

Likewise, a number of findings have demonstrated that emotional reactions to the suffering of others, and subsequent helping behaviour, are suppressed when people's working memory is taxed. In one experiment, cognitive load was varied through a digit span task, while participants were exposed to sounds of infant crying (or a neutral tone). Results showed that high compared to low cognitive load reduced empathic responses and caregiving intentions in response to the crying (Hiraoka & Nomura, 2016). Neuroimaging findings have corroborated these results, showing that high cognitive load generically suppresses neural responses to others in pain as well as associated helping behaviour (Gu & Han, 2007; Rameson, Morelli, & Lieberman, 2012). In a neuroimaging experiment on empathy for pain (Gu & Han, 2007), for example, participants watched pictures or cartoons of hands that were in painful or neutral positions while they either estimated the pain intensity felt by the model or counted the number of hands in the stimulus displays. Rating the pain intensity of painful pictures and cartoons increased activation in the 'pain matrix' of the brain. But when subjects merely counted the number of hands in the painful stimuli, activation in the pain matrix was eliminated. To explain their findings, the authors argued that counting relies more on 'cool' cognitive processes, for which performance does not depend on accurately assessing someone's pain (or may even suffer from empathic responses to others' distress taking up limited resources).

In another study (Meiring et al., 2014), participants performed a highly or mildly demanding counting task while viewing content-matched short film clips of both a member of their racial ingroup and a member of their racial outgroup who described a distressing experience. While viewing the film clips, participants' cardiovascular reactivity and empathic responses were assessed. The researchers found no evidence of differential empathic responding due to racial group membership of the target. Instead, they found that high concurrent working memory load attenuated participants' physiological responses to the suffering of the target and decreased their willingness to volunteer help, irrespective of the target's group membership. These findings thus further support the idea that demanding mental conditions 'crowd out' empathic (behavioural) tendencies.

Taken together, and as depicted in Figure 19.1, the above discussed findings suggest that at the intrapersonal level of moral behaviour, working memory processes play a central role in the regulation of emotional influences on people's moral choices and actions. Theoretical models have typically strongly emphasized the automatic and inflexible nature of emotional influences on people's moral behaviour (i.e. Haidt, 2001; Paxton & Greene, 2010), and the idea that, once aroused, the impact of emotions is difficult to constrain. Yet, the above-discussed findings show that taxing people's working memory resources with a focal task, down-regulates the influence of both negative and positive emotions on their moral choices and actions. This in turn weakens both punitive as well as prosocial moral tendencies. Such working memory influences seem 'blind' to the desirability of particular moral behaviours, or whether these involve the harm or care domain. Rather, they reflect a generic characteristic of our human cognitive architecture, namely how, for better or for worse, it deals with the limits on our information processing capacity. In the absence of demanding task conditions, findings have demonstrated that emotional processing, and subsequent influences on moral behaviours, can be both up- and down-regulated, the success of which depends on working memory-related individual differences such as attentional control skills.

Unresolved questions, and practical implications of a working memory model

The working memory model discussed before proposes that blocking one's mental capacity with a demanding task may 'neutralize' emotional influences on moral behaviour, which is highly relevant for decision-making contexts in which these influences are unwarranted, such as in certain professional contexts. For example, both incidental disgust and trait disgust sensitivity have been found to result in harsher punitive decisions, in particular in response to gruesome crimes, by both lay people and legal professionals (Van Dillen & Vanderveen, 2017). When confronted with arousing evidence during a criminal investigation or the subsequent trial, police officers, judges or juries may be offered a cool-off period that involves neutral distractions (such as Tetris) before they make important decisions to prevent emotional bias of their assessments and decisions. Likewise, when one's profession involves the intentional infliction of harm (as in surgery), affective responses should be kept to a minimum as not to interfere with task performance (Decety, Yang, Cheng, 2010). More generally, people may strategically implement cognitive distractions to temper excessive emotional reactions (Sheppes et al., 2014) in order (or in an attempt) to regulate their behaviour.

Yet, we've also seen how taxing working memory suppresses emotional influences on positive moral behaviour, such as prosocial tendencies, and empathic responses. Thus, other moral behavioural contexts, for example in the care domain, may call for minimal interference from competing task demands. When the just-described police officer reaches out to a crime victim, or the surgeon is about to meet with a patient, they may want to limit any distractions as to maximize rapport and sensitivity to their interaction partner's emotional needs (Fennern & Sur, 2022). On this note, a number of findings suggest that the suppressive effects of cognitive load seem to be weaker for individuals scoring high on trait empathy (Rameson et al., 2012; Hiraoka & Nomura,

2016). In one study, in which participants judged the intensity of the emotion when looking at facial expressions (empathize group), or with an additional eight-digit memory task (cognitive load group), it was found that perspective-taking and empathic concern were positively related to pain, fear, and happiness ratings *within* the cognitive load group (Meiring et al., 2014). These results reveal that high dispositional empathic concern and perspective-taking abilities could allow individuals to override the suppressive effects of cognitive load on empathy. Perhaps, for these individuals, empathic responses and perspective taking have become more habitual and, hence, less dependent on working memory resources (Rameson et al., 2012; Bajouk & Hansenne, 2019). However, it is also possible that highly empathic individuals were better able to focus their attention on the target's distress, in the presence of the concurrent memory task. Interestingly, a recent study has documented a positive relation between empathy and the capacity to maintain information about biological movements in working memory (Gao et al., 2016), indicating that highly empathic individuals may be better able to process social information in conditions that tax their working memory capacity. Likewise, neuropsychological findings showed that the more effective engagement of the frontoparietal working memory network—during a cognitively demanding task—correlated positively with self-reported empathy scores (Xin & Lei, 2015). Future research could examine the role of individual differences in working memory capacity and their association with empathy more systematically.

Whereas the short-term effects of taxing working memory on affective processing have been compellingly demonstrated, little is known about the long-term impact of distraction-based strategies that tax working memory. Some research points to more shallow information processing, and accordingly, memory impairments (Kron et al., 2010; Sheppes & Meiran, 2008). Because taxing working memory leaves the source of emotions unchanged, emotional reactions to more stable problematic situations could rebound once people no longer engage in distraction. Such affective processing costs may prevent important moral intuitions from informing people's decisions, whereas poor integration of affective experiences in moral contexts may thwart the development of more fine-grained moral identities and growth (Gummerum et al., 2020; Lefebvre, & Krettenauer, 2019; Pohling et al., 2018). This reasoning aligns well with recent theorizing that suggests that typical cognitive load tasks that tax working memory capacity, might inhibit processes of self-reflection, mental state attribution, or imagination (Jenkins, 2019). An important question for future research thus is when our feelings should inform our moral behaviours and when they shouldn't, and how we can strategically employ our working memory resources to that effect.

References

Algoe, S. B., & Haidt, J. (2009). Witnessing excellence in action: The 'other-praising' emotions of elevation, gratitude, and admiration. *The Journal of Positive Psychology*, 4(2), 105–127.

Bajouk, O., & Hansenne, M. (2019). Dispositional perspective-taking and empathic concern modulate the impact of cognitive load on empathy for facial emotions. *Psychological Reports*, 122(6), 2201–2219.

Barley, B., Bauer, E. A., Wilson, K. A., & MacNamara, A. (2021). Working memory load reduces the electrocortical processing of positive pictures. *Cognitive, Affective, & Behavioural Neuroscience*, 21(2), 347–354.

Baron, J., Gürçay, B. & Luce, M. F. (2018). Correlations of trait and state emotions with utilitarian moral judgements. *Cognition and Emotion, 32(1)*, 116–129.

Bradley, M. M. (2009). Natural selective attention: Orienting and emotion. *Psychophysiology, 46(1)*, 1–11.

Buhle, J., & Wager, T. D. (2010). Performance-dependent inhibition of pain by an executive working memory task. *PAIN®, 149(1)*, 19–26.

Bushman, B. J., Bonacci, A. M., Pedersen, W. C., Vasquez, E. A., & Miller, N. (2005). Chewing on it can chew you up: effects of rumination on triggered displaced aggression. *Journal of Personality and Social Psychology*, *88*(6), 969.

Cohen, N., Moyal, N., & Henik, A. (2015). Executive control suppresses pupillary responses to aversive stimuli. *Biological Psychology, 112*, 1–11.

Cushman, F. (2013). Action, outcome, and value: A dual-system framework for morality. *Personality and Social Psychology Review*, *17*(3), 273–292.

Decety, J., Yang, C. Y., & Cheng, Y. (2010). Physicians down-regulate their pain empathy response: an event-related brain potential study. *Neuroimage, 50(4)*, 1676–1682.

Derryberry, D. (2002). Attention and voluntary self-control. *Self and Identity, 1*(2), 105–111.

D'Esposito, M., & Postle, B. R. (2015). The cognitive neuroscience of working memory. *Annual Review of Psychology*, *66*, 115–142.

Ellemers, N., Van Der Toorn, J., Paunov, Y., & Van Leeuwen, T. (2019). The psychology of morality: A review and analysis of empirical studies published from 1940 through 2017. *Personality and Social Psychology Review*, *23*(4), 332–366.

Erber, R. & Tesser, A. (1992). Task effort and the regulation of mood: The absorption hypothesis. *Journal of Experimental Social Psychology, 28,* 339–359.

Erk, S., Kleczar, A., & Walter, H. (2007). Valence-specific regulation effects in a working memory task with emotional context. *Neuroimage*, *37*(2), 623–632.

Fennern, E., & Sur, M. D. (2022). Surgical Empathy. In *Difficult Decisions in Surgical Ethics* (pp. 131–143). Springer, Cham.

Gao, Z., Ye, T., Shen, M., & Perry, A. (2016). Working memory capacity of biological movements predicts empathy traits. *Psychonomic Bulletin & Review*, *23*(2), 468–475.

Glenberg, A. M., Schroeder, J. L., & Robertson, D. A. (1998). Averting the gaze disengages the environment and facilitates remembering. *Memory & Cognition, 26*(4), 651–658.

Gu, X., & Han, S. (2007). Attention and reality constraints on the neural processes of empathy for pain. *Neuroimage*, *36*(1), 256–267.

Gummerum, M., López-Pérez, B., Van Dijk, E., & Van Dillen, L. F. (2020). When punishment is emotion-driven: Children's, adolescents', and adults' costly punishment of unfair allocations. *Social Development*, *29*(1), 126–142.

Gummerum, M., Van Dillen, L. F., Van Dijk, E., & López-Pérez, B. (2016). Costly third-party interventions: The role of incidental anger and attention focus in punishment of the perpetrator and compensation of the victim. *Journal of Experimental Social Psychology, 65*, 94–104.

Haidt, J. (2001). The emotional dog and its rational tail: A social intuitionist approach to moral judgment. *Psychological Review, 108(4)*, 814.

Harlé, K. M., & Sanfey, A. G. (2007). Incidental sadness biases social economic decisions in the Ultimatum Game. *Emotion, 7*(4), 876.

Hiraoka, D., & Nomura, M. (2016). The influence of cognitive load on empathy and intention in response to infant crying. *Scientific Reports*, *6*(1), 1–9.

Hoffmann-Hensel, S. M., Sijben, R., Rodriguez-Raecke, R., & Freiherr, J. (2017). Cognitive load alters neuronal processing of food odors. *Chemical Senses*, *42*(9), 723–736.

Hofmann, W. & Van Dillen, L. F. (2012) Desire: The new hotspot in self-regulation research. *Current Directions in Psychological Science, 21*(5), 317–322.

Hur, J., Iordan, A. D., Dolcos, F., & Berenbaum, H. (2017). Emotional influences on perception and working memory. *Cognition and Emotion, 31*(6), 1294–1302.

Jenkins, A. C. (2019). Rethinking cognitive load: A default-mode network perspective. *Trends in Cognitive Sciences*, *23*(7), 531–533.

Keefer, L. A., Brown, M., Brown, F. L., & Sacco, D. F. (2020). Gratitude predicts selective moral concern about interpersonal harms. *The Journal of Positive Psychology*, *16*(5), 701–713.

Knudsen, E. I. (2007). Fundamental components of attention. *Annual Review of Neuroscience, 30*, 57–78.

Kron, A., Schul, A., Cohen, A., & Hassin, R. R. (2010). Feelings don't come easy: Studies on the effortful nature of feelings. *Journal of Experimental Psychology: General, 139,* 520–534.

Landy, J. F., & Piazza, J. (2019). Reevaluating moral disgust: Sensitivity to many affective states predicts extremity in many evaluative judgments. *Social Psychological and Personality Science*, *10*(2), 211–219.

Lefebvre, J. P., & Krettenauer, T. (2019). Linking moral identity with moral emotions: A meta-analysis. *Review of General Psychology, 23*(4), 444–457.

Liang, P., Jiang, J., Ding, Q., Tang, X., & Roy, S. (2018). Memory load influences taste sensitivities. *Frontiers in Psychology, 9*, 2533. doi: 10.3389/fpsyg.2018.02533

Ma, L. K., Tunney, R. J., & Ferguson, E. (2017). Does gratitude enhance prosociality?: A meta-analytic review. *Psychological Bulletin, 143*(6), 601.

Miller, G. A. (1956). The magical number seven, plus or minus two: Some limits on our capacity for processing information. *Psychological Review, 63*(2), 81.

Meiring, L., Subramoney, S., Thomas, K. G., Decety, J., & Fourie, M. M. (2014). Empathy and helping: Effects of racial group membership and cognitive load. *South African Journal of Psychology, 44(4),* 426–438.

Moretti, L., & Di Pellegrino, G. (2010). Disgust selectively modulates reciprocal fairness in economic interactions. *Emotion, 10*(2), 169.

Paxton, J. M., & Greene, J. D. (2010). Moral reasoning: Hints and allegations. *Topics in Cognitive Science, 2*(3), 511–527.

Pfattheicher, S., Sassenrath, C., & Keller, J. (2019). Compassion magnifies third-party punishment. *Journal of Personality and Social Psychology, 117*(1), 124.

Pohling, R., Diessner, R., & Strobel, A. (2018). The role of gratitude and moral elevation in moral identity development. *International Journal of Behavioural Development, 42(4),* 405–415.

Rameson, L. T., Morelli, S. A., & Lieberman, M. D. (2012). The neural correlates of empathy: experience, automaticity, and prosocial behaviour. *Journal of cognitive neuroscience, 24*(1), 235–245.

Rozin, P., Haidt, J., & McCauley, C. R. (2000). Disgust. In M. Lewis & J. Haviland (Eds.), *Handbook of emotions* (2nd ed., pp. 637–653.). New York, NY: Guilford.

Schnall, S., Haidt, J., Clore, G. L., & Jordan, A. H. (2008). Disgust as embodied moral judgment. *Personality and Social Psychology Bulletin, 34,* 1096–1109.

Sheppes, G., & Meiran, N. (2008). There is no such thing as a free lunch: Divergent cognitive costs for online reappraisal and distraction. *Emotion, 8,* 870–874.

Sheppes, G., Scheibe, S., Suri, G., Radu, P., Blechert, J., & Gross, J. J. (2014). Emotion regulation choice: a conceptual framework and supporting evidence. *Journal of Experimental Psychology: General, 143*(1), 163.

Van der Wal, R. C., & Van Dillen, L. F. (2013). Leaving a flat taste in your mouth: task load reduces taste perception. *Psychological Science, 24*(7), 1277–1284.

Van Dillen, L. F. & Derks, B. (2012). Working memory load reduces facilitated processing of threatening faces: An ERP study. *Emotion, 12,* 1340–1349.

Van Dillen, L. F., & Koole, S. L. (2007). Clearing the mind: A working memory model of distraction from negative feelings. *Emotion, 7,* 715–723.

Van Dillen, L.F., Heslenfeld D. J., & Koole, S.L. (2009). Tuning down the emotional brain. *NeuroImage, 45,* 1212–1219.

Van Dillen, L. F., & Hofmann, W. (2023). Room for FEELINGS: A "working memory" account of affective processing. *Emotion Review,* 17540739221150233.

Van Dillen, L. F., Enter, D., Peters, L. P., van Dijk, W. W., & Rotteveel, M. (2017). Moral fixations: The role of moral integrity and social anxiety in the selective avoidance of social threat. *Biological Psychology, 122,* 51–58.

Van Dillen, L.F., & Vanderveen, G.N.G. (2017). Gruwelijke beelden van plaatsen delict: kijkstrategieën, opgewekte emoties en oordeelsvorming, *Tijdschrift voor Criminologie 59,* 176–193.

Van Dillen, L. F., Van der Wal, R., & Van den Bos, K. (2012). On the role of attention and emotion in morality: Attentional control modulates unrelated disgust in moral judgments. *Personality and Social Psychology Bulletin, 38,* 1221–1230.

Van Dillen, L. F. & Van Steenbergen, H. (2018). Tuning down the hedonic brain. Cognitive load reduces neural responses to high-calorie food pictures in the nucleus accumbens. *Cognitive, Affective, and Behavioural Neuroscience, 18,* 447–459.

Van Leeuwen, F., Dukes, A., Tybur, J. M., & Park, J. H. (2017). Disgust sensitivity relates to moral foundations independent of political ideology. *Evolutionary Behavioural Sciences, 11*(1), 92.

Vayness, J., Duong, F., & DeSteno, D. (2020). Gratitude increases third-party punishment. *Cognition and Emotion, 34*(5), 1020–1027.

Wang, C. S., Sivanathan, N., Narayanan, J., Ganegoda, D. B., Bauer, M., Bodenhausen, G. V., & Murnighan, K. (2011). Retribution and emotional regulation: The effects of time delay in angry economic interactions. Organizational Behavior and Human Decision Processes, *116*(1), 46–54.

Xin, F., & Lei, X. (2015). Competition between frontoparietal control and default networks supports social working memory and empathy. *Social Cognitive and Affective Neuroscience, 10*(8), 1144–1152.

20
THE INTERPERSONAL LEVEL

Affirming transgressors' morality as a strategy to promote apologies and interpersonal reconciliation—the promise and potential pitfalls

Nurit Shnabel

Abstract

Individuals who harm others (i.e., transgressors) experience threat to their moral identity, which they often try to defend through moral disengagement (e.g., by denying their culpability). Optimistically, the needs-based model of reconciliation suggests that restoration of transgressors' moral identity can reduce their defensiveness and increase their readiness for reconciliation. Several studies supported this possibility, revealing that morally accepting messages from their victims, as well as self-affirmation exercises through which transgressors affirmed their morality and the values breached by the transgression, increased their tendency to offer genuine, non-defensive apologies and invest effort in reconciliation. In contrast, however, morally accepting messages by third parties are associated with transgressors' lower willingness to reconcile. Further research is needed to identify the conditions under which moral affirmation might lead to such 'moral licensing' effects, rather than to increased reconciliatory behavior. Understanding the effects of moral affirmation is practically important for structuring effective restorative justice procedures.

- When a person harms someone else, the threat to the transgressors' moral identity hinders their readiness to apologize to the victim.
- Restoring transgressors' moral identity increases their readiness to apologize and reconcile with their victims.
- Morality restoration can be achieved through transgressors' self-affirmation of their morality or through morally accepting messages from their victims.
- Morally accepting messages by third parties, however, lead to moral licensing effects.
- Further research is needed to identify the conditions under which moral affirmation leads to prosocial, conciliatory vs. antisocial, licensing effects.

Introduction

Humans are a social animal (e.g., Dunbar, 2009), and conflict and transgressions are an inevitable part of social life. To enjoy the evolutionary benefits of sociality, humans, like other social primates (Silk, 2002), have evolved mechanisms for restoring valuable relationships in the aftermath of conflict (McCullough et al., 2013). In the seminal book *Mea culpa: A sociology of apology and reconciliation* sociologist Nicholas Tavuchis (1991) argues that apologies constitute the main mechanism to achieve this goal of harmony restoration, and that using them can dramatically transform the relations between former adversaries. Nevertheless, perpetrators of interpersonal transgressions often refrain from apologizing to their victim (Schumann, 2018).

Why is this the case, and what can be done about it? In the present chapter I will discuss the threat to transgressors' moral identity as an obstacle to apologies and reconciliation and focus on moral affirmation as a means to increase transgressors' readiness to apologize, compensate, and reconcile with their victims. Because research on moral affirmation is still in its early stages, I will also discuss the several unresolved issues that need to be studied in future research and explain why studying them has important practical implications.

Obstacles to apology and reconciliation

Interpersonal transgressions almost by definition involve transgressors' violation of moral imperatives, such as fairness, loyalty, or prevention of harm. Such moral failures may occur because the transgressors hold low concern for the victims and the relationship with them, which is also a common reason for their reluctance to apologize (Schumann, 2018). However, even when transgressors do care about their victims, they may refrain from apologizing because they view their acts as justified or at least excusable under the circumstances (Schönbach, 1990). Indeed, there is a systematic 'magnitude gap' (a term coined by Baumeister et al., 1990) between victims and transgressors' estimations of the immorality of the transgression and the severity of its consequences, which led Baumeister (1997) to conclude that "evil is in the eye of the beholder." This may explain the counterintuitive finding that transgressors feel greater guilt for harm caused by unintentional rather than intentional acts (Schönbach, 1990)—although it is intentional rather than unintentional acts that meet the conditions for attribution of blame (controllability, foreseeability, and intentionality; Shaver, 1985). Whereas the unintentional harm transgressors have caused may catch them with their guards down, intentional acts—which were processed and thought about in advance—are more likely to be perceived by the transgressors as justified and acceptable under the circumstances. Nevertheless, even if the transgressors believe their acts to be justified, knowing that the victims (and possibly others in their moral community) perceive their behavior as immoral poses a threat to transgressors' identity.

Research on the 'Big Two' in social psychology (see Abele et al., 2021) suggests that individuals' and groups' identities are perceived and judged along two fundamental dimensions: a 'vertical' dimension, representing traits such as agency and competence that are crucial for 'getting ahead,' and a 'horizontal' dimension, representing traits such as sociability and morality that are crucial for 'getting along.' According to the needs-based model of reconciliation (Shnabel & Nadler, 2008) transgressors experience threat to the 'horizontal' dimension of their identity (whereas their victims experience threat to the 'vertical' dimension). Because people generally wish to maintain their positive identity (Steele, 1988), and because those who violate the moral standards of their community face the risk of social rejection (Tavuchis, 1991), transgressors experience a heightened need to restore their positive moral identity.

How can this need be addressed? One way through which transgressors can restore their moral identity is apologizing to the victims and receiving their forgiveness. Theorizing on forgiveness has likened it to a 'gift' that victims grant to those who have offended them (Enright et al., 1998), which mitigates the moral inferiority engendered by the role of transgressor and reassures that the transgressors belong to the moral community to which their membership was questioned

(Exline & Baumeister, 2000). The problem with apologies, however, is that they are risky. This is because rather than reciprocating with forgiveness the victim might use the apology, which serves as an acknowledgment of the transgressor's 'moral debt' to the victim (Minow, 1998), to further reproach the transgressor. Therefore, despite the common view of apologizing as a moral imperative (Benziman, 2009) and evidence for its effectiveness in promoting reconciliation (Schumann, 2018), transgressors often avoid taking this risk. They choose, instead, to defend their moral identity through moral disengagement, such as denying their culpability or minimizing the harm caused by the transgression (Bandura, 1999).

Optimistically, however, the needs-based model of reconciliation puts forward the hypothesis that addressing transgressors' need to restore their moral identity may increase their readiness to take the risk involved in apologizing and increase their reconciliation efforts. In the next section I will review the research that supports this hypothesis.

Addressing transgressors' need for positive moral identity can open them to apology and reconciliation

The hypothesis that satisfying transgressors' need for moral acceptance can open them to reconciliation was first put into an empirical test in a series of experiments using diverse methods, including transgressions 'orchestrated' in the lab, recollection of real-life transgressions, and role-playing scenarios (see Shnabel & Nadler, 2008). For the present chapter's purposes, I will briefly present the findings of the large-scale registered replication of one study in this series (Baranski et al., 2020), which was conducted as part of the Many Labs 5 project (Ebersole et al., 2020).

Participants in this replication study ($N = 2,738$) were undergraduates of seven American universities and one European university. They read a vignette about a recently unemployed college student who, upon returning from a two-week family visit, learns that their roommate found a new roommate who could commit to paying the next year's rent, and therefore the college student had to move out. Participants were randomly assigned either to the victim condition, in which they imagined themselves in the shoes of the roommate who had to leave the apartment, or to the transgressor condition, in which they imagined themselves in shoes of the roommate who stayed in the apartment.

Note that we intentionally chose a vignette that does not reflect vicious or inexcusable behavior: The transgressors can justify their behavior by claiming that staying with a roommate who cannot commit to pay the rent might get them in trouble. This choice stemmed from our theoretical stance that purely 'evil,' unjustifiable behavior (such as having sex with a friend's fiancé, as in a vignette used in previous research by Gonzales et al., 1992) is rare, and our wish to use a vignette that simulates real-life transgressions. Indeed, this particular vignette was developed based on a pilot study in which US undergraduates wrote about a transgression experienced in their own lives.

After the assignment to social roles (victims or transgressors), participants completed self-reported measures of their sense of agency, moral image, need for empowerment (wish to have greater control over the situation), need for moral acceptance (e.g., wish that the other roommate would perceive them as a moral person), and willingness to reconcile with their roommate. Next, participants received the second part of the vignette. It described a class on interpersonal dynamics, taken one week after the conflict, which both roommates attended and in which participants provided each other with feedback about their intellectual competencies and interpersonal skills. In the 'empowerment' condition the roommate was said to give the participant highly positive feedback about their intellectual competencies, whereas in the 'moral acceptance' condition the roommate was said to give the participant highly positive feedback about their interpersonal skills (e.g., warmth and niceness). Then, participants completed once again the measures of their sense of agency, moral image, and willingness to reconcile with their roommate.

The results for participants assigned to the transgressor condition[1] revealed that in the first ('before') measurement they reported a lower moral image and a higher need for moral acceptance as compared to participants in the victim condition. Participants in the transgressor condition also reported a higher willingness to reconcile than participants in the victim condition, consistent with Baumeister's (1997) observation that transgressors find it easier to 'move on' than victims. Comparing the 'before' and 'after' measurements revealed that the moral acceptance (but not the empowerment) message improved transgressors' moral image. Moreover, the change in transgressors' willingness to reconcile was higher in the moral acceptance than in the empowerment condition, such that ultimately transgressors' willingness to reconcile was higher following the receipt of a morally accepting as compared to an empowering message from their victims. These findings suggest that restoring transgressors' moral identity through an appropriate message from the victim can increase their goodwill towards the victim—even in comparison to a message that is highly positive in tone yet does not directly refer to their moral identity.

Further empirical support for the positive effect of restoring transgressors' moral identity on their goodwill towards their victims was provided by research conducted within the framework of self-affirmation theory (Steele, 1988). According to this theory, behavioral or cognitive events that bolster the perceived integrity of the self (i.e., the person's overall image as adequate) can protect individuals from psychological threats encountered in their environment. Self-affirmation interventions, which commonly involve short writing exercises (typically instructing participants to write about their most important value; McQueen & Klein, 2006), have been consistently found to reduce individuals' defensive responses to psychological threats (for a review see Cohen & Sherman, 2014). For example, writing about their important values reduced smokers' defensiveness in response to threatening health-related information (Crocker et al., 2008).

Applying this logic to the context of interpersonal transgressions, Schumann (2014) hypothesized that transgressors tend to offer their victim defensive, unsatisfying apologies because an apology inherently associates the transgressors with their wrongful behavior, thus further endangering their already shaken sense of being a good person. If so, then self-affirmation exercises may reassure the transgressors that they are 'good people' and improve the quality of the apologies they offer to their victim. To test this hypothesis, Schumann (2014) instructed participants to think about something that they had done that offended or hurt somebody else, and then write down what they would say to that person had he or she been there right now. As expected, affirmed (vs. non-affirmed) participants wrote messages that included fewer defensive strategies (excuses, justifications, victim blaming, and minimization of the harm) and more genuinely apologetic elements (expressions of remorse, responsibility taking, offer of repair, promise of forbearance, and request for forgiveness). The effect persisted even when controlling for mood, thus allowing to rule out positive mood as an alternative explanation.

A remaining question, however, was whether the positive effect of self-affirmation on transgressors' conciliatory messages indeed stemmed from the restoration of their moral identity or whether it was driven by their enhanced sense of connectedness due to the reassurance of their social bonds. The latter possibility is consistent with findings that when completing self-affirmation exercises participants typically write about their sense of belonging to significant others (such as friends and family members, Shnabel et al., 2013) and that sense of belonging may serve as a 'symbolic shield' that helps people cope with psychological threats (Mikulincer & Shaver, 2007). Indeed, both morality and belonging can be viewed as components of the 'horizontal dimension' of the 'Big Two,' representing one's communion and getting along with others (Abele et al., 2021). Nevertheless, the restoration of one's moral identity vs. one's sense of belonging and connectedness to significant others can be viewed as representing two distinct avenues for encouraging reconciliation.

To distinguish between these two avenues, Woodyatt and Wenzel (2014) compared between different types of self-affirmation exercises. Participants in Woodyatt and Wenzel's research had committed an interpersonal transgression a couple of days prior to study participation. They were then assigned to different affirmation conditions: In the morality affirmation condition, participants affirmed the value violated by the transgression by explaining why they felt this value was important to them and describing a time in the past in which they had behaved consistently with this value. In the two other affirmation conditions, participants affirmed either their sense of belonging (by writing about a time in which they felt loved or accepted), or a value that was important to them yet unrelated to the transgression. There was also control, no-affirmation condition in which participants wrote about the activities they were going to complete that day. The results revealed that, compared to the other experimental conditions, affirming the value violated by transgression led participants to process their feelings of shame, rather than leaving it unresolved. Processing their shame led, in turn, to genuine self-forgiveness; namely, transgressors' effortful act of processing their wrongdoing, as compared to pseudo, defensive self-forgiveness characterized by simple lack of self-condemnation. Genuine self-forgiveness, in turn, increased participants' trust that they would behave better in the future as well as their readiness to reconcile with their victim one week following the affirmation.

Notably, these results diverge from previous findings on self-affirmation interventions, in which threats to one's identity and self-worth in one domain were effectively removed through the affirmation of one's identity and self-worth in other domains (Cohen & Sherman, 2014). For example, Black students' affirmation of their sense of belonging (representing the 'getting along' dimension of their identity) buffered them against the impairment to academic performance (representing the 'getting ahead' dimension of their identity) resulting from stereotype threat (the fear of confirming the negative stereotype about their group's intelligence) (Shnabel et al., 2013). Woodyatt and Wenzel (2014) explain this discrepancy by arguing that in the traditional self-affirmation research, self-affirmation exercises are used to encourage perseverance in the face of negative feedback (e.g., about one's academic performance). Yet "moral failure is not about poor performance at a valued task or activity" (p. 132), because one's moral identity is intimately linked to their feeling as worthy and adequate (moreso than performance in academic tasks, for example). This argument underlines that morality is the most important dimension in people's identity (see Leach et al., 2007), which makes it unique and non-fungible in nature.

Taken together, Baranski et al.'s (2020), Schumann's (2014) and Woodyatt and Wenzel's (2014) findings are all consistent with the notion that 'what goes on between people, cannot be separated from what is going on within people' (Gopin, 2004): Transgressors need to feel good about themselves, that is, perceive themselves as good and moral people in order to be kind and moral towards their victims.

Unresolved issues concerning the positive effect of restoring transgressors' moral identity

The research reviewed so far has demonstrated that the restoration of transgressors' moral identity either through morally accepting messages from the victim, or through self-affirmation exercises (especially if focused on the values breached by the transgression), increases transgressors'

Interpersonal level: transgressors' morality as a strategy

genuinely conciliatory tendencies towards their victims. Research on identity restoration through messages conveyed by third parties, however, revealed a more complex picture. In this research (Shnabel et al., 2014, Study 2), participants read a vignette about an employee who took a two-week leave from work due to maternity leave or military reserve duty.[2] Upon returning to the office, the employee learned that a colleague who temporarily filled their position was ultimately promoted to their job, whereas they themselves were demoted. Participants assigned to the victim role were asked to imagine themselves as the demoted employee, and participants assigned to the transgressor role—as the promoted employee.

After the assignment to roles, participants were randomly assigned to three experimental conditions. In the control/no-message condition, the vignette ended at this point. In the two 'message source' conditions, the vignette continued to describe a subsequent staff meeting in which employees gave each other feedback. Transgressors assigned to the 'other party' condition read that the victim praised their interpersonal skills (e.g., mentioned incidents in which they were considerate of others at the workplace). For transgressors in the 'third party' condition, the same message was said to be conveyed by a colleague who was not involved in the conflict.[3] Finally, participants completed a set of measures including moral image in the eyes of the victim, moral image in the eyes of the third party (the colleague not involved in the conflict), trust in the victim, and willingness for reconciliation. While a detailed review of the results is beyond the scope of the present chapter, Figure 20.1 presents the findings most relevant to the current discussion:

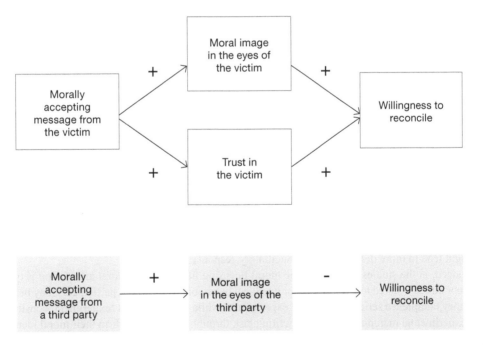

Figure 20.1 Main findings of mediation analysis: A morally accepting message from the victim restored transgressors' moral image in the eyes of the victim and trust in the victim, which was associated with the transgressor being *more* willing to reconcile (upper part of the figure). A morally accepting message from an uninvolved third party restored transgressors' moral image in the eyes of the third party, which was associated with the transgressor being *less* willing to reconcile (lower part of the figure).

217

The results revealed that a morally accepting message from the victim restored transgressors' trust in the victim (i.e., belief in the victim's good intentions) and moral image in the victim's eyes (but not in the eyes of the third party). Both trust in the victim and moral image in the eyes of the victim were associated with transgressors' greater readiness for reconciliation. In contrast, a morally accepting message from a third party failed to affect transgressors' trust in the victim or moral image in the victim's eyes. It did restore transgressors' moral image in the eyes of the third party, yet such restoration was *negatively* associated with transgressors' readiness for reconciliation. This result points to the potentially adverse effect on reconciliation of morality restoration interventions by third parties. From a broader perspective, it suggests that there are boundary conditions to the positive effect on reconciliation of affirming and restoring transgressors' moral identity.

Future research directions

An intriguing and important avenue for future research is to identify the conditions under which morality restoration effectively promotes transgressors' conciliatory tendencies, as well as the conditions under which it might hinder them. This may be achieved by integrating the assumptions of the needs-based model with the literature on moral licensing effects (e.g., Merritt et al., 2010), which shows that people's belief that they are good and moral people sometimes frees them to behave selfishly or immorally. The logic of this literature can explain the abovementioned finding that a morally accepting message from a third party was associated with transgressors' lower readiness to reconcile (Shnabel et al., 2014; Study 2). Possibly, the praise to their interpersonal skills by the third party provided the transgressors with 'moral credits'—by reassuring that their bad behavior toward the victim was balanced out by their other, positive behaviors, or with 'moral credentials'—by establishing their 'accreditations' as "good people" (see Monin & Miller, 2001).

A possible account for the discrepancy between the prosocial effects of morality affirmation reported in the reconciliation literature (except for Shnabel et al., 2014) and the antisocial effects reported moral licensing literature is that the effect of moral affirmation depends on the saliency of a threat to transgressors' moral identity. Perhaps transgressors show more conciliatory tendencies when *both* the threat to *and* the affirmation of their moral identity become salient at the same time. This could be the case, for example, when the victims themselves convey the morally reassuring message (as found by Baranski et al., 2020), or when transgressors write about why, despite the fact that they violated it, they do adhere to the value breached by the transgression (as found by Woodyatt & Wenzel, 2014). In contrast, when the affirmation occurs while the threat to transgressors' identity is not salient, for example, when the morally reassuring message is conveyed by a third-party who was not involved in the conflict (as found by Shnabel et al., 2014), it might lead to more defensive, non-conciliatory responses.

Indeed, in the studies reported in the moral licensing literature, the moral affirmation is typically not directly linked to the immoral or unethical behavior. To illustrate, participants may believe that they complete a series of unrelated experiments, while in fact the first 'experiment' constitutes the experimental manipulation (e.g., a writing task through which they affirm their moral identity) and the last 'experiment' constitutes the measurement of (im)moral behavior (e.g., defection in a commons dilemma; Sachdeva et al., 2009). While theoretically plausible, the possibility that the effect of moral affirmation depends on the saliency of a moral threat awaits direct empirical verification.

Notably, however, one of the difficulties that hinders the empirical testing of this theoretical account (or, in fact, other hypotheses about transgressors' moral behavior) is that assigning participants to the role of transgressors in lab experiments, which is the most preferred method in social psychological research, is tricky. While the victim's role is passive and therefore easy to produce in the lab (e.g., by having participants being mistreated by a confederate), the transgressor's role is active and therefore harder to orchestrate—as it paradoxically requires leading participants to transgress against others, yet making them do so *on their own volition*.

Classic paradigms that successfully lead most participants to transgress against other people, such as the "teacher-student" paradigm (Milgram, 1974), are ethically questionable. Recall of real-life transgressions has the advantage of participants' high degree of psychological involvement, yet the conclusions might be limited to past conflicts that have already been thought about and processed, and standardization is compromised because the transgressions recalled by participants vary in terms of severity, foreseeability, and elapsed time since the event. Vignette studies allow control and standardization, but compromise external validity because participants respond to imagined scenarios rather than to real-life events, and the dependent variables are assessed through self-reports rather than based on participants' actual behavior. Avoiding reliance on self-reports is possible through using behavioral economic games; however, this often necessitates focusing only on those participants whose behavior was transgressive (e.g., participants who breached their partners' trust in a modified trust game; Leunissen et al., 2012), which might result in a selection bias.

Encouragingly, technological advances allow the implementation of new methods, such as computerized pseudo-dyadic 'interactions,' in which participants falsely believe that they are interacting with a partner, that are programmed in a dynamic way. In one study, for example (SimanTov-Nachlieli & Shnabel, 2014; Study 1), transgressors were 'produced' in the lab by asking participants to allocate valuable resources between themselves and an (ostensive) partner and then giving them feedback on their allocation behavior. The feedback was pre-programmed such that participants who allocated the resources unequally were informed that the norm was to allocate the resources equally, whereas participants who allocated the resources equally were informed that the norm was to allocate the resources generously. Thus, regardless of their allocation behavior, participants perceived themselves as violating common moral standards. This paradigm, which allows to study participants' actual behavior under standardized conditions without the risk of selection bias, was originally used in the lab. Yet there is evidence that pseudo-dyadic 'interactions' can be effectively utilized in large-scale online platforms, such as MTurk (Summerville & Chartier, 2013). Hopefully, these technological tools and platforms will make it less challenging to experimentally study transgressors' moral behavior in the future.

Practical implications

Identifying the circumstances under which morality restoration strategies by different sources, that is, the transgressors themselves, their victims, or third parties, can promote (or hinder) the transgressors' efforts to apologize, compensate and reconcile with their victims has practical implications for mediators and facilitators of restorative justice practices. Such practices, which focus on rectifying the relationships and personal connections damaged by the transgression, rather than merely punishing the transgressors (Wachtel & McCold, 2001) are increasingly used in the legal and educational systems, as well as among families and communities (Boyes-Watson, 2008).

Participation in restorative justice procedures is typically not mandatory. For example, perpetrators of criminal offences in the Netherland voluntary choose whether to participate in victim-offender mediation (Jonas-van Dijk et al., 2020). The findings reviewed in this chapter suggest that transgressors' motivation to take part in these procedures should be higher if they provide them with an opportunity to address their need for moral acceptance. A study among 91 victim–offender mediation cases from a Dutch mediation agency (Zebel et al., 2019) provided initial support for this possibility. This study revealed that the need to restore their moral identity was an important underlying factor in offenders' decision to participate in VOM (victim–offender mediation) and intention to apologize and help their victims. Future research may examine whether the success of VOM (e.g., in reducing the risk of reoffending) is enhanced if encounters are structured such that offenders have an opportunity to address their need to restore their moral identity. Future research may also examine whether some offenders; for example, those who are dispositionally high on perpetrator sensitivity (more prone to feel guilt when transgressing against others; Baumert & Schmitt, 2016), are more likely to benefit from receiving an opportunity for moral restoration. Such future research may provide valuable insights for practitioners who engage in restorative justice encounters and real-life reconciliation efforts.

Conclusion

Based on the assumptions of the needs-based model of reconciliation, this chapter has put forward three arguments. First, the experience of threat to their moral identity is a common reason for transgressors' tendency to refrain from making sincere effort to reconcile and make amends to their victims. Second, removing the threat to transgressors' moral identity, which can be achieved through self-affirmation exercises that restore their moral image or through morally accepting message from their victims, increases transgressors' readiness to reconcile with their victims and offer them remorseful, non-defensive apologies. Third, that morally accepting messages from third parties were associated with transgressors' lower willingness to reconcile suggests that there are boundary conditions to the positive effects on reconciliation of morality affirmation, which should be identified in future research. I hope that the present chapter, and volume, will incite additional research on this socially and practically important topic.

Notes

1 Readers interested in the results for participants in the victim condition are kindly referred to Baranski et al. (2020).
2 Both are common reasons for absenteeism, for women and men respectively, in the Israeli context in which the study was conducted.
3 Participants in the victim condition received empowering messages, which praised their professional skills, from either the transgressor or a third party. Readers interested in these results are kindly referred to Shnabel et al. (2014).

References

Abele, A. E., Ellemers, N., Fiske, S. T., Koch, A., & Yzerbyt, V. (2021). Navigating the social world: Toward an integrated framework for evaluating self, individuals, and groups. *Psychological Review, 128*, 290–314. https://doi.org/10.1037/rev0000262
Bandura, A. (1999). Moral disengagement in the perpetration of inhumanities. *Personality and Social Psychology Review, 3*, 193–209. https://doi.org/10.1207/s15327957pspr0303_3
Baranski, E., Baskin, E., Coary, S., Ebersole, C. R., Krueger, L. E., Lazarevic´, L. B., ... Žeželj, I. (2020). Many Labs 5: Registered replication of Shnabel and Nadler (2008), Study 4. *Advances in Methods and Practices in Psychological Science, 3*, 405–417.
Baumeister, R. F. (1997). *Evil: Inside human violence and cruelty.* New York: Henry Holt.
Baumeister, R. F., Stillwell, A. M., & Wotman, S. R. (1990). Victim and perpetrator accounts of interpersonal conflict: Autobiographical narratives about anger. *Journal of Personality and Social Psychology, 59*, 994–1005.
Baumert A., & Schmitt M. (2016) Justice sensitivity. In: C. Sabbagh & M. Schmitt (eds) *Handbook of social justice theory and research.* Springer. https://doi.org/10.1007/978-1-4939-3216-0_9

Benziman, Y. (2009). *Forgive and not forget: The ethics of forgiveness*. Jerusalem: Van Leer [in Hebrew].

Boyes-Watson, C. (2008). *Peacemaking circles and urban youth: Bringing justice home*. Living Justice Press.

Cohen, G.L., & Sherman, D.K. (2014). The psychology of change: Self-affirmation and social psychological intervention. *Annual Review of Psychology, 65*, 333–371.

Crocker, J., Niiya, Y., & Mischkowski, D. (2008). Why does writing about important values reduce defensiveness? Self-affirmation and the role of positive other-directed feelings. *Psychological Science, 19*, 740–747.

Dunbar, R.I.M. (2009). The social brain hypothesis and its implications for social evolution. *Annals of Human Biology, 36*, 562–572. doi: 10.1080/03014460902960289

Ebersole, C.R., Mathur, M.B., Baranski, E.,… Szecsi, P. (2020). Many Labs 5: Testing pre-data-collection peer review as an intervention to increase replicability. *Advances in Methods and Practices in Psychological Science, 3*, 309–331.

Enright, R. D., Freedman, S., & Rique, J. (1998). The psychology of interpersonal forgiveness. In R. D. Enright & J. North (Eds.), *Exploring forgiveness* (pp. 46–62). Madison, WI: University of Wisconsin Press.

Exline, J. J., & Baumeister, R. F. (2000). Expressing forgiveness and repentance: Benefits and barriers. In M. E. McCullough, K. I. Pargament, & C. E. Thoresen (Eds.), *Forgiveness: Theory, research and practice* (pp. 133–155). New York: Guilford Press.

Gonzales, M. H., Manning, D. J., & Haugen, J. A. (1992). Explaining our sins: Factors influencing offender accounts and anticipated victim responses. *Journal of Personality and Social Psychology, 62*, 958–971.

Gopin, M. (2004). *Healing the heart of conflict: 8 crucial steps to making peace with yourself and others*. Emmaus, PA: Rodale Books.

Jonas-van Dijk, J. , Zebel, S., Claessen, J., & Nelen, H. (2020). Victim–Offender mediation and reduced reoffending: Gauging the self-selection bias. *Crime and Delinquency, 66*(6–7), 949–972. https://doi.org/10.1177/0011128719854348

Leach, C. W., Ellemers, N., & Barreto, M. (2007). Group virtue: The importance of morality (vs. competence and sociability) in the positive evaluation of in-groups. *Journal of Personality and Social Psychology, 93*, 234–249.

Leunissen, J. M., De Cremer, D., & Reinders Folmer, C. P. (2012). An instrumental perspective on apologizing in bargaining: The importance of forgiveness to apologize. *Journal of Economic Psychology, 33*, 215–222.

McCullough, M.E., Kurzban, R., & Tabak, B.A. (2013). Cognitive systems for revenge and forgiveness. *Behavioral and Brain Sciences, 36*, 1–58.

McQueen, A., & Klein, W.M.P. (2006). Experimental manipulations of self-affirmation: A systematic review. *Self and Identity, 5*, 289–354.

Merritt, A. C., Effron, D. A., & Monin, B. (2010). Moral self-licensing: When being good frees us to be bad. *Social and Personality Psychology Compass, 4*, 344–357. https://doi.org/10.1111/j.1751-9004.2010.00263.x

Minow, M. (1998). *Between vengeance and forgiveness: Facing history after genocide and mass violence*. Boston: Beacon Press.

Mikulincer, M., & Shaver, P. R. (2007). Boosting attachment security to promote mental health, prosocial values, and inter-group tolerance. *Psychological Inquiry, 18*, 139–156. https://doi.org/10.1080/10478400701512646

Milgram, S. (1974). *Obedience to authority: An experimental view*. New York: Harper Collins.

Monin, B., & Miller, D. T. (2001). Moral credentials and the expression of prejudice. *Journal of Personality and Social Psychology, 81*(1), 33–43. https://doi.org/10.1037/0022-3514.81.1.33

Sachdeva, S., Iliev, R., & Medin, D. L. (2009). Sinning saints and saintly sinners: The paradox of moral self-regulation. *Psychological Science, 20*, 523–528.

Schönbach, P. (1990). *Account episodes: The management or escalation of conflict*. New York: Cambridge University Press.

Schumann, K. (2014). An affirmed self and a better apology: The effect of self-affirmation on transgressors' responses to victims. *Journal of Experimental Social Psychology, 54*, 89–96.

Schumann, K. (2018). The psychology of offering an apology: Understanding the barriers to apologizing and how to overcome them. *Current Directions in Psychological Science, 27*, 74–78. https://doi.org/10.1177/0963721417741709

Shaver, K.G. (1985). *The attribution of blame: Causality, responsibility and blameworthiness*. New York: Springer.

Shnabel, N., & Nadler, A. (2008). A needs-based model of reconciliation: Satisfying the differential emotional needs of victim and perpetrator as a key to promoting reconciliation. *Journal of Personality and Social Psychology, 94*, 116–132. https://doi.org/10.1037/0022-3514.94.1.116

Shnabel, N., Nadler, A., & Dovidio, J. F. (2014). Beyond need satisfaction: Empowering and accepting messages from third parties ineffectively restore trust and consequent reconciliation. *European Journal of Social Psychology, 44*, 126–140. https://doi.org/10.1002/ejsp.2002

Shnabel, N., Purdie-Vaughns, V., Cook, J.E., Garcia, J., & Cohen, G.L. (2013). Demystifying values-affirmation interventions: Writing about social-belonging is a key to buffering against stereotype threat. *Personality and Social Psychology Bulletin, 39,* 663–676.

Silk, J.B. (2002). The form and function of reconciliation in primates. *Annual Review of Anthropology, 31,* 21–44.

SimanTov-Nachlieli, I., & Shnabel, N. (2014). Feeling both victim and perpetrator: Investigating duality within the needs-based model. *Personality and Social Psychology Bulletin, 40*(3), 301–314.

Steele, C.M. (1988). The psychology of self-affirmation: Sustaining the integrity of the self *Advances in experimental social psychology* (Vol. *21*: Social psychological studies of the self: Perspectives and programs, pp. 261–302). San Diego, CA: Academic Press.

Summerville, A., & Chartier, C. R. (2013). Pseudo-dyadic 'interaction' on Amazon's Mechanical Turk. *Behavioral Research Methods, 45***,** 116–124. https://doi.org/10.3758/s13428-012-0250-9

Tavuchis, N. (1991). *Mea culpa: A sociology of apology and reconciliation*. Stanford, CA: Stanford University Press.

Wachtel, T., & McCold, P. (2001). Restorative justice in everyday life. In H. Strang & J. Braithwaite (Eds.), *Restorative justice in civil society*. Cambridge University Press.

Woodyatt, L., & Wenzel, M. (2014). A needs-based perspective on self-forgiveness: Addressing threat to moral identity as a means of encouraging interpersonal and intrapersonal restoration. *Journal of Experimental Social Psychology, 50,* 125–135. https://doi.org/10.1016/j.jesp.2013.09.012

Zebel, S., Kippers, S., & Ufkes, E. (2019). Herstel van het morele imago van daders als drijfveer voor bemiddeling: De ervaringen van bemiddelaars, *Tijdschrift voor Herstelrecht, 19,* 22–35. DOI: 10.5553/TvH/1568654X2019019004004 [in Dutch]

21
THE INTRAGROUP LEVEL

When and why reputational concerns influence immoral behaviour

Bianca Beersma, Annika S. Nieper, Maria T. M. Dijkstra, and Gerben A. van Kleef

Abstract

Immoral conduct, such as tax evasion or corruption, can have tremendous societal costs. Public policies aimed at curtailing immoral behaviour often try to capitalize on the fact that people care about what others think of them. That is, policies are geared towards enhancing people's *reputational concerns*. However, research has yielded conflicting findings on the relationship between reputational concerns and immoral behaviour. In some situations, reputational concerns decrease immoral behaviour, whereas in other cases they are inconsequential or even counterproductive. This chapter reviews when and how reputational concerns influence people's immoral behaviour, considering when reputational concerns decrease immoral behaviour, when they have no influence on immoral behaviour, and finally, when they inadvertently increase immoral behaviour. As such, the chapter elucidates when and why public policies that enhance people's reputational concerns have desired consequences by decreasing immoral behaviour.

- People's concerns about what others in their group think of them (i.e., reputational concerns) influence their (im)moral behaviour.
- People want to make a favourable impression on their group members; having a negative reputation can have undesired consequences (e.g., exclusion from the group).
- Reputational concerns can therefore help to avoid these negative consequences by increasing moral behaviour.
- However, reputational concerns may also fail to affect (im)moral behaviour and may even increase immoral behaviour.
- Whether interventions that target reputational concerns have a positive, negative or no effect on (im)moral behaviour depends on the observability of people's behaviour, people's awareness of the consequences of their behaviour, and what behaviour is prescribed by social norms.

Introduction

In 2001, Norway implemented a radical shift in its tax policy: The country introduced a system of public disclosure of tax and income information (Bø et al., 2015). From then onwards, Norwegian tax payers could obtain each other's income and tax reports via an online system. The idea behind this is simple: If someone perceives that the income and taxes reported by a member of their social group do not correspond with that person's lifestyle, the observer could discuss this mismatch with other relevant group members or powerful strangers, potentially leading to a loss of reputation (and possibly formal sanctioning) of the target person. For instance, when a neighbour or acquaintance observes their group member driving an expensive car while also reporting a low income, they could discuss this with other neighbours, friends or parents, or public officials. Fear of such reputation loss should, in turn, stimulate taxpayers to minimize the possibility that other people would perceive differences between their reported and actual income, and thus, to honestly report their income.

The policy described above is an example of how reputational concerns, defined as people's concerns about what other people think about them (Caldwell, 1986), influence people's behaviour. Reputational concerns operate among individuals within groups and communities and are particularly relevant when it comes to immoral behaviour because morality is a fundamental dimension on which people judge others (Abele et al., 2021; Leach et al., 2007). In general, people want to make a favourable impression on others in their social group, and thus be seen as behaving morally, because having a negative reputation (i.e. group members believing that one behaves in an undesirable way or has negative attributes) can have serious consequences, such as direct confrontation, gossip, ostracism (Molho et al., 2020) or legal punishment (e.g., fines or imprisonment). As a result, people have developed reputational concerns to avoid these negative consequences and increase their chances of survival (Nowak, 2006; Nowak & Sigmund, 2005).

Because upholding moral behaviour is crucial for the functioning of social groups and societies at large (van Kleef et al., 2019), policies that affect people's reputational concerns, such as the Norwegian tax policy, could be a powerful tool. Indeed, research on moral behaviour has demonstrated that people are more likely to honestly report taxes when income reports are publicly disclosed (Bø, Slemrod, & Thoresen, 2015), and others can observe their behaviour (Coricelli, Rusconi, & Villeval, 2014; Andreaoni & Petrie, 2004; Köbis et al., 2019). However, reputational concerns do not always have the desired effect; sometimes, they fail to affect immoral behaviour and sometimes, they even increase it. This state of affairs makes managing immoral behaviour exceedingly difficult.

The purpose of this chapter is to shed light on the intricate effects of reputational concern on (im)moral behaviour and generate possible explanations for these inconclusive findings. We start with explaining how we delineate moral behaviour in the intragroup context in this chapter. Then, we review three recent strands of research on reputational concerns and moral behaviour. First, we discuss studies that have found the desired effect of reputational concerns decreasing immoral behaviour. Second, we discuss studies that found no effects of reputational concerns, allowing us to identify the conditions associated with this lack of effects. Third, we discuss studies that have found reputational concerns to increase rather than decrease immoral behaviour, enabling us to point to the factors that could explain such counterproductive effects. We then synthesize the insights derived from the three previous sections into an overview of the conceptual factors that explain when and why reputational concerns function as an effective means to discourage immoral behaviour. We end the chapter by discussing suggestions for future research and practical implications.

Moral behaviour viewed from an intragroup perspective

Before discussing pertinent research, it is important to clarify how we define moral behaviour. Morality refers to what is "right" and "wrong", and to a code of conduct that is accepted by society (Gert & Gert, 2020). According to Moral Foundations Theory, people generally consider at least five foundations as morally important. These are: care/harm, fairness/cheating, loyalty/betrayal, authority/subversion, and sanctity/degradation (Graham et al., 2013).[1] Whereas there are differences between social groups in the extent to which they regard violations of the last three foundations as immoral, the care/harm and fairness/cheating foundation are considered morally important across cultures and independent of political affiliation (Graham et al., 2013). Most research on the impact of reputational concerns on behaviour has focused on behaviours that relate to these two foundations. In this chapter, we focus on these two moral foundations in the context of social groups, and discuss research that addresses related behaviours—particularly prosocial versus proself behaviours, and fairness and cheating behaviours. In other words, we consider morality as individual prosocial behaviour and fair behaviour towards others in one's social community, and we consider reputation as the public image pertaining to such behaviour within the same community.

When reputational concerns decrease immoral behaviour

Numerous studies show that reputational concerns can decrease immoral behaviour. For instance, studies have found that reputational concerns increase prosocial behaviour. Wu et al. (2016) studied prosocial behaviour in a public goods game. In this game, participants were part of a group and had to decide to provide monetary benefits to the group or not. Participants would be better off individually if they decided to not benefit the group and keep the money for themselves. However, the group as a whole would be better off if everybody would invest all their money to the group, in which case the money would be multiplied and then distributed equally across the group members. Participants thus experienced a conflict between choosing selfishly and thereby maximizing their individual outcomes, versus cooperating (choosing to prosocially benefit their group members). Wu et al., (2016) manipulated whether participants could gossip about one another (i.e., exchange information about them behind their backs, Dores Cruz et al., 2021), and found that when the possibility to gossip existed, participants were more concerned about their reputation than when gossip was not possible. Increased reputational concern, in turn, led them to behave more prosocially in the public goods game by giving more money to the group and keeping less for themselves. Several other studies also indicate that gossip can increase prosocial behaviour (e.g., Beersma & Van Kleef, 2011, 2012; Molho et al., 2019; Wu et al., 2015, 2016), and that reputational concerns are an underlying mechanism explaining this relationship (Beersma & Van Kleef, 2011; Wu et al., 2016). Thus, manipulating reputational concerns via gossip can increase prosocial behaviour.

Not only in the domain of care/harm (as illustrated by the examples on prosocial behaviour) but also in the domain of fairness/cheating, studies illustrate that reputational concerns can decrease immoral behaviour. The die-rolling paradigm (Fischbacher & Föllmi-Heusi, 2013) is a widely used method to measure whether people behave honestly. In experiments using the die-rolling task, participants receive a fair die, and are asked to roll it and report the number they have rolled. They are incentivized to misreport the number, because they earn more money for reporting a higher number. If participants roll the die in private, it is not possible to directly observe if they reported truthfully or lied, but it is possible to compare the reported die-roll distribution to the expected distribution of die rolls of a fair die. If the reported die-roll distribution differs significantly from a distribution that would be expected based on chance, then it can be assumed that people were dishonest when reporting the die rolls. A meta-analysis summarizing 90 studies using the die-rolling task demonstrated that reputational concerns are an important reason why people behave honestly in this task (Abeler et al., 2019). As an example of a study demonstrating this, Bašić and Quercia (2022) found that the die-roll numbers people reported were more similar to a random distribution when their behaviour was observed than when it was not, indicating that people reported more honestly when their behaviour was observed.

Increasing reputational concerns has been shown to increase moral behaviour in other task contexts as well. For example, Mazar et al. (2008) had participants engage in a computational task in which they had to search two numbers that add up to ten from 20 matrices containing 12 three-digit numbers. After this, they had to report how many matrices they had solved successfully to receive bonus payment (the more matrices participants resolved, the more bonus payment they received). Mazar et al. (2008) manipulated whether participants' reports of the number of matrices they solved would be shredded (thereby making their behaviour not identifiable anymore and thus lowering reputational concerns) or not (making the behaviour identifiable, hence resulting in higher reputational concerns). Results showed that people lied more often in the shredder condition than in the no-shredder condition.

In sum, across two broad domains of moral behaviour, prosociality and honesty, there is evidence that reputational concerns, under the right conditions, can increase honesty and prosocial behaviour.

When reputational concerns do not influence immoral behaviour

Whereas the studies we discussed previously highlight the positive effects of reputational concerns on immoral behaviour in line with the Norwegian tax policy example we discussed earlier, there are instances when measures taken to increase reputational concerns were not found to influence immoral behaviour. One set of measures that was found to have no effect on moral behaviour concerns manipulations that suggest the mere presence of others, whereas these others cannot actually observe one's behaviour (i.e., the observers are present but unable to obtain information about one's actual behaviour). For example, a study examining whether the mere presence of others influences immoral behaviour found no impact at all (Köbis et al., 2019). In this study, participants rolled a die and reported the outcome, and earned more bonus payment the higher the number they reported. Köbis et al. (2019) manipulated whether somebody else was merely present with the participant in the room without this person being able to observe the participant's actual behaviour, versus whether somebody else was present and could observe how the participant behaved. They found that mere presence did not influence people's decisions to act morally (Study 3) while the direct observation of one's behaviour did (Köbis et al., 2019). Furthermore, studies using images of watching eyes found no impact of the presence or absence of such watching eyes on honest behaviour (Pfattheicher et al., 2019).

Another type of manipulation that has not been found to have an effect on immoral behaviour relates to the extent to which being observed can have consequences for the focal person. In Wu et al. (2016)'s experiment, participants engaged in a public goods game and could decide to benefit the group or to selfishly keep all the available money to themselves. The possibility that other participants could gossip about their behaviour increased prosocial behaviour but only in those situations in which the gossip was transmitted to somebody with whom participants would interact again. In a situation in which the gossip was sent to somebody with whom they would never interact, introducing gossip did not influence prosocial behaviour.[2]

In sum, when people performed incentivized tasks in the mere presence of another person who was unable to observe their behaviour, or when any information another person could transmit about them would not have any consequences, levels of honesty and prosociality were unaffected. Potentially, in situations in which another person is present but cannot see one's behaviour, people are not really concerned about their reputation. Similarly, watching eyes or inconsequential gossip, might not influence people's concern about their reputation and thereby not alter their behaviour.

However, it is important to note that while in the studies described here, no significant effects of reputational concern on immoral behaviour were found, this is not evidence for a null effect (see Lakens et al., 2018). For this conclusion, equivalence tests are necessary. Future studies including such equivalence tests are needed to further understand the non-significant effects of reputational concerns on immoral behaviour.

When reputational concerns increase immoral behaviour

Besides decreasing or not affecting immoral behaviour, reputational concerns may inadvertently increase immoral behaviour. One instance in which such an undesirable consequence of reputational concerns occurs is when a bad reputation, once earned, cannot be restored. In an experiment by Coricelli et al. (2014) participants could lie for their personal benefit, and in case their lie would be detected, a picture of them would be shown to all other group members along with the information that they lied. The authors compared two conditions: one in which the detected liar was pardoned after some rounds and reintegrated into the group, and one in which the liar wasn't reintegrated. In the treatment in which liars were not pardoned, lying increased in comparison to when liars where pardoned and reintegrated after their lie was made public.

Another adverse consequence reputational concerns can have is that when people are trying to maintain an honest reputation, they might actually lie in order to appear honest. Evidence for this comes from a set of studies that employed a die-rolling task in which the researchers programmed the die to roll specific numbers such that participants would be very lucky (i.e., the die would roll 5, 6, 6, 5) or not (die rolls would result in random numbers). Participants who were in the lucky condition lied "downward" (i.e., reported lower numbers than they actually rolled), forgoing bonuses in order to appear honest (Choshen-Hillel et al., 2020). This demonstrates that a concern to be perceived as dishonest can actually, paradoxically, increase dishonesty.

Lastly, differences in moral behaviour have been found between situations in which people were observed by peers (such as friends) versus other observers. In one experiment, peer presence increased cheating in a die-rolling task in comparison to doing the task alone, presumably because it increased competition among peers to earn more money in the experiment (Bäker & Mechtel, 2019). As such, in those situations, increasing reputational concerns via increasing observability does not decrease immoral behaviour, but rather increases it.

In the realm of prosocial behaviour, reputational concern has also sometimes been found to increase immoral behaviour. Steinel et al. (2010) found that people who occupied a marginal position in a group, yet had a high need to belong to that group, behaved more cooperatively as representatives in an intergroup negotiation when their fellow group members seemed to favour cooperation, but behaved more competitively when their fellow group members seemed to favour competition.

In sum, increasing reputational concerns can reduce honesty and prosociality and thus increase immoral behaviour. This can happen, first, when people are not reintegrated into their group after engaging in a misdeed; second, when engaging in moral behaviour makes one appear immoral (i.e., when being honest makes one appear dishonest or not helpful); third, when one is observed by peers with whom one is in competition; and lastly, when one's fellow group members support a competitive stance toward an outgroup member. In the following we will integrate these findings and discuss the conceptual factors that determine how reputational concerns influence immoral behaviour in the next section.

Emerging patterns, practical implications and future directions

Our review reveals that, in line with what policy makers intend when implementing policies to increase reputational concerns, in many situations reputational concerns decrease immoral behaviour. This happens, for example, when people know others can observe their behaviour and/or gossip about them. In other situations, measures intended to increase reputational concerns, although potentially costly, do not increase immoral behaviour. This happens, for instance, when people do not actually feel observed. Similarly, when people know gossip can be transmitted to another person, but they will never interact with that person, increasing reputational concerns do not influence immoral behaviour. Lastly, we reviewed studies that show that measures intended to increase reputational concern can inadvertently increase immoral behaviour. This happens, for instance, when a bad reputation, once earned, cannot be restored (see also Shnabel, this volume, for a discussion of restoration opportunities), when people feel they have to lie to appear honest, and in the context of peer competition. In those situations, rather than decreasing immoral behaviour, increasing reputational concerns can ironically increase immoral behaviour.

Researchers have manipulated reputational concern in various ways. These manipulations include, among others, being observed by others, others gossiping about one's behaviour or at least having the opportunity to do so, the mere presence of others, and being observed by watching eyes. The findings show that these different ways to trigger reputational concern are not equally successful in either bringing about the desired reputational concern and/or bringing about the desired decrease in immoral behaviour. Here, we summarize the key factors that emerge from our review as influencing reputational concern and/or immoral behaviour (see also Figure 21.1).

The first factor is the observability of people's actual immoral behaviour. The different manipulations researchers have used differ in terms of the extent to which others can really observe one's behaviour. For the watching eyes manipulation, the observability of one's behaviour is obviously low: a mere picture of watching eyes does not mean that one's behaviour is actually visible to someone else. The same applies to mere presence: When others are present while one is engaging in immoral behaviour, but they have no way of actually knowing how one behaved, observability of one's behaviour is low. In the die rolling game, when others are observing one's reports of the die rolls, but not the actual numbers one rolled, observability is arguably higher than for the two aforementioned manipulations. Observability is still not perfect, though; it would be at the highest possible level in case observers would be able to see both participants' actual die rolls and their reports of these die rolls. If the observability is high, reputational concerns have an impact on behaviour, while when observability is low (as it is the case for the "watching eyes" or "mere presence" manipulation), manipulations did not impact immoral behaviour.

The second factor that emerges from our review as potentially crucial is the extent to which observations of one's immoral behaviour are consequential. Manipulations aimed to increase reputational concerns only do so effectively when information about one's behaviour can

Intragroup level: reputational concerns and immoral behaviour

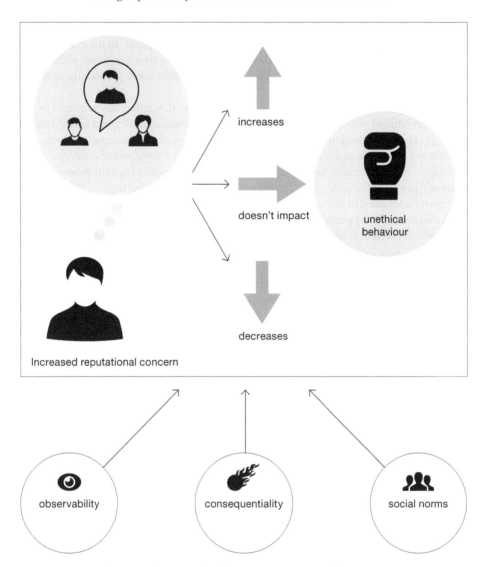

Figure 21.1 Interventions targeting reputational concerns can have positive, negative or no effect on (im) moral behaviour, depending on the observability of people's behaviour, people's awareness of the consequences of their behaviour, and what behaviour is prescribed by social norms.

potentially reach others that could impose consequences on the person deciding whether or not to behave immorally. When someone has the certainty that information about their immoral behaviour *cannot* reach others who could impose consequences on them, knowing that one is observed is unlikely to trigger reputational concerns.

The third factor that emerged from our review is the (implicit) social norm that is activated by a reputational concern manipulation or policy. Social norms are defined as principles or rules that are commonly accepted within a group and guide and/or constrain behaviour (Cialdini & Trost, 1998). The research demonstrating counter-productive effects of interventions that increased reputational concern we reviewed, showed that measures taken to increase reputational concern make people engage in those behaviours that they believe will make them "look good" in the eyes of observers. When there is an implicit norm of competition in the group, making behaviour visible to group members may make them behave more competitively rather than more prosocially or more honestly (Bäker & Mechtel, 2019; Steinel et al. 2010).

In summary, our review sheds light on three crucial factors that influence the effects of policies that target reputational concerns, namely observability, consequentiality and social norms (see Figure 21.1). These factors point to the essence of what can make reputational concerns work to reduce immoral behaviour and highlight the intragroup nature of reputational concerns. That is, in the context of a highly cohesive, small group, observability is typically high (members can observe one another's [im]moral behaviours). Consequentiality is typically also high, in that people know that the reputational damage that immoral behaviour could cause can have severe consequences—such as social exclusion or punishment. Finally, highly cohesive small groups tend to have salient social norms with regard to moral behaviour as this is in the interest of their survival (Feldman, 1984). Together, these factors should lead people to alter their behaviour in a way that is congruent with the group norms, and thus decrease the chance they would engage in immoral behaviour, in order to avoid being excluded from the group or punished by group members.

The factors explaining whether reputational concerns decrease immoral behaviour that emerged from our review fit theories about social norms (Bicchieri, 2016). In this chapter, we highlight an important, yet often overlooked, route for enforcing social norms: via reputational concerns. We highlight two factors, namely observability and consequentiality, that help explain when reputational concerns help to enforce social norms. Importantly, however, whether by increasing reputational concerns, one increases or decreases immoral behaviour, depends on the third factor that we identified: the salient social norm. If the underlying social norm prescribes engaging in moral behaviour, such as prescribing cooperation among group members, increasing observability and consequentiality will increase cooperation (see e.g., Wu et al., 2015). However social norms can also encourage immoral behaviour, by setting a norm to compete with others. In these settings, increasing observability and consequentiality will lead to the enforcement of norms that foster immoral rather than moral behaviour (see e.g., Abbink et al., 2017; Steinel et al. 2010).

With regards to practical implications of the findings discussed here and suggestions for future research, based on the research findings we reviewed, we argue that the higher interventions that aim to increase reputational concerns score on the observability they afford, the more effective they will be in increasing reputational concerns. Future studies should empirically test this idea. In many studies, researchers so far only assumed that their manipulations influenced reputational concerns, but did not actually measure reputational concerns. Comparing the effects of different manipulations on reputational concerns as measured by self-report scales (Beersma & Van Kleef, 2011; Wu et al., 2016) could help to pinpoint which ones actually increase reputational concerns and which ones do not. Insights derived from such studies will also be helpful for designing practical interventions that actually do what they are intended to do: increase reputational concern.

We also argue that the more interventions that are implemented to increase reputational concerns include the possibility that observations of one's current actions have future consequences, the more effective they should be in increasing reputational concern. There is one important caveat here: When the consequences of immoral behaviour are irreversible, once implemented, they will no longer decrease immoral behaviour. The study by Coricelli et al. (2014) showed that participants who were exposed for lying and not pardoned and reintegrated into the group, lied more rather than less over time. Therefore, in order to effectively stimulate positive consequences of reputational concern, policies have to make clear that moral transgressions are consequential, but transgressors have to be given the opportunity to redeem themselves and repair their reputation accordingly. Future studies could shed light on the ideal balance between severity of consequences and possibilities to repair one's reputation that is most successful in bringing about reputational concerns and moral behaviour. Specifically, studies might examine which combinations of consequences/punishment and reintegration are most successful in decreasing immoral behaviour by examining different forms of consequences (direct confrontation, gossip, ostracism, public exposure) and different time periods during which such consequences are effective. Obviously, insights generated by such studies are also directly relevant for designing practical interventions aimed to decrease immoral behaviour.

Furthermore, we argue that manipulations used in research, or policies implemented to increase reputational concern, are effective in decreasing immoral behaviour to the extent that the person deciding to engage in immoral behaviour perceives moral behaviour as the norm their group members want them to adhere to. When group norms implicitly or explicitly prescribe immoral behaviour, manipulations or policies that increase reputational concern may increase rather than decrease immoral behaviour. Future studies could test this by investigating the interactive effects of the social norm (such as being cooperative vs. competitive) and reputational concerns on moral behaviour. Policy makers can benefit from the insights generated by such research. For them, it is important to be aware of the social norms that are salient to people when interventions aimed to increase reputational concern are implemented. Only when these norms prescribe prosocial and honest behaviour, the intervention will solicit the desired effect.

Finally, a potentially important factor that we have not highlighted yet is group identification/belonging. If a specific individual does not need/want to belong to, or doesn't identify with, a specific group, then increasing reputational concerns is likely to have little effect on behaviour, as the individual does not fear to be excluded from the group. Future studies could test and extend this idea.

Conclusion

To decrease immoral behaviour and the societal costs it entails, many policies seek to make use of the fact that people care about what their group members think about them. As such, these policies are aimed at enhancing people's reputational concerns. This chapter revealed that some of these policies are more successful than others, and highlights observability, consequentiality and salient norms as three crucial factors that affect the extent to which reputational concern manipulations or policies are likely to trigger reputational concerns and decrease immoral behaviour. We hope these insights and the future research directions outlined above will stimulate further research on this important topic, so that humans' fundamental desire to uphold their reputation can be employed for the good of society.

Contributor statement

A.S.N. wrote a draft of this manuscript and B.B., M.T.M.D. and G.A.v.K. provided comments and improved the manuscript. A.S.N. and B.B. implemented the revision. All authors contributed to the writing of the manuscript and approved the final version of the manuscript for submission.

Notes

1 Graham et al. (2013) provide an overview of the adaptive challenges these five moral foundations provide a response to, as well as their triggers in our evolutionary history, their modern-day triggers, emotions that are related to each of them, as well as related relevant virtues. This overview falls outside the scope of this chapter but we refer readers to the table Graham et al. (2013) provide on page 68 and their discussion on pages 67–71.
2 It is important to note that in Wu et al.'s (2016) experiment, participants interacted anonymously, online. Thus, in both conditions, whether gossip was sent to a future interaction partner or not, participants were completely anonymous, and therefore anonymity cannot explain the findings.

References

Abbink, K., Gangadharan, L., Handfield, T., & Thrasher, J. (2017). Peer punishment promotes enforcement of bad social norms. *Nature Communications*, *8*(1), 1–8.

Abele, A. E., Ellemers, N., Fiske, S. T., Koch, A., & Yzerbyt, V. (2021). Navigating the social world: Toward an integrated framework for evaluating self, individuals, and groups. *Psychological Review*, *128*(2), 290–314. https://doi.org/10.1037/rev0000262

Abeler, J., Nosenzo, D., & Raymond, C. (2019). Preferences for truth-telling. *Econometrica*, *87*(4), 1115–1153. https://doi.org/10.3982/ECTA14673

Andreoni, J., & Petrie, R. (2004). Public goods experiments without confidentiality: A glimpse into fundraising. *Journal of Public Economics*, *88*(7), 1605–1623. https://doi.org/10.1016/S0047-2727(03)00040-9

Bäker, A., & Mechtel, M. (2019). The impact of peer presence on cheating. *Economic Inquiry*, *57*(2), 792–812. https://doi.org/10.1111/ecin.12760

Bašić, Z., & Quercia, S. (2022). The influence of self and social image concerns on lying. *SSRN Electronic Journal*. https://doi.org/10.2139/ssrn.3666771

Beersma, B., & Van Kleef, G. A. (2011). How the grapevine keeps you in line: Gossip Increases Contributions to the Group. *Social Psychological and Personality Science*, *2*(6), 642–649. https://doi.org/10.1177/1948550611405073

Beersma, B., & Van Kleef, G. A. (2012). Why people gossip: An empirical analysis of social motives, antecedents, and consequences. *Journal of Applied Social Psychology*, *42*(11), 2640–2670. https://doi.org/10.1111/j.1559-1816.2012.00956.x

Bicchieri, C. (2016). *Norms in the wild: How to diagnose, measure, and change social norms*. Oxford University Press.

Bø, E. E., Slemrod, J., & Thoresen, T. O. (2015). Taxes on the internet: Deterrence effects of public disclosure. *American Economic Journal: Economic Policy*, *7*(1), 36–62. https://doi.org/10.1257/pol.20130330

Caldwell, R. L. (1986). The deceptive use of reputation by stomatopods. In *Deception: Perspectives on human and nonhuman deceit* (S. 129–145).

Choshen-Hillel, S., Shaw, A., & Caruso, E. M. (2020). Lying to appear honest. *Journal of Experimental Psychology: General*, *149*(9), 1719–1735. https://doi.org/10.1037/xge0000737

Cialdini, R. B. & Trost, M. (1998) R. Social influence: social norms, conformity and compliance. In Gilbert, D.T., Fiske, S. T. and Lindzey, G. (Eds.) The handbook of social psychology 4th edn, *Vols. 1–2* (pp. 151–192). New York: McGraw-Hill.

Coricelli, G., Rusconi, E., & Villeval, M. C. (2014). Tax evasion and emotions: An empirical test of re-integrative shaming theory. *Journal of Economic Psychology*, *40*, 49–61. https://doi.org/10.1016/j.joep.2012.12.002

Dores Cruz, T. D., Nieper, A. S., Testori, M., Martinescu, E., & Beersma, B. (2021). An integrative definition and framework to study gossip. *Group & Organization Management*, 1059601121992887. https://doi.org/10.1177/1059601121992887

Feldman, D. C. (1984). The development and enforcement of group norms. *Academy of Management Review*, *9*(1), 47–53. https://doi.org/10.5465/amr.1984.4277934

Fischbacher, U., & Föllmi-Heusi, F. (2013). Lies in disguise-an experimental study on cheating. *Journal of the European Economic Association*, *11*(3), 525–547. https://doi.org/10.1111/jeea.12014

Gert, B., & Gert, J. (2020). The Definition of Morality. In E. N. Zalta (Hrsg.), *The Stanford encyclopedia of philosophy* (Fall 2020). Metaphysics Research Lab, Stanford University. https://plato.stanford.edu/archives/fall2020/entries/morality-definition/

Graham, J., Haidt, J., Koleva, S., Motyl, M., Iyer, R., Wojcik, S. P., & Ditto, P. H. (2013). Moral foundations theory. In *Advances in Experimental Social Psychology* (Bd. 47, S. 55–130). Elsevier. https://doi.org/10.1016/B978-0-12-407236-7.00002-4

Köbis, N., van der Lingen, S., Dores Cruz, T. D., Iragorri-Carter, D., van Prooijen, J.-W., Righetti, F., & van Lange, P. (2019). The look over your shoulder: Unethical behaviour decreases in the physical presence of observers [Preprint]. PsyArXiv. https://doi.org/10.31234/osf.io/gxu96

Lakens, D., Scheel, A. M., & Isager, P. M. (2018). Equivalence testing for psychological research: A tutorial. *Advances in Methods and Practices in Psychological Science, 1*(2), 259–269. https://doi.org/10.1177/2515245918770963

Leach, C. W., Ellemers, N., & Barreto, M. (2007). Group virtue: The importance of morality (vs competence and sociability) in the positive evaluation of in-groups. *Journal of Personality and Social Psychology, 93*(2), 234–249. https://doi.org/10.1037/0022-3514.93.2.234

Mazar, N., Amir, O., & Ariely, D. (2008). The dishonesty of honest people: A theory of self-concept maintenance. *Journal of Marketing Research, 45*(6), 633–644. https://doi.org/10.1509/jmkr.45.6.633

Molho, C., Balliet, D., & Wu, J. (2019). Hierarchy, power, and strategies to promote cooperation in social dilemmas. *Games, 10*(1), 12. https://doi.org/10.3390/g10010012

Molho, C., Tybur, J. M., Van Lange, P. A. M., & Balliet, D. (2020). Direct and indirect punishment of norm violations in daily life. *Nature Communications, 11*(1), 3432. https://doi.org/10.1038/s41467-020-17286-2

Nowak, M. A. (2006). Five rules for the evolution of cooperation. *Science, 314*(5805), 1560–1563. https://doi.org/10.1126/science.1133755

Nowak, M. A., & Sigmund, K. (2005). Evolution of indirect reciprocity. *Nature, 437*(7063), 1291–1298. https://doi.org/10.1038/nature04131

Pfattheicher, S., Schindler, S., & Nockur, L. (2019). On the impact of Honesty-Humility and a cue of being watched on cheating behavior. *Journal of Economic Psychology, 71*, 159–174. https://doi.org/10.1016/j.joep.2018.06.004

Steinel, W., Van Kleef, G. A., Van Knippenberg, D., Hogg, M. A., Homan, A. C., & Moffitt, G. (2010). How intragroup dynamics affect behavior in intergroup conflict: The role of group norms, prototypicality, and need to belong. *Group Processes & Intergroup Relations, 13*(6), 779–794. https://doi.org/10.1177/1368430210375702

van Kleef, G. A., Gelfand, M. J., & Jetten, J. (2019). The dynamic nature of social norms: New perspectives on norm development, impact, violation, and enforcement. *Journal of Experimental Social Psychology, 84*, 103814. https://doi.org/10.1016/j.jesp.2019.05.002

Wu, J., Balliet, D., & Van Lange, P. A. M. (2015). When does gossip promote generosity? Indirect reciprocity under the shadow of the future. *Social Psychological and Personality Science, 6*(8), 923–930. https://doi.org/10.1177/1948550615595272

Wu, J., Balliet, D., & Van Lange, P. A. M. (2016). Reputation management: Why and how gossip enhances generosity. *Evolution and Human Behavior, 37*(3), 193–201. https://doi.org/10.1016/j.evolhumbehav.2015.11.001

22
THE INTERGROUP LEVEL
The strategic use of morality in intergroup relations

Susanne Täuber

Abstract

Comparatively little is known about moral behavior in intergroup contexts. Extant research further approaches moral behavior mainly as a compensatory strategy aimed at preserving and defending moral image. Combining these two unchartered territories, the current chapter introduces a model of strategic use of morality in intergroup contexts. The model, which is informed by power dynamics between groups, allows for conceiving of morality as used proactively in order to push economic and political agendas, optimize impression management when external pressures require so, and to prevent changes to intergroup relations that afford a group with power and privilege. Allowing the examination of diverse research topics under one overarching framework, the model facilitates cross-fertilization between adjacent disciplines, diversification of methodologies, and novel areas of inquiry in the field of psychology of morality.

- Moral norms can be used strategically to maintain and reproduce power differences between groups.
- Because of the functions of moral norms, it is essential to examine who has the power to decide what issues and behaviors are considered moral.
- By defining what is moral (creating the moral landscape), powerful groups can influence intergroup relations to their own benefit.
- Society and other third parties can support or hinder powerful groups' (attempted) influence on the moral landscape.
- In the moral landscape, power can be exerted on a visible, hidden, as well as an invisible dimension.

Introduction

The strategic use of moral norms to navigate and negotiate power in intergroup relations is largely unchartered territory. Addressing this lacuna, the present chapter first introduces the three-dimensional perspective on power (Gaventa 2006; Lukes 2005). This perspective valuably extends the dominant approaches to intergroup behavior as preserving and defending moral image, by taking into account the deliberate creating, shaping, and negotiating of moral norms. Empirical studies are then reviewed from a range of areas to illustrate the strategic use of morality in intergroup relations and its contingency on power dynamics. Unresolved questions are then identified and routes for future theorizing and research are derived. Finally, the chapter discusses practical implications of an approach to morality in intergroup relations that is informed by power.

The main theoretical issues concerning morality in intergroup relations

Moral behaviors are socially defined and identity-affirming. Moral norms regulate our behavior individually, within the social groups we belong to, and determine how we behave towards other groups (Ellemers & van den Bos 2012; Ellemers et al. 2019). Moral norms differ across groups; conforming to some and deviating from other moral norms hence signals our belongingness to some but not other groups. Accordingly, what is considered moral is not universally shared: behavior considered moral by one group can be considered neutral or even immoral by another group (Ellemers & van den Bos 2012; Täuber 2018). Consequently, people should be able to flexibly construe issues as morally laden or morally neutral. This proposition has received empirical support across a variety of topics and research paradigms. Participants in experimental research (Van Bavel et al. 2012), for instance, flexibly shift their evaluation of issues in moral and non-moral terms on a trial-to-trial basis. Relatedly, when participants were asked to classify 40 diverse issues ranging from exercising over honesty to the death penalty, in terms of their moral or non-moral nature, no issue was unanimously classified as moral (Wright et al. 2008, Study 1). In addition to flexibly construing morality upon experimenter instructions, Rozin (1999) showed that previously morally neutral issues can attain moral connotations over time (moralization), just as issues that were construed as moral can lose their moral connotation over time (amoralization). Cigarette smoking and vegetarianism, for instance, have gained moral connotations over the past decades (Rozin et al. 1997; Rozin and Singh 1999). By contrast, divorce and homosexuality have lost their moral connotations (Rozin 1999).

How does this relate to moral behavior? Scholarship aiming to predict, explain and influence moral behavior mostly addresses how individual moral guidelines interact with social norms (Ellemers et al. 2019). Accordingly, the most impactful papers in moral behavior concern the relationship between moral self-conceptions and displays of moral behavior (Blasi 1980), strategies to maintain a moral self-image (Mazar et al. 2008) even after moral lapses and when confronted with challenges to one's moral self-concept (Monin & Miller 2001). Because being deemed immoral is an aversive experience (e.g., Wojciszke 1994, 2005), people have been shown to engage in various compensatory strategies, such as moral disengagement (Bandura et al. 1996), do-gooder derogation (Minson & Monin 2012), and moral hypocrisy (Valdesolo & DeSteno 2007). Such compensatory strategies have also been demonstrated in intergroup contexts, showing that, similar to findings in the interpersonal domain, moral behavior is motivated by concerns for the group's moral image (e.g., Täuber & van Zomeren 2013). Being made aware of moral lapses or shortcomings in intergroup contexts prompts compensatory strategies similar to those observed in interpersonal contexts (Ellemers et al. 2019; Täuber et al. 2015).

In sum, extant research suggests that what is considered moral is rather arbitrary. Individuals, groups, and society as a whole can construe the same issue in morally laden or morally neutral terms, depending on framing, time, and context. However, once established, people are highly motivated to conform to moral norms and protect their social image as being moral (Pagliaro et al. 2016; Van Nunspeet et al. 2015). Because they signal social categorization (van Leeuwen et al. 2012), moral norms have enormous potential to divide the social world into good and bad, making those who deviate outsiders worthy of rebuke (Wright et al. 2013), stigmatization (Skitka and Mullen 2002), intolerance (Haidt et al. 2003; Skitka et al. 2005; Wright et al. 2008), and exclusion (Opotow 1990; Täuber 2018).

Despite these insights, current scholarly insight into the role of moral behavior for intergroup relations is limited, particularly with regard to the mechanisms that lead to specific moral norms being created and endorsed when different groups are involved (Ellemers et al. 2019). Considering the malleability, motivational quality, and category-signaling function of moral norms, the lack of research and theorizing concerning who has the power to decide which norms are moral is surprising. Moral norms are excellently suited for strategic use in intergroup contexts. Our current understanding of how groups regulate their moral image through reactive responses and compensatory strategies can be valuably complemented by highlighting how groups proactively shape the moral landscape they operate in, for instance by using language to frame certain behaviors as moral, and how this influences other actors. This complementary perspective warrants analysis of power.

The main empirical insights

The analysis I'll describe here, is informed by the three-dimensional perspective on power as described by sociologist Lukes (2005). The three-dimensional view on power allows to systematize and analyze behaviors of powerful groups that are aimed at influencing intergroup relations to their benefit. The three dimensions refer to the exertion of power through visible (e.g., formal authority, physical constraint), hidden (e.g., agenda setting), or invisible means (e.g., internalized stereotypes). The point of departure, aligning with the status protection motive described by Social Identity Theory (e.g., Ellemers, 1993), is powerful groups' motive to maintain and reproduce their favorable position in stratified systems, which they achieve by exerting power. Social psychological research demonstrates that members of dominant groups do not willingly give up their privilege (Craig et al. 2018; Leach et al. 2002). In fact, powerful groups often resist potential changes of the power hierarchy because change affects them more negatively than powerless groups (Scheepers et al. 2009). In addition, change motives by powerful groups can aim to maintain or even increase the inequality that benefits them (Sweetman et al. 2013). Finally, powerful groups use backlash to regain power that is lost or threatened to be lost (Mansbridge and Shames 2008; Townsend-Bell 2020). In academia, for instance, backlash against gender equality can range from retaliation against reporters of harassment (Young Academy Groningen, 2021) to the physical destruction of women's research projects (Naezer, van den Brink, & Benschop, 2019).

Analyses typically focus only on the powerless and the powerful group. However, as I will elaborate below, the available empirical evidence suggests that more groups need to be considered in order to develop a comprehensive understanding of the strategic use of morality. Therefore, Figure 22.1 includes society and third parties as relevant actors (Panel A) who can be influenced by powerful groups. These actors can support or hinder powerful groups' (attempted) influence on the moral landscape. In principle, each of these actors can exert visible, hidden, and invisible forms of power (Panel B), thereby contributing to maintaining and reproducing the power differential in question. Visible power is the most obvious form of power exertion, whereby the interests of the parties are contested in public spaces and formal decision-making bodies (Gaventa, 2006). Importantly, despite the strong motive to protect their privileged position among powerful groups, power differentials can be maintained and reproduced even outside of people's awareness and deliberation. For instance, socialized norms as well as stereotypes about class, gender and race are often internalized and enacted without much deliberation by powerful and powerless groups

Intergroup level: the strategic use of morality

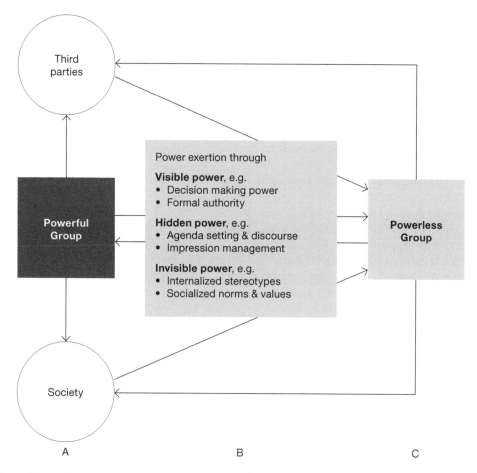

Figure 22.1 Different actors (A) involved in maintaining and reproducing existing power differentials through different forms of power exertion (Panel B). Responses to power exertion by the powerless group (Panel C) make these processes dynamic and interactive.

alike. In general, the strategic use of moral norms as an attempt to maintain and reproduce power is most likely when powerless groups challenge the power differential (Scott, 1990; Täuber & Moughalian, 2022). When power differentials are uncontested, powerful groups are more likely to exert hidden and invisible forms of power (e.g., Acker, 2006). Moral norms and behaviors are thus interactive and dynamic, and research should take into account powerless groups' reactions to power exertion (Panel C).

Visible power: moral framing as agenda-setting

Visible power refers to observable decision making and concerns influencing others through formalized authorities and rules (e.g., Dahl 1957; French et al. 1959; Lukes 2005). Such coercive power can be seen in making rules and laws, for instance. When members of powerful groups are in actual positions of political power, they will likely be perceived as interchangeably with "society." In such positions, the powerful group can decide that certain behaviors are moral, thereby directly influencing what is deemed moral. The pressure on the less powerful group to comply with the newly defined moral behavior then seems to consensually come from society itself. In order to push specific political or economic agendas, issues can be "made" moral through to taxes or legislation (Rozin 1999). Legislation in The Netherlands, for instance, was tailored to "catch" people who undeservingly receive childcare allowance, depicting people in that group as a potential profiteers and fraudsters. The algorithms resulting from this political agenda exacerbated racial discrimination and led to tens of thousands of parents from predominantly low-income families being falsely accused of fraud – they lost their homes, their children, their livelihoods, and their dignity in the process. Families from ethnic minorities were disproportionately affected (Amnesty International 2021).

Another example of visible power concerns moralization motivated by economic agendas, such as the Dutch transition from welfare state to "participation society". In the participation society, citizens are expected to assume individual responsibility for their health and well-being (Koster 2014). Participation now is considered a prerequisite for good citizenship, leaving those who lack the capacities for participation with a questionable status of citizenship and at the mercy of more self-reliant individuals, because the state considers itself as freed from responsibility. Observers state that "the Netherlands has introduced the idea of the 'participation society' to frame the impetus for its austerity measures" (Hoekman et al. 2018, p. 131). Similar narratives to legitimate cuts in public services were observed in the United Kingdom's "Big Society" (Bach 2012). Framing austerity measures in terms of citizens' responsibility for health and well-being contributed to a division of society into morally good and morally bad citizens, especially regarding health (Täuber 2018). The categorization of people with less healthy lifestyles as deviating from societally sanctioned moral norms leads to stigmatization, lower inclusion, and less solidarity, undermining social cohesion. In addition, the resulting "Us versus Them" categorization paves the way for harsh consequences, as evident in the childcare allowance scandal. Moralization can thus be used strategically to push economic agendas and to legitimize exclusion of groups that powerful groups seek to marginalize (Opotow 1990; Täuber 2017).

Hidden power: moral framing as impression management

Hidden power refers to being able to keep others from the decision-making table and to keep their concerns off the agenda (Gaventa 2006). Rather than directly influencing others, hidden power operates through manipulating discourse, reframing the grievances of the powerless, and thereby enabling the powerful to remain in power (Fairclough 2010; Scott 1990). This type of power exertion will often take place when, despite being powerful, groups are depending on other groups. Corporations, for instance, are dependent on their customers and on third parties such as shareholders and supervisory authorities. Similarly, governments are dependent on public trust and support. Pressure coming from other actors, who might be formally less powerful, can prompt symbolic compliance with the moral norms implied by these actors. The powerful group might feel compelled to favorably present themselves in the moral domain – regulating the impressions other groups form about them, rather than actually engaging in moral conduct.

For instance, the growing demand for organizations to consider economic, social, and environmental issues (Prasad & Holzinger 2013) has been accompanied by suspicions that companies' claims of corporate social responsibility (CSR) are insincere and mainly aim to increase profit ("CSR-washing", Pope & Wæraas 2016). Relatedly, advertisement highlighting female talent and messages countering gender stereotypes ("femvertising") can prompt backlash when the brands are not knowledgeable about real feminist values (Lima and Casais 2021). Using morality for impression management to influence intergroup relations, such as the relation between consumers and brands, favorably, is risky because of the comparatively stronger negative reaction to perceived hypocrisy. Accusations of corporate hypocrisy are particularly likely when companies fail to walk the talk in moral domains, leading to harsher punishment (Stiegert et al. 2021).

The above examples also suggest that the boundaries between hidden and invisible power are fluid. Organizations and institutions can be inclined to "doing the right thing" based on actual commitment, but also in order to influence brand loyalty, public trust, or employee satisfaction to their advantage. Using moral claims to demonstrate commitment to causes such as social justice and equality can be a particularly sinister way of preventing actual change, when such change threatens powerful groups' status (Täuber & Moughalian, 2022). This is mainly done through invisible power.

Invisible power: moral framing to preserve power and privilege

Invisible power is exerted by shaping the beliefs, wishes, and values of powerless groups (Lukes 2005). It is considered the most effective form of power exertion because it builds on manipulation rather than coercion and is consequently almost impossible to resist. Socialization can result in compliance with inequality and power differentials when it leads to the internalization of stereotypes and moral norms. Women and girls can be socialized to value staying at home more than paid labor, because they have been exposed to the women as caregiver discourse (Fernando & Prasad 2018). Acker (2006) refers to the resulting self-control as internalized controls. Similarly, Gaventa (2006) warns that the adoption of language of participation and inclusion by the powerful obscures the boundaries between the powerful and the powerless, potentially undermining struggles for progressive change: when powerful actors like the World Bank speak of "partnership," "shared ownership," or interaction on a "level playing field," they hide their greater access to resources and power. When the call for progressive change becomes louder, powerful groups can engage in change initiatives with the goal of being perceived as doing the moral thing while actually maintaining and reproducing the status-quo that benefits them.

The prevention of progressive change in order to safeguard own power and privilege is known as co-optation, and has been demonstrated in many areas. Examples concern the reliance on speech acts to show commitment, which lead to "doing the document" rather than doing the change (Ahmed 2007), and reliance on metrics that are easy to manipulate to prove successful change (Leslie 2019). Indeed, co-optation allows organizations and institutions to present themselves in morally flattering ways while preventing meaningful change. Giridharadas (2018) describes how those in power set up efforts to "change the world," while these efforts obscure their own role in causing problems like widespread inequality or poverty. He observes that global elites use progressive change initiatives to preserve the status quo by constantly seeking to do more good, but never less harm. Illustrating this, in a recent systematic review of the literature on sexual harassment in higher education, Bondestam and Lundqvist (2020) conclude that anti-harassment policy has had no discernible effect over the past thirty years. Considering the lack of meaningful change despite the myriads of zero-tolerance policy documents, the training and awareness sessions, and the promised political commitment, invisible power is likely at play. Understanding that change is prevented because it threatens the privilege afforded to the powerful by an inherently unequal system is crucial for designing more effective interventions.

The main controversies and unresolved questions

The above review shows that groups can use morality strategically in a number of ways, and that power provides a useful analytical lens to systematize inquiries into such strategies. Diverse phenomena such as agenda-setting and achievement of economic and political objectives, impression management, and preventing progressive change can all be meaningfully examined as power dynamics that motivate and curb the strategic use of morality in intergroup contexts. The proposed model (Figure 22.1) may guide more systematic research into the strategic use of morality because it addresses three lacunae of current scholarship in particular. First, the model can be applied to intergroup contexts consisting of multiple actors (Panel A), which is rarely done (Ellemers et al. 2019). Second, the model points towards the proactive – rather than reactive and compensatory – use of morality, which is under-researched so far (Panel B). Third, the model explicates the dynamic and interactive character of morality in intergroup contexts (Panel C).

Questions that go beyond the above review concern two broad areas in particular, namely mechanisms and processes. Regarding mechanisms associated with the strategic use of morality in intergroup contexts, relevant questions concern whether behaviors and strategies can be attributed more or less clearly to different types of power exertion and whether certain types of power exertion functionally relate to specific relationships or to certain strategic motives. For instance, will powerful groups aiming to preserve the status quo that affords them their privilege typically use invisible forms of power exertion? Is framing issues morally more effective in prompting compliance from less powerful groups compared to framing issues in non-moral ways? And which other ways of using morality strategically can be discovered in the different forms of power exertion?

Regarding processes, relevant questions concern how negotiations and disagreements over power unfold, how definitional power is acquired in order to influence the moral connotation of behaviors, but also how, by whom and under which circumstances such powers will be accepted or contested. Which role do third parties play in supporting versus contesting definitional power over moral norms and behavior? How do social actors negotiate double-standards that occur when one moral value is prioritized over another, such as illustrated by the discussion about the right to bodily integrity versus compulsory vaccination that emerged in the context of the COVID-19 pandemic? Research into the strategic motives for intergroup help might offer valuable guidance for inquiries into such topics. The field was strongly influenced by the pioneering work of Arie Nadler (2002), whose conceptualization of intergroup helping relations as power relations has stimulated an impressive body of supporting empirical and conceptual work. For instance, refusing help from another group can be an attempt to communicate disagreement with the power differential implied by the roles of help giver and help recipient (e.g., Täuber 2017). Does the rejection of moral connotations of norms and behaviors fulfil similar purposes?

The important practical implications of current insights on this topic and level

Considering morality as strategically used to maintain and reproduce power in intergroup contexts has important practical implications. First, it points to groups actively creating and shaping moral landscapes, rather than passively undergoing and responding to existing moral norms. Second, it underlines the value of adjacent disciplines for cross-fertilization. For instance, regardless of whether visible, hidden, or invisible power exertion is concerned, language fulfils an important signaling function when morality is used strategically. Discourse analysis should therefore play a role when investigating moralization and power dynamics in situ. To illustrate, a good indication that an issue is becoming moralized is name-calling. People who do not categorize themselves as belonging to the same group are often grouped together under a common denominator by other groups in society. This was evident during the COVID-19 pandemic, when people who were hesitant to getting vaccinated were categorized under names such as "covidiot" (English), "wappie" (Dutch) or "Querdenker" (German). While their hesitance to getting vaccinated was rooted in divergent reasons, they were all subsumed under a unifying label depicting them primarily as crazy believers in conspiracy theories.

In addition, name-calling itself points to power differentials, because typically, the groups that are seen as deviating from the moral norm will be labelled. For instance, when labels are used for only one group, the power dynamics are clear: there is no word for citizens who got vaccinated. Accordingly, in public perception, they are the morally good. However, when both groups use moralized labels to refer to each other, struggles over definitional power might still be ongoing. Therefore, the use of moral language and labels can have an important signaling function for social stability. For instance, the spaces in which labels are used might be significant: many labels are only used for the outgroup in closed spaces reserved for ingroup members. An example are the terms used by right-wing ideologists to characterize people perceived as belonging to the political left. These terms were present in the associated online platforms but did not infiltrate public discourse until recently. When moral qualifications of outgroups permeate boundaries from closed forums to public discourse, this may signify shifts from covert to overt power struggles. Investigating such propositions can help anticipate unstable social situations that may culminate in open conflict, such as the Capitol Insurrection or the widespread demonstrations against governments' measures to curb the pandemic.

In sum, heeding recent calls for the use of more varied methodologies in order to gain more systematic insights into the socially shared nature of moral norms (Ellemers et al. 2019), the current analysis suggests benefits from cross-fertilization with adjacent fields (e.g., sociology, human geography, political science, and linguistics) and the associated methods (e.g., participatory research, spatial analysis, and discourse analysis). The framework presented in this chapter allows to consider the strategic use of morality in intergroup contexts by accounting for human motivation to create, shape, and influence their social environment, including moral landscapes. This opens up exciting new routes for theory, research, and methods that can inform pressing societal questions.

References

Acker, J. (2006). Inequality regimes: Gender, class, and race in organizations. *Gender & Society, 20*: 441–464.
Ahmed, S. (2007). 'You end up doing the document rather than doing the doing': Diversity, race equality and the politics of documentation. *Ethnic and Racial Studies, 30(4)*, 590–609.
Amnesty International (2021). Dutch childcare benefit scandal an urgent wake-up call to ban racist algorithms. www.amnesty.org/en/latest/news/2021/10/xenophobic-machines-dutch-child-benefit-scandal/. Last accessed 0n 20.02.2022
Bach, S., 2012. Shrinking the state or the Big Society? Public service employment relations in an era of austerity. *Industrial Relations Journal, 43 (5)*, 399–415.
Bandura, A., Barbaranelli, C., Caprara, G. V., & Pastorelli, C. (1996). Mechanisms of moral disengagement in the exercise of moral agency. *Journal of Personality and Social Psychology, 71(2)*, 364.
Blasi, A. (1980). Bridging moral cognition and moral action: A critical review of the literature. *Psychological Bulletin, 88(1)*, 1.
Bondestam, F., & Lundqvist, M. (2020). Sexual harassment in higher education: A systematic review. *European Journal of Higher Education, 10*: 397–419.
Craig, M. A., Rucker, J. M., & Richeson, J. A. (2018). The pitfalls and promise of increasing racial diversity: Threat, contact, and race relations in the 21st century. *Current Directions in Psychological Science, 27(3)*, 188–193.

Dahl, R. A. (1957). The concept of power. *Behavioral Science, 2(3)*, 201–215.

Ellemers, N. (1993). The influence of socio-structural variables on identity management strategies. *European Review of Social Psychology, 4(1)*, 27–57.

Ellemers, N., & van den Bos, K. (2012). Morality in groups: On the social-regulatory functions of right and wrong. *Social and Personality Psychology Compass, 6(12)*, 878–889.

Ellemers, N., Van Der Toorn, J., Paunov, Y., & Van Leeuwen, T. (2019). The psychology of morality: A review and analysis of empirical studies published from 1940 through 2017. *Personality and Social Psychology Review, 23(4)*, 332–366.

Fairclough, N. (2010*). Critical discourse analysis: The critical study of language* (2nd edn). Harlow: Longman.

Fernando, D., & Prasad, A. (2018). Sex-based harassment and organizational silencing: How women are led to reluctant acquiescence in academia. *Human Relations, 72(10)*, 1565–1594.

French, J. R., Raven, B., & Cartwright, D. (1959). The bases of social power. *Classics of Organization Theory, 7*, 311–320.

Gaventa, J. (2006). Finding the spaces for change: a power analysis. *IDS Bulletin, 37(6)*, 23–33.

Giridharadas, A. (2018). *Winners take all: The elite charade of changing the world*. New York: Alfred A. Knopf.

Haidt, J., Rosenberg, E., & Hom, H. (2003). Differentiating diversities: Moral diversity is not like other kinds. *Journal of Applied Social Psychology, 33(1)*, 1–36.

Hoekman, R., van der Roest, J. W., & van der Poel, H. (2018). From welfare state to participation society? Austerity measures and local sport policy in the Netherlands. *International Journal of Sport Policy and Politics, 10(1)*, 131–146.

Koster, M. (2014). Bridging the gap in the Dutch participation society: New spaces of governance, brokers, and informal politics. *Etnofoor, 26(2)*, 49–64.

Leach, C. W., Snider, N., Iyer, A., & Smith, H. (2002). Poisoning the consciences of the fortunate. The experience of relative advantage and support for social equality. In I. Walker, & H. Smith (Eds.), *Relative deprivation: Specification, development and integration* (pp. 136–163). Cambridge: Cambridge University Press.

Leslie, L. M. (2019). Diversity initiative effectiveness: A typological theory of unintended consequences. *Academy of Management Review, 44(3)*, 538–563.

Lima, A.M. and Casais, B. (2021). Consumer reactions towards femvertising: A netnographic study. *Corporate Communications: An International Journal, 26(3)*, 605–621

Lukes, S. (2005). Power and the battle for hearts and minds. *Millennium, 33*(3), 477–493.

Mansbridge, J., & Shames, S. L. (2008). Toward a theory of backlash: Dynamic resistance and the central role of power. *Politics & Gender, 4(4)*, 623–634.

Mazar, N., Amir, O., & Ariely, D. (2008). The dishonesty of honest people: A theory of self-concept maintenance. *Journal of Marketing Research, 45*(6), 633–644.

Minson, J. A., & Monin, B. (2012). Do-gooder derogation: Disparaging morally motivated minorities to defuse anticipated reproach. *Social Psychological and Personality Science, 3(2)*, 200–207.

Monin, B., & Miller, D.T. (2001). Moral credentials and the expression of prejudice. *Journal of Personality and Social Psychology, 81*, 33–43.

Nadler, A. (2002). Inter–group helping relations as power relations: Maintaining or challenging social dominance between groups through helping. *Journal of Social Issues, 58*(3), 487–502.

Naezer, M. M., van den Brink, M. C. L., & Benschop, Y. W. M. (2019). Harassment in Dutch academia: Exploring manifestations, facilitating factors, effects and solutions. www.researchgate.net/publication/334989749_Harassment_in_Dutch_academia_Exploring_manifestations_facilitating_factors_effects_and_solutions

Opotow, S. (1990). Moral exclusion and injustice: An introduction. *Journal of Social Issues, 46(1)*, 1–20.

Pagliaro, S., Ellemers, N., Barreto, M., & Di Cesare, C. (2016). Once dishonest, always dishonest? The impact of perceived pervasiveness of moral evaluations of the self on motivation to restore a moral reputation. *Frontiers in Psychology, 7*, 586.

Pope, S., & Wæraas, A. (2016). CSR-washing is rare: A conceptual framework, literature review, and critique. *Journal of Business Ethics, 137*(1), 173–193.

Prasad, A., & Holzinger, I. (2013). Seeing through smoke and mirrors: A critical analysis of marketing CSR. *Journal of Business Research, 66(10)*, 1915–1921.

Rozin, P. (1999). The process of moralization. *Psychological Science, 10(3)*, 218–221.

Rozin, P., Markwith, M., & Stoess, C. (1997). Moralization and becoming a vegetarian: The transformation of preferences into values and the recruitment of disgust. *Psychological Science, 8(2)*, 67–73.

Rozin, P., & Singh, L. (1999). The moralization of cigarette smoking in the United States. *Journal of Consumer Psychology, 8(3)*, 321–337.

Scheepers, D., Ellemers, N., & Sintemaartensdijk, N. (2009). Suffering from the possibility of status loss: Physiological responses to social identity threat in high status groups. *European Journal of Social Psychology, 39(6)*, 1075–1092.

Scott, J. C. (1990). *Domination and the Arts of Resistance*. New Haven, CT: Yale University Press.

Skitka, L. J., Bauman, C. W., & Sargis, E. G. (2005). Moral conviction: Another contributor to attitude strength or something more?. *Journal of Personality and Social Psychology, 88(6)*, 895.

Skitka, L. J., & Mullen, E. (2002). The dark side of moral conviction. *Analyses of Social Issues and Public Policy, 2(1)*, 35–41.

Stiegert, P., Täuber, S., Leliveld, M. C., & Oehmichen, J. (2021). The stereotype rub-off effect–Organizational stereotypes modulate behavioural expectations, expectancy violation and punishment after transgressions. *Organizational Behavior and Human Decision Processes, 165*, 127–138.

Sweetman, J., Leach, C. W., Spears, R., Pratto, F. & Saab, R. (2013). "I have a dream": A typology of social change goals. *Journal of Social and Political Psychology, 1(1)*, 293–320.

Täuber, S. (2017). A conceptualisation of help avoidance as motivated inaction: Implications for theory, research and society. In *Intergroup helping* (pp. 223–246). Springer, Cham.

Täuber, S. (2018). Moralized health-related persuasion undermines social cohesion. *Frontiers in Psychology, 9*, 909.

Täuber, S. & Moughalian, C. (2022). Collective system-supporting inaction: A conceptual framework of privilege maintenance. *European Journal of Social Psychology*, 1–15. https://doi.org/10.1002/ejsp.2860.

Täuber, S., & van Zomeren, M. (2013). Outrage towards whom? Threats to moral group status impede striving to improve via out-group-directed outrage. *European Journal of Social Psychology, 43(2)*, 149–159.

Täuber, S., van Zomeren, M., & Kutlaca, M. (2015). Should the moral core of climate issues be emphasized or downplayed in public discourse? Three ways to successfully manage the double-edged sword of moral communication. *Climatic Change, 130(3)*, 453–464.

Townsend-Bell, E. (2020). Backlash as the moment of revelation. *Signs: Journal of Women in Culture and Society, 45(2)*, 287–294.

Valdesolo, P., & DeSteno, D. (2007). Moral hypocrisy: Social groups and the flexibility of virtue. *Psychological Science. 18(8)*, 689–690.

Van Bavel, J. J., Packer, D. J., Haas, I. J., & Cunningham, W. A. (2012). The importance of moral construal: Moral versus non-moral construal elicits faster, more extreme, universal evaluations of the same actions. *PloS One, 7(11)*, e48693.

Van Leeuwen, F., Park, J. H., & Penton-Voak, I. S. (2012). Another fundamental social category? Spontaneous categorization of people who uphold or violate moral norms. *Journal of Experimental Social Psychology, 48(6)*, 1385–1388.

van Nunspeet, F., Derks, B., Ellemers, N., & Nieuwenhuis, S. (2015). Moral impression management: Evaluation by an in-group member during a moral IAT affects perceptual attention and conflict and response monitoring. *Social Psychological and Personality Science, 6(2)*, 183–192.

Wojciszke, B. (1994). Multiple meanings of behavior: Construing actions in terms of competence or morality. *Journal of Personality and Social Psychology, 67(2)*, 222.

Wojciszke, B. (2005). Morality and competence in person-and self-perception. *European Review of Social Psychology, 16(1)*, 155–188.

Wright, J. C., Cullum, J., & Schwab, N. (2008). The cognitive and affective dimensions of moral conviction: Implications for attitudinal and behavioral measures of interpersonal tolerance. *Personality and Social Psychology Bulletin, 34(11)*, 1461–1476.

Wright, J. C., Grandjean, P. T., & McWhite, C. B. (2013). The meta-ethical grounding of our moral beliefs: Evidence for meta-ethical pluralism. *Philosophical Psychology, 26(3)*, 336–361.

Young Academy Groningen Report (2021). *Harassment at the University of Groningen*. www.rug.nl/research/young-academy/files/yag-report-harassment-at-the-ug.pdf

PART VI

Moral self-views

PART VIA

A vision on moral self-views

23
ON THE VERTICAL
How the moral self pursues its highest good

Karl Aquino

When I was a teenager, my father had a religious conversion. It was an unsettling time in our family because his language, his behavior, and his new way of dealing with worldly problems greatly changed. At the time, I thought of myself as an iconoclast and so I had many arguments with my father about the authenticity of his conversion and the logical incoherence of his emerging faith. As my father became more immersed in his religion, he grew closer to a community of like-minded people who I came to know over many years. Eventually, my father became a pastor, guiding a small flock who sought moral guidance from him and from something beyond themselves. All of the disagreements I had with my father, along with my occasional participation in his religious community's ceremonial observances, gave me many opportunities to observe and contemplate how people incorporate morality into their everyday lives. When I pursued an academic career, the contrast between the morality of the people I encountered in the academy and that of the less credentialed worshipers in my father's church became more glaring.

I learned over time that a fair number of my colleagues were either dismissive of or openly hostile towards religion. Others were indifferent to it, but charitable in their views of those who find solace in a simple though logically indefensible faith. The more zealous of the anti-religious types were convinced that religion was plague upon humanity and should be replaced as soon as possible with a rational, evidence-based system of morality built upon the findings of science and the faculties of reason. Having heard, deliberated, and studied many of the allegations they made against religion and its practitioners over my career, it is not obvious to me that the alternatives they offer for how to live one's life are any wiser, more nourishing, or more humane than the one my father discovered when he reached his moment of decision all those years ago.

The gulf between the thought world occupied by my father and his fellow believers and that of many with whom I shared an intellectual habitat largely inspired my interest in moral psychology. My naïve ethnography of faith and non-faith communities informed my theorizing along with the countless articles and books I consulted in my quest to unravel the mysteries of moral life. I studied how agnostics, believers, and atheists made sense of their earthly predicament, comported themselves in the face of personal tragedy or frustrated goals, and treated both friends and strangers during times of need and plentitude. I introspected regularly about my own moral thoughts, emotions, and behaviors as I bungled my way (often badly) through moral quagmires, deluded myself to avoid reckoning with my hypocrisy and malevolence, and projected my debased and impure motivations onto others.

Twenty years ago, I came across a concept that gave me a useful framework for studying morality and organizing my reflections into a coherent explanation for what I had noticed and observed. That idea was the moral self, which my colleague Americus Reed and I referred to in a paper we published in 2002 as a person's *moral identity*. Drawing from decades of theory and research on identity, we defined moral identity as the mental model a person holds about their moral character. This model can include traits they possess that are associated with morality such as honesty, compassion, or fairness. It can also include their values, beliefs, ideals, and narratives they construct about they have dealt with past moral dilemmas. In other words, moral identity is a capacious concept that can be summarized by the basic notion that it is how one thinks about themselves in the sphere of moral judgment, choice, and action.

When Americus and I first began exploring moral identity, only a handful of scholars in the social sciences had used the term, many of whom were developmental psychologists. Augusto Blasi was perhaps the most influential of the early moral identity theorists and his writings were invaluable for helping us develop our own conceptual definition. Professor Blasi's contributions to explaining how the self can be a source of sustained moral motivation were seminal and provocative, but his papers, and those of others who wrote about moral identity at the time, were largely theoretical or philosophical. Americus and I wanted to study moral identity empirically, so we developed a measure of its self-importance that has since been used in hundreds of studies

It is gratifying to see how the idea of the moral self has expanded beyond its early roots. I am grateful to the editors of this volume for giving me an opportunity to reflect upon the state of the research and to share my views on what territory remains unexplored. I would like to focus this introduction on what may be the most urgent question researchers might ask about the moral self in the current historical period. I present it by first alluding to the German philosopher Friedrich Nietzsche's famous assertion that God is dead.

When Nietzsche wrote these words at the end of the 19th century, he did not intend them to be a bland descriptive statement like "The rose is red." Rather, they were an ominous warning about the price humanity must pay for rejecting what until then had been the most important source of meaning and moral instruction for millions of people throughout history. What remains after the death of God was anyone's guess. Nietzsche spent the remainder of his sane life trying to answer this question. Unfortunately, madness ended his attempt. I submit, without any claim to originality, that the challenge facing billions of people around the world after the death of God is how to comprehend a self that has become the ultimate creator, arbitrator, and defender of the moral universe. It is a heavy burden. In a world without a transcendent, supreme authority to turn to for moral direction, the self can only either turn inward to its conscience or horizontally to the actions, exhortations, or commands emanating from mortal selves to help it navigate through the complex and seemingly intractable moral problems that confront the present age. Understanding how the self comes to know right and wrong when nihilism and a polytheistic worship of many gods, whether they be money, power, social status, hedonistic pleasure, a political ideology, or a charismatic leader, appears to be the prevailing psychological and cultural condition of people in the developed world.

Another way of stating this condition is that whatever morality the self generates or accepts from others as being the true and evident and worth following is increasingly a horizontal one, by which I mean it is a morality that instructs us about how we should relate to other terrestrial beings that are a part of the natural world. This perspective contrasts with one that views the self as connected in a vertical relationship to a being that exists outside of nature and time and to which it is subordinate. The shift from a moral self in vertical relationship to a supreme being to one that is largely conceived as being in a relationship of fundamental equality with other biological species, whether they be other humans, animals, or plants, is one of the hallmarks of the rationalization of nature that Max Weber described as producing a "disenchantment of the world." It is an orientation that arguably predominates among those who have received the gift of higher education and who, as a result, believe themselves better equipped than most to advance human welfare. I suggest that the change in the self's orientation for deriving the moral rules by which it should live can be analyzed in a novel way by invoking the idea of a *relational self*. The relational self refers to how a person thinks about their connection to other individuals with whom they have causal or intimate interactions. What distinguishes the relational self from other models of the self is that it is not focused on one's individual qualities or their membership in a larger collective. Rather, it describes one's role in a relationship with a singular other such as a friend, a team member, a neighbor, or a God.

My reading of the literature is that scholars have paid relatively less attention to the moral self as a relational identity compared to the attention devoted to studying the self as a set of individual attributes or as a member of a larger collective like an ethnic group or nation state. I was therefore encouraged to discover that one of the chapters selected for inclusion in this volume, written by Maryam Kouchacki and Rajen Anderson, focuses on moral self-views at the interpersonal level. This treatment of the moral self is much needed, and thoughtful readers of this chapter will be rewarded with many new insights about how our interactions with others in relational contexts shape our views of ourselves and our behavior.

Reviewing the content of all of the chapters regarding the moral self and writing this introductory reflection has been a valuable exercise because it forced me to consider what questions I might ask if I were to study the moral self with new and innocent eyes. Here are some of the questions I would ask:

1. How does a self that submits to no transcendent authority arrange its values into a hierarchy, and on what grounds does it justify this arrangement? Nietzsche asserted that humans are valuing creatures. If so, the question of how our minds deduce value from the clutter and chaos of everyday life, and how it decides which values it should raise to paramount importance warrants attention. For instance, does the brain have a "valuing module"? Are there connections among different brain systems that explain the process of valuing? Philosophers and theologians have debated the question of objective value for hundreds of years. Studies on the moral self can inform this conversation by discovering how the human brain goes about the task of valuing and revaluing. Toward this end, readers will find the chapter by Jennifer Jordan, Elizabeth Mullen, and Marijke Leliveld informative because it provides an intimation into how the self may go about arranging its value hierarchy to meet the requirements of different situations because it is malleable.
2. If the self has the capacity to internalize the moralities of many gods with different and often competing systems of value, how does it choose its allegiances? What mental mechanisms does it draw from to make peace among warring gods? The self is composed of ideologies, cultural expectations, transitory emotions, faith-based commitments, and other powerful forces that intrude into consciousness and make equally compelling demands. Jolanda Jetten and Charlie R. Crimston explore the question of how the self might adjudicate among its various gods by reviewing research and theory on intragroup dissent, which is the willingness by a group member to challenge or deviate from the demands for conformity imposed by a group. Social pressure imposed by people with whom one shares a common identity is among the most

demanding of gods, so understanding why some individuals do not yield to it has been an abiding interest of those who view dissent essential for a well-functioning democracy. Who will bear the costs of dissent when the expectation of conformity is intense and price of deviance is high remains almost impossible to predict. Sometimes those who appear least likely to dissent end up being the ones whose disobedience ignites a revolution. Part of the answer for why some conform and others do not may be found in how the dissenter views their moral self.

3. Walt Whitman presented a poetic defense of moral hypocrisy when he wrote that if he contradicts himself, so he contradicts himself. What is the problem, for as he defiantly proclaims: "I am large, I contain multitudes." Whitman did indeed have a complex self-understanding as anyone who has read his verse can attest. But what is the consequence of thinking that one contains a multitude of selves? Does it mean that one can casually and without any psychic cost shed, revise, or recreate any self that one desires? Reinventing the self is a modern trope and appears to heed the heroic Nietzschean call to become who one is. Yet is it conducive to the practice of morality to have a world of people trying to live out the ideal of a protean self and experimenting with different moral selves as they go along? What can we say about self-view that permits a person to behave like a de Sadian libertine at one moment and in another to perform an act of service compassion worthy of St. Francis? What kind of moral self would this be? Perhaps the ability to maintain an essentialist belief in one's moral goodness when confronted with evidence to the contrary is a psychic benefit of having a complex and malleable moral self-view. On the other hand, it is worth asking whether the capacity to execute such mental operations is conducive to the forming the sound and reliable moral character on which a well-functioning social order depends.

4. Related to the previous question is how might our delusions inform or misinform our understanding and appraisal of our moral actions? One of Nietzsche's most decisive blows against the vanities of those who seek truth is his assertion that the will to untruth has proven far more valuable to our species, and is also far more common. Moral psychology has revealed time and time again that we lie to ourselves and to others all the time to support a belief in our moral goodness. The chapter by Matthew J. Hornsey describes how this phenomenon occurs at an intergroup level. As Professor Hornsey explains, intergroup processes can allow people to evade moral self-reflection and rationalize immorality. This observation seems particularly timely for understanding how group polarization and rapid social change can lead people may have once shared a unifying creed begin to separate and view one another as enemies rather than partners in a worthy moral enterprise.

5. Eastern religious traditions counsel that the escape from suffering requires the extinction of the self. The literature on the moral self has been relatively silent about ways of conceiving the self as something to be annihilated rather than preserved. Is it even possible to know whether there is such thing as a non-self in the way a Buddhist monk might experience this state of being? Does a non-self have a moral identity? The Western mind and the psychological theories it has produced offers few empirical answers to these questions. Perhaps like the mysterious Zen koan they are beyond the reach of science, but it might be worth finding out if this is so.

6. Finally, I would be curious to learn about what the self is doing when it makes conspicuous displays of its moral *bona fides*? Social media allows people to present a persona of moral goodness to a global audience, but the image is often a grand façade concealing a less admirable reality. What are we to make of the behavior colloquially known as "virtue signaling"? What does it reveal about the values of a culture when many of its members believe it will bring psychological fulfillment and social rewards if they can effectively "brand" the self in the most flattering moral light? Are the motives for virtue signaling similar to those that explain

the conspicuous consumption of luxury goods that the economist Thorstein Veblen argued was a way for those who possesses a surfeit of wealth and leisure to distinguish the noble from the common? Does frequent virtue signaling indicate that one possesses morality in abundance, or is it more revelatory of its absence? Is a self that hungers for social validation of its moral worth a psychologically healthy one? Would a self that understands itself to be in a vertical relationship with a supreme being whose grace is lavish and whose love is infinite require such validation to experience itself as having value?

No doubt the reader's engagement with the chapters that follow will raise many more questions than these, which would be sign that the topic of the moral self will have a long intellectual life.

During my father's slow decline from dementia, I watched the moral self he fashioned from a lifetime of activities, memories, and shared experiences disintegrate and fade away. All the while, I saw the community of believers he had served and worshiped try to ease his passage to the other world. They would clean him when he soiled himself and lifted him from his bed to his wheelchair when he needed to travel. They sang him songs of praise, laughed at his repetitive and often unintelligible jokes, reminisced about past adventures, and prayed with him until the very end. I was told that he expired after one of the church members, who had been a constant companion in his last days, concluded a reading of one of his favorite psalms. I do not know what moral self-view these believers held, but what I infer from how they dedicated themselves to caring for my father over several years is that the moral universe they inhabited was not an indifferent and pitiless one. I may never acquire the spiritual clarity that characterized my father's faith, but I hope that before he died his last coherent experience of his moral self was one that stood looking upward, in a relationship of loving reverence, towards its beckoning God. My father was no Nietzschean superman. He chose not to kill God, and for him that made all the difference in this world – and maybe the next.

PART VIB

Empirical review chapters on moral self-views

24
THE INTRAPERSONAL LEVEL
The moral self

Jennifer Jordan, Elizabeth Mullen and Marijke C. Leliveld

Abstract

The moral self is an individual's dynamic and malleable moral self-concept. In this chapter, we describe how the moral self functions within the working self-concept, relates to an individual's broader identity, and is affected by and affects behavior and cognition. Specifically, we differentiate the moral self from related constructs such as moral identity, self-esteem, and actual, ideal and ought selves. We then discuss how the moral self serves to regulate individuals' moral behavior and review the literature on what shapes the moral self and what the moral self is likely to shape in return. We close by discussing future directions in research about the moral self.

- The moral self indicates how people think about themselves and their behavior.
- The moral self is malleable and resides in people's working self concepts.
- The moral self shapes and is shaped by moral cognition and behavior.
- The moral self functions to regulate moral behavior.
- Measuring the moral self can affect subsequent moral behavior and cognition; this makes it challenging to detect mediational effects of the moral self on prior to subsequent moral behavior and cognition.

Introduction

An individual's self-perception of his or her own morality is dynamic, meaning that it changes over time based on behaviors and contexts (Monin & Jordan, 2009). This dynamic and malleable moral self-concept is what we label as the moral self, also referred to as the moral self-image (MSI) (Jordan et al., 2015).[1] We view the moral self as a cognitive construct – meaning, it involves how people think about themselves and their subjective appraisals of their behavior. The moral self is affected by various influences and has important implications for how people think about themselves and the actions that they take (Jennings et al., 2015).

In this chapter, we define the moral self, distinguish it from related constructs, look at what variables have been found to affect (and are affected by) the moral self, explain how the moral self serves as a regulatory mechanism, and outline potential future directions for research. We primarily focus on moral self-views rather than on how others perceive a person's moral self.[2]

The moral self within the greater self concept

The moral self resides in individuals' working self-concepts (Kernis & Johnson, 1990). Being part of the working self-concept makes the moral self a malleable part of the self – particularly when compared to other more stable self constructs, such as trait self-esteem (Rosenberg, 1965) and moral identity (Aquino & Reed, 2002). As part of the working self-concept, the moral self shifts based on feedback from the social world and one's own actions (Monin & Jordan, 2009). For example, people's moral selves are responsive to social comparisons about the states of their moral selves, (bogus) feedback about the states of their moral selves, and their actual actions (Jordan et al., 2015) – three domains identified to affect people's self-concepts (Kernis & Goldman, 2003). Additionally, the moral self is completely subjective, meaning it is unrelated to one's objective moral standing; people who act in a way perceived as moral by others could still perceive their own moral self to be lacking. And vice versa. And while individuals differ in how highly they value their moral selves (Aquino & Reed, 2002), there is nearly a universal desire to perceive oneself as moral (Dunning, 2007). This desire to maintain a positive MSI coupled with the state of a person's current MSI, influences people's tendency to engage in (im)moral behavior.

We define the moral self as a "person's malleable moral self-concept", that is, their self-concept related to the traits of the prototypically moral person (i.e., *caring, compassionate, helpful, hardworking, friendly, fair, generous, honest, kind*) (Jordan et al., 2015). These nine traits were derived from the seven traits that Aquino and Reed (2002) found most exemplified a moral identity. And while not an exhaustive representation of the traits of the moral self, they represent people's prototype of the ideal moral self. In the following subsections, we differentiate the moral self from other related constructs.

Moral identity. The self-importance of moral identity, one of the most cited moral self-related constructs, is "a self-conception organized around a set of moral traits" (Aquino & Reed, 2002). It comprises two subdimensions: the importance to the self of possessing such traits (internalization) and the importance of demonstrating to others through behavior that one possesses those traits (symbolization). The moral self and moral identity are similar in two ways. First, they both regulate one's own behavior towards actions considered more morally appropriate. And second, they are both associated with moral-related beliefs, attitudes, and behaviors (Aquino & Reed, 2002). The biggest difference between the two constructs is their level of stability; moral identity is a trait, whereas, MSI refers to a state (Aquino et al., 2009).

Scores on the MSI scale are positively associated with symbolic moral identity, but are unrelated to internalized moral identity (Jordan et al., 2015). Thus, what people do to externally signal the strength of their moral selves (e.g., reading morally related publications, belonging to certain clubs or associations) is positively associated with their MSIs. But because there is an almost universal value of being a moral person (i.e., of having a high internalized moral identity), the temporary state of one's MSI is unrelated to the importance of possessing moral traits (i.e., to internalized moral identity); one can simultaneously acknowledge that their state MSI is low and that their moral identity is a key part of their self.

Self-esteem – state and trait. The MSI is also separate from trait and state self-esteem. Trait self-esteem indicates a person's global and stable feelings of self-worth (Kernis & Goldman, 2003). While trait self-esteem can change, unlike the moral self, it does not respond to single events within short time periods (Rosenberg, 1986). State self-esteem, is a more dynamic form of the trait-based construct (Heatherton & Polivy, 1991). But unlike state self-esteem, the moral self encompasses people's specific feelings of moral self-worth, rather than general feelings of self-worth. One can think about state self-esteem versus MSI as global versus specific state-based self-appraisals related to isolated events, with the former being based on a generalized emotional response and the latter being based on specific morally-relevant events (Brown, 1993). Indeed, the moral self has low to moderate correlations with state-based self-esteem (Jordan et al., 2015).

Actual, ought, and ideal selves. According to self-discrepancy theory, individuals have three "selves": the actual, the ideal, and the ought. The actual self represents the self that one perceives oneself to be. The "ought" self, is the self one perceives that one should be, and is mainly based on societal perceptions, norms, and perceived expectations about duties, roles, and responsibilities. Finally, the "ideal" self represents the self one aspires to be. Of course, these three selves are interconnected. Self-discrepancy theory proposes that people seek to align their actual with either their ideal or ought selves, and that misalignment results in negative emotions and discomfort. While similar in theory to the moral self, there are two major differences. First, self-discrepancy theory is about a general self-assessment rather than an appraisal of one's moral standing. Second, self-discrepancy theory proposes that the source of the self-discrepancy (i.e., being from either the ideal or ought selves) (Higgins, 1987) influences how the discrepancy impacts the individual. In contrast, Jordan et al. (2015) found that discrepancies with the ideal- or ought-moral selves did not differentially affect individuals' behavior. To conclude, given individuals' moral self aspirations come both from what they think society expects of them (the *ought*) (Hoffman, 1975; Kohlberg, 1971) and what they expect from themselves (the *ideal*) (Monin & Jordan, 2009) both constructs influence one's MSI.

The regulatory function of the moral self

People's moral behavior is in constant flux – both on the positive and negative sides of the continuum (e.g., Mazar et al., 2008; Shalvi et al., 2011), and these fluctuations influence and are influenced by people's MSIs. For example, people's moral selves are responsive to social comparisons about the states of their moral selves, (bogus) feedback about the states of their moral selves, and their actions (Jordan et al., 2015; Kernis & Goldman, 2003). Moreover, because people highly value their moral selves, and strive to see themselves as moral beings (Monin & Jordan, 2009), they will take (even costly) steps to preserve a positive MSI.

Thus, the moral self is often theorized to play an important role in regulating one's moral behavior (Monin & Jordan, 2009). In particular, the literatures on behavioral consistency, moral licensing and moral compensation all theorize that current levels of MSI, combined with the motivation to maintain a positive MSI, are predictive of future behavior.[3] Notably, although changes to the MSI, as a result of prior behavior, are not always empirically demonstrated in the literatures on moral consistency, licensing, and compensation, the mediational role of MSI between prior and subsequent behavior is often theorized and is therefore reviewed in this chapter. We discuss the issue of empirical versus theoretical support for the role of the MSI in the section on Future Directions.

Consistency. Research on behavioral consistency suggests that individuals' desires to maintain positive MSIs should lead them to consistently engage in moral behavior (Cornelissen et al., 2013). Indeed, when one's prior moral behavior is construed as evidence of commitment to the goal of being a moral person (rather than making progress toward that goal), initial moral behavior leads to subsequent moral behavior (Susewind & Hoelzl, 2014). Moreover, research on the slippery slope, a phenomenon wherein small transgressions gradually grow and lead to larger transgressions (Welsh et al., 2015), suggests that consistency can also lead people to engage in progressively more immoral behavior, due to the ease with which they can self-rationalize and hence maintain a positive MSI (Tenbrunsel & Messick, 2004).

Licensing and compensation. However, people do not always consistently display (im)moral behavior; sometimes an initial moral behavior can relax subsequent strivings to be a moral person. In particular, moral licensing (Monin & Miller, 2001) occurs "when past moral behavior makes people more likely to do potentially immoral things without worrying about feeling or appearing immoral" (Merritt et al., 2010, p. 344). One mechanism proposed for licensing effects is that a temporary boost to one's MSI, as a result of initial moral behavior, licenses subsequent immoral behavior (e.g., Khan & Dhar, 2006). In contrast, research on moral compensation (or moral cleansing) suggests that engaging in immoral behavior can lower people's MSIs which motivates corrective action. In particular, acting immorally (and presumably experiencing a threat to their MSI) motivates people to engage in actions that figuratively cleanse themselves of their past transgression and reassert their moral selves (cf. Mulder & Aquino, 2013; Tetlock et al., 2000).

Influences on and of the moral self

Building on the notion that the MSI serves a regulatory function, in this section we discuss which factors can influence the MSI and how this, in turn, affects subsequent behavior. See Figure 24.1 for a rough visual representation.

One's own behavior: real and imagined

People make inferences about their own morality by reflecting on their own behavior (Bem, 1972). Thus, one of the most common influences on the state of one's moral self is one's past behavior (both real and imagined) and reflecting on one's past behavior (Kernis & Goldman, 2003).

Actual and recalled behavior. Numerous scholars have theorized that engaging in moral behavior boosts one's MSI, engaging in immoral behavior decreases it, and that these changes to MSI predict subsequent behavior (for a review see Mullen & Monin, 2016).[4] Recently, Liu et al. (2019) empirically demonstrated that engaging in organizational citizenship behaviors increased

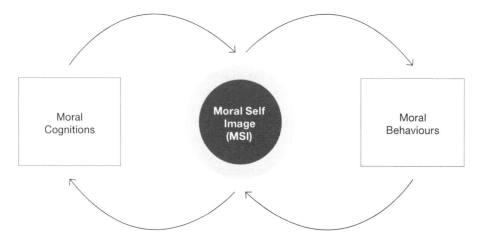

Figure 24.1 Moral self image.

people's MSIs, which licensed pro-social rule breaking in organizational contexts. And Mulder and Aquino (2013) found that people who lied in an initial task were more likely than those who did not lie in the initial task to be honest in a later task; this compensatory behavior was hypothesized to be driven by a desire to maintain a positive MSI.

Recalling one's own past moral or immoral behaviors is posited to have similar effects as performing actual behavior on one's MSI (Jordan et al., 2011). For example, in one study recollections of past moral behavior positively impacted the state of the moral self, whereas recollections of past immoral behavior negatively impacted it, and changes in MSI predicted subsequent compensatory behavior (Cornelissen et al., 2013). Similarly, Jordan et al. (2011) found that merely asking people to think about times that they helped or harmed others, led to changes in subsequent prosocial and cheating behavior (although MSI was not measured in these studies).

Imagined behavior. Merely imagining engaging in moral or immoral behavior can impact one's MSI. For example, Khan and Dhar (2006) found that participants who imagined themselves volunteering reported higher moral self-concepts (as measured by their endorsement of items such as "I am helpful") than did participants who did not imagine volunteering, and these changes in MSI predicted subsequent purchasing decisions (i.e., purchasing an indulgent or utilitarian good).

Counterfactual roads not taken. Similar to imagining behaving morally, refraining from engaging in unethical behavior may boost people's MSIs (Khan & Dhar, 2006). For example, White participants who had an opportunity to forego blatantly racist behavior, compared to those who did not have such an opportunity, subsequently expressed less racially sensitive views (Effron et al., 2012). It is plausible that such counterfactuals about unethical roads-not-taken may be sufficient to boost MSI (although this was not empirically tested in Effron et al., 2012). Similarly, when reflecting on their positive moral behaviors (rather than merely refraining from unethical behavior), counterfactuals may also influence people's MSIs; someone may get a bigger boost to their MSI for taking public transportation (a positive moral behavior to help the environment) if driving was an option relative to if it was not (i.e., when they could have taken a less virtuous mode of transportation, cf., Khan & Dhar, 2006, Study 4).

Others' behavior

A second major influence on the MSI is others' behavior. Given the inherent ambiguity in what constitutes moral behavior, others' behavior, particularly via social norms, vicarious processes, and social comparisons, can also inform one's judgments about one's own MSI.

For example, others' behavior can serve to influence the perceived norms for what constitutes moral or immoral behavior (Jordan et al., 2011; Reno et al., 1993). Individuals who fall short of moral standards, as signaled by others' actions, may perceive a threat to their MSIs, which may motivate corrective action. Similarly, observation of others' immoral actions is likely to have the reverse effect, boosting individuals' MSIs and potentially relaxing their subsequent moral behavior.

The behavior of (close) others can also influence one's MSI through vicarious processes (Kouchaki, 2011) – particularly, when the observer perceives him or herself as having the characteristics of, or shares an identity with, the other. For example, Lennartz and colleagues (2019) found that when a company successfully implemented an equal-opportunity hiring policy, this increased organization members' MSIs (Jordan et al., 2015), which subsequently licensed more covert forms of discrimination in hiring decisions.

Finally, social comparisons provide people with information about their own abilities and attitudes, which can influence their self-concepts (Festinger, 1954) – including their moral self-image (Jordan et al., 2015). Notably, social comparison processes in the moral domain may have similar effects as those in the non-moral domain on people's self-concepts (Monin, 2007). Whereas, downward social comparisons (e.g., comparing oneself to someone who has just engaged in unethical behavior) should provide a boost to one's MSI because the comparison may lead one to feel morally superior (Jordan et al., 2015), upward social comparisons (e.g., comparing oneself to someone who has engaged in significant moral deeds) may have a more complex impact on MSI. On the one hand, upward social comparisons may lower one's MSI; indeed, receiving false feedback that one was less moral than others decreased participants' MSIs (Jordan et al., 2015). On the other hand, given that individuals strive to maintain positive MSIs, the threat generated by upward social comparisons could also lead individuals to engage in cognitive distortions (e.g., derogating the target of the upward comparison) to protect their cherished MSIs (Minson & Monin, 2012; Monin, 2007). In the next section, we discuss the cognitive – rather than behavioral – route to maintaining a positive MSI.

Maintaining the moral self via cognitive processes

When people experience real or potential threats to their cherished MSIs they may increase their subsequent moral behavior (as reviewed above) in an effort to restore their MSI, or they may engage in cognitive distortions to alleviate the discomfort caused by threats to their MSIs without having to change their behavior (Minson & Monin, 2012). People can change their beliefs about their past behavior by, for example, reframing a moral decision into an amoral one. When positioning the decision out of the domain of morality, it has reduced, if any, effects on the MSI, a process known as moral disengagement (Bandura, 1990). Finally, people can also distort the good derived from their own past actions. For example, in one study, Effron (2014) found that participants who anticipated the possibility of receiving negative feedback on a test of their morality, overestimated the extent to which their prior decision to donate 50 cents to charity would provide evidence of their morality to an observer. In other words, when faced with a moral self threat, they inflated the impact that a small prosocial act would have on others' assessment of their own morality (and presumably also on their own MSI). In summary, people can, at times, engage in cognitive distortions by reappraising their own or others' (im)moral behavior in a more or less negative light in an effort to alleviate threats to their MSI without having to engage in actual moral behavior.

Future directions

One of the most important questions for future research on the moral self is *how best to measure the construct*? Many scholars have proposed that the moral self is the mechanism explaining various moral phenomenon – from moral compensation to licensing and consistency; however, only a few of these investigations have provided actual empirical evidence for this assertion (e.g., Cornelissen et al., 2013). One reason may be that until recently, there was not a validated self-report measure of MSI (Jordan et al., 2015). Additionally, capturing the MSI's role as a mediator could be challenging because the simple act of measuring the MSI (i.e., asking people to reflect and self-report on the state of their MSIs) may dilute any subsequent effects. For example, if a person does something moral and then is asked to reflect on the state of their moral self, the mere recording of one's increased MSI could subsequently restrict subsequent licensing effects by highlighting the importance of their moral identity. Alternatively, reflecting on one's MSI after an immoral act could instigate reframing processes of the immoral behavior through a form of rationalization (Tenbrunsel & Messick, 2004). Thus, one opportunity for future research is to generate a more implicit way of measuring the moral self; for example, measuring people's activation of either a moral or immoral mindset through a word completion task (c.f., Zhong & Liljenquist, 2006) or their speed of responding to various words, videos, or images (c.f., Aquino et al., 2011; Greene et al., 2001). Using an unobtrusive measure might obviate the limitations found with more conscious, explicit measures. Another method might be to use a mediation-by-causal-chain-approach (Spencer et al., 2005) where researchers identify the effects of the independent variable on MSI in a separate study from one assessing the effects of the independent variable on the dependent variable.

Another unanswered question about the moral self is if the state of the self is more a function of personal, internal perceptions or of social judgment and the desire to be perceived as moral by others. Having our behavior witnessed by others invites opportunities for praise and condemnation,[5] which may strengthen the impact observed behavior has on our moral self. But existing studies have shown that the moral self is responsive to private personal changes that only the individual has witnessed him or herself (Bryan et al., 2013; Monin & Miller, 2001). For example, in one study, participants received bogus feedback on the state of their moral selves based on some action they performed (Jordan et al., 2015). Even when they believed that only they could see this score, it affected the state of their moral selves. Other research indicates that even though people adjust the focus of their moral decisions to strategically affect the perceptions of others, they retain high personal self-perceptions of their moral selves regardless of their socially-motivated behavior (Rom & Conway, 2018). Taken together, these studies suggest that the state of the moral self is reactive to personal observations and not in need of public witness. Of course, the options can coexist; it is possible that the MSI is a self-driven, private phenomenon, and that the effects of one's behavior on the moral self are strengthened when witnessed and acknowledged by others. This is an empirical question that remains to be answered.

A third direction for future research is to examine the types of actions that are required to prompt changes in the moral self and if the amoral, immoral, or moral labeling of an action affects the magnitude of the subsequent alteration. That is, must actions be explicitly morally labeled (e.g., volunteering for a charity whose cause many identify as moral), be in the moral domain (e.g., planting trees in a deforested area), or merely perceived as moral by the person performing the action (e.g., wearing a t-shirt purchased in support of a charity, without any logos or text referring to the charity) for those actions to affect the moral self? Most research thus far has asked participants to recall incidents that they consider as moral or immoral – without, requiring some sort of external validation for the recall. In fact, it is rare that these stories are coded for their externally evaluated moral or immoral content. However, one study (Jordan et al., 2011) did find that the more moral or immoral these recalls were labelled by external coders, the more extreme the effects on subsequent behavior (although notably MSI was not measured in this study). And even when they are coded, as the participant never sees the actual coding (or the external labeling of the behavior), it is usually the participants' cognitive characterization of the behavior as moral or immoral that leads to the subsequent effects.

Fourth, there are a number of individual differences that may impact the extent to which people draw inferences about their MSI from their past behaviors. For example, it would be interesting to investigate if the state of the moral self is related to a person's stage of moral development (Kohlberg, 1971). Individuals progress through three stages (*preconventional* to *conventional* to *postconventional*) of moral development, which determine how they judge what is and is not morally right. Essentially, this progress is defined along the lines of judgment based on rewards and punishments (preconventional) to social norms (conventional) to universal principles of rights and justice (postconventional). It would be interesting to investigate how people's stage of moral reasoning affects the malleability of their moral selves. On the one hand, it is possible that pre-conventional and conventional reasoners have more sensitive moral selves because they are seeking external cues to determine if they are being moral people (i.e., either rewards and punishments or judgments from others). On the other hand, it is possible that the MSIs of post-conventional moral reasoners are more sensitive, as they are more attuned to the complexity of moral issues and more sensitive to moral issues in their environment.

Lastly, other individual-difference measures may also influence the extent to which individuals draw inferences about their own morality from their behavior. For example, moral chronics, that is, people with a trait-based tendency to have moral constructs chronically accessible, may be more likely to consider the relevance of behaviors to morality (Narvaez & Lapsley, 2009). Similarly, individuals scoring higher on moral attentiveness, or the extent to which they find morality salient in their everyday experiences, are more cognizant of the moral content of everyday behavior and may be more likely to reflect on the implications of various courses of action for their own morality (Reynolds, 2008). Future research may benefit from the inclusion of individual difference variables that may moderate the mediating effect of MSI on prior and subsequent behavior.

Conclusion

The moral self is a dynamic and malleable part of the working self-concept. A positive MSI is highly cherished by people, leading them to take meaningful steps to internally maintain it – even if only through cognitive rationalizations rather than real behavioral changes. Better understanding the MSI, particularly how to best measure it and examine its isolated effects on subsequent behavior, will aid scholars in better understanding the construct, as well as how to predict and influence individuals' (im)moral behaviors.

Notes

1. We use these two terms interchangeably throughout.
2. For a more detailed examination of the interpersonal factors that affect the moral self, see Chapter 25 of this volume, "Moral self-views, at the interpersonal level of analysis" by Maryam Kouchaki and Rajen Anderson.
3. See also the chapters in this volume by Beersma et al. and Shnabel.
4. Notably, some of these theorized influences of positive or negative initial behavior on the moral self have not been empirically demonstrated although the effects on subsequent behavior (i.e., licensing or compensation) have.
5. For more details, see the chapter in this volume on interpersonal influences on the moral self by Kouchaki and Anderson.

References

Aquino, K., Freeman, D., Reed II, A., Lim, V. K. G., & Felps, W. (2009). Testing a social-cognitive model of moral behavior: The interactive influence of situations and moral identity centrality. *Journal of Personality and Social Psychology*, *97*(1), 123–141. https://doi.org/10.1037/a0015406

Aquino, K., McFerran, B., & Laven, M. (2011). Moral identity and the experience of moral elevation in response to acts of uncommon goodness. *Journal of Personality and Social Psychology*, *100*(4), 703–718. https://doi.org/10.1037/a0022540

Aquino, K., & Reed, A. (2002). The self-importance of moral identity. *Journal of Personality and Social Psychology*, *83*(6), 1423–1440. https://doi.org/10.1037/0022-3514.83.6.1423

Bandura, A. (1990). Mechanisms of moral disengagement in terrorism. In W. Reich (Ed.), *Origins of Terrorism: Psychologies, Ideologies, States of Mind* (pp. 161–191). Cambridge: Cambridge University Press.

Bem, D. J. (1972). Self-perception theory. In L. Berkowitz (Ed.), *Advances in experimental social psychology* (Vol. *6*, pp. 1–62). Academic Press. https://doi.org/10.1016/S0065-2601(08)60024-6

Brown, J. D. (1993). Self-esteem and self-evaluation: Feeling is believing. In J. Suls (Ed.), *Psychological perspectives on the self* (Vol. *4*, pp. 27–58). Erlbaum.

Bryan, C. J., Adams, G. S., & Monin, B. (2013). When cheating would make you a cheater: Implicating the self prevents unethical behavior. *Journal of Experimental Psychology: General*, *142*(4), 1001.

Cornelissen, G., Bashshur, M. R., Rode, J., & Menestrel, M. L. (2013). Rules or consequences? The role of ethical mind-sets in moral dynamics. *Psychological Science*, *24*(4), 482–488. https://doi.org/10.1177/0956797612457376

Dunning, D. (2007). Self-image motives and consumer behavior: How sacrosanct self-beliefs sway preferences in the market place. *Journal of Consumer Psychology*, *17*(4), 237–249. https://doi.org/10.1016/S1057-7408(07)70033-5

Effron, D. A. (2014). Making mountains of morality from molehills of virtue: Threat causes people to overestimate their moral credentials. *Personality and Social Psychology Bulletin*, *40*(8), 972–985. https://doi.org/10.1177/0146167214533131

Effron, D. A., Miller, D. T., & Monin, B. (2012). Inventing racist roads not taken: The licensing effect of immoral counterfactual behaviors. *Journal of Personality and Social Psychology*, *103*(6), 916–932. https://doi.org/10.1037/a0030008

Festinger, L. (1954). A theory of social comparison processes. *Human Relations*, *7*(2), 117–140. https://doi.org/10.1177/001872675400700202

Greene, J. D., Sommerville, R. B., Nystrom, L. E., Darley, J. M., & Cohen, J. D. (2001). An fMRI investigation of emotional engagement in moral judgment. *Science*. https://doi.org/10.1126/science.1062872

Heatherton, T. F., & Polivy, J. (1991). Development and validation of a scale for measuring state self-esteem. *Journal of Personality and Social Psychology*, *60*(6), 895–910. https://doi.org/10.1037/0022-3514.60.6.895

Higgins, E. T. (1987). Self-discrepancy: A theory relating self and affect. *Psychological Review*, *94*(3), 319–340. https://doi.org/10.1037/0033-295X.94.3.319

Hoffman, M. L. (1975). Sex differences in moral internalization and values. *Journal of Personality and Social Psychology*, *32*(4), 720.

Jennings, P. L., Mitchell, M. S., & Hannah, S. T. (2015). The moral self: A review and integration of the literature. *Journal of Organizational Behavior*, *36*(S1), S104–S168. https://doi.org/10.1002/job.1919

Jordan, J., Leliveld, M. C., & Tenbrunsel, A. E. (2015). The moral self-image scale: Measuring and understanding the malleability of the moral self. *Frontiers in Psychology*, *6*, 1878. https://doi.org/10.3389/fpsyg.2015.01878

Jordan, J., Mullen, E., & Murnighan, J. K. (2011). Striving for the moral self: The effects of recalling past moral actions on future moral behavior. *Personality and Social Psychology Bulletin*, *37*(5), 701–713. https://doi.org/10.1177/0146167211400208

Kernis, M. H., & Goldman, B. M. (2003). Stability and variability in self-concept and self-esteem. In M. R. Leary & J. P. Tangney (Eds.), *Handbook of self and identity* (pp. 106–127). Guilford Press.

Kernis, M. H., & Johnson, E. K. (1990). Current and typical self-appraisals: Differential responsiveness to evaluative feedback and implications for emotions. *Journal of Research in Personality*, *24*(2), 241–257. https://doi.org/10.1016/0092-6566(90)90019-3

Khan, U., & Dhar, R. (2006). Licensing effect in consumer choice. *Journal of Marketing Research*, *43*(2), 259–266. https://doi.org/10.1509/jmkr.43.2.259

Kohlberg, L. (1971). Stages of moral development. In C. M. Beck, B. S. Crittenden, & E. V. Sullivan (Eds.), *Moral education: Interdisciplinary approaches* (pp. 23–92). Toronto: University of Toronto Press.

Kouchaki, M. (2011). Vicarious moral licensing: The influence of others' past moral actions on moral behavior. *Journal of Personality and Social Psychology*, *101*(4), 702–715. https://doi.org/10.1037/a0024552

Lennartz, C., Proost, K., & Brebels, L. (2019). Decreasing overt discrimination increases covert discrimination: Adverse effects of equal opportunities policies. *International Journal of Selection and Assessment*, *27*(2), 129–138. https://doi.org/10.1111/ijsa.12244

Liu, T., Liu, C., & Zhou, E. (2019). Influence of organizational citizenship behavior on prosocial rule breaking: Moral licensing perspective. *Social Behavior and Personality: An International Journal*, *47*(6), 1–9. https://doi.org/10.2224/sbp.8079

Mazar, N., Amir, O., & Ariely, D. (2008). The dishonesty of honest people: A theory of self-concept maintenance. *Journal of Marketing Research, 45*(6), 633–644. https://doi.org/10.1509/jmkr.45.6.633

Merritt, A. C., Effron, D. A., & Monin, B. (2010). Moral self-licensing: When being good frees us to be bad. *Social and Personality Psychology Compass, 4*(5), 344–357.

Minson, J. A., & Monin, B. (2012). Do-gooder derogation: Disparaging morally motivated minorities to defuse anticipated reproach. *Social Psychological and Personality Science, 3*(2), 200–207. https://doi.org/10.1177/1948550611415695

Monin, B. (2007). Holier than me? Threatening social comparison in the moral domain. *Revue Internationale de Psychologie Sociale, 1*, 53–68.

Monin, B., & Jordan, A. H. (2009). The dynamic moral self: A social psychological perspective. In D. Narvaez & D. K. Lapsley (Eds.), *Personality, identity, and character: Explorations in moral psychology* (pp. 341–354). Cambridge University Press.

Monin, B., & Miller, D. T. (2001). Moral credentials and the expression of prejudice. *Journal of Personality and Social Psychology, 81*(1), 33–43. https://doi.org/10.1037/0022-3514.81.1.33

Mulder, L. B., & Aquino, K. (2013). The role of moral identity in the aftermath of dishonesty. *Organizational Behavior and Human Decision Processes, 121*(2), 219–230. https://doi.org/10.1016/j.obhdp.2013.03.005

Mullen, E., & Monin, B. (2016). Consistency versus licensing effects of past moral behavior. *Annual Review of Psychology, 67*, 363–385.

Narvaez, D., & Lapsley, D. K. (2009). *Personality, identity, and character: Explorations in moral psychology*. Cambridge University Press.

Reno, R. R., Cialdini, R. B., & Kallgren, C. A. (1993). The transsituational influence of social norms. *Journal of Personality and Social Psychology, 64*(1), 104.

Reynolds, S. J. (2008). Moral attentiveness: Who pays attention to the moral aspects of life? *Journal of Applied Psychology, 93*(5), 1027–1041. https://doi.org/10.1037/0021-9010.93.5.1027

Rom, S. C., & Conway, P. (2018). The strategic moral self: Self-presentation shapes moral dilemma judgments. *Journal of Experimental Social Psychology, 74*, 24–37.

Rosenberg, M. (1965). *Society and the adolescent self-image*. Princeton University Press.

Rosenberg, M. (1986). Self-concept from middle childhood through adolescence. In J. Suls & A. G. Greenwald (Eds.), *Psychological perspectives on the self* (Vol. 2, pp. 107–136). Erlbaum.

Shalvi, S., Dana, J., Handgraaf, M. J., & De Dreu, C. K. (2011). Justified ethicality: Observing desired counterfactuals modifies ethical perceptions and behavior. *Organizational Behavior and Human Decision Processes, 115*(2), 181–190.

Spencer, S. J., Zanna, M. P., & Fong, G. T. (2005). Establishing a causal chain: Why experiments are often more effective than mediational analyses in examining psychological processes. *Journal of Personality and Social Psychology, 89*(6), 845.

Susewind, M., & Hoelzl, E. (2014). A matter of perspective: Why past moral behavior can sometimes encourage and other times discourage future moral striving. *Journal of Applied Social Psychology, 44*(3), 201–209. https://doi.org/10.1111/jasp.12214

Tenbrunsel, A. E., & Messick, D. M. (2004). Ethical fading: The role of self-deception in unethical behavior. *Social Justice Research, 17*(2), 223–236. https://doi.org/10.1023/B:SORE.0000027411.35832.53

Tetlock, P. E., Kristel, O. V., Elson, S. B., Green, M. C., & Lerner, J. S. (2000). The psychology of the unthinkable: Taboo trade-offs, forbidden base rates, and heretical counterfactuals. *Journal of Personality and Social Psychology, 78*(5), 853–870. https://doi.org/10.1037/0022-3514.78.5.853

Welsh, D. T., Ordóñez, L. D., Snyder, D. G., & Christian, M. S. (2015). The slippery slope: How small ethical transgressions pave the way for larger future transgressions. *Journal of Applied Psychology, 100*(1), 114.

Zhong, C.-B., & Liljenquist, K. (2006). Washing away your sins: Threatened morality and physical cleansing. *Science, 313*(5792), 1451–1452. https://doi.org/10.1126/science.1130726

25
THE INTERPERSONAL LEVEL
Moral self-views, at the interpersonal level of analysis

Maryam Kouchaki and Rajen Anderson

Abstract

In this chapter, we highlight the social and interpersonal nature of moral self-views. Across a variety of domains and contexts – including morality – people define themselves in relation to other people. In addition, people typically want to think of themselves as moral actors. We argue that a number of psychological and social processes – both in response to our own behavior and to the behavior of others – allow individuals to maintain such positive moral self-views. When we behave morally, praise from others boosts our self-esteem and self-concept. When we behave immorally, guilt and blame from others help to "recalibrate" individuals to behave more morally in the future. When others behave morally, we can draw closer to them and be inspired by them. When others behave immorally, we engage in condemnation and downward comparison. We end by highlighting several promising topics regarding the nature of interpersonal moral self-views for future research.

Highlights:

- Relations with other people impact on our moral self-views.
- People are motivated to maintain a positive moral self-view by referring to the moral behaviors of other people and through other people's reactions on their own moral behavior.
- Moral self-views can be maintained by drawing closer to others who behave morally and condemning others who behave immorally.
- Praise from others boosts moral self-views; guilt and blame from others helps us to behave more morally in the future.
- Lack of well-calibrated praise and blame can also impact moral self-views: understanding how and when feedback is given is crucial to understanding the interpersonal influences on moral self-views.
- Future research into interpersonal moral self-views should investigate the role of moral conversations (e.g., gossip, disagreements, advice giving/receiving) and how to integrate across multiple levels of analysis.

Introduction

In this chapter, we focus on the social nature of moral self-concepts and self-views. We address interpersonal processes in particular as we examine how other people (intentionally or not) can influence how we think about our moral selves and moral behavior. Before we elaborate on these issues, we first offer definitions of key constructs in our analysis. "Moral self-views" concern the self-reflective and self-justifying tendencies associated with moral behavior. Research on moral self-views addresses the mechanisms people use to think of themselves as moral persons, even when their behavior is not in line with their moral principles (Ellemers et al., 2019). In this chapter, we will take an "interpersonal" approach to this topic: that is, how individuals' moral self-views are impacted by other individuals.

People frequently define themselves based on their relationships and connections with other people, be they familial (e.g., parent and child), organizational (e.g., supervisor and subordinate), or based on group membership (e.g., nationality). In addition, the idea that our self-concept is defined and refined by others is not new, as thinkers starting with Cooley (1902), Mead (1934), and Festinger (1954) have all discussed the topic. Common to these different accounts is the idea that a person's self-concept – how they think of their own identity and behavior – is informed by how they think others think of them. More recent psychological research has also explored when and why people experience a "vicarious self-concept" (see also Jordan et al., Chapter 27 of this volume), whereby individuals incorporate the behaviors of others into their own self-perceptions and cognitions (e.g., Goldstein & Cialdini, 2007; Gunia et al., 2009; Kouchaki, 2011; Welten et al., 2012). That is, self-concepts and self-views can be subject to both how we think others think of us and our behavior and also to whether and when we incorporate others and their behavior into our self-perceptions. What we aim to contribute to this conversation is the uniquely *moral* angle that often plays a role in how people develop a social self-concept, providing a framework for considering the potential interpersonal influences on a person's moral self-view.

Morality is an especially relevant lens for understanding the social self-concept, as morality is typically defined in psychology as the set of norms, emotions, and cognitions that facilitate group cooperation and ensure a harmonious social life (Curry et al., 2019; Greene, 2015; Haidt, 2007; Janoff-Bulman & Carnes, 2013; Rai & Fiske, 2011; Tomasello & Vaish, 2013). Given that morality is *about* the way we treat other people, it seems fitting that moral self-views should be influenced by other people. Morality also plays a central role in how we think about individuals – as moral judges, humans care not just about *what* was done (e.g., "is this a moral action?") but *who* was involved and how that action reflects on them (e.g., "is this a moral person?"; Helzer & Critcher, 2018; Pizarro & Tannenbaum, 2012; Uhlmann et al., 2015). Observers prioritize moral traits over other important traits like warmth in their evaluations of others (Goodwin et al., 2014), a target's moral qualities play a critical role in how much others like and respect that person (Hartley et al., 2016), and people rank their in-group's morality as more important than its competence or sociability (Leach et al., 2007). Finally, morality is seen as central to a person's identity (Heiphetz et al., 2018; Strohminger & Nichols, 2014). Our moral views of each other are therefore critical for our broader social understanding of each other – put simply, who someone is as a person largely depends on other people's views of their morality.

We are especially keen on maintaining a positive self-view and as seeing ourselves as moral (Aquino & Reed, 2002); much like with other desirable traits, people rate themselves as more moral, honest, and ethical than the average person (Alicke, 1985; Epley & Dunning, 2000). People are also flexible in their ability to feel good about their moral behavior and to excuse their moral transgressions. For example, a number of studies have identified a phenomenon of "unethical amnesia" (Kouchaki & Gino, 2016), whereby individuals report lower memory recall of their past misdeeds compared to other behaviors (Shu et al., 2011). Interpersonally, people remember being victims of harm rather than being perpetrators of harm, and such memory asymmetries appear to be due to how features of the harm (e.g., intensity, intention) are weighted based on perspective (Helion et al., 2020). Beyond simply being motivated to perceive themselves as moral, people's memory may assist in maintaining a positive moral self-view: forgetting the harms we have done to others and highlighting the harms they have done to us (thus making the self relatively more moral in comparison). Critically, maintaining a positive moral self-view does not happen in a vacuum – people are embedded in their relationships to others. In addition, these other people provide a variety of inputs in defining and refining a moral self-view, both through their responses to our moral actions and their own moral actions.

An interpersonal framework for understanding moral self-views

The focus of this chapter will be on the interpersonal processes that allow us to think of ourselves as moral. As a framework for understanding the interpersonal processes involved in developing and maintaining moral self-views and self-concepts, we can consider two broad categories: others' reactions to our own morally-relevant behaviors (i.e., how people think about what I have done) and the morally relevant behaviors of others (i.e., how what other people do reflects upon my own behavior) (see Figure 25.1). Within each of these categories, we can examine both moral actions (i.e., doing good) and immoral actions (i.e., doing bad). This framework organizes multiple streams of psychological processes to understand the interpersonal nature of our moral self-views (see Table 25.1).

This table summarizes our framework for understanding interpersonal influences on moral self-views. Different rows refer to the particular person that has performed a moral behavior, along with a complementary observer who is reacting to that behavior. Different columns refer to whether the morally-relevant behavior was moral and prosocial or immoral and antisocial.

Reactions to our actions

Consider the last time you did something morally good (or morally questionable). How did others react to you and your behavior? Morally relevant behavior is sometimes met with some form of

Table 25.1 Interpersonal influences on moral self-views

	Moral behavior	Immoral behavior
Others' reactions to your … behavior	- Feeling self-affirmed (e.g., from receiving praise)	- Feeling guilt and embarrassment (e.g., from receiving blame)
Your reactions to others' … behavior	- Feeling virtuous/moral (e.g., through vicarious self-concepts as a result of others' action) - Feeling elevated/inspired by others (e.g., experiencing awe from their exceptional behavior) - Feeling threatened and reacting negatively (e.g., derogating highly moral others)	- Feeling virtuous/moral (e.g., from condemning others)

feedback: approval and praise for doing good or disapproval and condemnation for doing bad. Such feedback (even if only anticipated; Ellingsen & Johannesson, 2008) can act as a direct learning mechanism, serving to reinforce positive behaviors and discourage negative behaviors (e.g., Choi & Ahn, 2013; Stajkovic & Luthans, 2003). Additionally, moral feedback can serve communicative functions, whereby the very presence of feedback acts a signal to the receiver on what the desired behavior is (Ho et al., 2019; Sarin et al., 2021). Receiving moral feedback from other people can therefore shape both our own future behavior but also how we think of ourselves morally, in light of how others seem to think about us.

Reactions to morality: positive self-esteem and praise

After performing some good deed, our moral behavior may be met with praise or approval from others. In this way, moral praise can provide direct feedback (and reinforcement) to moral agents about their positive behavior. When others praise us, this both feels good as a social reward and reaffirms a positive moral self-view. Other people seem to like what we have done morally, so that must mean that we are morally good. This idea stems from research on self-esteem, in particular the "sociometer" hypothesis of self-esteem (e.g., Leary et al., 1995). Under this account, our experience of self-esteem is our assessment of how much other people seem to like us (i.e., accept or reject us as a social interaction partner).

However, the way in which moral praise is expressed likely plays an important role in exactly how the moral self-view is modified. For example, marketing messages that praise customers for their good deeds can increase subsequent self-interested and self-indulgent behaviors through changes in one's self-concept (Kouchaki & Jami, 2018). In addition, developmental research has found that morally praising a child's self and identity (e.g., "you are such a good helper") may increase subsequent helping behavior compared to praising a child's action (e.g., "you did such a good job helping"; Bryan et al., 2014). Thus, self-directed praise may offer a benefit over action-directed praise in encouraging future moral behavior. However, praising a child for being a "good helper" can hinder children's subsequent moral behavior if the child encounters obstacles that cause them to fail at their goal of helping (Foster-Hanson et al., 2020). Assuming such results replicate with adults, this research suggests that interpersonal feedback to our moral behavior is contextually dependent based on how it is expressed, with implications for our future behavior and self-views.

Reactions to immorality: guilt, embarrassment, and blame

Inevitably, we all do things that might harm someone else. If we are caught and reprimanded by others for our harmful behavior, moral emotions like guilt, embarrassment, and shame may be triggered (Eisenberg, 2000; Tangney et al., 2007). Such emotions may serve to redirect and "recalibrate" the offender's moral judgments and future moral behavior so as to protect one's moral self-views. Agents who experience more embarrassment tend to behave more prosocially than those less prone to embarrassment, and observers treat embarrassed targets as more prosocial (Feinberg et al., 2012). Embarrassment in response to an external sanction may also form a kind of internal sanction that focuses attention on what went wrong and revises how the agent makes such decisions in the future (Warren & Smith-Crowe, 2008). Thus, direct feedback from others to our own moral behavior may actually cause shifts in perceptions of the moral self so as to avoid such image threats in the future.

Interpersonal level: moral self-views

What happens if people *don't* respond to our immoral behavior? As indicated above, people often downplay or even forget their own misdeeds (Helion et al., 2020; Kouchaki & Gino, 2016; Shu et al., 2011). At the interpersonal level, we argue that a similar failure to speak up may also occur: Even if someone transgresses, social concerns may cause others to refrain from extending negative feedback, allowing people to maintain a positive view of the self. For example, those in leadership positions often do not receive candid feedback from subordinates regarding their unethical decisions, freeing them to make ever more selfish decisions (Oc et al., 2015).

Why might people feel disinclined to provide proper negative feedback? Recent research suggests that moral blame and condemnation likely have greater potential interpersonal costs than positive feedback like praise (for a review of differences between praise and blame, see Anderson et al., 2020). For example, blame that is considered unjustified or miscalibrated can result in retaliation and resentment (Aquino et al., 2001; Dreber et al., 2008) and lower group commitment (Podsakoff et al., 2006) from the accused party. Even blame that is viewed as deserved by third parties may feel undeserved by the recipient – as has been argued above, people frequently judge their own misdeeds as less blameworthy than the misdeeds of others (Elshout et al., 2017; Stillwell et al., 2008). In addition, blaming others opens a person up to potential accusations of hypocrisy if they engage in that same behavior (Jordan et al., 2017). In comparison, positive moral feedback like praise is relatively costless: people enjoy receiving praise and the consequences for erroneously applied praise are minimal. All of these reasons can lead to people to more narrowly assign blame for misdeeds compared to praise for equivalent positive acts (Schein et al., 2020), meaning that people may not always receive the negative moral feedback that would be appropriate. This relative lack of negative moral feedback from others may thus allow people to maintain a positive view of their moral standing, even after behaving immorally.

Others' actions

Moral behavior is all around us (Hofmann et al., 2014). On the way to work, we might see a driver hit a parked car and then drive off without leaving any note. On the news or social media, we might read about corrupt politicians and activists campaigning for justice. When we are with friends, we might gossip about what another friend did (or perhaps failed to do). Other people and their moral actions can serve as normative influences, demonstrating what others tend to do morally, and as moral examples to be either praised and mimicked (if positive) or condemned and shunned (if negative). In both cases, interpersonal processes are at play that can both influence our own moral self-views and trigger motivational processes to maintain a positive moral self-view. As a general note, how we process the moral behavior of others (both positive and negative) is filtered through the lens of our own moral self-concept and identity (Helzer et al., 2022) – even at the neural level, our moral self influences how we automatically process information about moral events (Pletti et al., 2019). As a starting disclaimer then, the impact of others' moral behavior on our self-views is partially a function of our own moral self-views.

Moral actions: exemplars, vicarious self-concepts, and reactance

We often want to affiliate, cooperate, or otherwise be associated with others who behave morally. We like and respect moral people, and attaching ourselves to them can then potentially reflect well on us. Such moral exemplars can serve as guides and targets of inspiration, allowing us to refine our moral self-view in light of how others morally behave. The prosocial behavior of others can be contagious and serve as a form of normative influence on how people tend to and should behave and thus benefits their moral self-views. For example, people donate more to charity if they hear that others have already done so (Shang & Croson, 2009). In addition, prosocial conformity need not be limited to the specific modeled behavior but can also extend to other prosocial behavior (Nook et al., 2016), suggesting that such enriched moral self-views may be quite expansive. However, the extent to which exemplars influence our own morality likely depends on the relationship to and nature of the exemplar and the behavior. Motivation to engage in voluntary prosocial behavior was more effectively promoted by relevant and attainable moral exemplars (i.e., exemplars that are similar to the agent with behavior that is relatively easy to achieve) than irrelevant or less attainable moral exemplars (Han et al., 2017). People can also experience "moral elevation" and awe in response to others' exceptional acts of moral goodness, and such experiences can directly impact moral identity and self-views (e.g., Aquino et al., 2011). This suggests that by surrounding ourselves (or at least orienting towards) individuals we view as relevant moral exemplars can be morally motivating and help in refining our self-view as a moral individual.

Beyond just serving as guides for our own moral behaviors, others' prosocial actions can also trigger motivated reactions in observers to regulate and maintain their own positive self-view. For example, past research has identified a moral licensing effect, whereby individuals behave more unethically after previously behaving ethically (for a meta-analysis on the effect, see Blanken et al., 2015). Additional research has found that such effects can even occur at the interpersonal level through *vicarious* licensing – the positive behavior of another group member may allow individuals to then behave more unethically (Kouchaki, 2011). As noted above, our moral selves can have a vicarious component whereby other people are part of those moral selves. This suggests that our moral self-views are not only *influenced* by those around us but may even partially *include* how we view those around us – if we are members of the same group or socially close, their behavior can serve as our own moral credentials.

In contrast to the positive influences described above, one alternative method by which observing another's prosocial behavior can trigger motivated regulation is through potential backlash against the moral agent. For example and counter-intuitively, high cooperators are often punished, usually by low cooperators so that they themselves don't look bad in comparison (Pleasant & Barclay, 2018). In general, extreme do-gooders may be threatening to the moral self-view and thus also receive derogation, criticism, and ridicule by others (Minson & Monin, 2012). When faced with the extremely positive moral behavior of others, instead of being inspired by such agents, individuals may instead react negatively in order to preserve their own moral standing, both to themselves and to others.

Immoral actions: condemnation, downward comparison, and gossip

Unfortunately, people often behave immorally – harming or cheating others or otherwise failing to meet common ethical standards. Assuming the moral agent meets certain levels of perceived responsibility and intentionality, people frequently condemn and blame such actions (Malle et al., 2014), which can often lead to punishment and sanctions levied against the agent (e.g., Cushman, 2008; Fehr & Gächter, 2000; Hofmann et al., 2018; McAuliffe et al., 2015). In this way, when faced with the immoral behavior of others, people may both physically and psychologically distance themselves from the immoral agent so as to not be associated with them – allowing them to protect their moral self-views. Engaging in third-party punishment may even serve to signal one's own moral goodness (Jordan et al., 2016). Distancing from and explicitly condemning immoral agents may thus be one way with which people work to preserve (and signal) their own positive

Interpersonal level: moral self-views

moral self-view – they are moral both in comparison to that harmful person (often because of motivated processes; Barkan et al., 2012) *and* because they have expressed condemnation or a desire to punish that harmful person.

People may also be especially prone to downward comparisons in the moral domain, comparing themselves against those that they feel are less moral, often as a means of preserving their own self-esteem (Fleischmann et al., 2021). It is also worth highlighting that how people evaluate the immoral actions of others is different from how they evaluate their own immoral actions (Tappin & McKay, 2017). When thinking about their own misdeeds people tend to be much more flexible in their moral thinking and less inclined to endorse generalized moral principles (e.g., stealing is wrong) than when considering the misdeeds of others (Stanley et al., 2021). As alluded to above, even the way in which people consider the immoral behavior of others, compared to their own moral behavior, allows them to maintain a positive view of their own moral standing.

At the interpersonal level, gossip seems especially important for understanding the influence of immoral others on our self-views. Gossip is necessarily comparative in nature (for a review, see Wert & Salovey, 2004) – when gossiping, we compare what someone has done to what others have done or what that person should have done. To the extent that the shared information is true, gossip likely aids in our ability to gain information about others (both the gossiped-about regarding what they did and the gossiper regarding what they may value) and about ourselves in relation to these others (e.g., Feinberg et al., 2012). For more discussion on the role of social reputations (as informed by gossip) in adapting moral behavior, please see Beersma et al., Chapter 21 of this volume. As we will discuss in more detail below, gossip and moral conversations are a relatively underexplored area of research that may yield important insights about how moral norms are transmitted along social networks and in how people develop their moral self-views (e.g., Fernandes et al., 2017).

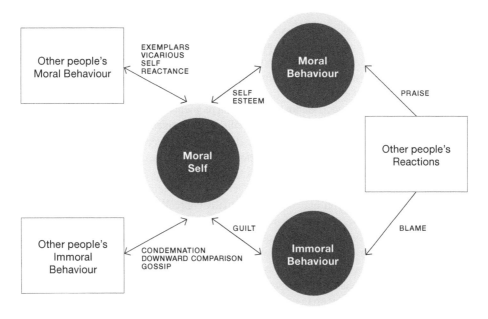

Figure 25.1 Moral behavior, moral self, and immoral behavior.

Directions for future research

As we have indicated above, there is still a great deal of research to be done in the space of interpersonal approaches to moral self-views. We believe that the uniquely social aspect of this approach offers a guiding framework for new research to better understand how people form and maintain positive moral self-views. We highlight two general approaches below.

Moral conversations

A promising avenue for future research involves moral conversations - how, when, and for what purposes do people talk to each other about moral matters? How do such moral discussions shape our moral beliefs, attitudes, and sense of self? Morality is not simply about the overt actions that people do to each other, but includes the words and language that people express to each other (Bollich et al., 2016). There is some work on moral conversations with children that highlights the importance of parents having moral conversations with their children to encourage moral development (Recchia et al., 2014; Reese et al., 2007). However, additional work should investigate how moral instruction like this may continue into adulthood and how same-age peers (both children and adults) converse with each other about moral guidelines.

As mentioned above, moral gossip (e.g., Feinberg et al., 2012; Fernandes et al., 2017) is one form of moral conversation, but moral conversations can also be more broadly construed, including discussion of moral disagreements (e.g., having a moral argument), direct expressions of moral feedback (e.g., approval or condemnation), moral persuasion (e.g., attempting to convince another person to hold the same moral position), and moral advice-seeking (e.g., seeking advice from another person on moral matters). As such, conversation and other linguistic expressions can be both a vehicle for discussing morality (e.g., two people expressing their opinions on a moral topic) and act as a moral behavior itself (e.g., one person emotionally harming another person by verbally insulting them). We briefly highlight two specific topics: moral disagreements and moral advice-seeking.

Moral disagreements may arise for a variety of reasons. People may agree that a global or social problem requires a solution but disagree on which solution will produce the most good while minimizing harm. Alternatively, people may even disagree on whether such a problem exists, based on differing standards of benefits and harms. However the disagreement arises, such arguments may likely evoke strong emotions, given how strongly people feel about their moral beliefs (Skitka, 2010). For understanding moral disagreements, a related body of work exists in political disagreements. For example, work on political conversations amongst family members has found that cross-ideology conversations (i.e., discussions between people of opposing political beliefs), compared to within-ideology conversations, are often more contentious and shorter (Chen & Rohla, 2018; Frimer & Skitka, 2020). Given that political beliefs and moral beliefs are often linked together (e.g., Everett et al., 2021; Hatemi et al., 2019; Schein & Gray, 2015), these findings suggest that moral disagreements may consist of equally contentious and short conversations. For more discussion on the interplay between moral attitudes and politics, please see Bauman and Helzer, Chapter 10 of this volume. Open questions remain regarding how such disagreements may serve to reinforce one's own moral self-view: in contrast to the person you are disagreeing with, your own moral principles may stand out as being more righteous in comparison. Alternatively, moral disagreements may spark genuine moral change and updating – understanding the conditions under which disagreements lead up to updating and revising one's moral views also offers a promising direction for future research.

Along similar lines, moral conversations can take the form of advice giving and receiving, whereby one individual seeks out – and another person conveys – advice, wisdom, or guidance. In times of uncertainty or with ambiguous decisions, people may seek advice from a trusted friend or colleague, from a family elder, or from a religious or spiritual leader. There is a great deal of research in general judgment and decision-making to understand when, why, and from whom people seek advice (e.g., Barnett White, 2005; Gino, 2008; Gino et al., 2012). Such insights can likely be applied to understanding moral advice seeking as well. However, one potential, underexplored difference between getting advice about, say, what product to purchase versus what ethical decision to make is that the latter may include a more generalizable principle or social norm. That is, moral advice could take the form of a universalizable rule about how to make a decision both in this context and in other contexts, while nonmoral advice may include such rules less frequently. Thus, understanding when and how people incorporate the moral advice of others, as a form of moral conversation, may prove an especially potent role for understanding how people revise their moral self-views.

Integrating across multiple levels of analysis

This chapter has focused on the interpersonal level of analysis for understanding how people form and maintain moral self-views. While we believe that this approach is especially potent for understanding moral self-views due to the strong social influences on self-views, it is just one level of analysis. Additional research should investigate how within-person processes (e.g., memory and attention; Helion et al., 2020; Kouchaki & Gino, 2016) interact with between-person processes. For example, do people also experience unethical amnesia when considering the misdeeds of close others (e.g., romantic partners, family members)? What aspects of moral conversations do people remember and how are such conversations integrated into how people form their moral self-view? Expanding to the group level, research may also consider the role of moral circles, or how "far" and to what degree do individuals extend moral concerns to others (e.g., Graham et al., 2017; Waytz et al., 2019). Individuals who draw relatively tight moral circles around themselves (compared to those who draw relatively more expansive circles) may hold more positive self-views of their morality, as there are comparatively fewer individuals to have moral concerns about. We believe that integrating across multiple levels of analysis and employing a diversity of theoretical approaches and methods (e.g., cultural, developmental, social network analysis) will be especially fruitful and helpful for the emerging study of moral self-views.

Conclusion

Compared to other aspects of human psychology, moral self-views are particularly subject to social and interpersonal processes. Such interpersonal processes are often recruited to serve motivational aims, allowing individuals to maintain a positive view of their moral self. To understand how such processes can occur, we provide an interpersonal framework that considers reactions from different agents to behaviors of different valences. We note that different psychological processes are at play based on whether the moral agent is the self or another person, and whether the morally relevant act is positive or negative. Looking ahead, we believe that there is more work to be done – we are especially excited by emerging work on moral praise and other forms of direct moral feedback, moral conversations, and attempts to integrate across multiple levels of analysis.

References

Alicke, M. D. (1985). Global self-evaluation as determined by the desirability and controllability of trait adjectives. *Journal of Personality and Social Psychology*, *49*(6), 1621–1630. https://doi.org/10.1037/0022-3514.49.6.1621

Anderson, R. A., Crockett, M. J., & Pizarro, D. A. (2020). A theory of moral praise. *Trends in Cognitive Science*, *24*(9), 30–39. https://doi.org/10.1016/j.tics.2020.06.008

Aquino, K., McFerran, B., & Laven, M. (2011). Moral identity and the experience of moral elevation in response to acts of uncommon goodness. *Journal of Personality and Social Psychology*, *100*(4), 703–718. https://doi.org/10.1037/a0022540

Aquino, K., & Reed, A. (2002). The self-importance of moral identity. *Journal of Personality and Social Psychology*, *83*(6), 1423–1440. https://doi.org/10.1037/0022-3514.83.6.1423

Aquino, K., Tripp, T. M., & Bies, R. J. (2001). How employees respond to personal offense: The effects of blame attribution, victim status, and offender status on revenge and reconciliation in the workplace. *Journal of Applied Psychology*, *86*(1), 52–59. https://doi.org/10.1037/0021-9010.86.1.52

Barkan, R., Ayal, S., Gino, F., & Ariely, D. (2012). The pot calling the kettle black: Distancing response to ethical dissonance. *Journal of Experimental Psychology: General*, *141*(4), 757–773. https://doi.org/10.1037/a0027588

Barnett White, T. (2005). Consumer trust and advice acceptance: The moderating roles of benevolence, expertise, and negative emotions. *Journal of Consumer Psychology*, *15*(2), 141–148. https://doi.org/10.1207/s15327663jcp1502_6

Blanken, I., van de Ven, N., & Zeelenberg, M. (2015). A meta-analytic review of moral licensing. *Personality and Social Psychology Bulletin*, *41*(4), 540–558. https://doi.org/10.1177/0146167215572134

Bollich, K. L., Doris, J. M., Vazire, S., Raison, C. L., Jackson, J. J., & Mehl, M. R. (2016). Eavesdropping on character: Assessing everyday moral behaviors. *Journal of Research in Personality, 61*, 15–21. https://doi.org/10.1016/j.jrp.2015.12.003

Bryan, C. J., Master, A., & Walton, G. M. (2014). "Helping" versus "being a helper": Invoking the self to increase helping in young children. *Child Development*, *85*(5), 1836–1842. https://doi.org/10.1111/cdev.12244

Chen, M. K., & Rohla, R. (2018). The effect of partisanship and political advertising on close family ties. *Science*, *360*(6392), 1020–1024. https://doi.org/10.1126/science.aaq1433

Choi, J.-K., & Ahn, T. K. (2013). Strategic reward and altruistic punishment support cooperation in a public goods game experiment. *Journal of Economic Psychology, 35*, 17–30. https://doi.org/10.1016/j.joep.2013.01.001

Cooley, C. H. (1902). *Human nature and the social order*. New York: Scribner's

Curry, O. S., Mullins, D. A., & Whitehouse, H. (2019). Is it good to cooperate? Testing the theory of morality-as-cooperation in 60 societies. *Current Anthropology*, *60*(1), 47–69. https://doi.org/10.1086/701478

Cushman, F. (2008). Crime and punishment: Distinguishing the roles of causal and intentional analyses in moral judgment. *Cognition*, *108*(2), 353–380. https://doi.org/10.1016/j.cognition.2008.03.006

Dreber, A., Rand, D. G., Fudenberg, D., & Nowak, M. A. (2008). Winners don't punish. *Nature*, *452*(7185), 348–351. https://doi.org/10.1038/nature06723

Eisenberg, N. (2000). Emotion, regulation, and moral development. *Annual Review of Psychology*, *51*(1), 665–697. https://doi.org/10.1146/annurev.psych.51.1.665

Ellemers, N., van der Toorn, J., Paunov, Y., & van Leeuwen, T. (2019). The psychology of morality: A review and analysis of empirical studies published from 1940 through 2017. *Personality and Social Psychology Review*, *23*(4), 332–366. https://doi.org/10.1177/1088868318811759

Ellingsen, T., & Johannesson, M. (2008). Anticipated verbal feedback induces altruistic behavior. *Evolution and Human Behavior*, *29*(2), 100–105. https://doi.org/10.1016/j.evolhumbehav.2007.11.001

Elshout, M., Nelissen, R. M. A., & van Beest, I. (2017). Your act is worse than mine: Perception bias in revenge situations. *Aggressive Behavior*, *43*(6), 553–557. https://doi.org/10.1002/ab.21713

Epley, N., & Dunning, D. (2000). Feeling "holier than thou": Are self-serving assessments produced by errors in self- or social prediction? *Journal of Personality and Social Psychology*, *79*(6), 861–875. https://doi.org/10.1037/0022-3514.79.6.861

Everett, J. A. C., Clark, C. J., Meindl, P., Luguri, J. B., Earp, B. D., Graham, J., Ditto, P. H., & Shariff, A. F. (2021). Political differences in free will belief are associated with differences in moralization. *Journal of Personality and Social Psychology*, *120*(2), 461–483. https://doi.org/10.1037/pspp0000286

Fehr, E., & Gächter, S. (2000). Cooperation and punishment in public goods experiments. *American Economic Review, 90*(4), 980–994. https://doi.org/10.1257/aer.90.4.980

Feinberg, M., Willer, R., & Keltner, D. (2012). Flustered and faithful: Embarrassment as a signal of prosociality. *Journal of Personality and Social Psychology, 102*(1), 81–97. https://doi.org/10.1037/a0025403

Fernandes, S., Kapoor, H., & Karandikar, S. (2017). Do we gossip for moral reasons? The intersection of moral foundations and gossip. *Basic and Applied Social Psychology, 39*(4), 218–230. https://doi.org/10.1080/01973533.2017.1336713

Festinger, L. (1954). A theory of social comparison processes. *Human Relations, 7*, 117–140. https://doi.org/10.1177/001872675400700202

Fleischmann, A., Lammers, J., Diel, K., Hofmann, W., & Galinsky, A. D. (2021). More threatening and more diagnostic: How moral comparisons differ from social comparisons. *Journal of Personality and Social Psychology, 121*(5), 1057–1078. https://doi.org/10.1037/pspi0000361

Foster-Hanson, E., Cimpian, A., Leshin, R. A., & Rhodes, M. (2020). Asking children to "be helpers" can backfire after setbacks. *Child Development, 91*(1), 236–248. https://doi.org/10.1111/cdev.13147

Frimer, J. A., & Skitka, L. J. (2020). Are politically diverse Thanksgiving dinners shorter than politically uniform ones? *PLOS ONE, 15*(10), e0239988. https://doi.org/10.1371/journal.pone.0239988

Gino, F. (2008). Do we listen to advice just because we paid for it? The impact of advice cost on its use. *Organizational Behavior and Human Decision Processes, 107*(2), 234–245. https://doi.org/10.1016/j.obhdp.2008.03.001

Gino, F., Brooks, A. W., & Schweitzer, M. E. (2012). Anxiety, advice, and the ability to discern: Feeling anxious motivates individuals to seek and use advice. *Journal of Personality and Social Psychology, 102*(3), 497–512. https://doi.org/10.1037/a0026413

Goldstein, N. J., & Cialdini, R. B. (2007). The spyglass self: A model of vicarious self-perception. *Journal of Personality and Social Psychology, 92*(3), 402–417. https://doi.org/10.1037/0022-3514.92.3.402

Goodwin, G. P., Piazza, J., & Rozin, P. (2014). Moral character predominates in person perception and evaluation. *Journal of Personality and Social Psychology, 106*(1), 148–168. https://doi.org/10.1037/a0034726

Graham, J., Waytz, A., Meindl, P., Iyer, R., & Young, L. (2017). Centripetal and centrifugal forces in the moral circle: Competing constraints on moral learning. *Cognition, 167*, 58–65. https://doi.org/10.1016/j.cognition.2016.12.001

Greene, J. D. (2015). The rise of moral cognition. *Cognition, 135*, 39–42. https://doi.org/10.1016/j.cognition.2014.11.018

Gunia, B. C., Sivanathan, N., & Galinsky, A. D. (2009). Vicarious entrapment: Your sunk costs, my escalation of commitment. *Journal of Experimental Social Psychology, 45*(6), 1238–1244. https://doi.org/10.1016/j.jesp.2009.07.004

Haidt, J. (2007). The new synthesis in moral psychology. *Science, 316*(5827), 998–1002. https://doi.org/10.1126/science.1137651

Han, H., Kim, J., Jeong, C., & Cohen, G. L. (2017). Attainable and relevant moral exemplars are more effective than extraordinary exemplars in promoting voluntary service engagement. *Frontiers in Psychology, 8*. https://doi.org/10.3389/fpsyg.2017.00283

Hartley, A. G., Furr, R. M., Helzer, E. G., Jayawickreme, E., Velasquez, K. R., & Fleeson, W. (2016). Morality's centrality to liking, respecting, and understanding others. *Social Psychological and Personality Science, 7*(7), 648–657. https://doi.org/10.1177/1948550616655359

Hatemi, P. K., Crabtree, C., & Smith, K. B. (2019). Ideology justifies morality: Political beliefs predict moral foundations. *American Journal of Political Science, 63*(4), 788–806. https://doi.org/10.1111/ajps.12448

Heiphetz, L., Strohminger, N., Gelman, S. A., & Young, L. L. (2018). Who am I? The role of moral beliefs in children's and adults' understanding of identity. *Journal of Experimental Social Psychology, 78*, 210–219. https://doi.org/10.1016/j.jesp.2018.03.007

Helion, C., Helzer, E. G., Kim, S., & Pizarro, D. A. (2020). Asymmetric memory for harming versus being harmed. *Journal of Experimental Psychology: General, 149*(5), 889–900. https://doi.org/10.1037/xge0000691

Helzer, E. G., Cohen, T. R., & Kim, Y. (2022). The character lens: A person-centered perspective on moral recognition and ethical decision-making. *Journal of Business Ethics*. https://doi.org/10.1007/s10551-021-05010-z

Helzer, E. G., & Critcher, C. R. (2018). What do we evaluate when we evaluate moral character? In K. Gray & J. Graham (Eds.), *Atlas of moral psychology* (pp. 99–107). New York: Guilford Press.

Ho, M. K., Cushman, F., Littman, M. L., & Austerweil, J. L. (2019). People teach with rewards and punishments as communication, not reinforcements. *Journal of Experimental Psychology: General*, *148*(3), 520–549. https://doi.org/10.1037/xge0000569

Hofmann, W., Brandt, M. J., Wisneski, D. C., Rockenbach, B., & Skitka, L. J. (2018). Moral punishment in everyday life. *Personality and Social Psychology Bulletin*, *44*(12), 1697–1711. https://doi.org/10.1177/0146167218775075

Hofmann, W., Wisneski, D. C., Brandt, M. J., & Skitka, L. J. (2014). Morality in everyday life. *Science*, *345*(6202), 1340–1343. https://doi.org/10.1126/science.1251560

Janoff-Bulman, R., & Carnes, N. C. (2013). Surveying the moral landscape: Moral motives and group-based moralities. *Personality and Social Psychology Review*, *17*(3), 219–236. https://doi.org/10.1177/1088868313480274

Jordan, J. J., Hoffman, M., Bloom, P., & Rand, D. G. (2016). Third-party punishment as a costly signal of trustworthiness. *Nature*, *530*(7591), 473–476. https://doi.org/10.1038/nature16981

Jordan, J. J., Sommers, R., Bloom, P., & Rand, D. G. (2017). Why do we hate hypocrites? Evidence for a theory of false signaling. *Psychological Science*, *28*(3), 356–368. https://doi.org/10.1177/0956797616685771

Kouchaki, M. (2011). Vicarious moral licensing: The influence of others' past moral actions on moral behavior. *Journal of Personality and Social Psychology*, *101*(4), 702–715. https://doi.org/10.1037/a0024552

Kouchaki, M., & Jami, A. (2018). Everything we do, you do: The licensing effect of prosocial marketing messages on consumer behavior. *Management Science*, *64*(1), 102–111. https://doi.org/10.1287/mnsc.2016.2571

Kouchaki, M., & Gino, F. (2016). Memories of unethical actions become obfuscated over time. *Proceedings of the National Academy of Sciences, 113*(22), 6166–6171. https://doi.org/10.1073/pnas.1523586113

Leach, C. W., Ellemers, N., & Barreto, M. (2007). Group virtue: The importance of morality (vs. competence and sociability) in the positive evaluation of in-groups. *Journal of Personality and Social Psychology*, *93*(2), 234–249. https://doi.org/10.1037/0022-3514.93.2.234

Leary, M. R., Tambor, E. S., Terdal, S. K., & Downs, D. L. (1995). Self-esteem as an interpersonal monitor: The sociometer hypothesis. *Journal of Personality and Social Psychology*, *68*(3), 518–530. https://doi.org/10.1037/0022-3514.68.3.518

Malle, B. F., Guglielmo, S., & Monroe, A. E. (2014). A theory of blame. *Psychological Inquiry*, *25*(2), 147–186. https://doi.org/10.1080/1047840X.2014.877340

McAuliffe, K., Jordan, J. J., & Warneken, F. (2015). Costly third-party punishment in young children. *Cognition, 134*, 1–10. https://doi.org/10.1016/j.cognition.2014.08.013

Mead, G. H. (1934). *Mind, self, and society*. Chicago: University of Chicago Press.

Minson, J. A., & Monin, B. (2012). Do-gooder derogation: Disparaging morally motivated minorities to defuse anticipated reproach. *Social Psychological and Personality Science*, *3*(2), 200–207. https://doi.org/10.1177/1948550611415695

Nook, E. C., Ong, D. C., Morelli, S. A., Mitchell, J. P., & Zaki, J. (2016). Prosocial conformity: Prosocial norms generalize across behavior and empathy. *Personality and Social Psychology Bulletin*, *42*(8), 1045–1062. https://doi.org/10.1177/0146167216649932

Oc, B., Bashshur, M. R., & Moore, C. (2015). Speaking truth to power: The effect of candid feedback on how individuals with power allocate resources. *Journal of Applied Psychology*, *100*(2), 450–463. https://doi.org/10.1037/a0038138

Pizarro, D. A., & Tannenbaum, D. (2012). Bringing character back: How the motivation to evaluate character influences judgments of moral blame. In M. Mikulincer & P. R. Shaver (Eds.), *The social psychology of morality: Exploring the causes of good and evil* (pp. 91–108). Washington: American Psychological Association. https://doi.org/10.1037/13091-005

Pleasant, A., & Barclay, P. (2018). Why hate the good guy? Antisocial punishment of high cooperators Is greater when people compete to be chosen. *Psychological Science*, *29*(6), 868–876. https://doi.org/10.1177/0956797617752642

Pletti, C., Decety, J., & Paulus, M. (2019). Moral identity relates to the neural processing of third-party moral behavior. *Social Cognitive and Affective Neuroscience*, *14*(4), 435–445. https://doi.org/10.1093/scan/nsz016

Podsakoff, P. M., Bommer, W. H., Podsakoff, N. P., & MacKenzie, S. B. (2006). Relationships between leader reward and punishment behavior and subordinate attitudes, perceptions, and behaviors: A meta-analytic review of existing and new research. *Organizational Behavior and Human Decision Processes, 99*(2), 113–142. https://doi.org/10.1016/j.obhdp.2005.09.002

Rai, T. S., & Fiske, A. P. (2011). Moral psychology is relationship regulation: Moral motives for unity, hierarchy, equality, and proportionality. *Psychological Review, 118*(1), 57–75. https://doi.org/10.1037/a0021867

Recchia, H. E., Wainryb, C., Bourne, S., & Pasupathi, M. (2014). The construction of moral agency in mother–child conversations about helping and hurting across childhood and adolescence. *Developmental Psychology, 50*(1), 34–44. https://doi.org/10.1037/a0033492

Reese, E., Bird, A., & Tripp, G. (2007). Children's self-esteem and moral self: Links to parent-child conversations regarding emotion. *Social Development, 16*(3), 460–478. https://doi.org/10.1111/j.1467-9507.2007.00393.x

Sarin, A., Ho, M. K., Martin, J. W., & Cushman, F. A. (2021). Punishment is organized around principles of communicative inference. *Cognition, 208*, 104544. https://doi.org/10.1016/j.cognition.2020.104544

Schein, C., & Gray, K. (2015). The unifying moral dyad: liberals and conservatives share the same harm-based moral template. *Personality and Social Psychology Bulletin, 41*(8), 1147–1163. https://doi.org/10.1177/0146167215591501

Schein, C., Jackson, J. C., Frasca, T., & Gray, K. (2020). Praise-many, blame-fewer: A common (and successful) strategy for attributing responsibility in groups. *Journal of Experimental Psychology: General, 149*(5), 855–869. https://doi.org/10.1037/xge0000683

Shang, J., & Croson, R. (2009). A field experiment in charitable contribution: The impact of social information on the voluntary provision of public goods. *The Economic Journal, 119*(540), 1422–1439. https://doi.org/10.1111/j.1468-0297.2009.02267.x

Shu, L. L., Gino, F., & Bazerman, M. H. (2011). Dishonest deed, clear conscience: When cheating leads to moral disengagement and motivated forgetting. *Personality and Social Psychology Bulletin, 37*(3), 330–349. https://doi.org/10.1177/0146167211398138

Skitka, L. J. (2010). The psychology of moral conviction. *Social and Personality Psychology Compass, 4*(4), 267–281. https://doi.org/10.1111/j.1751-9004.2010.00254.x

Stajkovic, A. D., & Luthans, F. (2003). Behavioral management and task performance in organizations: Conceptual background, meta-analysis, and test of alternative models. *Personnel Psychology, 56*(1), 155–194. https://doi.org/10.1111/j.1744-6570.2003.tb00147.x

Stanley, M. L., Henne, P., Niemi, L., Sinnott-Armstrong, W., & De Brigard, F. (2021). Making moral principles suit yourself. *Psychonomic Bulletin & Review, 28*(5), 1735–1741. https://doi.org/10.3758/s13423-021-01935-8

Stillwell, A. M., Baumeister, R. F., & Del Priore, R. E. (2008). We're all victims here: Toward a psychology of revenge. *Basic and Applied Social Psychology, 30*(3), 253–263. https://doi.org/10.1080/01973530802375094

Strohminger, N., & Nichols, S. (2014). The essential moral self. *Cognition, 131*(1), 159–171. https://doi.org/10.1016/j.cognition.2013.12.005

Tangney, J. P., Stuewig, J., & Mashek, D. J. (2007). Moral emotions and moral behavior. *Annual Review of Psychology, 58*(1), 345–372. https://doi.org/10.1146/annurev.psych.56.091103.070145

Tappin, B. M., & McKay, R. T. (2017). The illusion of moral superiority. *Social Psychological and Personality Science, 8*(6), 623–631. https://doi.org/10.1177/1948550616673878

Tomasello, M., & Vaish, A. (2013). Origins of human cooperation and morality. *Annual Review of Psychology, 64*(1), 231–255. https://doi.org/10.1146/annurev-psych-113011-143812

Uhlmann, E. L., Pizarro, D. A., & Diermeier, D. (2015). A person-centered approach to moral judgment. *Perspectives on Psychological Science, 10*(1), 72–81. https://doi.org/10.1177/1745691614556679

Warren, D. E., & Smith-Crowe, K. (2008). Deciding what's right: The role of external sanctions and embarrassment in shaping moral judgments in the workplace. *Research in Organizational Behavior, 28*, 81–105. https://doi.org/10.1016/j.riob.2008.04.004

Waytz, A., Iyer, R., Young, L., Haidt, J., & Graham, J. (2019). Ideological differences in the expanse of the moral circle. *Nature Communications, 10*(1), 4389. https://doi.org/10.1038/s41467-019-12227-0

Welten, S. C. M., Zeelenberg, M., & Breugelmans, S. M. (2012). Vicarious shame. *Cognition & Emotion, 26*(5), 836–846. https://doi.org/10.1080/02699931.2011.625400

Wert, S. R., & Salovey, P. (2004). A social comparison account of gossip. *Review of General Psychology, 8*(2), 122–137. https://doi.org/10.1037/1089-2680.8.2.122

26
THE INTRAGROUP LEVEL
Morally motivated intragroup deviance and dissent

Jolanda Jetten and Charlie R. Crimston

Abstract

What motivates a moral rebel? Why do whistleblowers risk it all for their cause? In this chapter, we take a deep dive into the morally motivated reasons why individuals defy group pressures to conform and engage in intragroup dissent. Contrary to early social psychology narratives around the sheep-like nature of group members, there is considerable evidence that individuals will consciously deviate from group norms for moral reasons. For instance, rebels might risk group punishment and expulsion to stay true to their personal moral convictions or highly identified group members might be driven to challenge the status quo because they feel that is the right thing to do. We also discuss the varied ways in which groups respond to moral rebellion, including when rebels are more (e.g., they threaten a group's identity) or less (e.g., when they raise the moral image of the group) likely to be punished for their 'transgressions'.

- People's moral self-views are impacted by intragroup dissent on the morality of group norms.
- Group members who consciously and deliberately deviate from group norms for moral reasons are 'moral rebels'.
- Group members can become moral rebels because of personal reasons such as their moral concerns, or because of group-related reasons such as their position in the group
- Moral rebellion is likely to be punished by the group when it seems to threaten the group's identity.
- Moral rebellion can be welcomed when it liberates other group members, raises the moral image of the group, or contributes to group success.

Introduction

While early work in social psychology promoted a narrative around the sheep-like nature of group members (expressed as blind obedience and conformity, Asch, 1956; Milgram, 1963), there is considerable evidence that group members frequently engage in deviance and dissent within the group. For instance, group members blow the whistle on malpractices in the group or they decide to prioritize moral standards over conformity to group norms. In these instances, rather than being driven by nefarious means, dissent and deviance seem to be motivated by a desire to 'do the right thing'. Such intragroup rebellion represents an attempt to live up to a higher moral standard (Jetten & Hornsey, 2014). Consistent with this reasoning, a substantial body of recent work highlights how intragroup deviance and dissent are not just normal and healthy aspects of group life, but – in particular when a group is on a path of running off course – are at the core of a group's ability to restore a group's moral status or realign its moral compass (Jetten & Hornsey, 2014; Packer, 2008).

In this contribution, we focus on processes within groups (i.e., intragroup processes) and we define moral deviance and dissent as group members who consciously and deliberately deviate from group norms for moral reasons (i.e., moral rebels). Drawing on a broad body of empirical findings (including our own), we aim to answer two questions relevant to the impact of moral rebels on people's self-views. First, why might group members become moral rebels? Second, how do other group members respond to moral rebels in their midst? We finish this contribution by outlining directions for future research and highlight the important role moral rebels play in social change initiatives.

Why group members might become moral rebels

What makes people want to defy group pressure to conform and become moral rebels? This question is not easy to answer because research on rebels has typically focused on rebels more generally (i.e., those that break generic group or societal norms) with only a handful of studies looking at morally motivated rebellion. Moreover, the two sets of findings may not simply generalise across these different forms of non-conformity because there are some important differences between '*ordinary* rebels' and '*moral* rebels'. For instance, the large body of work on dissent and deviance more generally has often assumed that individuals are mostly accidentally placed in the rebel role. In other research it has been proposed that these individuals become deviants because they fail to live up to important group goals (e.g., black sheep), they simply do not care about conforming to group norms because the group is not important to them (see Packer, 2008), they want to express their difference, individuality and uniqueness (Jetten et al., 2001), they do not necessarily want to be included in the group and therefore do not feel the need to conform (Ellemers & Jetten, 2013), or because norm violations are associated with tangible rewards, making the costs of punishment less of a deterrent (e.g., crime, fraud, see Jetten & Hornsey, 2011; 2014 for an overview of motives).

While these motivations may explain many forms of deviance and dissent, we argue that moral rebels are different from 'ordinary' deviants and dissenters in that moral rebels actively take a stance against the group and they often have deliberately chosen to play the role of rebel within the group as a way to challenge the moral self-views of its members (see Monin & O'Connor, 2011). We propose that moral rebels intentionally deviate from group norms and, crucially, their dissent and deviance imply not just difference from group norms but active defiance against those norms (Monin & O'Connor, 2011). As a result, individuals may not necessarily see themselves as victims who are unable to live up to the norms of the group or society, but as those at the forefront of social change. Consider, for example, Swedish Greta Thunberg, Australian Grace Tame, or Dr Martin Luther King in the US – all individuals whose activism (calling out climate change inaction, sexual violence against women, or racism, respectively) represents principled or moral objection of current group practices and their dissent and deviance is aimed at demanding group or societal change for moral reasons. For these moral rebels, their activism is not motivated by nefarious desires or personal gain motives but by aiming to be a force for good and moral improvement within groups and society at large. These individual's moral rebellion and their deviance and dissent should be seen as a reflection of (a) personal moral beliefs, (b) high group identification with their group or society at large, or both. Let us unpack these arguments in more detail.

(a) Moral rebellion for personal reasons

Starting with personal reasons for moral rebellion, there are several processes that may motivate these rebels. First, people might deviate or dissent because, in relation to a particular issue, they feel it is more important to act in accordance with their personal moral convictions than to fall in line with (potentially outdated) group norms (Hornsey et al., 2003; Monin et al., 2008; Skitka & Mullen, 2002). For example, people might resist expressing racist comments in the face of group pressure to go along with them or they might call out group practices they perceive to be harming someone else in line with personal moral norms. In two studies examining moral attitudes toward gay law reform and toward an Australian government apology to First Nation Australians for past wrongdoing, Hornsey et al. (2003) found that individuals with a weak moral basis for their attitudes were more likely to publicly conform to group norms, whereas those with a strong moral basis for their attitudes were more likely to publicly challenge group norms. The latter finding was stronger for group members who only identified weakly with the group. In contrast, those who identified more strongly with the group – presumably because they were more concerned with showing ingroup loyalty – were more willing to express opinions that ran counter to their privately held moral convictions. It appears, as Hornsey et al. (2003) argued, that those with a stronger moral basis for their views (and those who are less identified with the group) were keen to signal to other group members (who disagreed with them) what they stood for even if that meant facing ridicule and rejection for being different and standing out. This process was also described in Milgram's obedience studies reporting on participants who refused to go to the highest shock levels justifying their resistance by referring to moral mandates: "I'd like to continue, but can't do that to a man" or "I can't go on with this; no, this is not right" (Milgram, 1963, p. 376).

Second, in addition to the extent to which a particular topic is moralized for an individual, we can also assess the breadth or expansiveness of an individual's moral concern toward others (see Crimston et al., 2018). That is, individuals may differ in the extent to which they feel that moral standing applies more broadly beyond 'traditional' boundaries. For instance, they may perceive their moral concern should not just be reserved for ingroup members (e.g., family and friends) but extend it to include outgroup members, diverse entities such as animals, plants and even villains. In fact, some may decide to flip the script entirely by prioritizing the needs of distant entities (e.g., animals and ecosystems) over those generally considered more proximal (e.g., vulnerable human groups; Rottman et al., 2021). In line with this conceptualization, Crimston, Bain, Hornsey, and Bastian (2016) developed the Moral Expansiveness Scale to assess the relative size of an individual's moral world. They found that individuals with expanded moral circles showed higher prosocial intentions and willingness to prioritise humanitarian and environmental concerns over personal and national self-interest. Such individuals were also more likely to be willing to make costly personal self-sacrifices and engage in volunteering to comply with their own moral mandates. Put differently, those with more expansive moral circles define their ingroup as more inclusive whereby everyone within the moral circle is defined as 'one of us' and therefore worthy of protection even if that comes at a high personal cost. It follows that such individual-level moral rebellion is not so much driven by an obligation to adhere to specific moral norms, but by the extent to which they perceive that all entities in the world are within their moral circle and thus deserve to be treated with care and consideration. In this sense, these individuals may hold up their own moral self-views for other group members to follow.

Finally, we would like to draw attention to impostors who represent a specific form of moral rebel. That is, to obtain social or financial advantage, these individuals break group norms by passing themselves off as genuine group members even though they do not meet criteria for group membership (e.g., someone claiming to be a vegetarian but secretly eats meat; Hornsey & Jetten, 2003). In other words, impostorism allows people to cross what are normally impermeable group boundaries (e.g., race or class; Griffin, 1977) and is a way to obtain access to groups, professions or classes that could not be legitimately claimed otherwise. Being an impostor rebel can be said to be morally defiant in that these individuals lie about who they truly are because they see barriers for belonging to the group as illegitimate restrictions to their preferred self-views whereby their defiance reflects attempts to 'right a wrong'. Interestingly too, impostorism is different from other types of moral rebellion in that the impostor's rule-breaking is hidden from others. This form of deviance is often only apparent and public if/when the impostor is unmasked. Given that impostors often violate various normative expectations and rules (e.g., it is wrong to lie about who you truly are, or to illegitimately claim membership in a group that prides itself in holding high moral standards), as we discuss further below, their transgressions may evoke strong responses from other group members, even if they are morally justified (e.g., because current criteria for group inclusion are unfair).

(b) Moral rebellion for reasons relating to group concerns

Moral rebels' behaviour may also be driven by group concerns. In particular, group members may engage in moral rebellion in an attempt to align or redefine group norms and beliefs in line with their own morally mandated beliefs about right and wrong (see Skitka & Mullen, 2002; Skitka et al., 2005). They may also seek to change group norms or behaviour that they see as detrimental to group functioning. In such cases, group members may dissent because they care for the group and are concerned about the course of action that other group members are taking (e.g., see Packer, 2008). In these contexts, it is concern about norm violations within groups or group functioning more generally that lead highly identified individuals to challenge the status quo in ways that may represent less of a choice and more of a moral imperative (Ellemers & Jetten, 2013; Jetten & Hornsey, 2014).

Such motives may underlie the behaviour of whistleblowers – group members who are willing to publicly or privately disclose rule violations by other individuals or by the group to outsiders, often at substantial personal risk (Mesmer-Magnus & Viswesvaran, 2005). For example, a medical doctor may notice that her colleagues are breaking codes of conduct by not treating a terminally ill patient and report them, or a bank employee may disclose to official regulators that he discovered irregularities in the bank's financial transactions. In these instances, individuals need to decide whether norm violations within the group should be reported or whether, perhaps for fear of repercussions, it is better for them to keep quiet about the fact that an important rule or norm has been violated. Here whistleblowers have to weigh up the costs versus benefits of their actions (Gundlach et al., 2003) because, as we will outline further below, they are seldom heralded as heroes by other ingroup members – whose self-views they challenge.

Ironically, it is at times easier for those at the periphery of the group to engage in moral rebellion than it is for those at the core of the group. This is because occupying a marginal position within the group may make it easier for individuals to challenge group norms (Packer, 2008) because they do not attract the limelight as much as core group members. That is, their nonconformity might be less likely to be noticed which, at times, allows them to successfully enact their moral mandates to drive positive group change (Ellemers & Jetten, 2013). However, it is also important to consider that, whether core or peripheral, most group members are reluctant to become a moral outcast in their group (Ellemers et al., 2013; van Nunspeet et al., 2015). Indeed, given the importance of seeing the self as a loyal group member and the risks associated with challenging group norms, it is likely that individuals will avoid being the moral rebel in their group whenever possible. To better understand this point, it is constructive to examine contexts when people would like to deviate and dissent but decide against such action and instead (at least publicly) conform to group norms. It has been found that such strategic conformity is particularly likely to occur when dissent might jeopardize acceptance or support from other group members (Jetten et al., 2003; Matz & Wood, 2005), when addressing a high status audience who can affect an individual's outcomes (Jetten et al., 2006) or when costs of dissent are perceived to be too high because responses are public rather than private (Barreto & Ellemers, 2000; Jetten et al., 2010). One of the few studies concerned with moral rebellion intentions looked at whether newcomers are more likely to blow the whistle than old-timers when confronted with rule violations by other ingroup members (i.e., rule violations that are morally not condoned). In a study examining rule-breaking among rugby-players (e.g., witnessing dirty tackles on the field that have gone unnoticed by a referee), compared to old-timers, newcomers' whistleblowing intentions were more sensitive to the social context when confronted with rule violations. Newcomers were more likely to blow the whistle when the audience was high status, and when there was little risk of alienating other ingroup members. Newcomers refrained from whistleblowing when an ingroup rule breaker had to be directly confronted, presumably because the perceived costs of doing so exceeded the potential benefits of ingratiating oneself to the high status audience. In contrast, old-timers expressed relatively high whistleblowing intentions regardless of the context.

Interestingly too, while it is mostly those lower in group identification or newcomers who will engage in strategic conformity whereby they fail to enforce and live up to moral group norms, higher identifiers or old-timers might also decide to turn a blind eye to rule violations. Such so called "uneasy conformity" might occur when group members perceive that the group has been harmed due to the violation of norms or when they are concerned that the moral dissent and rebellion that is needed to call out the rule-breaking might not be effective in bringing about desired social change (Packer, 2008).

All in all, it is clear that there are myriad justifications for moral rebellion, some motivated by personal reasons and some driven by a concern to stop rule violators in the group from harming group interests. In the latter case, it is important to be mindful of the broader context and intragroup dynamics that determine whether moral rebellion might occur. Whether moral rebels decide to call out moral norm violations depends, among other things, on whether responses are public or private, the intragroup position of the group member to be reprimanded, the intragroup position of the moral rebel and the level of group identification with the group (see Figure 26.1).

Responses to moral rebels

Moral rebellion may come at a cost. In the interpersonal domain, research has shown that moral dissenters can face rejection if their rebellion threatens the positive self-image of individuals who choose not to rebel (Cramwinckel et al., 2015; Monin et al., 2008). This is particularly likely to occur if moral rebels present themselves as morally superior to those who decide to endorse the status quo (Ellemers & Jetten, 2013; Skitka et al., 2005). Within groups (i.e., in intragroup contexts), there is evidence that moral rebels may at times face rejection, but at other times they encounter admiration. What then are conditions under which moral rebels will be condemned and face negative responses from other group members, and what are the conditions under which they

Intragroup level: intragroup deviance and dissent

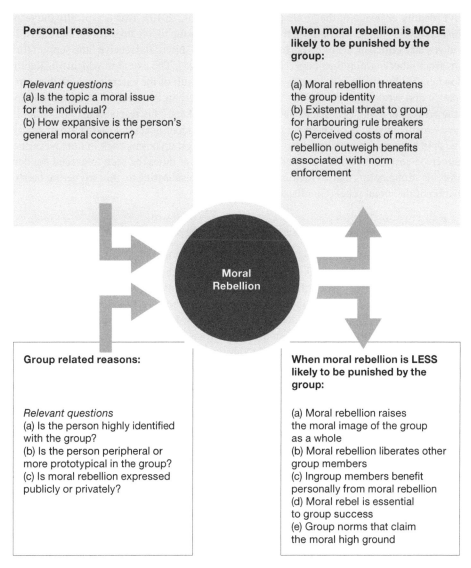

Figure 26.1 Questions to consider that might help to determine the drivers of why someone becomes a moral rebel.

might be silently condoned or even actively encouraged to engage in moral rebellion by others in the group?

When moral rebellion is MORE likely to be punished by the group

There are several reasons why moral ingroup rebels might face rejection from the group for their rebellious behaviour. Most importantly, moral rebels may face negative responses, hostility and downgrading from other ingroup members when their behaviour is seen as threatening the positive identity or image of the group (see Brambilla et al., 2013). This is typically the response to whistleblowers – those who expose the failings of the group to live up to moral standards. These individuals face criticism, are often portrayed as disloyal, a snitch, and receive little support for their actions from other ingroup members (Near & Miceli, 1995). The extent to which whistleblowers are downgraded by others in the group is often a direct result of the extent to which they are seen to threaten and weaken group identity and whether the group is perceived as being able to survive the process of being exposed as harbouring rule breakers. This response may be rather ironic because whistleblowing is often an act of loyalty or high identification with the group, motivated by a wish to bring group members who violate important group norms back in line. Nevertheless, the perceived costs of hanging out the dirty laundry may, at times, be seen to exceed the benefits of enforcing group norms that all members are expected to subscribe to, thus triggering harsh condemnation of the moral rebel (Gundlach et al., 2003).

When moral rebellion is LESS likely to be punished by the group

However, there are also instances when moral rebels may be tolerated, accepted or even admired for taking their principled, yet risky, moral stance. Moral rebels may encounter such responses by other ingroup members when they (a) are seen to raise the moral image of the group as a whole (Ellemers et al., 2012), (b) liberate other group members from the pressure of conformity or obedience to immoral norms and demands (Asch, 1956; Monin & O'Connor, 2011), (c) when ingroup members benefit personally from the rebel's transgressions (Bocian & Wojciszke, 2014), or (d) when the moral rebel may be essential to group success and backing them serves a strategic purpose of progressing the collective (e.g., Abrams et al., 2008; Ellemers & Jetten, 2013; Morton et al., 2007).

Broader group norms also determine how other group members respond to moral rebels. In particular, some groups might take the moral high ground and their perceived moral superiority might make them blind to the digressions of individual group members who break moral codes of conduct (e.g., failure by the Catholic Church to punish sexual abuse by priests). For instance, Iyer, Jetten and Haslam (2012) found that group members who have taken the moral high ground differ in their judgement of the extent to which deviant behaviour is damaging and should be punished, compared to groups that do not place themselves on a moral pedestal. Indeed, in particular, when a group takes a priori a moral stance, group members are more likely to struggle in determining the appropriate response to those who break that moral norm. As Erikson (1966) argues, such norm transgressions are difficult to navigate for group members because they are so bound up with the core identity of the group. In Erikson's words:

> The thief and his victim share a common respect for the value of property; the heretic and the inquisitor speak much to the same language and are keyed to the same religious mysteries; the traitor and the patriot act in reference to the same political institutions, often use the same methods, and for that matter are sometimes the same person.
>
> (1996, p. 20)

Because of this, when a group that claims the moral high ground is confronted with a transgression against this moral norm, group members may find it difficult to detect that wrongdoing has occurred because the high moral position is immune to doubt or challenge.

Iyer, Jetten and Haslam (2012) tested this reasoning in two studies where academics were presented with a scenario asking them to consider and evaluate a hypothetical ingroup member who violated ethical principles in his research (Study 1) and among British undergraduate students who were asked to evaluate British soldiers who violated rules of war when they abused prisoners of war in Iraq (Study 2). In both studies, moral group superiority was manipulated. In Study 1, moral superiority condition participants were told that the psychology department prides itself on the high ethical and moral standards it adheres to. In Study 2, participants in the moral superiority condition read about the "superior moral conduct" of the British armed forces relative to other countries, stating that "British soldiers are trained to treat people from other cultures with dignity and respect, and are required to follow the codes of the Geneva Convention when on active duty." Both studies included control conditions where only factional information was presented and there was no mention of the moral superior stance of the ingroup.

In both studies, results showed that when the ingroup was not presented as taking the moral high ground, high and low identifiers did not differ in their evaluations and punishment of the rule breakers. However, when the ingroup was in a position of perceived moral superiority, high and low identifiers responded in markedly different ways to the rule breaking. Specifically, those who were less identified with their university department (Study 1) and those less identified as British (Study 2) were more likely to report the inconsistency between the rule breaker's behaviour and the high moral stance of the group. However, in both studies, those higher in social identification (with the university or country) perceived the rule breaking as less damaging for the group and evaluated the rule breaker more positively. In Study 2, when it came to assigning punishments to the three British soldiers who were charged with abusing Iraqi prisoners, low identifiers recommended a harsher punishment for the rule breakers than did the high identifiers. Taken together, the results suggested that high identifiers were more forgiving of rule breaking than were low identifiers when the group claimed the moral high ground. High identifiers appeared to see the rule breakers as generally good people whose rule breaking constituted an isolated action. For them, the group's position of moral superiority appeared to act as a protective buffer limiting the negative impact of group members' rule breaking.

Other research has shown that high identifiers are far less forgiving of a rule breaker when it is the rule breaker (and not the group) who takes the high moral stance. Hornsey and Jetten (2003) found that vegetarian participants confronted with an impostor (i.e., a vegetarian who secretly ate meat occasionally) were sensitive to the size of the gulf between the target's claims for identity and their behaviour. In other words, impostors who made public claims about being a vegetarian and who moralised the issue of being a vegetarian were evaluated more negatively when their impostorism became public than were targets who kept their claims about their identity private. Furthermore, vegetarian participants downgraded the impostor more strongly and experienced more negative affect when they identified more strongly as vegetarians (compared to moderate identified vegetarians and non-vegetarians). These findings suggest that rebels that take the form of impostors might be rated more harshly when they claim the moral high ground or when they threaten the integrity of group identities (for those vegetarians who identify more strongly with the group). However, those who are less invested in the group might be more accepting of ingroup rebels and the target's rule breaking might even be met with tolerance for drawing attention to problematic group norms and for enhancing diversity within the group (see also Hutchison et al., 2006).

Practical implications and future research

Research exploring the responses to moral rebels (as opposed to ordinary rebels) is rather limited. And, because the origins and motives of 'ordinary' and 'moral' rebels are rather different (i.e., passive responding rather than active, principled choices by a group member to break with group norms), it is important to develop a better understanding of undertaking morally motivated rebellion. This is particularly relevant because social change is typically brought about by individuals who challenge the status quo and who speak out; often compelled by moral agendas about what is right and what is wrong (as an example, sexism and racism in the workplace or in society more generally). Indeed, moral rebellion can be an effective way to counter power abuse or corruption in the group. Furthermore, it is these individuals that draw attention to the faults of their group and their critical stance makes the group less vulnerable to suboptimal decision making (Postmes et al., 2001).

However, whereas at times moral rebellion may be motivated by noble and prosocial intentions, there is a dark side to morally mandated behaviour. When strong moral convictions underlie attitudes and behaviour, people are at times more interested in the outcome of their actions than the process through which that outcome is achieved. As Skitka and Mullen (2002) argue, at times, this provides a recipe for extreme, undemocratic, and even terrorist behaviour, where achieving morally mandated outcomes becomes more important than following fair and just procedure to achieve that outcome.

In sum, though not always without risks and not always motivated by the right reasons, if done well, expressions of moral deviance and dissent can be a powerful force for social change. If we stand in their way, the necessary action that might lead to desired social change and an improved moral self-image might not materialize (Bashir et al., 2013). Therefore, future research should focus on developing a better understanding of when and why group members welcome moral rebels within groups, how moral rebels propel social change, and how to avoid the dark side of moral rebellion. It is the development of this research agenda that promises to be an important avenue for future work.

Final words

Groups need moral rebels because their transgressions are important for groups to understand and negotiate its identity. As Erikson (1966) argues, boundary transgressions invite responses (i.e., tolerance or rejection) thereby allowing groups to make statements about what is normative within the group (Peters et al., 2017) and distinguish themselves from other groups (Jetten et al., 2001). This enhances norm clarity and helps to define the group's identity, which in turn increases group stability and consistency. In this contribution, we aimed to develop a better understanding of these dynamics by outlining the motives for becoming a moral rebel within a group and by exploring when and why moral rebels might be tolerated or rejected by other group members.

References

Abrams, D., Randsley de Moura, G., Marques, J. M., & Hutchison, P. (2008). Innovation credit: When can leaders oppose their group's norms? *Journal of Personality and Social Psychology, 95*(3), 662–678. https://doi.org/10.1037/0022-3514.95.3.662

Asch, S. E. (1956). Studies of independence and conformity: I. A minority of one against a unanimous majority. *Psychological Monographs: General and Applied, 70*(9), 1–70. https://doi.org/10.1037/h0093718

Barreto, M., & Ellemers, N. (2000). You can't always do what you want: Social identity and self-presentational determinants of the choice to work for a low-status group. *Personality and Social Psychology Bulletin, 26*(8), 891–906. https://doi.org/10.1177/01461672002610001

Bashir, N. Y., Lockwood, P., Chasteen, A. L., Nadolny, D., & Noyes, I. (2013). The ironic impact of activists: Negative stereotypes reduce social change influence. *European Journal of Social Psychology, 43*(7), 614–626. https://doi.org/10.1002/ejsp.1983

Bocian, K., & Wojciszke, B. (2014). Self-interest bias in moral judgments of others' actions. *Personality and Social Psychology Bulletin, 40*(7), 898–909. https://doi.org/10.1177/0146167214529800

Brambilla, M., Sacchi, S., Pagliaro, S., & Ellemers, N. (2013). Morality and intergroup relations: Threats to safety and group image predict the desire to interact with outgroup and ingroup members. *Journal of Experimental Social Psychology, 49*(5), 811–821. https://doi.org/10.1016/j.jesp.2013.04.005

Cramwinckel, F. M., van den Bos, K., & van Dijk, E. (2015). Reactions to morally motivated deviance. *Current Opinion in Psychology, 6*, 150–156. https://doi.org/10.1016/j.copsyc.2015.08.007

Crimston, C. R., Bain, P. G., Hornsey, M. J., & Bastian, B. (2016). Moral expansiveness: Examining variability in the extension of the moral world. *Journal of Personality and Social Psychology, 111*(4), 636–653. https://doi.org/10.1037/pspp0000086

Crimston, C. R., Bain, P. G., Hornsey, M. J., & Bastian, B. (2018). Toward a psychology of moral expansiveness. *Current Directions in Psychological Science, 27*(1), 14–19. https://doi.org/10.1177/0963721417730888

Ellemers, N., & Jetten, J. (2013). The many ways to be marginal in a group. *Personality and Social Psychology Review, 17*(1), 3–21. https://doi.org/10.1177/1088868312453086

Ellemers, N., Pagliaro, S., & Barreto, M. (2013). Morality and behavioural regulation in groups: A social identity approach. *European Review of Social Psychology, 24*(1), 160–193. https://doi.org/10.1080/10463283.2013.841490

Ellemers, N., & van den Bos, K. (2012). Morality in groups: On the social- regulatory functions of right and wrong. *Social and Personality Psychology Compass, 6*(12), 878–889. https://doi.org/10.1111/spc3.12001

Erikson, K. T. (1966). *Wayward puritans: A study in the sociology of deviance*. Wiley & Sons.

Griffin, J. H. (1977). *Black like me*. Houghton Mifflin.

Gundlach, M. J., Douglas, S. C., & Martinko, M. J. (2003). The decision to blow the whistle: A social information processing framework. *Academy of Management Review, 28*(1), 107–123. https://doi.org/10.5465/amr.2003.8925239

Hornsey, M. J., & Jetten, J. (2003). Not being what you claim to be: Impostors as sources of group threat. *European Journal of Social Psychology, 33*(5), 639–657. https://doi.org/10.1002/ejsp.176

Hornsey, M. J., Majkut, L., Terry, D. J., & McKimmie, B. M. (2003). On being loud and proud: Nonconformity and counter-conformity to group norms. *British Journal of Social Psychology, 42*(3), 319–335. https://doi.org/10.1348/014466603322438189

Hutchison, P., Jetten, J., Christian, J., & Haycraft, E. (2006). Protecting threatened identity: Sticking with the group by emphasizing ingroup heterogeneity. *Personality and Social Psychology Bulletin, 32*(12), 1620–1632. https://doi.org/10.1177/0146167206292235

Iyer, A., Jetten, J., & Haslam, S. A. (2012). Sugaring o'er the devil: Moral superiority and group identification help individuals downplay the implications of ingroup rule-breaking. *European Journal of Social Psychology, 42*(2), 141–149. https://doi.org/10.1002/ejsp.864

Jetten, J., Branscombe, N. R., Schmitt, M. T., & Spears, R. (2001). Rebels with a cause: Group identification as a response to perceived discrimination from the mainstream. *Personality and Social Psychology Bulletin, 27*(9), 1204–1213. https://doi.org/10.1177/0146167201279012

Jetten, J., Branscombe, N. R., Spears, R., & McKimmie, B. M. (2003). Predicting the paths of peripherals: The interaction of identification and future possibilities. *Personality and Social Psychology Bulletin, 29*, 130–140. https://doi.org/10.1177/0146167202238378

Jetten, J., & Hornsey, M. J. (Eds.). (2011). *Rebels in groups: Dissent, deviance, difference and defiance*. Wiley-Blackwell.

Jetten, J., & Hornsey, M. J. (2014). Deviance and dissent in groups. *Annual Review of Psychology, 65*, 461–485. https://doi.org/10.1146/annurev-psych-010213-115151

Jetten, J., Hornsey, M. J., & Adarves-Yorno, I. (2006). When group members admit to being conformist: The role of relative intragroup status in conformity self-reports. *Personality and Social Psychology Bulletin, 32*(2), 162–173. https://doi.org/10.1177/0146167205279904

Jetten, J., Hornsey, M. J., Spears, R., Haslam, S. A., & Cowell, E. (2010). Rule transgressions in groups: The conditional nature of newcomers' willingness to confront deviance. *European Journal of Social Psychology, 40*(2), 338–348. https://doi.org/10.1002/ejsp.627

Matz, D. C., & Wood, W. (2005). Cognitive dissonance in groups: The consequences of disagreement. *Journal of Personality and Social Psychology, 88*(1), 22–37. https://doi.org/10.1037/0022-3514.88.1.22

Mesmer-Magnus, J. R., & Viswesvaran, C. (2005). Whistle-blowing in organizations: An examination of correlates of whistle-blowing intentions, actions, and retaliation. *Journal of Business Ethics, 62*, 277–297. https://doi.org/10.1007/s10551-005-0849-1

Milgram S. (1963). Behavioral study of obedience. *The Journal of Abnormal and Social Psychology, 67*(4), 371–378. https://doi.org/10.1037/h0040525

Monin, B., & O'Connor, K. (2011). Reactions to defiant deviants: Deliverance or defensiveness? In Jetten, J., & Hornsey, M. J. (Eds.), (2011). *Rebels in groups: Dissent, deviance, difference and defiance* (pp. 261–280). Wiley-Blackwell.

Monin, B., Sawyer, P. J., & Marquez, M. J. (2008). The rejection of moral rebels: Resenting those who do the right thing. *Journal of Personality and Social Psychology, 95*(1), 76–93. https://doi.org/10.1037/0022-3514.95.1.76

Morton, T. A., Postmes, T., & Jetten, J. (2007). Playing the game: When group success is more important than downgrading deviants. *European Journal of Social Psychology, 37*(4), 599–616. https://doi.org/10.1002/ejsp.385

Near, J. P., & Miceli, M. P. (1995). Effective-whistle blowing. *Academy of Management Review, 20*(3), 679–708. https://doi.org/10.5465/amr.1995.9508080334

Packer, D. J. (2008). On being both with us and against us: A normative conflict model of dissent in social groups. *Personality and Social Psychology Review, 12*(1), 50–72. https://doi.org/10.1177/1088868307309606

Peters, K., Jetten, J., Radova, D., & Austin, K. (2017). Gossiping about deviance: Evidence that deviance spurs the gossip that builds bonds. *Psychological Science, 28*(11), 1610–1619. https://doi.org/10.1177/0956797617716918

Postmes, T., Spears, R., & Cihangir, S, (2001). Quality of decision making and group norms. *Journal of Personality and Social Psychology, 80*(6), 918–930. https://doi.org/10.1037/0022-3514.80.6.918

Rottman, J., Crimston, C. R., Syropoulos, S. (2021). Tree-huggers versus human-lovers: Anthropomorphism and dehumanization predict valuing nature over outgroups. *Cognitive Science: A Multidisciplinary Journal, 45*(4), e12967. https://doi.org/10.1111/cogs.12967

Skitka, L. J., Bauman, C. W., & Sargis, E. G. (2005). Moral conviction: Another contributor to attitude strength or something more? *Journal of Personality and Social Psychology, 88*(6), 895–917. https://doi.org/10.1037/0022-3514.88.6.895

Skitka, L. J., & Mullen, E. (2002). The dark side of moral conviction. *Analyses of Social Issues and Public Policy, 2*(1), 35–41. https://doi.org/10.1111/j.1530-2415.2002.00024.x

van Nunspeet, F., Derks, B., Ellemers, N., & Nieuwenhuis, S. (2015). Moral impression management: Evaluation by an in-group member during a moral IAT affects perceptual attention and conflict and response monitoring. *Social Psychological and Personality Science, 6*(2), 183–192. https://doi.org/10.1177/1948550614548076

27
THE INTERGROUP LEVEL
Moral self-views

Matthew J. Hornsey

Abstract

Groups are motivated to think of themselves as moral: at least as moral as relevant outgroups, if not more so. This motivation nudges groups toward developing moral cultures, but also incentivizes group members to deny, rationalize, or trivialize immoralities that exist. Because of this, the task of identifying sub-optimal cultures and triggering reform is sometimes left to agents of change who are members of the outgroup. Providing moral feedback like this is a fraught endeavour: the intergroup context presents powerful psychological obstacles to creating change, and failure to understand the psychology of intergroup communication can cause more damage than good. This chapter details the intergroup factors that lead to defensiveness in the face of moral feedback. Lessons from this research highlight common mistakes people make when communicating between groups on morally charged issues, while also pointing to concrete and actionable steps for triggering positive change.

- Groups are motivated to think of themselves as moral.
- This incentivizes group members to deny, rationalize, or trivialize immoralities that exist.
- Moral feedback from the outgroup can damage intergroup relations rather than reforming sub-optimal group cultures.
- Research points to concrete and actionable communication strategies for triggering positive change.

Introduction

Humans have a talent for morally justifying even the most abhorrent practices. Defenders of slavery, for example, did not just rely on economic arguments, they also relied on moral ones: that enslaved groups are infantile in their development and so need protection, or that slavery was an escape from extreme poverty. In South Africa, apartheid was defended as a method of liberating Afrikaners from British domination and reducing inter-racial conflict. In Australia, when laws were changed to force refugees into detention and to deny them basic civil liberties, it was defended on the grounds that it was a way of punishing "queue-jumpers", smashing a corrupt people smuggling trade, and "saving lives at sea".

These examples highlight three features of group psychology. First, people are motivated to see their groups as moral and can engage in elaborate mental gymnastics to do so. Second, the job of calling out immorality and pushing for positive change frequently falls to outgroup members; witnesses to a morally questionable culture whose perception is unmuddied by group loyalties and absorption of inappropriate norms. Third, groups are mindful of maintaining a moral self-image not just to themselves but to the world at large: to the extent that ingroup members *are* motivated to express moral compunction, they may be constrained in doing so by the reputational concerns associated with highlighting shameful features of the culture in front of relevant outgroups.

This chapter examines each of these phenomena, mostly drawing on theory and data from social psychology. After reviewing literature on the need for moral enhancement within groups, I examine work on the intergroup sensitivity effect: the phenomenon that it is disproportionately difficult to push for positive change when the source of the message is an outgroup member. I then discuss how willingness to embrace ingroup dissent – and willingness to express compunction for immoral practices – shifts as a function of the intergroup audience. The chapter concludes by examining unresolved questions, theoretical controversies, and practical implications for constructing a more moral society.

Moral self-enhancement: an intergroup approach

Social identity theory is an ambitious and multi-faceted theory but is probably best recognized for this simple psychological prescription: people are motivated to think of their groups as good groups (Tajfel and Turner 1979), a collective enhancement motive that provides purpose, meaning, validation, and positive self-regard. There are multiple dimensions on which groups may judge their collective self-worth, but morality seems to be the most important. People self-report that they care primarily about group morality, morality judgements are especially central predictors of identification levels, and groups are more reluctant to accept future members when those individuals display moral lapses as compared to other lapses (Leach et al. 2007; Ellemers et al., 2008; Van der Lee et al. 2017). This is perhaps not surprising: morality has an especially strong relevance in terms of maintaining norms, regulating relations between individuals, and signalling potentially harmful intentions of others (Brambilla et al. 2021; Ellemers et al. 2019).

On face value this should be a positive characteristic of group psychology, nudging groups to uphold more virtuous cultures and practices. While this is no doubt true, it is also true that group members (like individuals; Shalvi et al. 2015) have a suite of strategies to rationalize, minimize, or distract from their collective moral lapses (see Ellemers et al., 2019, for an overview). Some of these tools – such as censorship and propaganda – can operate at the system level and might be outside any one individual's control. Other tools, however, can be switched on and off by individuals. These include avoidance of morally threatening information, denial in the face of morally threatening information, an emphasis on historical victimhood as a distraction from current perpetration, moral licensing, moral hypocrisy, and moral disengagement (see also Jordan et al., this volume; Shnabel, this volume). Another way of rationalizing intergroup immorality is to victim-blame (implying that the outgroups deserved the treatment) or sanctification of one's group mission that leads to an ends-justifies-the-means culture (e.g., rationalization of war as holy). From this latter perspective, intergroup aggression can occur not *despite* a group's collective moral self-image, but rather *because* of it.

The challenges of creating moral reform as an outgroup member.

When a person or group "calls out" another group for practices that are morally sub-optimal, under what circumstances do people accept these criticisms, as opposed to denying or rationalizing them away? One major factor is the group membership of the messenger. In short, group-directed criticisms and recommendations for change are much more likely to be taken on board when the comments are made by an ingroup member than when an outgroup member says exactly the same thing. This phenomenon – referred to as the intergroup sensitivity effect – is large, robust, and resilient across multiple contexts.

The typical approach to examining the intergroup sensitivity effect is to give participants what they are led to believe is a real statement (e.g., an extract from an interview) in which the speaker makes a criticism of the participant's group. For example, Australians may receive the criticism that Australian culture is racist. The content of the message is equivalent across conditions: all that changes is the group membership of the speaker (in the case above, the criticisms might be attributed to an Australian or to a foreigner).

The typical finding is that people rate both the speaker and the comments more positively when they are attributed to an ingroup member than when the same comments are attributed to an outgroup member. Furthermore, participants are more likely to agree with the criticism and to intend to reform when the comments are made by an ingroup member. Recent evidence indicates that people are also more likely to pay to punish outgroup critics and to behaviourally discriminate against outgroup critics compared to ingroup critics (Thürmer and McCrea 2018). Indeed, group members prioritize counterarguing outgroup criticism over getting their work done (Thürmer et al. 2019).

The effect is consistently strong for both low and high identifiers (Morier et al. 2013), persists over time (Hiew and Hornsey 2010), and has been detected using diverse arguments: for example, Muslims hearing they are too fanatical and intolerant (Ariyanto et al. 2010); Italians hearing they are racist and prone to corruption (Moscatelli et al. 2019); maths–science students hearing they are arrogant and lacking in social conscience (Hornsey et al. 2002); and meat-eaters hearing their diets are unsustainable (Thürmer et al. 2022). Furthermore, the messenger effect typically does *not* emerge when the speaker is praising the group, which suggests that the intergroup sensitivity effect is not a reflexive tendency to derogate outgroup speakers. When it comes to morally laden criticism, group members appear to be saying "It's OK if *we* say it, but *you* can't".

Clearly, the intergroup sensitivity effect is pessimistic news for anyone who strives to push for positive change from the outside. Of even greater concern, the reception for criticisms tends to be more negative when the comments are made by an outgroup member than when they are attributed to no-one (Hiew and Hornsey 2010). One implication of this is that outgroup criticisms might be *creating* resistance: that in the face of pressure from the outside, recipients sink into a state of denial about problems and failings that they would otherwise admit to. When trying to point out moral failings from the outside, then, one should not be primarily concerned that the attempts will not work; the more concerning possibility is that the comments will make things worse.

The most intuitive explanation for the intergroup sensitivity effect is expertise: Ingroup members have privileged access to the group and to its culture, so on face value should be more credentialled than outsiders to make an informed criticism (a "what would they know?" response). However, the data suggest this is *not* a driver of the effect. People who self-identify as outgroup members – but who have years of experience with the group they are criticizing – are received just as negatively as those with no experience (Hornsey and Imani 2004).

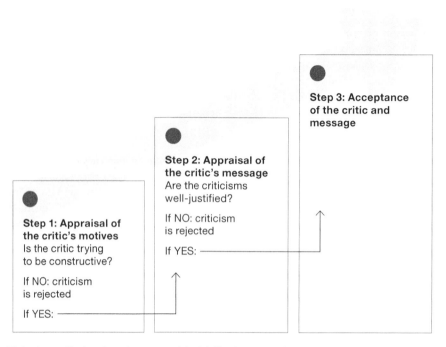

Figure 27.1 An attributional gatekeeper model of delivering moral feedback to groups.

Instead, the intergroup sensitivity effect appears to be partly driven by basic intergroup biases with respect to trust and motive (Hornsey et al. 2004). This notion is presented in Figure 27.1. From this perspective, the first thought that recipients of group criticism ask themselves about the critic is not "Are they right or wrong?" but rather "Why would they say that?" Here, the attributional question – Is the speaker trying to be constructive? – is a gatekeeper question, the answer to which may render other considerations irrelevant. Only if recipients receive a satisfactory answer to this question will they engage in a rational examination of the merits of the argument.

When gauging whether a speaker is motivated by constructive reasons, group members fall back on a simple social identity heuristic: ingroup members can be trusted, outgroup members cannot. So when ingroup members criticize a group, the default response is to assume that the critic is motivated for constructive reasons: they criticize because they care. Having won the benefit of the doubt on motive, insiders' criticisms are more or less likely to be listened to depending on traditional criteria such as the objective credibility of the argument and the skill with which they make the persuasive case. When outsiders say the same thing, however, people are more likely to assume bad faith; for example, that the comments are merely insults as part of a cynical strategy to exert intergroup dominance. Unconvinced of the purity of the outgroup critic's motives, the audience shuts down and become immune to what should technically be persuasion assets such as evidence, expertise, and experience. As will be seen later, this model has implications for how to overcome defensiveness in the face of intergroup moral feedback.

How intergroup audiences shape willingness to give and receive moral feedback

Moral feedback is not typically made in a vacuum: rather, people are mindful of audiences and the reputational capital implied by those audiences. Calling out one's own group for morally dubious actions is a combustive act, one that can potentially damage the group's reputation in the eyes of others (see also Jetten and Crimston, this volume). According to the needs-based moral of reconciliation, for example, a concern for public image and moral redemption in the eyes of others is a *primary* motivation for a perpetrator group to engage in apologies and other reconciliation attempts (Shnabel and Nadler 2015). To the extent that these needs are met, perpetrator group members will support public expressions of moral compunction. But where these needs are denied – or where the needs are complicated by perceptions of rejection from the outgroup – perpetrator group members may withhold gestures of reconciliation or even lash out (Gausel and Leach 2011; Harth et al. 2011).

Similar reputational concerns have been uncovered in the literature on group criticism. Consistent with everyday phrases like "keep it in-house" and "don't air your dirty laundry", ingroup members are indeed less likely to engage in internal criticism when the comments could be heard by outsiders (Packer 2014). Furthermore, ingroup members who criticize their group publicly are liked less and arouse more defensiveness than those who keep it in-house (Ariyanto et al. 2006; Elder et al. 2005; Hornsey et al. 2005). These effects are not explained by attributions of motive; the data show no evidence that the ingroup critic is perceived as a traitor or as malicious. Rather, participants question the *appropriateness* of crossing intergroup boundaries with one's criticism, and fret about the reputational consequences of having done so (as elaborated later in the chapter, these reputational consequences might be particularly acute when a group's morality is being called into question as opposed to other dimensions such as competence; Rösler et al. 2021).

Interestingly, there is some evidence that this concern for reputational damage might be misplaced. On occasions, intergroup antipathy is fuelled by the perception that the outgroup is homogeneous, inflexible, and blinded by moral conviction. Hearing that the outgroup is capable of intragroup criticism can be a stereotype-busting event, one that can "unfreeze" intergroup hostilities. For example, several studies have shown that Israelis show more openness to the Palestinian cause when they hear examples of Palestinians criticizing their own group (McDonald et al. 2018; Saguy and Halperin 2014). This suggests an irony: although normative constraints against public criticisms are driven by strategic concerns for reputation, on a deeper level there can be strategic *advantages* in allowing an outgroup to hear that your group is capable of healthy internal dissent.

Further demonstrating these complex cost-benefit analyses, Ashokkumar et al. (2019) showed that strongly identified members of a political party will pivot in their response to an immoral act depending on who is watching. When the act was hidden from public view, deeply aligned group members were reluctant to publicly report the transgression, a tendency that was attributed to reputational concerns. When the transgression had already been made public, however, the same constituency encouraged the party to openly denounce the transgressor.

Another important caveat is that reputational concerns can sometimes trigger change. There are several studies showing that *intentions to reform* are particularly strong among high identifiers who receive criticisms that are made to outgroup audiences (Ariyanto et al. 2006; Hornsey et al. 2005; Rabinovich and Morton 2010). This is despite the fact that the same respondents often report high levels of global negativity and discomfort with the criticisms. When responding to reputational damage associated with public criticism of morality, high identifiers may decide that structural reform might be a better long-term strategy instead of (or perhaps in parallel to) anger and defensiveness.

Unresolved questions

Research and theory reviewed above falls into two broad categories: (1) literature on the need for moral enhancement within groups (and how this is maintained) and (2) literature on the psychology of communicating negative moral feedback to groups. The former literature is older and more mature, benefitting not just from social psychological research but also from literature in the broader social sciences. Stitching together insights from experiments, surveys, case studies and even pure intellectualization has resulted in a broad and detailed tapestry, built up over decades.

In contrast, research on intergroup criticism has to date operated in a relatively narrow lane. In the early days of establishing theory and principles, adherence to a single paradigm has its benefits, allowing insights to accumulate in an orderly and programmatic way. It would be ideal, however, if these insights could be blended with different approaches and methodologies to produce a more three-dimensional picture. One limitation of an over-reliance on lab-based experimental work is the focus on self-report: the performative aspect of responding to criticism in public has been under-examined, and it is only recently that there has been an examination of how "defensiveness" plays out in terms of behaviour (see work by Thürmer and colleagues). It is also important to gain a stronger sense of how intergroup communication plays out "in the wild", including the macro-factors that lab-based studies struggle to tap into (e.g., media effects, political factors, cultural influences).

The main theoretical controversy surrounding intergroup criticism work has been the question of mechanism (which in turn has implications for practical interventions, discussed in the next section). The standard approach to understanding responses to group criticism is that the effects are steeped in social identity considerations; for example, the intergroup sensitivity effect is described as an identity-based attributional bias. However, some have argued that the effect can be explained by the enforcement of social conventions around criticism in a way that is potentially unrelated to identity. Specifically, the intergroup sensitivity effect can be explained as an enforcement of a rule to never level criticisms of groups other than your own, one that is not a reflection of "sensitivity" per se. Consistent with this view, studies confirm that one does not have to be a member of the criticized group to show effects that resemble the intergroup sensitivity effect. For example, bystanders (those who are members of neither the criticized or the criticizing groups) *also* express more negativity when moral criticisms are delivered across intergroup boundaries as compared to intragroup criticisms (McCrea et al. 2021; Sutton et al. 2006; Thürmer and McCrea 2021). Participants have even been shown to penalize ingroup members who criticized outgroups more so than ingroup members who criticized their own group (Adelman and Verkuyten 2020).

Implicit in some of this debate is the notion that the intergroup sensitivity effect is *either* an identity-driven defensiveness response *or* it is an identity-neutral social convention. However, it could easily be that both processes are operating in parallel. It is possible, for example, that people instinctively understand that intergroup criticisms are combustive and hostility-inducing acts, ones that trigger identity-related defensiveness. As a result, a politeness norm has emerged that you should not do it, and this social convention is recognized by everyone regardless of whether they are the targets of the criticism. From this perspective, receivers and bystanders may both show the same results, but for different reasons.

The notion of parallel processes provides a better fit to the data than the notion that one process is pre-eminent. An identity-based process cannot explain the bystander effects. But a social convention explanation alone cannot readily explain the fact that the intergroup sensitivity effect is eliminated when group members are induced to feel social threat (Adelman and Dasgupta 2018; Ariyanto et al. 2010). Perhaps most importantly, strategies to overcome defensiveness in the face of moral criticism from the outside tend to be effective when they take identity considerations into account and tend to be ineffective when they do not. This research is detailed below.

Practical implications

The fact that outsiders are routinely discredited when they attempt to create positive change in a group culture is not just theoretically interesting, it carries real practical importance. If the job of reforming or reinvigorating a group culture is left exclusively to ingroup members, the job may never get done because insiders have a propensity to justify – and habituate to – the status quo. Understanding how outsiders can best get their message across is one part in the puzzle of creating a more moral society.

In grappling with this question, one needs to remember that the psychology of influencing groups from the outside is a distinctive psychology: many intuitive – and even many empirically validated – tools of persuasion are not equipped to deal with this specific case. As mentioned earlier, experience with the group does not seem to help (Hornsey and Imani 2004). Furthermore, outgroup critics arouse just as much defensiveness when they make well-researched, high-quality arguments than when they make sloppy, low-quality arguments (Esposo et al. 2013). Hornsey et al. (2008) tested two theoretically driven strategies that outsiders can use: "sugaring" (adding praise to the negative comments) and "spotlighting" (i.e., the messenger making it explicit that they intend their comments to apply to just a portion of the group, not the whole group). Neither strategy was effective in reliably reducing negativity toward an outsider's critical message.

The failure of these strategies is well-anticipated by Figure 27.1 because they do not address the attributional bias that drives the defensiveness in the first place. From the perspective of the attributional gatekeeper model, outgroup critics should spend their time building their attributional credentials – responding to the "Are they trying to be constructive?" question – and only then attend to issues of experience and argument quality.

In this spirit, Hornsey et al. (2008) tested a strategy of "sharing"; that is, outgroup critics acknowledging that the problems they identified in the target group were shared also by their own ingroup. Compared to a no-strategy control, outgroup critics were liked more and aroused less negativity when they used this strategy. Similarly, newcomers to a group are more able to win support for their criticisms when they also criticized the group they recently left (Hornsey et al. 2007; Experiment 3). Finally, Hornsey et al. (2004) examined how Asian-Australians could sell the message to Anglo-Australians that they have a problem with anti-Asian prejudice. One successful technique for reducing defensiveness was when the speaker located themselves within a shared, superordinate identity (i.e., "*I feel we Australians are racist and intolerant*") than when they situated themselves as outsiders ("*I feel Australians are racist and intolerant*").

In each case, the mechanism for success was that these strategies helped convince the recipients that the speaker's motives were constructive: they were making these comments because they cared, not because they were trying to signal their rejection of the group (in the case of the superordinate identity technique) or because they were trying to signal the group's inferiority relative to other groups (in the case of sharing). Having anticipated and defused suspicion of motives, the critics were better able to guide the audience to listen to the message. More recently, Moscatelli et al. (2019) argued that the content of the message can signal attributions of motive. In two studies they found that outgroup criticisms phrased in concrete terms provoked less attributions and (consequently) fewer negative reactions compared with outgroup criticisms formulated in abstract terms (which signal greater generalizability and stability of the claims).

Another potentially successful strategy is to frame a criticism in ways that do not explicitly call into question morality. Morality is an especially important dimension of self-regard, one that can easily trigger defensiveness and denial (Täuber et al. 2015), and so there may be benefits in using non-moralized communication frames. In line with this, Rösler et al. (2021) asked participants to recall a criticism that was framed either in terms of their competence or their morality. Even when delivered by an outgroup member, participants made fewer negative attributions and (as a result) indicated that they changed their behaviour more when their competence was criticized relative to their morality.

In sum, it is sometimes important to deliver uncomfortable moral feedback across intergroup boundaries: indeed, at the essence of much political activism is the efforts of bystanders and outsiders to call out moral failings in groups to which they do not belong. Intuitively, outgroup critics may choose to spend a lot of time credentialling by demonstrating their experience, the quality of their argument, and the quantity of their evidence. These intuitive efforts may fall on deaf ears, however, if the speaker does not first attend to the suspicion about motive inherent to intergroup communication about morality. Once these issues are addressed, outgroup critics may find that they have a much easier time getting their message across, with everything that implies in terms of constructing a more moral society.

References

Adelman, L., & Dasgupta, N. (2018). Effect of threat and social identity on reactions to ingroup criticism: Defensiveness, openness, and a remedy. *Personality and Social Psychology Bulletin, 45*, 740–753.

Adelman, L., & Verkuyten, M. (2020). Rules of engagement: Reactions to internal and external criticism in public debate. *British Journal of Social Psychology, 59*, 405–424.

Ariyanto, A., Hornsey, M.J., & Gallois, C. (2010). United we stand: Intergroup conflict moderates the intergroup sensitivity effect. *European Journal of Social Psychology, 40*, 169–177.

Ariyanto, A., Hornsey, M.J., & Gallois, C. (2006). Group-directed criticism in Indonesia: Role of message source and audience. *Asian Journal of Social Psychology, 9*, 96–102.

Ashokkumar, A., Galaif, M., & Swann, W.B.Jr. (2019). Tribalism can corrupt: Why people denounce or protect immoral group members. *Journal of Experimental Social Psychology, 85*, 103874.

Brambilla, M., University, S.S., Rusconi, P., & Goodwin, G.P. (2021). The primacy of morality in impression development: Theory, research, and future directions. *Advances in Experimental Social Psychology, 64*, 187–262.

Elder, T.J., Sutton, R.M., & Douglas, K.M. (2005). Keeping it to ourselves: Effects of audience size and composition on reactions to criticism of the ingroup. *Group Processes & Intergroup Relations, 8*, 231–244.

Ellemers, N., Pagliaro, S., Barreto, M., & Leach, C.W. (2008). Is it better to be moral than smart? The effects of morality and competence norms on the decision to work at group status improvement. *Journal of Personality and Social Psychology, 95*, 1397–1410.

Ellemers, N., van der Toorn, J., Paunov, Y., & van Leeuwen, T. (2019). The psychology of morality: A review and analysis of empirical studies published from 1940 through 2017. *Personality and Social Psychology Review, 23*, 332–366.

Esposo, S.R., Hornsey, M.J., & Spoor, J.R. (2013). Shooting the messenger: Outsiders critical of your group are rejected regardless of argument quality. *British Journal of Social Psychology, 52*, 386–395.

Gausel, N., & Leach, C.W. (2011). Concern for self-image and social image in the management of moral failure: Rethinking shame. *European Journal of Social Psychology, 41*, 468–478.

Harth, N., Hornsey, M.J., & Barlow, F. (2011). Emotional responses to rejection of gestures of intergroup reconciliation. *Personality and Social Psychology Bulletin, 37*, 815–829.

Hiew, D. N., & Hornsey, M.J. (2010). Does time reduce resistance to out-group critics? An investigation of the persistence of the intergroup sensitivity effect over time. *British Journal of Social Psychology, 49*, 569–581.

Hornsey, M.J., de Bruijn, P., Creed, J., Allen, J., Ariyanto, A., & Svensson, A. (2005). Keeping it in-house: How audience affects responses to group criticism. *European Journal of Social Psychology, 35*, 291–312.

Hornsey, M. J., Grice, T., Jetten, J., Paulsen, N., & Callan, V. (2007). Group directed criticisms and recommendations for change: Why newcomers arouse more resistance than old-timers. *Personality and Social Psychology Bulletin, 33*, 1036–1048.

Hornsey, M. J., & Imani, A. (2004). Criticizing groups from the inside and the outside: An identity perspective on the intergroup sensitivity effect. *Personality and Social Psychology Bulletin, 30*, 365–383.

Hornsey, M. J., Oppes, T., & Svensson, A. (2002). "It's ok if we say it, but you can't": Responses to intergroup and intragroup criticism. *European Journal of Social Psychology, 32*, 293–307.

Hornsey, M. J., Robson, E., Smith, J., Esposo, S., & Sutton, R. (2008). Sugaring the pill: Assessing rhetorical strategies designed to minimize defensive reactions to group criticism. *Human Communication Research, 34*, 70–98.

Hornsey, M. J., Trembath, M., & Gunthorpe, S. (2004). 'You can criticize because you care': Identity attachment, constructiveness, and the intergroup sensitivity effect. *European Journal of Social Psychology, 34*, 499–518.

Leach, C.W., Ellemers, N., Barreto, M., Leach, C.W., Ellemers, N., & Barreto, M. (2007). Group virtue: the importance of morality (vs. competence and sociability) in the positive evaluation of in-groups. *Journal of Personality and Social Psychology, 93*, 234–249.

McCrea, S.M., Erion, C.J.G., & Thürmer, J.L. (2021). Why punish critical outgroup commenters? Social identity, general norms, and retribution. *British Journal of Social Psychology.* https://doi.org/10.1111/bjso.12508

McDonald, M., Brindley, S., Halperin, E., & Saguy, T. (2018). Outgroup members' internal criticism promotes intergroup openness: The role of perceived risk. *British Journal of Social Psychology, 57*, 95–111.

Morier, D., Bryan, A.E.B., & Kasdin, L. (2013). The effects of group identity, group choice, and strength of group identification on intergroup sensitivity. *Group Dynamics: Theory, Research, and Practice, 17*, 14–29.

Moscatelli, S., Prati, F., & Rubini, M. (2019). If you criticize us, do it in concrete terms: Linguistic abstraction as a moderator of the intergroup sensitivity effect. *Journal of Language and Social Psychology, 38*, 680–705.

Packer, D.J. (2014). On not airing your dirty laundry: Intergroup contexts suppress ingroup criticism mong strongly identified group members. *British Journal of Social Psychology, 53*, 93–111.

Rabinovich, A., & Morton, T.A. (2010). Who says we are bad people? The impact of criticism source and attributional content on responses to group-based criticism. *Personality and Social Psychology Bulletin, 36*, 524–536.

Rösler, I.K., Van Nunspeet, F., & Ellemers, N. (2021). Don't tell me about my moral failures but motivate me to improve: Increasing effectiveness of outgroup criticism by criticizing one's competence. *European Journal of Social Psychology, 51*, 597–609.

Saguy, T., & Halperin, E. (2014). Exposure to outgroup members criticizing their own group facilitates intergroup openness. *Personality and Social Psychology Bulletin, 40*(6), 791–802

Shalvi, S., Gino, F., Barkan, R., & Ayal, S. (2015). self-serving justifications: Doing wrong and feeling moral. *Current Directions in Psychological Science, 24*, 125–130.

Shanbel, N., & Nadler, A. (2015). The role of agency and morality in reconciliation processes: The perspective of the needs-based model. *Current Directions in Psychological Science, 24*, 477–483

Sutton, R.M., Elder, T.J., & Douglas, K.M. (2006). Reactions to internal and external criticism of outgroups: Social convention in the intergroup sensitivity effect. *Personality and Social Psychology Bulletin, 32*, 563–575.

Tajfel, H., & Turner, J. C. (1979). An intergrative theory of intergroup conflict. In W. G. Austin & S. Worchel (Eds.), *The social psychology of intergroup relations* (pp. 33–47). Monterey, CA: Brooks/Cole.

Thürmer, J.L., & McCrea, S.M. (2021). Disentangling the Intergroup Sensitivity Effect: Defending the ingroup or enforcing general norms? *European Journal of Social Psychology.* https://doi.org/10.1002/ejsp.2748

Thürmer, J.L., & McCrea, S.M. (2018). Beyond motivated reasoning: Hostile reactions to critical comments from the outgroup. *Motivation Science, 4*, 333–346.

Thürmer, J.L., McCrea, S.M., & McIntyre, B.M. (2019). Motivated collective defensiveness: Group members prioritize counterarguing out-group criticism over getting their work done. *Social Psychological and Personality Science, 10*, 382–392.

Thürmer, J.L., Stadler, J., & McCrea, S.M. (2022). Intergroup sensitivity and promoting sustainable consumption: Meat eaters reject vegans' call for a plant-based diet. *Sustainability, 14*, 1741. www.mdpi.com/2071-1050/14/3/1741

Täuber, S., van Zomeren, M., & Kutlaca, M. (2015). Should the moral core of climate issues be emphasized or downplayed in public discourse? Three ways to successfully manage the double-edged sword of moral communication. *Climatic Change, 130*, 453–464.

Van der Lee, R., Ellemers, N., Scheepers, D., & Rutjens, B.T. (2017). In or out? How the perceived morality (vs. competence) of prospective group members affects acceptance and rejection. *European Journal of Social Psychology, 47*, 748–762.

PART VII

A concluding vision

28
HOW MORALITY SHAPES RESEARCH
A conversation with the editors

Susan T. Fiske

Susan T. Fiske (Eugene Higgins Professor, Psychology and Public Affairs, Princeton University) has shaped the field of social psychology in many ways. Throughout her career, her work has revolved around issues of fairness and legitimacy, which are central to morality and moral judgments. Besides her own pathbreaking research on stereotyping, prejudice, and discrimination, she has edited multiple editions of the *Handbook of Social Psychology* (Gilbert, Fiske, & Lindzey, 1998) and served for many years as editor of the highest impact outlet in our field, the *Annual Review of Psychology*. Generations of psychologists across the world have been trained to consider the way people make social judgments and think about themselves and others through the lens of the landmark textbook 'social cognition,' now in its sixth edition across publishers (Fiske & Taylor, 2020).

Recurring research topics in Fiske's work include gender inequality (Glick & Fiske, 2001), prejudice and discrimination (Fiske, 1998), power (Fiske, 1993), stereotyping (Fiske, Cuddy, Glick & Xu, 2002) and infrahumanization (Harris & Fiske, 2009). She also did pioneering work to bring the insights from her research to practitioners who might benefit from them. A groundbreaking example is her work as an expert witness for the Ann Hopkins anti-gender discrimination lawsuit (Fiske, Bersoff, Borgida, Deaux, & Heilman, 1991). Other examples include her efforts to make available scholarship on subjective legitimacy and biased judgments for legal practitioners (Borgida & Fiske, 2008; Krieger & Fiske, 2006), her book targeting marketeers on how organizational misbehavior impacts brand reputations and customer support (Malone & Fiske, 2013), and the work she has done as a founding editor for Policy Insights from the Behavioral and Brain Sciences to reach out and inform broader audiences of these and other insights. Furthermore, Fiske has made tremendous efforts to promote equal treatment of scholars, for instance through her work at the US National Academy of Sciences. Enough reason, therefore, to ask her about her views on the topic of morality.

Fiske does not refer to her work as being on the topic of morality per se. She indicates that her interest in topics like fairness and equality was sparked by social events she witnessed, for instance during the time when she grew up as a young adult.

Fiske:

It was an era when we felt that social justice needed to be advanced. So we were in favor of peace, of equality, of a certain amount of freedom. Those all seemed to me fair, and legitimate, and morally right. Things to believe in. However, I do not think that, back then, I thought of these issues as 'morality' exactly. Rather, I thought of it as fairness: Giving everybody the same chance.

Fiske was willing to do a lot for her beliefs. Fiske:

During the antiwar movement, I went to jail for blocking an Army induction bus. We sat down on the highway blocking the buses that were going to take the men for their physical examinations, and we got arrested for blocking traffic. We would either get a $20 fine or 20 days in jail. So we went to jail for one night in order to get in the newspaper, and then they bailed us out the next day for $19. If commitment is indicated by doing something a little risky, I was willing to do that at the time. I would think twice now, but in essence, it was (and still is) important to me.

Another reason Fiske became interested in the topics of fairness and equality was when she realized, during college, that the researchers who were developing scales did so from their own point of view. She noted they implicitly made assumptions about which end of the scale was the 'right' or 'better' end.

Fiske:

For example, take 'locus of control': the idea being that it's better to have an internal locus of control than an external locus of control. Field independence was better than field dependence, those kind of things. And so I'm reading these things and I'm thinking, isn't this interesting? The guy who made the scale thinks there's a good end. But if you look where women and minorities end up, they're always on the other end of the scale. So it seems to me that the topics that you study, and how you study them (how you define and label your concepts, and how you analyze them), and hence what is implied to be the 'good end of a scale' is determined by who you are, by your identity. So, it seemed to me that the field needed some people who had different identities than the vast majority of the field at that time. My joining the field was not because they were wrong, but to complement their view to create a more complete picture. I don't want to be essentialist about people's research interests and their group identity, because I think that would be a mistake, but there is a tendency to notice things if you live your life from a certain point of view and so it's important to have a counterpoint. My view was to contribute my perspective—not just by having an opinion, but also by acquiring the methods training to be taken seriously.

A key recurring theme in Susan's scientific and applied work revolves around issues of social biases, power and stereotyping, and prejudice and discrimination. One of her most influential contributions to social psychological theory is the Stereotype Content Model (Fiske, Cuddy, & Glick, 2007). The model maps social perceptions of different groups in society (e.g., 'men', 'women', 'elderly', 'poor') along two core dimensions, warmth and competence, which are associated with the perception of people's intentions versus their abilities, respectively. The first rendition of this model originated from rather pragmatic reasons (Fiske: "I had a publication deadline"), but clearly resulted from her 'moral concerns' about how stereotyping (most often negatively) impacts the way people are perceived and treated in society.

Fiske:

I was writing a handbook chapter on bias, prejudice, discrimination, and stereotyping (Fiske, 1998), and I was trying to do something beyond White and Black racism, which is where most of the work was. So I started writing about what we know about stereotypes of African Americans, and about stereotypes of women generically, and stereotypes of Latinos. And I began to realize that we have been assuming that the processes of social perception and stereotyping are all the same, regardless of which group you examine. For instance, there is a stereotype of Latinos that they are fun loving and harmless. And there's a stereotype of certain kinds of women that they are fun loving and harmless—almost as if they are viewed as being a clown. But then there are Black Americans who are seen as angry. For me, the similarities seem to boil down into two clusters: I thought at first we would find (all) groups to either be perceived as high in terms of warmth and low in terms of competence or the other way around. Thus, warm but stupid, or as smart but cold. However, we found that there were also groups who were perceived as high on both warmth and high on competence, or low on both warmth and low on competence. Chick Judd [the research methods expert and author of many textbooks on data analysis] reassured me that this was really fine, the fact that we had groups in all the different quadrants, and he went on to do research with Vincent Yzerbyt saying that social perception is apparently mostly ambivalent.

Together with colleagues, Fiske replicated and extended her Stereotype Content Model around the world (Cuddy et al., 2009). At the same time, she encountered fellow researchers who questioned her work. Topics of fairness, sincerity, and a search for the truth and what is right, also come into play when Fiske opens up about how she felt about her own work being reevaluated.

Fiske:

There once was this graduate student in Cologne [Alex Koch] who, in all sincerity, was trying to replicate the Stereotype Content Model using a different methodology, multidimensional scaling. And he did a great job, but he got different results. When we talked about why and how he might alter how he collected or analyzed the data, he was very cooperative and did all the things I suggested. But still, he kept getting these other dimensions than I was getting. I was annoyed that he was not showing what we show, and that he was getting lots of credit for that. I was happy for him, but I was also afraid that people would think this other model is really true, and the Stereotype Content Model is not. I did not think that was right, because we had the data. So we had a scientific puzzle, which is always fun. When he asked if he could come over to work in my lab for a semester, I initially thought "oh no ...!", but I said yes, because I'm a scientist, and I want to know the truth—and maybe we could get to the truth together. Eventually he and others got an incredible amount of work done that semester. And together, we came up with the idea that our different findings probably had to do with differences in level of abstraction: They seemed to examine social perception by looking down on a country from 30,000 feet, and observing how people are organized, or organize themselves, into groups based on different dimensions. Which is different from our approach, which seemed to examine social perception more like a neighborhood: Somebody new is coming to your neighborhood, what do you think they are going to be like to interact with? So that's why we seemed to get the differences, because of a difference in level of construal.

The different methodological approach was not the only way in which other researchers expanded the theory of social perception. Whereas Fiske included perceptions of trustworthiness, sincerity, and honesty as part of the 'warmth dimension'—indicating people's good intentions—she did not consider this to be a distinctive factor driving its effects. Yet others published research claiming that social perception is really all about morality (Leach, Ellemers, & Barreto, 2007).

Fiske:

My reaction was again annoyed at first. But then I realized that we hadn't really parsed it that way, we did not think about separating friendliness from morality. But then I thought, of course, I'm an American: I think people who are friendly are trustworthy. Whereas Europeans might be wiser than that and realize that somebody might be being friendly but is actually out to get you. By and large, this is a big overgeneralization of course. But in the end, the distinction between morality and friendliness seemed to me to be a sophisticated distinction that I should have thought of but had not.

The different viewpoints on social perception were recently integrated based on a successful adversarial collaboration (Abele et al., 2021; Koch et al., 2021). An enterprise consistent with Fiske's ideology of defining and collecting different perspectives, and looking for a more objective truth collaboratively than a scholar can obtain on its own (Ellemers et al., 2020). Again, it was a process in which Fiske considered the search for the truth, and everyone having an equal share in the available resources (e.g., research funding) and acknowledgement of valuable output (e.g., rotating first authorship on the different papers that resulted) to be most valuable. Fiske recounts how the collaboration came about:

First, there was a meeting at the European Association of Social Psychology conference, and somebody said we should have a panel on the different viewpoints on the social perception of individuals and groups in society. So Alex (Koch) and I were obviously in, and we invited Naomi Ellemers and Colin Leach, as they disagreed with us too. And Andrea Abele got involved, too, because she's had her model on communion and agency for a long time— maybe even longer than the Stereotype Content Model—but it was a parallel invention. So we had all these people on the panel and then graduate students came up to us afterwards, and they asked 'what do I do? If I want to study this area, what dimensions do I need to take into consideration, what traits do I use and what terms for those traits are most appropriate? This all seems to be too confusing, perhaps I should not study this topic at all'. To me, this was a very bad sign. As terrible as it would have been to have the Stereotype Content Model go away and lose out totally to another model, it would have been much worse if everybody just said 'forget it, it's too hard'—I really saw a train wreck coming. So then we decided to get together. Everyone being fun, sincere, and trustworthy, as well as competent and warm. We locked ourselves in a hotel room for five days and decided we could not come out till we had specified our agreements and disagreements. We worked really hard, but also made sure (especially thanks to Naomi) that everyone had a fair chance by ignoring rank as much as possible and giving everyone the same amount of time and space. It was an illustrative process of what I've always tried to do, which was to get adversaries to talk to each other in a constructive way.

Fiske clearly is someone who believes in engaging different levels of analysis to study complex social phenomena from different angles. This clearly matches a key aim of the current handbook—which is to highlight the breadth of issues relating to morality, ranging from relatively concrete emotions, behaviors, and self-views to more abstract reasoning and overall judgments, and considering these at the four classic levels of analysis in social psychology (intrapersonal, interpersonal, intragroup, intergroup).

Fiske:

I think science is not just about facts. Science is about how you approach the problem, how you decide about methods, how you analyze your data according to the principles that everybody agrees on. You should be open about that and then frame your conclusions. So all the things that I was worried about as a college sophomore, I still believe. And I think that taking a broad approach like this and looking at it from the different perspectives that you do, it creates that diversity of ideas that really get around the whole problem, look at it from all sides and give all sides a chance to make the best case they can and then see what people find useful. I wouldn't say what's 'right', because we often discover 50 years later that it might have been otherwise. But it's right and wrong in a different way: Just because somebody finds a different answer from everybody else doesn't mean that they're immoral. So I think it's good to give every approach its day, as long as it's a reasonable approach. The way in which you've organized this book gives people a chance to look at a lot of different features of morality that might interest them. I think it's a very approachable, comprehensive, interesting way to organize the book and the topics. I can imagine hundreds of dissertations being launched by this book. And although I've stayed away from using labels like 'morality' and 'morals' in my own work—as those sound judgmental to my ear—I would want to be a moral psychologist when I see all the wonderful chapters you have in this book.

References

Abele, A. E., Ellemers, N., Fiske, S. T., Koch, A., & Yzerbyt, V. (2021). Navigating the social world: Toward an integrated framework for evaluating self, individuals, and groups. *Psychological Review*, *128*(2), 290.

Borgida, E., & Fiske, S. T. (Eds.). (2008). *Beyond common sense: Psychological science in the courtroom*. Oxford: Wiley Blackwell.

Cuddy, A. J., Fiske, S. T., Kwan, V. S., Glick, P., Demoulin, S., Leyens, J. P., ... & Ziegler, R. (2009). Stereotype content model across cultures: Towards universal similarities and some differences. *British Journal of Social Psychology*, *48*(1), 1–33.

Ellemers, N., Fiske, S. T., Abele, A. E., Koch, A., & Yzerbyt, V. (2020). Adversarial alignment enables competing models to engage in cooperative theory building toward cumulative science. *Proceedings of the National Academy of Sciences*, *117*(14), 7561–7567.

Fiske, S. T. (1993). Controlling other people: The impact of power on stereotyping. *American Psychologist*, *48*(6), 621.

Fiske, S.T. (1998). Stereotyping, prejudice, and discrimination. In D.T. Gilbert, S.T. Fiske, & G. Lindzey (Eds.). *The handbook of social psychology* (Vol. 2, pp. 357–411). Oxford: Oxford University Press.

Fiske, S. T., Bersoff, D. N., Borgida, E., Deaux, K., & Heilman, M. E. (1991). Social science research on trial: Use of sex stereotyping research in Price Waterhouse v. Hopkins. *American Psychologist*, *46*(10), 1049.

Fiske, S.T., Cuddy, A.J.C, & Glick P. (2007). Universal dimensions of social cognition: Warmth and competence. *Trends in Cognitive Sciences*, *11* (2), 7–83.

Fiske, S. T., Cuddy, A. J. C., Glick, P., & Xu, J. (2002). A model of (often mixed) stereotype content: Competence and warmth respectively follow from perceived status and competition. *Journal of Personality and Social Psychology*, *82*(6), 878–902.

Fiske, S.T. & Taylor, S.E. (2020). *Social cognition: from brains to culture* (4th ed). Thousand Oaks, CA: Sage.

Gilbert, D. T., Fiske, S. T., & Lindzey, G. (Eds.). (1998). *The handbook of social psychology*. New York: Oxford University Press.

Glick, P., & Fiske, S. T. (2001). An ambivalent alliance: Hostile and benevolent sexism as complementary justifications for gender inequality. *American Psychologist*, *56*(2), 109–118.

Harris, L. T., & Fiske, S. T. (2009). Social neuroscience evidence for dehumanised perception. *European Review of Social Psychology*, *20*(1), 192–231.

Krieger, L. H., & Fiske, S. T. (2006). Behavioral realism in employment discrimination law: Implicit bias and disparate treatment. *California Law Review*, *94*(4), 997–1062.

Koch, A., Yzerbyt, V., Abele, A., Ellemers, N., & Fiske, S. T. (2021). Social evaluation: Comparing models across interpersonal, intragroup, intergroup, several-group, and many-group contexts. *Advances in Experimental Social Psychology*, *63*, 1–68.

Leach, C. W., Ellemers, N., & Barreto, M. (2007). Group virtue: the importance of morality (vs. competence and sociability) in the positive evaluation of in-groups. *Journal of Personality and Social Psychology*, *93*(2), 234.

Malone, C., & Fiske, S. T. (2013). *The human brand: How we relate to people, products, and companies*. San Francisco: Jossey-Bass.

INDEX

Note: Page numbers in *italic* refer to Figures; those in **bold** refer to Tables.

Abele, A. E. 80, 99, 306
abortion 97–8
Acker, J. 239
action tendencies 33, 103, 140, 149
activism 13, 281, 298
affective processing: dual process model 29–30, *32*, 34–6; fear 24; moral outrage 23–4; working memory and 203–9
age-morality hypothesis 152
allyship 179–81, 184–7
altruism 47–8, 121, 179, 184–6
amoralization 57, 235
Anderson, C. 90, 93
Anderson, N. H. 80
Anderson, R. 251
anger 103, 140, 206, 207
animal rights 41, 43, 47
antisocial behavior 33–4, 161–2
apology 173, 212–20
approach-inhibition theory 88, 90
Aquino, K. 258, 261
artificial intelligence (AI) 13, 130, 197
Ashokkumar, A. 295
attributional processes 79, *99*, 102–4
avoidance action-tendencies 63, 64, 65–6, 68–9

Bain, P. G. 282
Bandura, A. 23
Baranski, E. 216, 220
Baron, J. 10
Barranti, M. 100
Barreto, M. 1

Barry, B. 197
Bašić, Z. 226
Bastian, B. 282
Batson, C. D. 140
Bauman, C. W. 97, 274
Baumeister, R. F. 213, 215
Baumgartner, T. 127
Bazerman, M. H. 195, 196
Beersma, M. 264, 273
behavioral ethics 195–9
Behavioral Immune System 147, 149, 151–3, 175
bias 55, 122, 123, 196
Big Two 78, 79, 80, 213, 216
Billig, M. 121
Black Lives Matter (BLM) movement 180, 184
black sheep effect 55, 281
blame 23, 101, 103, **269**, 271
Blasi, A. 250
Bondestam, F. 239
Bowes-Sperry, L. 197
Brion, S. 89, 90, 92, 93
Byrd, N. 36
bystanders 197, 296, 298

Caldwell, D. F. 56–7
care/harm 12, 22, 225
caring responses 140, 206, 258
Carlson, E. N. 100
Challenger disaster 22
character traits: antisocial 33–4; positive/negative 80, 90; prosocial 100; trait inference 101, 104
cheating 88, 225, 227

Index

children 10–11, 47, 173, 270
Chin, M. K. 196
Chomsky, N. 10
Cialdini, R. B. 140
cognitive load 36–7, 55, *204*, 207–9
cognitive moral development theory (CMD) 21–2
cognitive processing 22–3, 35–7, 46
collective action 114, 179, 183–8
collective guilt 168–9, 171–3, 175
collective identity 51–5
competence 2, 78, 88–9, 110–15, 157, 298, 304–5
competition 87–8, 91–4
computational modelling 121, 127–8
condemnation 67, 147, 150–3, 159, 263, 270–4
conformity 52, 56, 102, 235, 252, 280–8
consequences norms inaction (CNI) model 33
consequentialism 30, 115, 197
construal level theory (CLT) 66, 69, 70, 104
contaminant proximity 63–70
contempt 140, 141
Conway, P. 33, 36, 42
Cooley, C. H. 268
cooperation 87–8, 91–4, 118–30, 230–1
Coricelli, G. 227, 230
corporate social responsibility (CSR) 196, 238
COVID-19 pandemic 9, 47, 98, 151, 240, 241
crime 67–8, 90, 208, 219–20
Crimston, C. R. 252, 282
crowd 66, 69
cultural beliefs 53, 79, 164
cultural psychology 11
cultural values 79, 122
culture wars 12, 13

Damasio, A. 11, 12
Dearing, R. L. 161
decision making 195–8; *see also* moral decision making
default-interventionist model 34–5
De Hooge, I. E. 160
dehumanisation 63–4, 65, 69–70, 170–1, 175
deindividuation 63, 65, 69
deliberative processing 29, 35–6, 42, 45–6
deontological reasoning 12, 33–4, 42, 66–7, 115
deontology, principle 30–1
Desai, S. D. 196
deviance 280–8
de Waal, F. 11
Dhar, R. 261
die-rolling paradigm 225–8
discrimination 122, 129, 130
disease avoidance 147, 149–51
disgust: distal condition 65–70; as driver of intergroup processes 170–1; influence on moral behavior 206–8; as moral emotion 139–40; physiological indicators 171; role in moral judgments 147–54
disinterest 140
dissent 252, 280–8
distal norms 66–7
divorce 57, 235
dual process model (DPM): "hard" vs "soft" 29–30, *32*, 34–6, 42, 45; impression formation 110; and social identity 53
Du Plessis, C. 90, 92

Effron, D. A. 262
elevation 24, 148, 206, 272
Ellemers, N. 1–2, 3, 139, 203, 306–7
embarrassment 148, **269**, 270
emotional intuitions 51, 53, 58
empathy 45, 54, 168–75, 207–9
Erber, R. 205
Erikson, K. T. 286, 288
ethics 21–4, 31, 43, 56, 195–9
ethnic identity 182–3
evaluative judgments 111–13, 115, 122–4
Everett, J. 30, 34
evolutionary psychology 11, 63–4, 70
Eyal, T. 70

face perception 123, 170–1
fairness: emotional influences on response to 206; group perspectives 118–30, 225; moral judgment of 80–1, 88; reflections 303–5; reputational concerns and 225
favoritism 55, 118, 121–2, 126, 129
fear of retaliation 24
Festinger, L. 268
Fiske, S. T. 170, 303–7
Flynn, F. J. 90, 92
fMRI 12, 35, 170, 173
forgiveness 213–16
fraud 23, 89, 238
Freud, S. 10, 11
friendliness 78, 80
Fulmer, I. S. 197
functionalism 112, 141
Furr, R. M. 100

Gaventa, J. 239
Gawronski, B. 33
gender 2, 77, 119, 196, 236, 239
genocide 69, 70, 171
Gilligan, C. 77
Gino, F. 196
Gioia, D. 22
Giridharadas, A. 239
God/gods 148, 250–3
Goffman, E. 196
gossip 11, 224, 225–8, 231, 273–4

310

Index

Graham, J. 12, 232
gratitude 140, 148, 206
Greene, J. D. 12, 34, 42, 196
Group Bounded Reciprocity Theory (GBRT) 122
group identity 123, 125, 171, 174, 285–8, 296–7
group image 113, 114, *115*, 280, 285–6, 292
group membership: advantaged vs disadvantaged 179–88; empathic response and 207–8; intergroup decision making 118–30; moral circles 275, 282; moral rebels 280–8; shared identity 51–2, 54, 55–6
group norms 51–4, 56, 127, 231, 234–41, 280–8
group perception 109–15
Guglielmo, S. 80, 103
guilt: collective guilt 168–9, 171–3, 175; group-based 179, 181; impact on moral self-view **269**, 270, *273*; moral disengagement and 23; as moral emotion 139–41, 148; vs shame 158, 161–3

Haidt, J. 69, 139, 140–1, 148, 204
Hardin, A. E. 197
harm/care 12, 40–8, 208, 213, 225
harm rejection 29, 31–4
Harris, L. T. 170
Haslam, S. A. 286
health 148–53, 238
Heltzel, G. 150
honesty 115, 225–8
Hornsey, M. J. 252, 282, 287, 297
Hughes, B. L. 125
Hughes, J. S. 47
humanization 63–70
Hume, D. 51, 148

immigrants 70, 112, 114
immoral behaviors 3, 223–31, 260–2, 267–73
immorality 77, 79, 80, 101, 113–14
impartial beneficence 40–8
impostorism 283, 287
impression formation 99–101, 109–15
inaction parameter 33
individual difference 23, 31, 35–6, 40–8, 154, 203–9, 263–4
inequality 88, 179–88
inequity 126, 130, 173
inference 101, 104
ingroup members: acceptance of others 168–75; considered humanity 63–70; evaluating 111–13; favoritism 118–30; group pride 1, 183; harm rejection 31; identification 187; moral feedback 293–7; moral rebellion 280–8; norm violation 55–6, 281, 283–4; trustworthiness 294
instrumental harm 40–8
integrative functional theory (IFT) 140
integrity 3, 89, 94, 113, 159, 287

intergroup mechanisms: bias 122, 123; boundary conditions 63–70, 288; decision making 118–30; group-based criticism 293–8; inequality and 179–88; moral emotions 179–88; moral enhancement 292; moral feedback 291, 294–7; moral self-views 252, 291–8; neuroscientific research 118–30; social identity 54–5; strategic use of morality 234–41; trust and cooperation 125–7
Intergroup Moral Value Computation Model 118, 127–8
intergroup sensitivity effect 293–4, 296
interpersonal mechanisms: moral conversations 274–5; moral dissent 284; moral feedback 270–1, 274, 275; morality and 102–3, 268; moral judgments 97–105; moral praise 54, 56, 80–1, 103, 140, 267–75; moral self-views 251, 264, 267–75; reconciliation 212–20; shame 157–65
intragroup mechanisms: deviance and dissent 252, 280–8; moral behavior 225; moral character in group perception 109–15; moral self-views 280–3; reputational concerns 223–31; social identity and 51–8; social neuroscience perspectives 168–75
intrapersonal mechanisms: moral behavior 203–9; moral emotions 147–54; moral reasoning 29–37; power and 87–94
Iyer, A. 286

Jetten, J. 252, 286, 287
Jordan, J. 251, 259, 261
Joseph, C. 12
Judd, C. 305
justification (of moral judgments) 51

Kant, I. 43, 51, 140
Khan, U. 261
Köbis, N. 226
Koch, A. 305, 306
Kohlberg, L. 10–11, 21, 22, 24, 77
Kouchacki, M. 251, 264

LaFrance, M. 196
language 22–3, 80, 119, 236, 239–41
Laurent, S. M. 170
Law, K. F. 47
Leach, C. W. 1, 111, 306
leaders 2, 47, 57, 101–2
Leliveld, M. 251
Lennartz, C. 261
Lewis, H. B. 161, 163
Liu, T. 260
logical reasoning 34, 36
Løkkeberg, S. T. 160
Long, D. A. 197
Lukes, S. 236

Lundqvist, M. 239
lying 164, 173, 197, 227, 231, 252

Malle, B. 80, 103
mathematical reasoning 36
Mazar, N. 226
McDougall, W. 10
Mead, G. H. 268
Menegatti, M. 101
mere liking effect 101
Messick, D. 195
methodology 24
Milgram S. 282
Moberg, D. 56–7
modelling approaches 33–4
Mooijman, M. 89, 92
moral behavior: defined 3–4, 225; emotional influences 203–9; ethics of 195–8; influence of moral self-view 267–72; interpersonal reconciliation 212–20; moral self-image and 257–64; observability/consequentiality 223, 227–31, 263; reputational concerns and 223–31
moral beliefs 10, 97–8, 100–3
moral clarity 90
moral concern 29–30, 34, 55
moral conflict 13, 124
moral conversations 267, 273–5
moral convictions 34, 57, 100, 101
moral criticism 3, 296, 297
moral decision making: decision-making paradigms 120; ethical aspects 21–4, 56; intergroup 121–2; neuroscientific/computational methods 12, 35, 120–1, 196–7; sacrificial dilemmas 29–37; value-based models 53, 57
moral development 10–11, 47, 263, 270, 274
moral dilemmas 29–37, 41–2, 97, 101
moral disagreement 101–5
moral disengagement 23, 65–6, 69, 235
moral domains 12, 99, 148
moral dumbfounding 70
moral emotions: and attributional certainty 103; defined 3, 139–42; disgust in 147–54; influence on moral behavior 203–9; intergroup relations 141, 179–88; intragroup relations 168–75; moral feedback and 270–1; role in moral judgments 11, 147–8; and sacrificial harm 35; social neuroscience perspectives 168–75; threat monitoring 147–54
Moral Expansiveness Scale 282
moral failure 159–60, 162, 163–4, 213, 216
moral feedback 270–1, 291, 294–7
moral foundations 67, 70, 104
Moral Foundations Theory 12, 99, 115, 225
moral framing 105, 196, 235, 237–40
moral identity 34, 206, 212–20, 250, 252, 257–8, 262

moral image 214–15, 217–20, 234–6
moral imagination 56–7
moral intuitions: affective processing and 209; moral emotions and 147–8, 204; vs reasoning 34, 66; social identity and 51–4; utilitarianism and 43, 45–6
morality: vs competence 2, 157; cultural differences 11; defined 78–9, 98; evolutionary perspectives 63–70; and group evaluation 109–15; historical perspectives 11, 51; and intergroup relations 234–41, 292, 295, 298; interpersonal perception 98–100, 268; normative standards 79, 102–3; restoration of 212–20; and the self 149–53; self-views 267–75; social intuitionist model 12; valence and 80
moralization 57, 235, 238, 240
moral judgments: children 47; defined 3, 98; interpersonal consequences 97–105; neuroscientific perspectives 122–7; power and 87–94; reputational issues 81; role of moral emotions in 11, 147–8; social context 52, 54–8, 91–3; threat monitoring 148–54; uniqueness of 77–81
moral licensing 197, 212, 218, 259–60, 262, 272
moral motives 2, 99
moral norms 158–60, 164–5, 234–41
moral outrage 23–4, 98, 180, 206
moral philosophy 11, 40, 148
Moral Primacy Model (MPM) 78, 111, 112, 113
moral psychology, historical perspectives 9–14
moral purity 104, 148–52
moral reasoning: affective processes 23–4; cognitive processes 22–3; defined 3, 65; gating of 65–8; influence of proximity 67–8; intrapersonal models 29–37; theoretical models 34–6
moral rebellion 280–8
moral transgressions: disgust and 149–50; emotional response to 206–7; historical 171–2; judgment of 102–3, 121, 149–53; morality restoration 212–20; of moral rebels 280, 283, 286, 288; social identity and response to 54–5; "unethical amnesia" 268–9, 275
moral tuning 51, 52, 53
moral values 3, 251–2
Moscatelli, S. 297
motivation 34, 122–5, 127, *159*, 179–88
Mulder, L. B. 261
Mullen, E. 251, 288

Nadler, A. 240
name-calling 240–1
Navarette, C. D. 70
Neale, M. 195
negative evaluations 123, 124–5
negativity effect 103
Nietzsche, F. 250, 251, 252, 253

nonverbal behaviors 101
norms parameter 33

obesity 170, 171
O'Leary-Kelly, A. M. 197
organizational behavior 21–2, 196, 238–9
others' behavior 261–2, 267–75
ought behavior 65, 259
outcome-maximization 31–6
outgroup members: considered humanity 63–70; derogation of 104; evaluating 111–13, 122–4; harm rejection 31; name-calling 240–1; norm violation 55–6; outgroup criticism 293–8; as prepared stimuli 69–70

Pagliaro, S. 2
Patil, I. 42
Peabody, D. 80
personal/impersonal distinction 31, 35, 42
person-perception 98–100
perspective differences 79, 81
Piaget, J. 10, 77
political ideology 45, 79, 196, 274, 295
political polarization 13
positive–negative asymmetry 77, 80, 81
power 87–94, 179–1, 185–6, 234–41
prediction 13, 127–8
prejudice: and allyship 185; outgroup prejudice 70, 119, 123–5, 297; regulation/reduction 172, 175; stereotyping and 305; towards obese people 170
prepared stimuli 63, 66, 69–70
pride 140, 141, 180–3
primatology 11, 212
priming 46
process dissociation 33
prosocial behavior: emotional influences 206–7; influence of past behavior 261, 263; ingroup favoritism and 126; moral exemplars 271–2; power and 92; prosocial outcome 140–1; reputational concerns and 225–8; shame and 161–2; social identity and 54, 57
psychopathy 33, 44–5
punishment: emotional influences 206–7; group membership and 55, 129, 230–1; influence of proximity 67–8; moral rebellion 285–7; moral self-image and 263–4; of positive moral behavior 272; power and 89–90

Quercia, S. 226

race 182–3, 207–8, 216
racial discrimination 238
racial evaluations 119, 122–3, 170, 172
racism: intergroup decision making 122; intergroup sensitivity 293; moral rebellion against 281, 282, 288; and moral self-image 261; outgroup critics 297; stereotyping and 305; utilitarianism and 43
Radke, H. R. 181–2
rational morality 52, 119
reasoning 51
reconciliation 212–20, 295
Reed, A. 250, 258
relational self 251
relative preferences 29, 31–4
religiosity 45, 79, 161, 249–53
reputation 81, 223–31, 295
resource-protection 92
responsibility 3, 23, 94, 162, 171–3, 185, 238
Rest, J. 21, 22
restorative justice 212, 219–20
reward-based decision making 88, 125, 127–30
Reynolds, C. J. 36
Rösler, I. K. 298
Rozin, P. 235
rule-based decision making 45, 92, 115

sacrificial dilemmas 29–37, 41–2
Sargis, E. G. 97
schadenfreude 54, 168–9, 173–4
Schilke, O. 89, 92
Schlink, B. 171
Schumann, K. 215, 216
Schwartz, S. H. 79
self *64*, 197
self-affirmation 212, 215–16, 220
self-categorization 53
self-concept: challenges to 235; groups 109–10, 113–14; moral self within working self-concept 257–8, 261–2, 264; social nature of 267–72
self-criticism 158–60, 162, 164
self-discrepancy theory 259
self-esteem 257–9, 267, 270, 273
self-image 164, 185–6, 235, 257–64
self-reflection 124, 209, 252
self-views: defined 4, 257–9; impact of group dissent 280–3; interpersonal nature 267–75; moral feedback and 291–8; reflections 249–53
self-worth 216, 258–9, 292
sexism 43, 288
sexual harassment 196, 197, 236, 239
sexual morality 142
sexual orientation 111, 119, 120, 122, 235, 282
Shamay-Tsoory, S. G. 173
shame 139–41, 157–65, 181–3
shaming 160–1, 165
Shnabel, N. 220, 264
Shweder, R. 12
Singer, P. 43, 45
Skinner, B. F. 10
Skitka, L. J. 97, 100, 288
slavery 57, 171, 180, 291

Smith, R. H. 160
smoking 57, 235
sociability 111–15
social categorization 122–4, 172, 235
social change 281, 288
social cognition theory 68
social comparison 113, 173, 258–9, 261–2
social criticism 159–60
social dilemmas 54, 55, 92, 142
social evaluation 78, 81
social identity: groups 111, 119, 122–3, 130, 292, 294; and moral cognition 51–8; power and 94, 236
social intuitionism 12, 53, 148
social judgment 3, 77–9, 113, 141, 263, 303
social media 9–10, 13, 98, 253
social neuroscience 2–3, 118–30, 168–75, 196–7
social norms: intergroup decision making 118, 120, 122, 124, 127–9, 170; moral judgments and 3, 88; power and 91–4; reputational concern and 229–30; violations and disgust 149
social orientation 99–100
social partners 46, 101
social perception 111, 115, 304–6
social preferences 54–5
social relationships 100, 152–3
social status 1, 2, 122, 251
Steckler, C. M. 150
Steinel, W. 227
Stereotype Content Model (SCM) 110, 170, 304–6
stereotyping: gender-based 239, 304–5; intergroup value computations 127; and moral evaluations 123–5; power differentials and 236; psychological distance and 66; racial 305; situational explanations 104; use of ERP methodology 172
stigmatization 140, 168–70, 175, 236, 238
suppression 31, 33, 34
sympathy 11, 140
Szameitat, D. P. 174

Tajfel, H. 121
Tangney, J. P. 161, 163
Tavuchis, N. 213
taxes 89, 224, 238
Telzer, E. H. 125

Tesser, A. 205
Tetlock, P. 13
threat monitoring 147–54
Tracy, J. L. 150
traits *see* character traits
Trevino, L. K. 195
trolley dilemma 12, 30, 31, 41–2, 43, 66–7
trustworthiness 78, 89, 92, 112, 118–30, 185, 294
Turiel, E. 12

Uhlmann, E. L. 101
utilitarian philosophy 30–1, 40–1, 43
utilitarian reasoning: distal condition 66–7; group evaluation 115; harm rejection 33–4; impartial beneficence 41–8; two-dimensional model 43–7

valence 80
value-based judgments 54, 57, 77, 79
value computations 52–5, 57, 127–8
values 3, 251–2
van Nunspeet, F. 2–3
van Prooijen, J. W. 90, 92
Vartanian, L. R. 170
Vaughn, D. 23
Veblen, T. 253
vegetarianism 57, 235, 287
violence 2, 159, 165, 281
virtual reality 149, 197
virtue signaling 253

warmth 110–11, 115, 170, 268, 304–6
Watanabe, S. 170
Weber, M. 251
Wenzel, M. 216
whistleblowing 280, 283–4, 286
Whitman, W. 252
Wilson, E. O. 11
Wiltermuth, S. S. 90, 92
Wojciszke, B. 80, 99
Woodyatt, L. 216
Woodzicka, J. A. 196
working memory 203–9
Wu, J. 225, 226, 232

Yzerbyt, V. 305